The Sea Hunters II

The Sea Hunters II

Clive Cussler

and Craig Dirgo

arrow books

Published by Arrow Books in 2003

14

Copyright © 2002 by Sandecker, RLLLP

Clive Cussler and Craig Dirgo have asserted their right under the Copyright, Designs and Patents Act 1988 to be identified as the authors of this work

First published in Great Britain in 2002 by
Century
Random House, 20 Vauxhall Bridge Road,
London SW1V 2SA

www.penguin.co.uk

Addresses for companies within The Random House Group Limited can be found at: www.randomhouse.co.uk/offices.htm

The Random House Group Limited Reg. No. 954009

A CIP catalogue record for this book
is available from the British Library

ISBN 9780099445555

Typeset by SX Composing DTP, Rayleigh, Essex

Penguin Random House is committed to a sustainable future for our business, our readers and our planet. This book is made from Forest Stewardship Council® certified paper.

MIX
Paper from
responsible sources
FSC® C018179

Printed and bound in Great Britain by Clays Ltd, Elcograf S.p.A.

For Barbara, always for Barbara.

C.C.

For my mother, who raised six children
and dozens of dogs, we miss you.

C.D.

IN MEMORY OF . . .

WILLARD BASCOM
Ocean pioneer of the first magnitude.

ROBERT FLEMING
A great researcher.

RICHARD SWETE
Exceptional historian and nautical archaeologist.

DONALD SPENCER
Who inspired a legion of divers.

&

GERALD ZINSER
Last surviving crew member of PT-109.

Acknowledgments

The authors are extremely grateful to the kind and gracious people who helped to make this book possible. Their efforts and considerations are deeply appreciated. Ralph Wilbanks of Diversified Wilbanks, John Davis of ECO-NOVA Productions, Bill Nungesser, Wes Hall, Connie Young, Robert Fleming, Richard DeRosset, Emlyn Brown, Gary Goodyear, Graham Jessop, Elsworth Boyd, Carole Bartholmeaux, Colleen Nelson, Susan MacDonald, Lisa Bower, John Hunley, and Wayne Gronquist.

Contents

PART FOUR: U.S.S. Mississippi

PART FIVE: The Siege of Charleston: *Keokuk, Weehawken,* and *Patapsco*

PART SIX: The Cannon of San Jacinto

PART SEVEN: *Mary Celeste*

PART EIGHT: The Steamboat *General Slocum*

PART FOURTEEN:
America's Leonardo da Vinci

Introduction

WE ALL HAVE A FASCINATION WITH THE SEA and the mysteries that lie in the deep. It is still one of the great unknowns. Adventurers climb the highest mountains in order to reach the summits and feast on the horizons fifty miles away. A diver does not share that pleasure. Unless he is diving in the clear water of the tropics, his visibility is seldom more than twenty feet. He can only wonder what lies in the murk beyond.

Men and women have hiked over most of the world's landmass, and what little we have encountered has been photographed from satellites. Giant observatories and the Hubble telescope have shown us the wonders of deep space. But the human eye and the camera lens have recorded less than 1 percent of the wonders that lie hidden below the surface of the seas.

The deep liquid void is still a great enigma.

Thanks to mushrooming scientific interest, however, deepwater technology has awakened. Probes have studied everything from bottom storms and the migration of sea life to currents, geology, underwater acoustics, and the increasing bugaboo of pollution. Because of new, sophisticated equipment that can probe thousands of feet down, great shipwrecks of history have been discovered in the silent darkness, after lying centuries in unmarked watery graves.

Men like Bob Ballard and companies like Nauticos have reached and photographed several of these lost wrecks, but many lie there yet, waiting. That's what we do: We try to find them. The National Underwater & Marine Agency (NUMA) searches for lost ships of historic significance, in the hopes of finding and surveying them before they have deteriorated and are gone forever. Since we are a shoestring operation funded mostly by my book royalties, our expeditions concentrate solely on wrecks in shallow water.

NUMA was formed in 1978 after our first venture— the unsuccessful hunt for John Paul Jones's *Bonhomme Richard*—and while we were preparing for our second crack at the same ship. Wayne Gronquist, a prominent Austin attorney, suggested that it would be more advantageous as a legal entity if we incorporated as a not-for-profit foundation. I agreed, and Wayne, who served twenty years as NUMA's president, filed the documents. And, yes, it is the same name as the government agency in my Dirk Pitt adventure books. The trustees thought it would be sporting to name the foundation after my own fictional creation, so I could say, "Yes, Virginia, there really is a NUMA."

When it comes to salvage, we leave that to others. No member of NUMA has ever kept an artifact. People who visit my home and office are always surprised to find only models and paintings of the ships we have discovered, never any relics. Any item brought up from a wreck is preserved and turned over to the state in whose waters it was found. For instance, the artifacts from the Confederate raider *Florida* and the Union frigate *Cumberland*—both NUMA finds—were preserved by the College of William and Mary before they were put on public display at the Norfolk Naval Museum in Virginia.

My desire is that our discoveries should be followed by federal, state, or local governments; by corporations, universities, or historical organizations with the funding either to raise the wrecks or retrieve the artifacts for exhibit in museums.

In the twenty-three years of its existence, NUMA's search and survey teams have conducted more than a hundred and fifty expeditions and have discovered or surveyed sixty-five wreck sites. We've also searched for a lost locomotive, a pair of cannon, an airplane, and a zeppelin. The successes, I'm sad to say, have been outnumbered by the failures. When you tackle the hunt for a lost object on land or sea, you quickly learn that the odds against finding it are far steeper than your chances of winning at a Las Vegas roulette table.

To look for a shipwreck is at best a crapshoot, and to launch and fund a search, it helps to be the headmaster of the village idiot school or else the kind of stubborn lunatic who tries to walk through walls simply because they're in the way. I probably fall in the latter group.

You have to live with failure—all too often, it seems. Let me describe just a few of our recent disappointments.

In 2000, we hunted for John Holland's sixteen-foot,

one-man submarine in New York's East River. Along with his competitor Simon Lake, John Holland is considered to be the father of the modern submarine. Their designs established the underwater navies of Europe and America just around the turn of the century.

Holland's tiny submarine was thought to be quite sophisticated for its time. Unfortunately, plans and reports on her construction are sparse. She was lost when she was stolen by the Fenian Brotherhood, an early parent organization of the Irish Republican Army, who funded Holland's early experiments with submarines for the express purpose of putting the British navy out of business. For the Brotherhood, Holland designed and built the most advanced sub of the time, aptly titled the *Fenian Ram*. Though never created to ram a steel-hulled ship, the three-man, 19-ton boat was 31 feet in length, with a 6-foot beam, and was propelled by a 15-horsepower Brayton twin-cylinder gas engine.

Not content with merely developing an efficient undersea boat, Holland conceived and perfected the instrument that turned the submarine into one of the most devastating weapons of warfare. Taking advantage of a missile developed by John Ericsson, the famed creator of the Civil War *Monitor*, who graciously allowed the sub builder to use copies of his experimental models, Holland fitted the missiles to a weapon of his own design in a 6-foot-by-9-inch tube. This gun, as it was called, was fired pneumatically by high-pressure air. The brilliant concept has changed little over the past 120 years.

The sub and its weapon worked incredibly well during tests conducted by Holland, tests that irritated the impatient Fenians. Angered because they felt he was taking too much time with his experiments and trial runs with the ram, the Fenians decided to snatch it. On a dark night in November of 1883, a group of maddened Irish tanked up on good whiskey at a Brooklyn saloon. After becoming properly fortified, they borrowed a tugboat and sneaked up to the dock where the *Fenian Ram* was moored and towed her away.

Enjoying the moment in an alcoholic haze, they became carried away and decided to make off with the small experimental sub, too. Then they headed up the East River toward Long Island Sound, intending to hide the two subs up a small river near New Haven, Connecticut.

By the time they reached Whitestone Point, the wind had begun to blow strongly from the north and heavily buffeted the small convoy. The Fenians failed to notice that the model boat's hatch cover on the turret had not been tightened down, and water began spilling through the cracks. Rapidly filling, the little sub foundered in the rising waves, snapped her towline, and headed to the bottom, 110 feet below. Unaware of the loss, they calmly continued on their way to New Haven.

Happily, the *Fenian Ram* still survives in a museum in Paterson, New Jersey.

I took up the challenge of searching for the little sub. Ralph Wilbanks hauled his boat, *Diversity*, up to New York from Charleston, and we stayed on the New York Maritime College cadet training cargo ship in the passengers' staterooms and ate with the cadets in their cafeteria. I am indebted to Admiral David Brown, dean of the college, whose courtesy and hospitality were a godsend to the project. The college maintenance people helpfully lifted Ralph's boat in and out of the water and provided space at the dock.

This sidescan sonar revealed many pieces of junk on the river bottom in the area off Whitestone Point, where the sub reportedly sank—though how the Fenians could claim they knew the spot, during a dark and windy night in choppy water in the days before depth sounders, is a mystery to me. I doubt whether they even knew the sub was missing until they reached New Haven.

Many of the anomalies the sidescan picked up were fifty-five-gallon steel drums. We could not help but wonder if one of them contained Jimmy Hoffa. We also recorded a few small cabin cruisers and sailboats on the bottom and imagined them with missing bodies inside. No one was in the mood to dive and find out. The riverbed was littered with so much metallic trash, it was difficult to pick out a small sub under the river mud with the magnetometer since no sign of it appeared on the sonar. After three days of fruitlessly cruising up and down the scenic East River, we packed up and called it a day.

Was the little sub covered over by mud? Did it lie under the Whitestone Bridge, whose steel girders threw the mag into hysterics? Or does it lie farther out in Long Island Sound?

I'm not ready to throw in the towel just yet. I hope to return someday and pick up the search where the river fans out into the Sound.

Continuing my self-inflicted orgy of shipwreck hunting, I then launched a search for the Confederate raider *Georgia*, which had a short but successful career, capturing nine Union merchant ships from 1862 to 1864. Though not quite as fascinating as that of

Alabama or *Florida*, which we found under the James River in Virginia in 1984, her history made her famous, and, as one of the first sea raiders, her exploits inspired the German raiders of two world wars.

During her cruise, she almost started a war with Morocco, when a group of her officers went ashore and were assaulted by the locals before they barely escaped back to the ship with their bodies still intact. Disturbed by the indignity, the captain of the *Georgia* ordered the guns manned and brought to bear. He then blasted the Moroccans until they dispersed.

A few months later, no longer considered fit to sail the seas as a raiding cruiser, she was sold and put into service as a mail packet between Lisbon and the Cape Verde Islands, where she was soon captured by a ship of the Union navy as a prize of war and returned to the United States. After a legal battle between the United States and Britain, she was sold to a series of shipping companies, before finally being bought by the Gulfport Steamship Company for passenger and cargo service between Halifax and Portland, Maine.

When on a passage south from Nova Scotia in January of 1875, the old steamship, still named *Georgia*, struck the rocks known as the Triangles ten miles west of Tenants Harbor, Maine. The crew and passengers took to the lifeboats and rowed through a snowstorm to shore. No lives were lost, but the ship became a total wreck and was abandoned. She was the last of the Confederate raiders to die.

Historian Michael Higgins produced a small mountain of research on *Georgia* and her grounding, contacted me, and, soft touch that I am, I agreed to arrange a search off Maine for the remains of the fabled ship. After arriving in Tenants Harbor with Ralph, Wes Hall, and Craig Dirgo, we settled into a hotel reminiscent of a Steinbeck Monterey fish cannery. We passed time throwing rocks from one side of town to the other and watching the rails rust at the train depot, before finding an old-fashioned drugstore with ancient white octagonal tile on the floor and a genuine antique soda fountain.

I ordered my all-time favorite from my childhood, a chocolate malt with chocolate ice cream churned in a metal canister by a 1930s mixer. One sip and I was in paradise.

Early next morning, with Ralph at the helm, *Diversity* swept out toward Triangle Rocks, dodging literally hundreds of colorfully painted buoys attached to lobster traps. Every lobsterman has his own distinct color-coded buoy, and more and more they are being purchased by collectors.

Wes manned the sonar and I watched the magnetometer, and Ralph threaded *Diversity* in and around the rocks, while Craig kept a wary eye for lobster buoys or scallop divers. Waves were washing over the rocks all around us, but Ralph seemed oblivious to them as he grimly studied the echo sounder. At times, they seemed so close you could spit on them, and yet they yielded no hint of *Georgia*.

There were a few small mag hits, but nothing showed on the sidescan sonar. After crisscrossing the Triangles three times, we stared at one another in surprised disappointment. We had come up empty. There was no indication of a shipwreck to be found.

We knew we were in the right spot. The only other rocks were too far out of the area, according to the old reports. Just to play it safe, we checked those out, too. How could an iron-hulled wreck the size of *Georgia* simply disappear?

The answer came from local historians whom we consulted after the unsuccessful hunt. Since urchin and scallop divers had been all over those rocks for many years without sighting wreckage, the only answer was that *Georgia* had been salvaged. Records from the 1870s and 1880s are sparse, but it was suggested that, owing to the extreme economic hardships of the citizens of Maine at the time, they'd pulled up almost every pound of her, including the keel and boilers, which they sold for scrap.

Curses, foiled again.

Shipwreck junkies that we were, the gang continued on to Saybrook, Connecticut, to take a stab at finding David Bushnell's famous Revolutionary War submarine, the *Turtle*. This was the first practical submarine in the world at the time—every submarine built in the following centuries owes its ancestry to the *Turtle*.

The son of a Connecticut Yankee farmer, Bushnell had a creative mind and was self-taught in his early years. Entering Yale at the advanced age of thirty-one, he roomed with Nathan Hale, who later became America's most famous patriot-spy. While in school, Bushnell became fascinated with the untried concept of producing underwater explosions with gunpowder. He was perhaps the first in history to devise and build a powder-filled container that had a clockwork timer capable of being exploded underwater. Not content simply to allow his mines to float against enemy vessels, which he accomplished successfully by blowing up a

British schooner and a smaller boat whose crew made the mistake of trying to pull one of the mines aboard, he decided the only effective way to sink a warship was to come up with a means of placing the mine directly against the hull.

His solution was the *Turtle*, a technological marvel of the time. In a barn next to the house where he lived with his brother Ezra, the brothers constructed a submarine that looked like two turtle shells standing on end. The hull was carved out of solid wood and actually resembled a child's toy top, set on a flattened lower point. David and Ezra designed a ball type of snorkel valve for air, a vertical-bladed propeller to pull the craft toward the surface, as well as a larger propeller in front for forward motion, an innovation that was seen on ships for fifty years. For submersion, they crafted water ballast tanks as well as detachable ballast weights.

The pilot entered and exited through a raised brass hatch and sat inside in an upright position. He steered with a stern rudder while he turned the forward horizontal propeller. The torpedo, a container with 150 pounds of gunpowder, a flintlock for detonation, and a clockwork mechanism that delayed the explosion until the *Turtle* had backed away for safety, was connected to the upper section of the submarine by a detachable twist lever that turned a screw that was supposed to penetrate the copper sheathing on the hull of an enemy ship. Once the screw penetrated the sheathing and the gunpowder container was gripped in place, the pilot frantically reversed his forward motion with the hand crank to make his escape.

A soldier from George Washington's army by the name of Ezra Lee volunteered to become the first man in history to attack a submarine against a warship. The target was British Admiral Richard Howe's flagship, the frigate *Eagle*, which was lying in the Hudson River off Manhattan Island. The *Turtle* worked flawlessly. Lee gave it his best shot and came within a hair of becoming the first submarine to sink a warship, but, unable to see underwater at night, he failed to deploy the explosive device properly. Its attaching screw struck an iron bracket holding the rudder instead of the soft copper nailed to the hull. Unable to attach the gunpowder container, Lee aborted the mission.

A second attempt was made, but Lee dove too deep, and the current was too strong for him to make headway. The third and final effort failed when the British sentries fired on the craft as it escaped. A week later, a British sloop fired on and sank the sloop carrying the *Turtle* up the Hudson River. The British failed to recognize the *Turtle* as an advanced instrument of war and left it aboard the half-sunken sloop.

In a letter written by Bushnell to Thomas Jefferson, he stated that he had raised the *Turtle* but, in his words, "was unable to prosecute the design any further." Bushnell then experimented with floating mines in the Delaware River, with little success. After the war, he entered medicine and became a physician, practicing while teaching at an academy in Georgia. He died in 1824 at the ripe old age of eighty-five, without leaving a clue as to what he did with the *Turtle*.

After he recovered it from the Hudson River, did he take it back to Saybrook and scuttle it in the Connecticut River, or did he simply chop it up into firewood and burn it to keep it out of British hands? Neither he nor his brother Ezra left any mention in their correspondences regarding the fate of the famed *Turtle*.

And so the world's first practical submarine became lost in the mists of time.

Well aware that it was an exercise in futility, we decided to make a search of the Connecticut River where Bushnell had built the *Turtle,* desperately clinging to the notion that if you don't seek, you won't find.

After our routine consultation with local historians, who were as much in the dark as anyone else about what Bushnell had done with the *Turtle*, we studied a working replica of the submarine that had been re-created by Frederic Frese and Joseph Leary at the Connecticut River Museum at Essex. The two men had actually performed open-water dives in it. Having soaked up all the available data on Bushnell and his extraordinary vessel, we then launched our boat and began a sidescan survey up and down the river. We were lucky to have a ballpark grid in which to search, since the house where David and Ezra Bushnell had lived while building the *Turtle* still stands about two hundred feet from the river's west bank. We did not use a magnetometer, because there was very little iron on the *Turtle* for it to detect. The ballast was lead and the hatch and fittings mostly brass.

We swept the entire river a good mile in either direction from the Bushnells' construction site. But the sonar recorded nothing that remotely resembled the *Turtle*. If Bushnell did indeed scuttle the *Turtle* off his old workshop—and that is a very big *if*—it could lie under a four-acre swamp that is impenetrable to man or boat, or it could be covered over with silt. Should that be the case, every target recorded by the magnetometer, no matter how small, would have to be dredged. It's not an impossible situation, but it is costly and most inconvenient.

Once again, we chalked one up to disappointment. As we are so fond of saying in the shipwreck business, "We still don't know where it is, but we well know where it ain't."

THOSE ARE the defeats, and they're pretty frustrating. It's the occasional successes that inspire us to sail onward.

Some of them we described in the first *Sea Hunters*, and some of them are in this book (though they're not all successes, as you'll see). But probably the most satisfying one of all was the discovery of the Confederate submarine *Hunley* and her heroic crew, hidden in the silt off Charleston, South Carolina. I was convinced she had to be there, even though several NUMA search expeditions had failed to find her, and I simply refused to give up.

The story of her discovery was told in the first *Sea Hunters*. After running 1,154 miles of search lanes dragging a magnetometer sensor, an anomaly that indicated the mass and dimensions of the *Hunley* was finally discovered. Marine surveyor Ralph Wilbanks and marine archaeologists Wes Hall and Harry Pecorelli III then excavated and made a positive identification of the long-lost sub.

If we hadn't found it in May of 1995, I'd still be out looking for it.

What couldn't be told then is what happened afterward. Due to the efforts of South Carolina state senator Glenn McConnell, and of Warren Lasch—who launched the Friends of the *Hunley* and acquired the funds to raise and preserve the vessel so future generations may view this remarkably advanced craft that became the first submarine in history to sink an enemy warship—the *Hunley* was raised from the water.

The day she was lifted from her watery shroud of 28 feet and saw the sun for the first time in 136 years, no one present will ever forget.

The recovery team, the true unsung heroes in the drama, labored for months in round-the-clock shifts, excavating and building a truss around the hull so it could be lifted onto a barge. This was no easy feat, especially when it was found that the sub was filled with silt that quadrupled its weight. The international salvage companies that performed the magnificent recovery effort and directed the lift were Oceaneering and the Titan Corporation.

When the moment came, the lifting cables became taut, and the little submarine began to rise from the silt where she had lain for so long. There was hushed expectation from the divers, the engineers, and the thousands of people who had gathered in hundreds of boats for the landmark event. Every eye was on the huge crane that stood on the great salvage barge, its own great pilings driven into the sea bottom. When the sub's dripping hull, supported by the truss and foam cushions, appeared under a cloudless blue sky, cheers, whistles, and air horns shattered the early-morning calm, while the stars and bars of the Confederacy flew from a forest of masts.

Standing on the press boat and leaning over the railing, I felt an indescribable thrill. Finally, I would lay eyes on her. My son, Dirk, friend and cowriter Craig

Dirgo, and I had hoped to dive on her soon after Ralph, Wes, and Harry made the discovery, but several days of rough weather and high seas beat us out. By then it was too late. A Charleston press conference was scheduled to announce the discovery, and we could not venture to the site again for fear of giving away her location to shady Civil War artifact collectors who were already offering $5,000 for a hatch cover and $10,000 for the propeller to anyone who would dive to the wreck and remove them. The *Hunley* hung poised and elegant, coated in rust and ancient sea life that had attached to her iron plates before the silt covered her entirely. She was gently lowered onto a smaller barge and then towed by two tugboats on her final, belated voyage into Charleston Harbor. Flags on Fort Sumter were lowered to half-mast, as reenactors in authentic Civil War uniforms, both Union and Confederate, shot volleys to the sky, accompanied by muzzle-loading cannon, whose salutes filled the air with puffs of black powder smoke. Women lined the shore wearing antebellum dresses, nine of the garments black in honor of the submarine's nine dead crew. Thousands of spectators lining the shores cheered as the barge, with its precious cargo, and the fleet of pleasure craft made their way past the town Battery and up the Cooper River to the old navy yard.

The men behind the project had pulled off an amazing feat. The entire operation had gone as smoothly as a ticking clock on the dashboard of a Rolls Royce. A crane lifted the sub off the barge onto a rail car that carried her into the Warren Lasch Conservation Center, where she will spend the next several years in a tank. Here, during her preservation process, her hull plates will be removed so the interior can be excavated and all artifacts and the crew's remains can be removed and studied. Eventually, *Hunley*, in all her glory, will be put in a museum for permanent public display.

I was numb with disbelief and exhilaration that the event had actually happened, as numb as I was the day five years earlier when Ralph Wilbanks had awakened me at 5 A.M. and told me he wasn't going to search for the *Hunley* anymore—because he and Wes and Harry had just touched its hull!

Dr. Robert Neyland, the naval archaeologist who was in charge of the investigation, graciously allowed me to go up now and touch the sub. After fifteen years and a share of my children's inheritance spent on the long search, I felt as if an electric shock were running through me as I laid my hands on the propeller. Close up, the vessel looked longer and narrower than I had imagined, far more streamlined and aerodynamically designed to reduce water resistance than anyone had suspected. *Hunley* was truly a marvel of Civil War engineering and technology.

A photographer asked Ralph, Wes, Harry, and me to stand in front of the sub as it hung suspended in its sling, before it was lowered into the preservation tank. After we posed for a few minutes, the entire building suddenly erupted in cheers and applause. Totally unexpected, it was truly an emotional and cherished moment, a fulfillment to a dream. We all fought back the tears, proud that this moment existed because of us. The years of effort and expense had been worth it.

But, as with a triumphant army after a great victory, the moment soon passed. That was then. Now is now.

It was time to plan the next expedition in hopes of finding another historically significant shipwreck.

Perhaps it'll be the *Pioneer II*—or *American Diver*, as she was sometimes called. It was the predecessor to *Hunley* and was built by the same group of men in Mobile, Alabama. While being towed from the harbor in an attempt to sink one of the blockading Union fleet, she was hit by a squall, and she began to take on water through an improperly sealed hatch until she slipped under the waves. Fortunately, none of her crew accompanied her into the deep. Scientists and archaeologists are anxious to see the technology that was used as a foundation to modify and refine the *Hunley* into an undersea vessel considered state-of-the-art in 1863.

We've just received a permit from the state of Alabama to conduct a search and excavation. Yes, we're positive this is another wreck that is buried deep in the sand and silt, and so is probably unrecoverable. But if we never make the attempt, we will never succeed.

Much water has passed the bows since Craig Dirgo and I wrote the first *Sea Hunters*. Since then NUMA has found the wrecks of *Carpathia*, the ship that rescued *Titanic*'s survivors and was torpedoed by a German U-boat six years later; the *General Slocum*, an excursion steamboat that burned and sank in the East River of New York, with a loss of more than one thousand people, mostly women and children; and the *Mary Celeste*, the famous ghost ship that was found floating off the Azores in 1876 with no one on board, the first great mystery of the seas.

The following narratives chronicle the most recent searches by NUMA crews who dragged sensing equipment through eight-foot seas, found themselves inundated by tidal waves, dove in water so dirty they couldn't see the fingernails on the hands in front of them, and excavated tons of mud and sand under the worst conditions imaginable, all in an effort to identify a long-lost shipwreck. The people who are portrayed here, both past and present, were and are real. The historical events depicted are also factual but have been slightly dramatized to make the ships, and all who voyaged in them, more immediate to today's reader.

There is no monetary profit to this ship-hunting madness. I do what I do purely out of a love for our country's maritime history and to preserve it for future generations. It's rich and worth cherishing.

Each day is future history. So don't step lightly. The trick is to leave tracks that can be followed.

PART ONE

L'Aimable

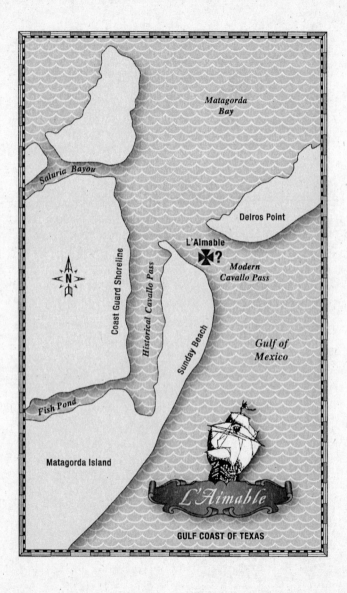

Matagorda
Bay

Saluria Bayou

Delros Point

L'Aimable

Modern
Cavallo Pass

Coast Guard Shoreline

Historical Cavallo Pass

Sunday Beach

Gulf of
Mexico

Fish Pond

Matagorda Island

L'Aimable

GULF COAST OF TEXAS

I

The Father of Waters

1684–1685

"THE FOOL!" RENÉ-ROBERT CAVELIER DE LA Salle shouted as he stood helpless on the desolate shore and watched his flagship, *L'Aimable*, veer out of the buoyed channel toward what he knew was certain destruction.

Earlier, over the protests of *L'Aimable*'s captain, René Aigron, La Salle had ordered the 300-ton French ship loaded with stores for a new colony to sail across the bar of Cavallo Pass into Matagorda Bay—a body of water that would become part of the state of Texas 157 years later.

Aigron stared menacingly, demanded La Salle draw up a document absolving him of any responsibility, and insisted the explorer sign it. La Salle, still recovering from an illness, was too weary to argue the point and reluctantly agreed to the terms. Fearing the worst, Aigron then transferred his personal possessions to a smaller ship, *Joly*, which had already crossed the bar and was safely anchored inside.

Now, with the sails unfurled and billowing from a following breeze, *L'Aimable,* to the horror of La Salle, was sailing into oblivion.

THE MAN who would claim the new world for France was born in Rouen, France, on November 22, 1643. After an unsuccessful attempt to become a Jesuit priest, he left France seeking a new life in New France, now known as Canada, then a French colony. After a few false starts, La Salle established a thriving fur-trading business, an endeavor that allowed him to develop his budding passion for exploration.

When Louis de Buade Comte de Frontenac became the new governor of Canada, La Salle nurtured a friendship with him. In time, the Canadian governor introduced La Salle to King Louis XIV, who granted the explorer a patent, or royal license, to explore the western regions of New France. In effect, La Salle now became France's approved explorer in the New World. La Salle, in debt, wasted little time before exploiting the honor.

Expanding his fur trade to the west and into Lake Michigan, La Salle set out to change the way the business was conducted. Most fur trappers headed into the wilds until they had secured sufficient pelts to load a birch-bark canoe, then they set off on a long journey to a major town where they could sell their bounty. La Salle saw that the Great Lakes needed larger vessels, so he built one. In August 1679, he launched *Le Griffon,* a rigged vessel of sixty tons mounting seven guns, into Lake Erie. *Griffon* amazed the Indians in the area, who had never seen a large ship. Unfortunately, the vessel was not long for this world.

In defiance of Louis XIV's order not to trade with the Indian tribes in the western regions, La Salle set out to do just that. After transporting people to Fort Michilimackinac, near where Lake Huron and Lake Michigan meet, *Griffon* was sent across Lake Michigan to Green Bay. There the ship was loaded with furs and goods for the trip back to Fort Niagara at the eastern end of Lake Erie.

With no explanation, *Griffon* disappeared into the mists of history.

The loss of *Griffon*, and another ship loaded with supplies in the Saint Lawrence River, brought La Salle to the edge of financial ruin. To complicate matters, in 1680, just after the loss of the ships, the men assigned to La Salle's Fort Crèvecoeur at the mouth of the Illinois River mutined and destroyed the outpost. Never lucky, La Salle saw his world collapsing.

Rather than admit defeat, he pressed on with his plans to discover the mouth of the Mississippi River. In February 1682, La Salle started down the upper waters of the Mississippi in an expedition consisting of twenty elm-bark canoes. By March, the expedition had reached present-day Arkansas and established contact with the Indians, who welcomed the French explorers. With the weather improving, the expedition pressed south, and on April 6 they finally reached the mouth of the great river.

La Salle was a pompous man given to ego, and the ceremony on April 9 reflected this. Standing next to a towering live oak and dressed in scarlet robes, La Salle had the men sing hymns while standing in front of a cross that had been carved from a large pine tree. Then he claimed all the land lining the Mississippi River for France.

In honor of the king he served, he called the land Louisiana.

Without a war and with hardly a single shot fired, La Salle made a claim to an area that doubled the size of New France. From the Appalachian Mountains to the east, south to the territories claimed by Spain, the land comprised some 909,000 square miles.

Now he needed to establish a base far to the south so he could exploit his discovery for profit: a base far away from his growing list of enemies in New France and far from his creditors. La Salle's friend Frontenac had been replaced as governor of New France by Antoine Levebre Sieur de La Barre, who, like most, cared little for the arrogant La Salle. His last chance was to return to France and convince King Louis XIV to support his efforts to colonize the southern end of the Mississippi River Valley. In this, he was successful.

On July 24, 1684, La Salle left France with four ships and four hundred colonists.

RENÉ-ROBERT Cavelier de La Salle never would have won a popularity contest.

On the lee side of Hispaniola Island in the country of Santa Domingo at the port of Petit Goave, the commander of the French thirty-six-gun warship *Joly*, Captain Andre Beaujeu, was airing his grievances about La Salle to Captain René Aigron of the supply ship *L'Aimable*. Aigron, whose ship was anchored off Port-de-Paix, was separated from the other ships of the fleet by a mix-up in orders. He had traveled by donkey to the other side of the island for the conference.

"La Salle is touched," Beaujeu said. "First he refuses permission for us to stop in Madeira, then he bans the sailors from baptizing the passengers as we cross the line into the tropics. Those two rituals are time-honored nautical traditions."

Aigron was a short man, just over five feet in height and weighing 120 pounds. Pursing his lips, he puffed on a long thin pipe. The bowl of the mahogany pipe had been carved into the shape of a jellyfish. Waving away the smoke, he pointed to a crude chart on the table in *Joly*'s captain's quarters.

"I'm more than a little concerned," Aigron noted. "Nowhere on this crude chart do I see where La Salle has marked the great river running into the Gulf of Mexico."

"I asked him before we left La Rochelle," Beaujeu said as he sipped from a silver flute of wine, "what exactly was our intended course. Then as now, he refused to disclose the route."

Aigron nodded and waited for Beaujeu to continue.

"Honestly, I don't believe La Salle knows where we are going," Beaujeu concluded.

Aigron stared at Beaujeu. His fellow captain was not a handsome man. His left cheek sported a dark red birthmark that was roughly the shape of the British Isles. Half his front teeth were missing, and the rest were stained from the wine Beaujeu habitually drank.

"I agree with you, Captain," Aigron said. "I believe La Salle is bluffing. Even though he claims to have traveled to the mouth of the river by land, I don't think he has a chance of finding it from sea. Navigating on land is much easier than over water."

"It will become extremely dangerous once we enter into the gulf," Beaujeu noted. "From there on, we'll be sailing under the Spanish death sentence."

For the last hundred years, the Spanish Crown had made it known that any foreign vessels found in the Gulf of Mexico would be impounded and their crews killed. That was the primary reason no navigational charts were available. The Spanish alone had charts, and they were not about to share them with another country.

"La Salle must be losing his mind," Aigron said.

Beaujeu nodded and took another puff. At this very instant, La Salle was bedridden with the fevers, so it was hard to argue with Aigron on that point.

"Then we need to make plans to ensure the safety of our ships and our sailors," Beaujeu said.

"Understood," Aigron agreed.

Then he reached for a flask of brandy to toast their treasonous alliance.

As La Salle lay in his sickbed, the fact that his expedition was already fractured was the least of his worries. Surely, the lies he had told his king must have topped the list.

Specifically, to receive the funding necessary to the venture, La Salle had told Louis XIV three lies.

The first lie was that the savages in the new land sought conversion to Christianity. The truth was far from that—other than a few scattered pockets where the Jesuits had made inroads, the Indians had resisted any attempts at salvation. Second, La Salle had boldly claimed he could raise an army of 15,000 savages to stave off any attacks from the Spanish, who currently claimed the area. That was simply not true. The Indian tribes in America were scattered and warring among themselves. The third, and probably the most important, was his representation that the return to the mouth of the great river was a foregone conclusion. The truth was that his knowledge of the river came only from land—finding it from sea was an entirely different matter altogether. He clung to the hope that he could locate the muddy brown stain where the river mixed with the salty water of the gulf. And that would prove as easy as finding a pin in a hayfield the size of Belgium.

The date was December 1684, two months after their arrival in Hispaniola.

"I FEEL stronger now," La Salle said to Tonty, who sat in a chair near his bed.

Tonty was the son of a Neapolitan financier who was La Salle's closest friend and adviser. A French soldier until the loss of his hand to a grenade, he was now fitted with a crude iron device where his hand had been.

La Salle was still far from healthy. He was worried that, if the expedition did not sail soon, it might never make it off the island. Spanish buccaneers had already captured *St. François,* the expedition's thirty-ton ketch assigned to carry fresh meat and vegetables for the colony. In addition, the French sailors had spent most of the last two months in Haiti, drunk and disorderly. To compound the troubles, the settlers, who were tasked with forging a colony in the New World, were at odds with the sailors. Of the more than three hundred that had left La Rochelle, sickness and desertion had taken a third. And then there was the festering revolt by the captains. Word had leaked back to La Salle about the frequent meetings between them, and he feared the worst.

The situation for the expedition was grim—and growing more deplorable by the hour.

"We must sail in the morning," La Salle murmured weakly. "We cannot wait another day."

"My friend," Tonty said, "if that is your desire, I will alert Captain Beaujeu."

Leaving the house in Port-de-Paix, Tonty descended the hill to the port. A stiff wind was blowing from the north, and the temperature, which usually hovered near ninety degrees, had dropped into the low sixties. Rounding a curve in the cobblestone street, Tonty stared at the three remaining ships anchored in the bay. The thirty-six-gun ship of the expedition, *Joly*, was farthest to sea. The *Belle*, a small frigate mounting six guns, was closer to shore. The 300-ton store ship for the expedition, *L'Aimable*, lay just off the docks at anchor. As the sun slipped behind the clouds, the water in the bay turned a midnight black. Tonty continued to the dock. Once there, he boarded one of *L'Aimable*'s launches for the short ride out to the vessel.

Captain Aigron had been alerted by the lookout that Tonty was on his way out. Defiantly, instead of leaving his cabin to stand on deck as a show of respect, he remained below until Tonty was led down.

"Monsieur Tonty," the sailor said, after knocking on the captain's door.

"You may enter," Aigron said quietly.

The sailor opened the door, then stepped aside to allow Tonty entrance. *L'Aimable*'s captain's cabin was high in the rounded stern of the vessel. Though not particularly large, the cabin was fitted out in a splendor not seen in the rest of the ship. Several brass whale-oil lamps were mounted on swivels that rocked with the ship. One lamp was placed near the berth, another near the table where Aigron sat, and another near an angled shelf mounted to the wall where the navigation charts were kept. A finely woven Persian rug, now becoming moth-eaten and worn from foot traffic, lay on the floor. To the right was Aigron's berth. Little more than a wooden shelf with high sides to prevent a person from rolling out as the ship rocked, it was fitted with linen sheets and a pair of feather pillows.

Atop one of the pillows lay the ship's cat. The aged feline looked worse for wear. He was a dusty yellow-and-brown color with a missing ear, the result of a rat attack deep in *L'Aimable*'s hold. The cat hissed as Tonty entered the cabin.

"Monsieur Tonty," Aigron said, still sitting at the table, "what brings you here?"

"La Salle orders you to prepare *L'Aimable* to sail in the morning," Tonty said evenly.

Tonty did not care for Aigron, and the feeling was mutual.

"Captain Beaujeu and I have been talking," Aigron said haughtily, "and before we will set sail we must see Monsieur La Salle's charts. We have no idea of the location of the river. More important, we need a solid course to sail."

"I see," Tonty said quietly. "So you and Beaujeu have decided this?"

"Yes, we have," Aigron said forcefully.

"Then you leave me little choice," Tonty said.

Tonty took two steps closer to Aigron, then grabbed him with his iron hand by the neck and held tightly. Dragging him along the passageway to the ladder, he pulled him topside to the deck. Once on the main deck, he shouted to the closest sailor.

"Who is the second in command?" Tonty asked.

A tall, thin man stepped forth. "I am, Monsieur Tonty."

"Scrub this ship from stem to stern," Tonty said. "We sail in the morning with La Salle as your captain. Is that understood?"

"Yes, sir," the second officer said.

Aigron started to speak, but Tonty squeezed his Adam's apple tighter.

"Captain Aigron will be going ashore with me," Tonty said, as he led the captain to the ladder going down to the shore boat. "La Salle will be back in a few hours. We weigh anchor at first light."

"As you wish, sir," the second in command said solicitously.

Tonty dragged Aigron across the deck to the ladder and then down the few feet to the shore boat. Stepping into the boat, he pulled the captain into a seat and motioned for the sailor to shove off. The boat was halfway to the dock before Tonty released his grip on Aigron's neck.

Staring straight into the captain's eyes, he spoke in a low voice. "You may take over command of *Belle* or I'll toss you into the drink right now. What is your choice?"

The hook had crushed his voice box—Aigron could barely speak.

"The *Belle*, please, Monsieur Tonty," Aigron said in a hoarse whisper.

The shore boat was pulling abreast of the dock.

"You defy La Salle's orders again," Tonty said, "and your neck will feel my cutlass."

Aigron gave a tiny nod.

Then Tonty climbed from the shore boat and walked

down the dock without looking back. His friend La Salle dreamed of conquering a continent for his king.

But dreams do not always come true.

FOR LA SALLE, the last two weeks had been a living hell. The fevers had returned and, with them, his feelings of isolation and indecision. Once the trio of ships rounded Cuba and entered the Gulf of Mexico, the tension of the Spanish death sentence made matters worse. At sea any ill will or imagined slights are magnified a hundredfold, and that was the case for La Salle's expedition. Sailors barely talked to settlers—La Salle and the captains had taken to communicating only through intermediaries.

Just in the nick of time, on January 1, 1685, the bottom soundings turned up land.

In *L'Aimable*'s cabin, La Salle, Tonty, and their faithful Indian guide, Nika, held a hushed meeting. The success of the whole expedition hinged on what these men would decide. It was a decision made under pressure, and those rarely are fruitful.

"What are your thoughts, Nika?" La Salle asked the taciturn guide.

"I think we are close," Nika noted, "but we have yet to see the brown streak from the muddy waters of the great river."

La Salle mopped his sweating brow with an embroidered handkerchief. The temperature outside was barely fifty degrees, but he could not stop sweating.

"Tonty?" he asked.

"I say we continue sailing due north until we make landfall, then send a party ashore," Tonty said logically. "That should give us an idea where we are."

"My thoughts exactly," La Salle said.

Three hours later, the dim outline of land was spotted by the crow's-nest lookout. La Salle went ashore to explore. From land, the area looked different from what he remembered, but there could be good reasons for that. First, the flat marshland featured less vegetation in January than in springtime, which was the only time he had seen it. Second, approaching from water was always tricky; the perspective was different, and landmarks were harder to identify.

Unless the expedition made land near the Head of Passes and could spot the brown outflow, the land might look the same from the Florida panhandle to the Red River. Whatever La Salle decided, it could go either way. The shore boat slid to a stop up a small tributary. The tangled growth of cypress trees and underbrush nearly blotted out the sun. Mullet splashed on top of the water. La Salle brushed a black fly from his neck, then dipped his hand into the water and tasted.

"Fresh and sweet," he noted. "We are near the fabled rivers of north Florida."

"I don't think so, master. I think we are close to the Mississippi," Nika said.

"It looks different," Tonty said, "from what I remember."

A fever racked La Salle's body. He shivered like a dog climbing from an icy stream. For a moment, he saw stars and heard voices. A vision entered his mind.

"I'm sure the river is over there," he said, pointing. "Let's return to *L'Aimable*. We'll sail west. If we hug the shoreline, we should see the muddy waters."

In his feverish mind, La Salle was convinced they

were somewhere near the Florida panhandle. In fact, they made land only a few miles to the west of the Mississippi River. Going east, they would have seen the brown water by lunchtime.

Another wrong decision would doom the expedition to failure.

"LA SALLE HAS no idea where we are," Beaujeu noted.

"Placing a non–navy man in charge of navigation is both unheralded and unwise," Aigron said.

Beaujeu nodded. "Return to your ship. Short of mutiny, we must follow the order."

"Mutiny might be wise," Aigron said, rising to return to *Belle*. "The damned settlers are eating my sailors' rations. If we don't make land and get a hunting party ashore, we may all starve to death."

The next morning, the trio of ships began sailing west. The tiny *Belle* hugged the shoreline, while *L'Aimable* stayed in the middle. The gunship *Joly* stayed farther out to sea to defend in case a Spanish ship happened past. A week passed, with the Father of Waters falling farther off their stern. When the expedition finally arrived off Texas, it was low on food and lower still on morale. Events were quickly turning worse.

"These barrier islands must have been farther out to sea," La Salle said.

"Then behind the islands is where we planted the French flag?" Tonty asked.

"I believe so," La Salle said.

Nika sat silently, brooding. Their current location was different from what he remembered. Here, the species of birds were not the same. Not only that, the beasts he glimpsed on land were more like those that graced the Great Plains.

Even so, the taciturn Indian said nothing. No one had asked his opinion.

"Even if the lagoons are not the outflow of the Mississippi, they must be a tributary that the river empties into," La Salle said. "We will make land, send out hunters, erect a fort for protection, then set out exploring. I have a good feeling."

His feeling came from the fever, but there was no one to second-guess his decision.

BELLE HAD PASSED the bar. *L'Aimable* and *Joly* remained outside.

"Sir," Aigron said, "I must protest. The water is shallow and the currents tricky."

It was the first face-to-face meeting between the two men in months.

"*Belle* has been inside," La Salle noted.

"A smaller, shallow draft vessel," Aigron said. "*L'Aimable* is three hundred tons."

"I am ordering you to take command of *L'Aimable* and take her inside," La Salle said, "or face charges of mutiny."

Aigron stared at the menacing presence of Tonty only feet away.

"I will draw up orders absolving me of any responsibility," Aigron said, "which you must sign. Then I am transferring my personal possessions to *Joly* outside the bar."

"I will agree to those terms," La Salle said wearily.

Aigron turned to his second in command. "Have

sailors sound the bottom and lay a string of buoys lining each side of the channel. We enter at high tide tomorrow."

La Salle rose. "I am turning over command of this vessel. Have a shore boat drop our possessions on land. Tonty, Nika, and I will stay on land tonight."

"As you wish, Monsieur La Salle," Aigron said.

LA SALLE, his two trusted companions, and a small party of settlers and sailors spent the night on land. The twentieth day of February 1685 dawned clear. Only a few scattered gusts of wind marred what appeared to be an otherwise perfect day. La Salle was tired. Indians from a nearby tribe had approached twice. So far the savages had remained peaceful, but they spoke a dialect neither La Salle nor Nika could understand.

Their intentions remained an unknown.

La Salle ordered a party of men to a small forested area nearby to fell a tree to be used to construct a dugout canoe for exploring the shallow waters. Staring out to sea, La Salle could see *L'Aimable* weigh anchor. At just that instant, a sailor jogged over to where he was standing. He was breathless and required a second to catch his wind.

"The savages," he gasped at last, "they came and took our men."

La Salle stared out to sea. The *Belle* was supposed to tow *L'Aimable* through the gap, but she remained away. Was the pilot intending to take *L'Aimable* in on sail against orders? There was no time for La Salle to find out. Together with Tonty and Nika, he ran toward the Indian encampment.

Looking over his shoulder, La Salle watched as *L'Aimable*'s sails were unfurled.

It wasn't the wine as much as the brandy that gave pilot Duhout and Captain Aigron their courage. With sails to the wind, they closed the distance. On old sailing vessels the pilot faced backward, staring at the horizon behind. With masts, riggings, and supplies stacked on deck, there is little to see facing forward.

"Port a quarter," Duhout shouted to Aigron, who adjusted the wheel.

"Starboard an eighth."

And so it went.

Aigron steered *L'Aimable* through the first shoals successfully. Lining up with the buoys, he began his run past the reef. In a few minutes, he would be inside.

"One ax and a dozen needles," La Salle offered as trade for his men.

Nika translated as best he could, then waited to see if it was understood.

The Indian chief nodded his assent and motioned for the men to be released.

La Salle and Tonty stepped outside to stare at the water at *L'Aimable*.

"If they hold the present course, they'll run her aground," La Salle said to Tonty.

"I fear you are right," Tonty said, "but there is nothing we can do."

La Salle was completing the negotiations when he heard the cannon shot the expedition had agreed upon as a sign of distress. *L'Aimable* had run aground.

*

WOOD RUBBING against a reef makes the sound of a screaming infant.

In the lower hold, the supplies to sustain the expedition were already becoming damp. If they were not quickly removed and dried, they would be lost.

"She's hard aground," Aigron said to Duhout. "The reef has holed the bottom."

"The wine and brandy," Duhout said, "should be salvaged first."

LA SALLE MADE his way back to the coast with his freed men as quickly as he could. As he rounded a corner and climbed up a small rise, his eyes met a grim sight. L'Aimable was hopelessly aground atop the reef, the tear in her side discharging the cargo into the water. To make matters worse, out in the Gulf of Mexico the sky was turning an angry black.

All that remained was to salvage what they could and pray for better luck, but luck would prove elusive. The rest of the day, the crew salvaged what goods they could by loading them onto small boats and transferring them to shore. At nightfall they set up camp.

Tomorrow, God willing, they would return for the rest.

The winds and the waves came calling that night, battering the stationary L'Aimable like a punching bag being pummeled by a prizefighter, and the ship was ripped to shreds. The morning sky dawned red. At first light La Salle stood silently, watching as wave after wave washed over the few sections of L'Aimable's hull that remained above water.

Little remained but to add up the losses.

Nearly all the expedition provisions were gone,

along with all the medicines. Four cannon and their shot, four hundred grenades, and small arms to protect the settlers. Iron, lead, the forge, and the tools. Baggage and personal items, books and trinkets.

The loss of *L'Aimable* was the deathblow, but La Salle had yet to realize it.

With what goods could be salvaged, La Salle moved inland and constructed a fort he named for the king of France. Fort Saint Louis gave La Salle a base from which to explore. With the few sailors and settlers still loyal, he began his search for the elusive Father of Waters.

But fate was a cruel mistress.

With La Salle's permission, Captain Beaujeu took all the settlers wanting to leave aboard *Joly*. In March of 1685, he returned to France. The next year was one of hardship and disappointment for La Salle. His inland expeditions made him realize he was hundreds of miles from the Mississippi River Delta.

After months of hardships, he returned to Fort Saint Louis to regroup. Upon arriving, La Salle received word that *Belle* had run aground and sunk.

The loss of *Belle* added fuel to the disillusionment of the remaining settlers and soldiers. The little ship was the only visible lifeline to France. With *Belle* destroyed, the settlers were little more than stranded visitors in a savage and cruel new world.

It was the final straw.

"I'LL TAKE a few men and set off for Canada," La Salle told Tonty. "You remain here so I have someone in control."

"That's a thirty-five-hundred-mile trip on foot," Tonty said. "Are you sure?"

"What other choice do we have?" La Salle said. "If we don't get some supplies soon, we all die. I've made it down the Mississippi before."

Tonty nodded. That had been years before, when La Salle was younger and healthier.

"How many men will you need?" Tonty asked.

"Less than a dozen," La Salle said, "so we can move quickly."

"I shall arrange it immediately," the always-loyal Tonty said.

IN MARCH of 1687, La Salle set out, but an old wound would bring death.

Duhout was the pilot of *L'Aimable* when she ran aground. Those who stayed behind blamed him for the expedition's failure. Because of that fact it was strange that La Salle allowed him to go along on the trip to Canada. The truth was that the settlers who would remain at Fort Saint Louis didn't want him around—Duhout had been acting increasingly strange as time passed.

La Salle figured that if he led Duhout to Canada he could wash his hands of him.

But Duhout's mind was fast fading into madness. He was beset by paranoia and voices in his head—evil thoughts that floated on the wind. At first, Duhout believed La Salle was talking about him behind his back. Within a few days, he thought La Salle was plotting to trade him to the Indians as a slave. By the time they reached the Trinity River, Duhout was sure La Salle was planning to kill him, so he moved first. He killed La Salle and left his body by the river.

The man who had set out to claim a continent died alone and disillusioned. His grave has yet to be found.

Within months of La Salle's death, Indians attacked Fort Saint Louis. Weakened by disease, the settlers could barely put up a fight, and they were slaughtered. The French plans for a settlement in the New World had been savagely crushed by weather, distance, and discord. When it was all said and done, only a dozen people had survived.

La Salle was a visionary, but, like so many other explorers, his vanity got the best of him. And yet his place in American history is secure. Only Lewis and Clark covered more territory than the aristocrat from France.

II

Out of Reach

1998–1999

HOW I WAS BEGUILED INTO LOOKING FOR *L'Aimable* (pronounced "la amaablea") is still a mystery to me. In my mind it was not a ship that held great interest. It had great historical significance, to be sure, but there was little romance or tragedy tied to it. Besides, NUMA had never searched for a ship that had been lost for three hundred years. However, like a trout that hasn't eaten all winter, I took the bait, rounded up a team, and began studying the historical records on La Salle's fatal expedition.

It all began when Wayne Gronquist, then-president of NUMA, met with Barto Arnold, who was then-director of the Underwater Archeological Research Section of the Texas Antiquities Commission. Arnold had achieved a remarkable accomplishment in recovering La Salle's smallest ship, *Joly*, which had grounded inside Matagorda Bay and had been abandoned. Building a cofferdam around the wreck,

Arnold and his team recovered hundreds of artifacts from La Salle's doomed 1685 expedition.

Arnold had conducted a magnetic survey of the area in 1978 and had hoped to initiate a major investigation of the myriad targets he had found. Texas Antiquities did have the funds and came to NUMA. Barnum was right: There's a sucker born every minute. Caught in an unguarded moment, I succumbed and offered to fund the survey and expedition, never dreaming it would take months and a boatload of currency.

The services of World Geoscience Inc., of Houston, were enlisted for an in-depth aerial magnetic survey using technology that was unavailable to Arnold twenty years earlier. The plan was to conduct a follow-up project to excavate and identify the magnetic anomalies located from the air.

Good old steadfast Ralph Wilbanks, a respected marine surveyor and valued trustee of NUMA, along with marine archaeologist Wes Hall, were called in to execute the survey. Ralph and Wes are the two men who discovered the Confederate submarine *Hunley* in 1995.

The historical data was accumulated and analyzed by respected historian Gary McKee. Douglas Wheeler, a NUMA trustee and a dedicated shipwreck hunter, generously provided funding for the first survey. Doug's only return on his investment was a remarkable painting of *L'Aimable*, by marine artist Richard DeRosset, that hangs in his office.

Contemporary reports on La Salle's ill-fated expedition were studied. The journals of Henri Joutel described a detailed account of the loss of *L'Aimable*. Minet, La Salle's chief navigator, drew contemporary charts that accurately illustrated Cavallo Pass as it appeared in 1685 and indicated the position of the wreck. Minet's charts show the wreck of *L'Aimable* lying on the eastern side of the old channel. The only predicament was that Minet seemed to have trouble measuring distances over water. He had a tendency to overestimate, a common error made by people judging distance over water by eye. Still, it isn't often that you can be lucky enough to find an eyewitness account that puts you in the ballpark.

The area to be investigated was determined at 4.81 nautical miles north to south and 2.12 nautical miles east to west, more than covering the documented wreck site. By making transparencies of Minet's charts to scale and then overlaying them with modern charts and aerial photographs, we could see that the shorelines had changed considerably over three hundred years. The southern tip of Matagorda Island has eroded significantly, up to a thousand feet, whereas the Matagorda Peninsula's erosion has not been as extreme. Though Minet's channel width seems too wide, it would be logical to assume that he simply misgauged the distance, since most charts from between 1750 and 1965 do not vary by more than a hundred yards.

The major frustrations we faced were the changes in the channel that had occurred over the last thirty-five years. In 1965, the U.S. Army Corp of Engineers opened a new shipping channel through the Matagorda Peninsula to the Intracoastal Waterway a few miles northeast of Cavallo Pass. The new channel changed the dynamics of the water flow out of the bay and altered the pass dramatically. These changes made it difficult to make exact comparisons between the modern charts and the older ones.

If we had come along before 1965, our job would have been much simpler. After the new channel was dredged, the original thirty-foot-deep channel began to "sand in." This transformation deeply buried most of the shipwrecks in our search grid, making it all the more difficult to reach them.

In February 1998, Ralph and Wes began the first survey, using Ralph's reliable twenty-five-foot Parker he had named *Diversity*. Naturally, the rest of us refer to it as *Perversity*. No more practical boat ever sailed the water in search of shipwrecks, but luxury yacht comfort she ain't. If you'll pardon a dry description of the technical equipment, the boat carried two marine cesium magnetometers, a handheld proton procession magnetometer, a NAVSTAR differentially corrected global positioning system (GPS), Coastal Oceanographics navigation and data-collecting software, and a small induction dredge.

The search team operated out of Port O'Connor, Texas, a town of friendly, warm people but not much else. There is a gas station, a nice motel, Josie's Mexican Restaurant—run by the wonderful Elosia Newsome—and 560 bait shacks. There is no main street. Next to Port O'Connor, Mayberry was a metropolis. I don't possess much insight into people's souls, so I am still baffled as to why Ralph bought a house there. I suppose one reason is that the local citizens think the world of Ralph and look upon him as the best thing to hit the town since grits.

Diversity left the port in the month of February. Each anomaly that was detected during the aerial surveys was located from the water surface as directed by the navigation computer software operating in conjunction with the differential global positioning system. Once the target was confirmed by the magnetometer, it was marked with a buoy. Next, the divers went over the side and examined the bottom. If the target was buried, the diver used a handheld proton to pinpoint the exact spot. Then a thin metal probe or water-jet probe was used to find out how deep the target was buried. Once the dimensions and depth were established, the induction dredge was lowered and the sand blown away, as a crater was dug over the target. Once an artifact or a wreck was revealed, a study was made to date it. A boiler meant a nineteenth- or twentieth-century wreck. Same with the remains of paddle wheels from an old steamship. Capstans, bronze propellers, deck winches, various pieces of ship's machinery, and anchors along with their chains were uncovered. Fascinating discoveries, but no blue ribbon or trophy.

A shipwreck was soon discovered and marked as Target 4. It was routinely marked with a buoy, and the drivers deployed to investigate the site. Two artifacts were found exposed and recovered for investigation. They appeared to be badly encrusted firearms, a flintlock pistol, and a flintlock musket.

Hopes were high that *L'Aimable* had been found, as Ralph sent the artifacts to the conservation laboratory at Texas A&M for preservation and identification. Sadly, our hopes were dashed when an X-ray evaluation revealed them to be from the late eighteenth to early nineteenth century. While of historical importance, they were not from *L'Aimable*.

Thus ended phase one.

I have been in contact with the Texas Antiquities Commission and Texas A&M University about the possibility of archaeology students excavating the artifacts on the wreck as a school project. Though I have offered to fund the effort, as of this writing I've yet to hear anything.

In September of the same year, Ralph set out again and launched phase two, lasting most of the fall and into the winter. Bad weather caused countless delays. I can't imagine the jolly times they must have had in Port O'Connor while waiting days and weeks for the weather to clear. I heard that one of their pastimes was going down to the nearest bait shack and counting worms.

I flew into San Antonio and had a pleasant two-hundred-mile drive to Port O'Connor for the next phase of the search. I met Ralph at the motel and had dinner at Josie's, where the meals are really belly-busters.

We set out the next day with a relatively calm sea and clear skies. I have always felt as though I was coming home when I stepped aboard *Diversity*. She is as rugged as they come, as well as stable and fast, its 250-horsepower Yamaha shoving her through the waves. *Diversity* and I have a love-hate relationship. I never fail to bang my shins on her many flanges, sharp edges, and pointed knobs, causing me to bleed all over Ralph's clean deck. Ralph always has a cooler of beer and soda pop, along with strange munchies from food manufacturers no one has ever heard of, such as Magnolia's Spicy Pickled Okra and Carl's Crunchy Pig Parts.

Wes Hall was working on another survey on the East Coast, so Mel Bell and Steve Howard, two very efficient and affable guys, filled in as dive crew for the second phase. Several targets were marked and probed before the dredge was unleashed, and we dug through the silt to see what turned up. Still no *L'Aimable*.

One evening during the operation, the leading citizens of Port O'Connor threw a barbecue party in our honor. A fun time was had by all, and I found it interesting to hear about the hefty amount of funding that was to be raised to aid in the recovery and preservation of any artifacts that would be put on display at a facility in town. I keep looking, but I haven't found a check yet. Help did come, however, in the form of contacts for additional equipment, which proved invaluable.

Target 2 appeared that it might be *L'Aimable*. She had the right magnetometer readings and after being probed was found to lie twelve feet under the sand, definitely an old wreck and a likely prospect. She could not be revealed just yet, since the dredge aboard *Diversity* was not up to the job of blowing a twelve-foot-deep crater. I had to return home because of writing commitments. Ralph received the generous assistance of Steve Hoyt and Bill Pierson of the Texas Historical Commission (THC), who brought their boat, *Anomaly*, a state marine survey boat with reverse prop-wash thrusters that could blow a larger hole through the sand. Not much progress could be made, due to poor weather conditions, and it was decided to cease operations until the weather improved.

Phase three began in June of 1999, as the sea turned fairly smooth. A veritable fleet set out for Target 2. Besides Ralph and his *Diversity* team, there was the Texas Historical Commission crew and its survey boat *Anomaly*, and a new arrival, the sixty-five-foot *Chip XI*, owned by the Ocean Corporation of Houston, a school for commercial divers. This boat was more than well equipped to reach through the silt to investigate the target. Jerry Ford, chief dive instructor for OC, brought along a team of dedicated students who volunteered to work the project on their own time.

Over the next several days, Target 2 was partially exposed. She was indeed a very old shipwreck. A cannonball was recovered, and then the divers exposed a cannon. I was immediately phoned and asked to provide the necessary financial support to conserve it. I was more than willing to comply, and the THC agreed to permit the recovery. But, while this was going on, the weather turned bad again, and the recovery was postponed for three weeks to await clearer seas. Unfortunately, as usually happens, the crater containing the cannon filled in with sand.

When the climate became congenial once again, *Diversity* and *Anomaly* returned to the scene of the wreck, then blew another huge hole until the cannon was exposed for the second time since it had sunk into the seafloor. Then it was raised with lift bags from its twelve-foot-deep hole and laid on the surface of the bottom.

The next day, Chief Kevin Walker graciously offered the Coast Guard's assistance, and he arrived at the site on a fifty-five-foot buoy tender. The crane used to lift buoys was activated, and the cannon was raised into the sun for the first time in more than two hundred years and lowered onto the deck. From the site, it was then carried to the Coast Guard base in Port O'Connor and immersed in shallow water for temporary preservation until it could be transported, along with the cannonball, to Texas A&M University for conservation.

James Jobling of the conservation lab eventually identified what turned out to be a British navy twenty-four-pounder carronade and dated it from the late seventeenth or early eighteenth century. Several months later, Jobling called and said that he and A&M had never received the check for $3,000, the cost of preserving the cannon. I checked with Wayne Gronquist, who assured me that the elite of Port O'Connor would take care of it. Another three months and Jobling had yet to be paid, so I sent him a check. My next call was to Steve Hoyt at the Texas Historical Commission. Even though the state had jurisdiction regarding the final placement of the cannon, I politely asked that it go anywhere but Port O'Connor, since all had run and hid when it came time to pay the bill. The last I heard, it was still in the conservation lab.

MISSED AGAIN.

But not entirely.

When the legendary pirate Jean Laffite was ordered out of Galveston in 1821, he engaged in a few piratical operations that angered not only the Americans but the British as well. Combined naval units of both countries chased him down the coast of Texas, pressing him hard. Reaching Cavallo Pass, his fleet of pirate ships was chased by five British frigates and several American armed sloops. His band of pirates was in a desperate situation. Throwing caution to the wind, during a violent storm he ordered his fleet to run over the bar at the entrance to the Pass, into the inner channel. With fortitude and luck, Laffite made it into Matagorda Bay with all his ships intact. The British frigates tried to follow him in, but two grounded and were lost.

Laffite, so the story goes, having achieved a short reprieve, divided up the booty among his pirate crews, burned his ships, and vanished. Rumors put him in South Carolina, where he married Emma Mortimer of Charleston, who knew him as successful merchant Jean Lafflin. After several years in the South, he and his wife moved to St. Louis, where it is said he manufactured gunpowder. On his deathbed he confessed to his wife that he was Jean Laffite the pirate, and was buried in Alton, Illinois, sometime in 1854.

Target 2, where the flintlock firearms were found, and Target 4, the wreck that produced the British cannon, intrigued everyone. Could these be the lost British frigates? There is little doubt that both were early warships. Future research and excavations by Texas archaeologists may well identify them.

That left us Target 8.

This was the most elusive, engaging, and enticing anomaly of them all. She gave a large magnetic signature of 560 gammas, which is consistent with a shipwreck with three to five tons of ferrous metal on board. Ralph conducted four underwater surveys with the handheld proton magnetometer. Each pass put the magnetic mass in the same area. The site was then probed with a twenty-six-foot jet probe. After several tries, the probe became lodged in something under the sand and was abandoned.

The location is also in the approximate latitude of *L'Aimable* and buried far deeper than the other wrecks Ralph found, a sure indication of an old vessel that has every potential of coming from the seventeenth century. She remains the most promising of all and the most obstinate to reach. Uncovering her for identification would take a major excavation effort.

As they say, so near, yet so far.

DISCOVERING KING TUT'S tomb was scooping ice cream compared to the hunt for La Salle's flagship *L'Aimable*. This was the toughest survey NUMA ever tackled. No search in a cemetery full of unmarked graves for a particular body could have been more formidable or challenging than this one. Ralph Wilbanks worked incredibly hard and left a legacy of investigative marine survey that will take a while to equal.

His long and arduous search resulted in the identification of sixty-six targets. Every magnetic anomaly in the entire Cavallo Pass area, including targets on shore, was surveyed and pinpointed on GPS. Eighteen were identified as shipwrecks or potential wreck sites. Ten shipwrecks were dated to the twentieth century, five are from the nineteenth, two are from the eighteenth century, and one, Target 8, has the potential to be a seventeenth-century wreck. If she is *L'Aimable*, she is beckoning and daring us to reach down and touch her.

Now all we have to do is go back and dig a bigger hole.

PART TWO

The Steamboat *New Orleans*

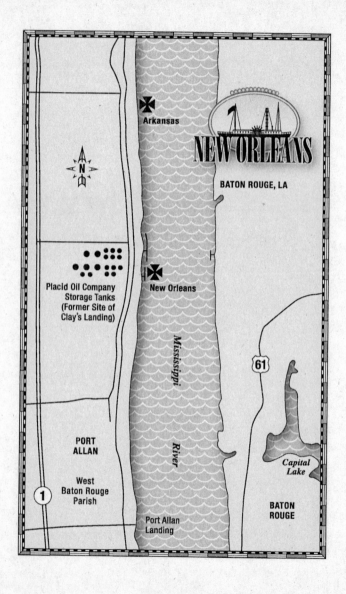

NEW ORLEANS

BATON ROUGE, LA

Arkansas

Placid Oil Company
Storage Tanks
(Former Site of
Clay's Landing)

New Orleans

Mississippi

61

River

PORT
ALLAN

West
Baton Rouge
Parish

1

Port Allan
Landing

Capital
Lake

BATON
ROUGE

I

Penelore

1811–1814

"Good Lord," Nicholas Roosevelt said.

A giant comet was hurtling through space on an elliptical orbit back to the sun. The diameter of the orb was estimated to be more than 400 miles, with a gaseous tail stretching back nearly 100 million miles. The comet moved slowly and steadily through its orbit—an orbit that required more than three thousand years to complete. The comet had last been seen on earth during the reign of Ramses II.

The date was October 25, 1811. The time, 10:38 P.M.

Roosevelt was medium height, about five feet six inches, and medium weight, around 150 pounds. His hair was brown, not favoring blond or drifting toward black, but a single shade like a varnished walnut log. His eyes, which twinkled when he became excited, were green and flecked with gold dots. In general, his appearance was average. What set Roosevelt apart from his fellowman was an undefined and indescribable demeanor, a zest for life that oozed from him like sap from a tree. Call it confidence, attitude, or ego—whatever it was, Roosevelt had it in spades.

STANDING ON the steamboat *New Orleans*, Lydia Roosevelt stared overhead in awe.

Lydia was dressed in a high-necked dress with a hoopskirt accented by a white straw hat interwoven with wild flowers. Her attire was out of place given her rough surroundings. She was graced with a face that was one of extremes. Her eyes were large, her mouth surrounded by puffy lips, and her nose slightly wider than usual. She was young and filled with life. Her chest was heavy and wide, her hips broad but without fat, her legs thick but shapely. She was not a delicate miniature rose but instead a robust sunflower in bloom. Lydia was eight months pregnant with her second child. The Roosevelts' first child, a daughter named Rosetta, was three. The Roosevelts had been married five years. Nicholas was forty-three, Lydia twenty.

For nearly an hour, the crew of *New Orleans* watched as the massive orb crossed from east to west like God's own exclamation point. The crew watched the spectacle in bemused amazement as the comet moved soundlessly through space. Even Tiger, the Roosevelts' Newfoundland dog, was strangely quiet.

"One more strange occurrence," Lydia said, as the comet faded from view. "First, northern lights and rivers out of their banks, then squirrels and pigeons. Now this."

Lydia was referring to a recent rash of strange events.

The spring floods of 1811 had been worse than usual. After the water finally retreated, sickness from the stagnant water left behind had gripped the land. Shortly thereafter, the aurora borealis became visible farther to the south than usual. To compound the odd turn of events, the strange flickering lights were visible for months. Then even more strange phenomena: On the day *New Orleans* left Pittsburgh, the crew had witnessed thousands of squirrels, an undulating wave of fur, traveling south as if being chased by a coordinated pack of dogs. The squirrels seemed hell-bent on escaping something, and the sight had been mildly disturbing to all aboard.

Then, a few days later, the crew witnessed another bizarre incident.

While everyone on *New Orleans* was asleep, the leading edge of a flock of passenger pigeons crossed over the river. The flock flew from north to south, a mass of birds stretching some 250 miles from Lake Erie into Virginia. The next morning when the crew woke, the decks of the *New Orleans* were spotted with droppings, and the sky overhead was still dark.

"What do you make of it?" Roosevelt asked Andrew Jack, the pilot.

"Sometimes these migrations can take days to pass," Jack said.

Lydia waddled down the walkway and now stood outside the door as well.

"I don't like that sound," she said. "Like the beating of tiny drums."

"A few more minutes and we'll be under way," said Jack. "Once we're a few miles downstream, we should be out of the migration path."

That night, after they tied up alongshore, Roosevelt supervised the deckhands as they washed *New Orleans*

from stem to stern. Tomorrow they would stop for a
few days in Henderson, Kentucky, to visit friends.
Roosevelt wanted *New Orleans* to look her best. Even
with all the strange events, his enthusiasm was
undiminished.

Nicholas Roosevelt was a constant source of
optimism.

New Orleans's itinerary was Pittsburgh to New
Orleans—a trip never before attempted by a steamship.
The trip was part of a well-funded and well-planned
play for Roosevelt and his partners. Their goal was to
secure a patent on western steamboat traffic. At the time
of the voyage, laws pertaining to steamships were still
in their infancy. In New York State, Robert Fulton's
company had managed to patent steamboat travel on
the Hudson River, creating, at least for a time, an
extremely lucrative monopoly. Now Fulton, along with
partners Robert Livingston and Nicholas Roosevelt,
wanted to do the same on the Mississippi River. The
planning for his trip had been meticulous and detailed.
First, the trip needed to be successfully completed. If
the boat sank, no investor would want to ante up.
Second, the trip needed to be completed quickly, to
prove to investors the economic benefit of steam over
paddle.

Robert Fulton, the inventor of the world's first
functional steamboat, had designed *New Orleans,* while
Robert Livingston, a wealthy New York businessman
who was a confidant of Thomas Jefferson, had
provided the funding. Roosevelt, himself no slouch
when it came to powerful contacts, was a descendant of
the Dutch settler who had purchased Manhattan Island
from the natives, as well as a close friend of John

Adams. The previous year, Nicholas and Lydia had made a test journey down the river on a flatboat, stopping to visit influential people along the way.

Nothing was left to chance, but there are some things that cannot be predicted.

NEW ORLEANS was 116 feet in length with a 20-foot beam. Constructed of yellow pine—not Roosevelt's first choice, but the only wood available within their rushed timetable—the vessel featured a rounded belly like that of a trout.

The middle section of *New Orleans*'s deck was open, housing the 160-horsepower steam engine, copper boilers, and walking beam that transferred power to the pair of side-wheel paddles. Having the machinery in the open gave the ship an unfinished appearance. Two masts with wrapped sails were stationed to each side of the open engine pit. From the stern mast flew the flag of the United States, a red, white, and blue cloth featuring seventeen stars and seventeen stripes. A pair of rectangular cabins, men's forward and women's aft, sat on the deck to each side of the engine pit. In the forward cabin was an iron cooking stove, and atop the ladies' cabin were a table and chairs covered by an awning. In the stern, constantly diminishing piles of firewood gave the boat a rough edge. All in all, *New Orleans* was a crude but functional-looking affair.

The morning after the comet passed, *New Orleans* continued downriver. By ten that morning, the ship was fifty miles from Cincinnati and steaming at eight miles per hour. This was the third day since leaving Pittsburgh, and the crew was finding a routine. Andrew Jack, the pilot who was guiding the newfangled steamship downriver, was tall, nearly six feet five inches in his work boots. Lean, with long narrow feet, he came across as a bit of a stork. His cheekbones were pronounced and his jaw square and defined. Jack had sandy-colored hair combed to the left. Bushy eyebrows topped pale gray eyes that looked far into the distance. He was twenty-three years old.

Belowdecks was the domain of Nicholas Baker, a dark-haired man who stood five feet nine inches and weighed 150 pounds. Baker had a face that was square and sturdy and without contrasts. His appearance might be called plain, save for his bright smile and warm eyes. With help from the six Cajun and Kaintuck deckhands, Baker tended to the engines and kept the boiler's fires stoked and the steam at a steady 60 pounds.

At least *New Orleans* was blessed with an experienced crew.

Painted an unusual sky-blue, the vessel steamed around the port bend in the Ohio River above Cincinnati. The pile of firewood on the rear deck was less than four feet by four feet, barely enough to make the city docks, since *New Orleans* burned fuel at the rate of six cords a day. A single cord of wood measures four feet high by four feet wide by eight feet long. When the steamboat was fully stocked with a full day of fuel, she looked like a lumber barge on her way to the mill.

"Sweep up the scraps of bark," Roosevelt said to one of the Cajun deckhands, "and straighten the rear deck."

"Yes, sir," the man drawled.

"We need the boat to look her best," Roosevelt said as he walked forward, "for as of this instant she's the most famous ship in the Western Territories."

At that instant, the shriek of the steam whistle ripped

through the air.

"Cincinnati dead ahead," Jack shouted from the pilothouse door.

As soon as *New Orleans* was tied fast to the dock, a crowd of citizens went to the waterfront to view the oddity up close. Nicholas Roosevelt was in rare form, and the bizarre events of the journey so far seemed behind them. With a showman's zeal, he led groups aboard the steamboat.

"Come one, come all," he shouted, "see the future of travel firsthand."

As the crowds filtered aboard, Engineer Baker explained the workings of the steam engine while Captain Jack demonstrated the steering from the pilothouse. Roosevelt even allowed the guests to tour the cabins and dining room. Other than the grumbling of a spoilsport, who claimed the vessel would never make it upstream against the current, the visit was proving successful.

It was dark and growing cold by the time the last guests left.

A chill wind blew from the east. The pregnant Lydia was tired and cold. She was resting in the dining room with a blanket around her legs. Her feet were propped up on a chair. Nicholas chased the last of the guests off *New Orleans*, then pulled the gangplank back aboard. Entering the dining room, he walked over to his wife.

"We couldn't fire the cookstove because of all the people aboard," Lydia said, "so we're having cold roast beef sandwiches for dinner."

Nicholas nodded wearily.

"The cook did have a chance to slip ashore and buy milk, however," Lydia said, "so you can have a cold glass of milk with your sandwich."

Nicholas pushed the clasp on his gold pocket watch, and the top popped open. Staring at the roman numerals inside, he could see it was nearly 7 P.M. "I need to go ashore for pipe tobacco. The store closes soon. Do you need anything?"

Lydia smiled. "If there's a pickle barrel, a few dills would be good."

"The baby, my dear?" Roosevelt asked.

"Yes," Lydia agreed, "it seems he craves sour."

"Be right back," Roosevelt said.

"I'll be waiting with your sandwich," Lydia shouted after her retreating husband.

Nicholas leapt the short distance to the receiving pier, then hurried up the cobblestone street to the store. Cincinnati was a frontier town. No streetlights lined the avenue, and what scant illumination was available came from candles and fuel oil lamps inside the shops lining the road. Half of the shops were closed for the night, and the cobblestones were a patchwork of light. Finding the mercantile, Nicholas entered, made his purchases, then started back for the boat.

Roosevelt was bone-tired. The excitement of the last few days, combined with the fact that he had yet to eat dinner, was dragging him to the edge of exhaustion. He walked with his head down as he descended the hill to the river.

Roosevelt did not see the approaching man until he was already upon him.

"The end is near," the man shouted, as Roosevelt nearly bumped into him.

Nicholas raised his eyes and took in the stranger. The man was bedraggled and badly in need of a bath.

His hair was long, halfway down his back, and matted. His face was deeply tanned, as if he lived outdoors. What few remaining teeth he had were stained from chewing tobacco. It was his eyes that Roosevelt focused on. They burned with an intensity of conviction or madness.

"Back away, my good man," Roosevelt said, as the man edged closer.

"The squirrels, the birds, a fiery comet," the man muttered. "How much more proof does man need? Repent. Repent."

Nicholas passed the man and continued down the hill.

"Bad things are coming," the man shouted after him. "Mark my words."

Strangely shaken by the bizarre exchange, Roosevelt returned to the *New Orleans*, quickly finished his sandwich and milk, then crept into bed. Hours passed before he found the release of sleep. It would be nearly two months before he knew what the strange man had meant.

TWO DAYS LATER, *New Orleans* bid farewell to Cincinnati, bound for Louisville, Kentucky. At this time the Ohio River was untamed. It featured many stretches with white water and small falls. Luckily, Jack had navigated a variety of flatboats and barges down this part of the river. He stood at the wheel and steered toward the correct channel. Like a kayak through rapids, the steamboat threaded past menacing rocks as the river's rushing current hurtled it through the narrow channel at twice the speed she was capable of reaching on her own.

In the ladies' cabin, Lydia calmly knitted while her servants nervously clutched railings, the rough ride throwing them about the cabin. Everyone sighed with relief when the steamboat finally found calm water again.

The maelstrom passed, and *New Orleans* reached Louisville under a pale harvest moon.

"Well," Jack said, as they pulled in front of the city. "We made it."

Then he released the steam valve. A shriek filled the air. The citizens of Louisville climbed from their beds at the unnatural sound. Wearing nightclothes and carrying candles, they sleepily made their way toward the river and stared at the bizarre beast that had arrived in the middle of the night.

"Looks like you woke the entire town," said Baker.

"Mr. Roosevelt likes to make a grand entrance," Jack said.

Just below Louisville the following day, Roosevelt, Jack, and the mayor of Louisville stood staring at the falls of the Ohio River just outside town.

"I've seen your vessel," the mayor said, "and I concur with Mr. Jack. She draws too much to safely navigate the falls. I'd wait until the water rises."

"When is that?" Roosevelt asked.

"The first week in December," the mayor said.

"Winter rains and snow raise the water level?" Jack asked.

"Exactly," the mayor said.

"That's nearly two months from now," Roosevelt said. "What do we do until then?"

"The crew of *New Orleans* will be our guests," the mayor said.

So that is what they did.

From the start of the voyage, a romance between Maggie Markum, Mrs. Roosevelt's maid, and Nicholas Baker had been blooming. The pair found time for stolen kisses and furtive groping while aboard the ship. More serious physical pursuits took place during their daily walks in the country. They were madly in love, and it would have been hard for the rest on the boat not to notice.

Their love affair was not the only event that took place while *New Orleans* was tied up at Louisville.

The first baby born on a riverboat, Henry Latrobe Roosevelt, arrived at sunrise.

The next few weeks in Louisville passed with cleaning and maintenance. *New Orleans*'s slate-blue paint was touched up and the brightwork was polished. The sails, as yet unused, were unfurled and checked for tears or moth damage, then refolded and stowed on the masts. Andrew Jack studied the measurements on a sheet of paper, then tossed a stick into the middle of the falls and watched its rate of travel. It was late November, and a light chill frosted the air.

"We can make it," he said at last, "but we'll need to traverse at full speed so we have steering control."

Nicholas Roosevelt nodded. A few days earlier, he had received a letter from his partners in the Ohio Steamboat Navigation Company. They'd expressed concern about the delay—the monopoly was in jeopardy. *New Orleans* needed to get under way. Once they had passed the falls, it would be smooth sailing.

Or at least that's what Roosevelt thought.

Nicholas sat inside the dining room, spooning a deer

stew into his mouth. Dabbing a cloth napkin at his lips, he then sipped from a tin cup filled with steaming coffee.

"The river is fullest in about two hours," he said. "I'll have a deckhand take you by wagon to the bottom of the falls, where you'll meet up with us."

"Is this for our safety?" Lydia asked.

"Yes," Nicholas said.

"Then the boat might overturn?" Lydia asked.

"The chance is slim," Nicholas admitted, "but it might."

"Then you would be killed and I'd be alone with a new baby," Lydia said.

"That's not going to happen," Nicholas said.

"I know it's not," Lydia said defiantly. "We're going with you. All or none."

So it was settled. *New Orleans* left the dock in early afternoon.

"I'll run upstream about a mile," Jack said, "then turn down and run her full-out."

Roosevelt stood outside the door to the pilothouse as *New Orleans* pulled into the current. Jack's face was a mask of tension and concern. A thin trickle of sweat ran down his neck, no mean feat with the temperature outside in the forty-degree area.

The steamboat was strangely quiet. The deckhands had secured themselves in the forward cabin. The women huddled together in the aft cabin, lining the windows to watch. Baby Roosevelt lay in a bassinet braced against a bulkhead, sound asleep.

"I'm going to turn now," Jack said.

He spun the wheel. *New Orleans* turned slowly in an arc and faced downstream. Then Jack pulled the whistle, rang the bell for full steam, and said a prayer.

Atop the rock outcropping on the south side of the falls, Milo Pfieffer and his best friend Simon Grants were pouring red paint into the water from a bucket they had stolen from the hardware store. The thin stream of tinted water widened as it neared the top of the falls, then spread across the water as it fell, finally completely tinting the discharge a light pink for a mile downstream.

"Okay," Milo said, "you go watch now."

"What's that?" Simon said, as he heard a noise coming from upstream.

"Ditch the paint," Milo said, "there's grown-ups coming."

Simon stashed the stolen paint, then turned to the crowd that was slowly advancing on the falls. Thirty of Louisville's finest citizens left the dock before *New Orleans*. They planned to watch the steamboat shoot the falls or break up trying.

"What's happening?" Simon asked.

"There's a steamboat going to try and shoot the falls," a man answered.

Milo ran upstream until he spotted *New Orleans* racing downstream. He stared in awe. The slate blue of the hull seemed to blend with the blue of the river water. Sparks and smoke poured from the stack and trailed to the rear like a signal fire run amok. The twin paddle wheels chopped at the river, flinging sheets of water high in the air. No one was visible on deck save for the big black dog atop the bow sniffing the air. In fact, the vessel looked like a ghost ship. Suddenly, the steam whistle shrieked, and Milo watched as *New Orleans* entered the middle channel of the falls.

"Back left wheel," Jack shouted, "full starboard."

New Orleans leaped sideways.

"Full on both wheels," Jack said a second later.

Spray washed through the open windows in the aft cabin, wetting Lydia's and Maggie's faces. To each side of the vessel were rocks and churning waters. They braced themselves as *New Orleans* took a sharp turn from left to right. In the pilothouse, Nicholas Roosevelt peered downstream.

"Looking good," he shouted over the roar of the water.

Engineer Baker poked his head into the pilothouse. "How much longer?"

"Two, maybe three minutes," Jack said.

"Good," Baker said. "I'll rupture a boiler if it's much longer."

"Twenty yards ahead is a series of boulders we need to avoid," Jack said.

"What's the sequence?" Roosevelt shouted.

"Hard left, right half, left half, then full to the right and hug that side of the river until we're in the clear," Jack said.

"Here they go," Milo shouted as *New Orleans* lined up to tackle the last rapids.

"He had better get her over to the left," Simon added.

The mayor of Louisville crested the rocks. He panted from the exertion of the climb. Stopping to catch his breath, he pulled the stub of a cigar from his vest pocket and crammed it in the corner of his mouth before speaking.

"Hard to believe," he said. "They just might make it after all."

Inside the pilothouse, the mood was tense but optimistic. Eighty percent of the falls had been navigated already. All that remained was a small series of rocky outcropping at the outflow. Then they would be in the clear.

"We're almost through," Jack said.

"The river narrows a bit right ahead," Roosevelt noted.

"And the current becomes stronger," Jack noted. "I'll need to steer at the rocks to the right, then let the current swing the bow around. Once she's straight, give her full steam. We should pop right out the other side."

"Should?" Roosevelt asked.

"We will," Jack said.

Inside the aft cabin, Lydia Roosevelt, Maggie Markum, and the heavyset German cook, Hilda Gottshak, were huddled together alongside the windows on the starboard side. Henry the baby was awake, and Lydia held him up to see.

"Looks like we're headed right for the wall," Lydia said, pulling the baby closer.

Gottshak hugged her Bible. "I pray the rest of this trip goes smoothly."

"Pray the engines keep running," Lydia said to her.

At that instant, the current grabbed hold of the bow and swung the vessel around.

"Bully of a job," Nicholas said, as they cleared the last of the falls. "Maxwell will bring you a snifter of brandy."

"The river is smooth from here to the Mississippi," Jack noted.

"How long until we reach Henderson?" Roosevelt asked.

"Barring any problems, we'll be there tomorrow afternoon," Jack said.

"QUIET," LUCY BLACKWELL SAID, "or you will scare it away."

Blackwell was Lydia Roosevelt's best friend. She was also the wife of artist John James Audubon, who would become famous for his sketches, drawings, and paintings of birds. Lydia Roosevelt was the daughter of Benjamin Latrobe, surveyor general of the United States. Nicholas had known the Latrobe family before Lydia was born, and he had watched her grow into womanhood. Though there was more than a twenty-year age difference between the two of them, Lydia was a happy wife.

"Carolina Parrot," Lucy said.

"Beautiful," said Lydia.

Half a mile away, in the Audubons' store in Henderson, Kentucky, Nicholas sat in front of a checkerboard. He glanced over at Audubon, then made his move.

"We are 150 miles below Louisville," Roosevelt said. "So far, so good."

Audubon studied Roosevelt's move. Reaching onto the table, he removed a deerskin pouch of tobacco and filled his pipe. Tamping down the tobacco, he lit it with a nearby candle. "From here downstream," Audubon said, "the river widens and the current slows."

"So you think we'll make New Orleans?" Roosevelt asked.

"Sure," Audubon said. "I made it to the Gulf of Mexico once in a canoe."

Roosevelt nodded and watched as Audubon made his jump.

"Did a painting of a pelican there," he finished, "with a fish hanging from his bill."

On December 16, *New Orleans* left Henderson and continued downstream.

Inside a buffalo-skin tepee near present-day East Prairie, Missouri, a Sioux Indian chief drew in smoke from a long pipe, then handed it to his Shawnee visitor.

"General Harrison defeated the Shawnee at Tippecanoe?" the Sioux chief asked.

"Yes," the Shawnee messenger noted. "The white men attacked the morning after the harvest moon. Chief Tecumseh rallied his braves, but the white men attacked and burned Prophet's Town. The tribe has retreated from Indiana."

The Sioux took the proffered pipe and again inhaled the smoke. "I had a vision yesterday. The white man has harnessed the earth's power for his own evil purposes. He has rallied the beasts to his cause, as well as controlling the comet in the heavens."

"One of the reasons I came," the Shawnee explained, "is that our braves witnessed a Penelore on the river above here. It might try to enter the Father of Waters."

"A Fire Canoe?" the Sioux chief asked. "Must be part of the burning star."

The Shawnee exhaled smoke from his lungs before answering. The Sioux had powerful tobacco, and his head was spinning. "Smoke trails from the center of the canoe like from the middle of a thousand tepees. And it roars like a wounded bear."

"Where did you see this beast last?" the Sioux said.

"It was still at the city by the falls when I left," the Shawnee said.

"Once it comes down my river," the Sioux chief said, "we will kill it."

Then the chief rolled over onto a pile of buffalo robes and closed his eyes. He would seek the answer from the spirits. The Shawnee opened the flap of the tepee and stepped out into the bright light reflected off the early snow.

DEEP INSIDE the earth below New Madrid, Missouri, all was not well. The layers forming the first thousand feet of overburden were twitching like an enraged lion. Molten earth, heated by the immense temperatures below ground, mixed with water from the thousands of springs and dozens of tributaries along the Mississippi River. This superheated, black, slippery liquid worked as a lubricant on the plates of the earth that were held in place under great tension. Earth had given fair notice of the wrath it was about to unleash. The birds and animals had sensed the danger. A great burp from the earth was building. And the burp would soon erupt.

New Orleans was steaming right toward the inevitable eruption.

The Ohio River current ran faster nearing the Mississippi River, and *New Orleans* was steaming smoothly. In a few moments, the ship would arrive at the confluence of the two rivers, hours ahead of schedule. The mood aboard the steamboat was one of happy contentment. The deckhands went about their duties with gusto. Markum had already cleaned the cabins and was hanging the sheets from a clothesline stretched between them. Andrew Jack was taking a short nap on the bow while Nicholas steered. When

Roosevelt sent word that they were at the confluence, he would go to the pilothouse to direct the passage.

Hilda Gottshak was putting the finishing touches on a dozen meat pies for lunch.

"What's wrong, boy?" Lydia asked Tiger.

The Newfoundland had started whining. Lydia checked and found no obvious injuries. Tiger kept up the low, relentless howl. Lydia chose to ignore the animal, hoping he would quiet down on his own.

In the corner of the pilothouse, Roosevelt was figuring the profits *New Orleans* could generate. From the start he'd envisioned the steamboat running from Natchez, Mississippi, to New Orleans. That route would ensure the vessel a ready supply of cargo—bales of cotton and a fair amount of passenger traffic. Roosevelt and his partner, Robert Fulton, figured to pay off the construction costs in eighteen months. Nothing Roosevelt had learned on the journey had made him alter this opinion. Folding up his charts, he slipped them back into his leather satchel.

The smell of the meat pies piqued his appetite. Roosevelt figured that once Jack resumed control of the helm, he would wander into the kitchen and see what Helga had to tide him over until lunch.

He was sure the worst was over, and his appetite had returned with a vengeance.

At the sight of the mighty river, Jack took the wheel from Roosevelt. As he made a sweeping turn into the muddy waters flowing from the north, the Roosevelt baby awoke screaming. At almost the same time, Tiger began to howl as if his tail were caught in a bear trap. To compound matters, the river was rougher than usual, and the boat was suddenly rocking to and fro. Stepping out the pilothouse door, Jack stared at the sky above. A flock of wrens darted back and forth as if their leader had no idea of their intended flight direction. Along the shoreline, the trees began to shake as if responding to an unseen gale.

Though it was not yet noon, the sky to the west was an unearthly orange color.

"I don't like this," Jack shouted, "there's some—"

But he never finished the sentence.

Deep below ground, where the sun will never reach and the cool of a light breeze will never be felt, the temperature was six hundred degrees Fahrenheit. A river of wet, molten earth one hundred feet in diameter roared toward a just-opened fissure. Slipping into the opening, the wet slop acted like Vaseline on glass. The plates of the earth, at this point just barely held in place, slipped like a skater on clear ice.

The earth snapped and stung at the surface.

"Good Lord, what is happen—" Nicholas Roosevelt started to say.

He was standing in the kitchen, trying to talk Helga out of a slab of cheese. Staring out the window for a second, he watched as a geyser of brown water shot eighty feet in the air. Then the water arced over the decks of *New Orleans*, as dozens of fish, turtles, salamanders, and snakes rained down. Then a rumbling was felt through the decks in the hull.

Back in the pilothouse, Jack struggled to keep the steamboat on course.

On the shore, undulating waves swept across the earth like someone shaking a bedspread. The trees along the bank swayed back and forth until their branches intertwined and locked in place. Then they snapped like breadsticks in a vise. Branches were turned into spears and shot across the water like a gauntlet of arrows. Fissures dotted the ground along the river. Streams of water ran into the low-lying areas. Then, seconds later, the ground belched as torrents of shale rock, dirt, and water blasted in the air.

"The river is out of its banks," Jack shouted.

Engineer Baker walked into the pilothouse.

From deep beneath the river's former channel, the blackened trunks of decomposing trees that had become waterlogged and sunk into the mud now shot up into the air with a smell akin to that of putrefied flesh. Baker watched a family of black bears hiding high atop a cottonwood tree, trying to escape the devastation. Suddenly the tree shattered as if a bomb had exploded at the base. He watched as the bears fell to the ground. They began to run west as fast as they could shuffle.

At that instant, Roosevelt burst into the pilothouse.

"It's either an earthquake," he said quickly, "or the end of the world."

"I think the former," Jack said. "I felt one in Spanish California a few years ago."

"How long did it last?" Roosevelt asked.

"That one was small," Jack said. "Only lasted ten minutes or so."

"I'm going to check on my wife," Roosevelt said, as he turned to leave.

"Could you ask Miss Markum to come in here?" Baker asked.

"I will," Roosevelt said, as he sprinted away.

Just then, the earth twitched, and the river began to flow backwards from south to north.

Markum poked her head inside the pilothouse door, her face white with fear.

"If we make it out of this alive—will you marry me?" Baker asked.

"Yes," Markum said without hesitation, clutching Baker around the waist.

Deep below the river, the liquid was squeezed from between the plates, and the grinding together of coarse rock stopped. The first shock had ended, but there was much more to come.

Jack spun the wheel completely to its stop as the Mississippi River changed direction again and returned to a north-to-south flow. Gazing through the window of the pilothouse, he saw that the boat was traversing a farmer's field. Fifty feet off the right side of the boat's hull was the upper story of a large red barn. Several milk cows and a lone horse were huddled on the upper loft, avoiding the rushing water. No trace of a farmhouse could be seen.

When Roosevelt came into the pilothouse, Jack was intent on staring off the right side of the bow far in the distance. There was an opening in the ground ahead that was swallowing up most of the river flow. As the land on the far side of the opening came into view, he could see puddles of water and acres of mud where the riverbed used to lie.

New Orleans was less than a hundred yards from the chasm and was being sucked closer. With only seconds to spare, Baker managed to get the beams reset for reverse running. Inch by inch, the steamboat began to back away from the tempest in the water. Twenty minutes later, *New Orleans* was nearly a mile upstream. Scanning the unearthly landscape, Jack found a tributary that had eroded a straight path through what had once been the river bend. Slipping the boat into the current, he steered past the void and then into the main channel once again.

CROUCHED IN the thick brush of Wolf Island, the Indian braves were as frozen as petrified wood. They had paddled their canoes out to the island before the first shock of the earthquake. When the worst of the tremors struck, their resolve was only strengthened. The Penelore was wreaking havoc across their land, and it needed to be killed. Straining to hear, the chief caught a faint unknown sound coming from upstream. With a series of hand signals, he motioned for his braves to climb into their canoes for the attack.

LYDIA RUSHED to the pilothouse and stuck her head in the door. "The baby has started to cry, and Tiger is whining up a storm."

Roosevelt turned to Jack. "That's the signal another shock is coming. Keep to the main channel to give yourself as much leeway as possible."

Jack pointed through the pilothouse front window. "An island coming up."

Roosevelt scanned through *The Navigator*, the chart book of the river written by Zadoc Cramer. "A lot of this has changed since the earthquake," he said, "but if I had to guess, I'd say it was Wolf Island."

"Which side is the best channel?" asked Jack.

"The left channel has the deepest water."

"The left channel it is."

"How long before the next shock?" Roosevelt asked Lydia.

"Judging by Tiger's howls, not long."

*

A GHASTLY SOUND reached the ears of the Sioux braves hidden on Wolf Island. The grinding of metal, the hissing of steam, the thumping of the walking beam. The great beast grew larger as it neared. The beast was blue like the sky—but this was nothing that came from the heavens. An ugly, pointed nose gave way to two waterwheels halfway down the trunk of the beast. Just behind them were a pair of black tubes where the smoke from the fires of hell spewed forth.

A few white men walked on the decks—dark lords of this evil creature.

First they would kill the white men. Then they would run the beast onto land and put the fire to her skin. When the Penelore was twenty yards upstream, their leader gave the signal, and the braves rose as one. With a war cry, they ran for the water.

The Mississippi River running underground added more much-needed lubricant to the jumble of opposing plates. Once again the earth let loose in a spasm. This tremor would last longer.

At the same instant that the Sioux braves were sprinting to the water, the ground nearby opened up as if it had been pierced by a thousand spears. Funnel-shaped holes in the earth spewed hot jets of water, and the jets formed an arc nearly one hundred feet overhead. Larger craters opened up in the ground, then spewed forth all manners of woody material: trees, branches, coal. It was a bizarre sight.

"Indians approaching from the island!" Roosevelt shouted.

Jack glanced toward Wolf Island and saw a group of braves carrying canoes racing toward the water.

Wearing full headdress, they carried bows on their backs.

Then, all at once, the downstream end of the island collapsed into the water.

The screams from the Sioux braves filled the air. Scalded by the hot water shooting from the ground, they let go of their canoes and stumbled into the cool water for relief. Twenty of them managed to launch a few canoes unscathed and began paddling into the river with every ounce of their strength, determined to destroy the monster they believed was the cause of the tempest.

They began to close the gap, gaining on *New Orleans*.

"Pour on the steam!" Roosevelt shouted to Baker. "They mean to have our scalps."

Baker and his stokers began throwing wood in the firebox like madmen, building up to a full head of steam. Slowly, *New Orleans* began increasing speed. But the Indians were gaining. Putting their backs into it, they could paddle their canoes at a rapid pace.

One canoe slowed as its occupants dropped their paddles, took up their bows, and shot a flight of arrows at the riverboat. Several arrows struck the rear cabin, giving it the look of a porcupine. Tiger ignored the threat and stood on the stern, barking at the attackers.

The first canoe was only twenty feet behind the stern now. Roosevelt and three of his crew loaded their flintlock muskets and prepared to fire point-blank when the Indians came alongside.

The boarding assault never came. Baker had the steam pressure wavering at the red line, and *New Orleans* began to pull away, black smoke pouring from her funnel. Seeing the frustrated Indians falling behind, he couldn't resist adding to Tiger's barking with a series of shrieks through the steam whistle.

Soon the Penelore had disappeared around the next bend, and there was no way for the Sioux to catch the beast.

The series of unforeseen dangers past, Jack glanced to the river ahead. The sun looked like a smoking copper plate framed by a purplish haze of atmosphere. Jack glanced at the shoreline ahead. The earthen hills alongside the great river were tumbling down like sand castles in a tsunami. Large chunks of peaty soil floated on the water, along with downed trees, part of a house, and what looked like a floating casket wrested free from the earth.

"The channel's shifting," Roosevelt said easily. "I'd steer to starboard now."

New Orleans would be miles downstream before the quaking stopped. Amazingly, she made it through the holocaust with minimal damage.

IN MISSISSIPPI you can sweat even in January. Particularly if you are dressed in a wool band uniform left over from the Revolutionary War and are carrying a tuba. Cletus Fayette and the rest of the makeshift band hurried toward the waterfront.

A tuba, a single large drum, and a fiddle—not really a band, more of a trio.

Word of the dramatic voyage of *New Orleans* had reached Natchez three days before. The mayor had wasted no time assembling a suitable welcome. Along with the band, Titus Baird, the mayor, was planning to give Roosevelt the key to the city. Two city councilmen were pressed into service for the obligatory speeches. Several of the local girls had been rounded up to present flowers to the brave women aboard. A banquet would follow in the evening.

Nearly a hundred citizens stood on the hill and glanced upriver for sign of the steamboat.

"Yes," Nicholas said, "we'll be in Natchez at least a week."

"I'll bank the fires, then. The boilers need a break."

"Fine," Roosevelt said, "we should have sufficient steam to reach the dock."

Nicholas climbed from the engine pit and glanced at the scenery. The virgin forest of the upper Ohio River, the falls near Louisville, the terrible cataclysm of weeks of earthquakes and aftershocks were still a vivid memory. His ship and crew had survived the trials with courage and conviction. He and Lydia had grown closer, and Engineer Baker still planned to marry Maggie Markum when they reached New Orleans. Andrew Jack had started to exhibit a hidden sense of humor.

New Orleans rounded the last bend, and Roosevelt glanced toward Natchez.

Baird signaled for the band to begin playing as soon as the steamboat came into sight. The band kept repeating the only song they knew, a crude rendition of "God Save the Queen," but, for some reason, the steamboat stayed away.

Mayor Baird watched as the ship began a turn to make its way to the dock, then began to drift with the downstream current.

"I don't have enough steam to make the dock," Jack said.

Nicholas Roosevelt could only laugh. The steamboat had successfully navigated a thousand miles of toil and trouble. With salvation only yards away, they had run out of steam. The situation was so ludicrous as to be humorous. Baker walked into the pilothouse. He was already dressed in a clean white shirt, and his hands and face looked freshly washed. The grimace on his face was barely hidden.

"I'll take care of it," he said quietly.

Cletus Fayette's head was spinning. A man could play a tuba only so long before he needed a break and a cigar. Fayette had reached his limit.

"We need to take a break, Mayor Baird," he shouted.

"Okay, Cletus," Baird said, "but hurry up. Smoke is coming from the stacks again."

Fifteen minutes later, *New Orleans* was tied to the dock in Natchez. The weary crew walked down the gangplank and made their way through the reception committee to a local hotel and a hero's welcome. The remainder of the journey would be a cakewalk.

In the dead of winter, the trees in the forests surrounding Natchez were devoid of leaves. From the bluff outside town, Nicholas Baker looked north. He could see where the river made a giant loop before passing the city and flowing downstream. A stiff wind blew west, bringing the smell of fields in Alabama being cleared with fire.

"I made arrangements with a preacher in town," Baker said eagerly. "We can be married this afternoon—if you still want me, that is."

"Of course," Markum said, "but what brought this on?"

"I just don't want to wait any longer," Baker said.

"Have you told the Roosevelts?" Markum asked.

"No," Baker admitted, "but I thought we could both tell them right now."

"Now?" Markum said.

"Yes, now," Jack said, "if you want them at the service."

A little over an hour later, on the deck of *New Orleans*, moored just off Natchez, Nicholas Baker stood next to Nicholas Roosevelt. Lydia Roosevelt, holding Henry the baby, wrapped in a clean white blanket, stood next to Maggie.

"Do you, Maggie Markum," the preacher said solemnly, "take Nicholas Baker to be your lawfully wedded husband?"

A yes and a kiss sealed the deal.

The first marriage on a steamboat turned out to be brief.

A few days later, the first cargo of cotton was loaded aboard *New Orleans*. Once the bales were secured on deck and the wood for the boiler secured in the hold, there was little else to do. They left for New Orleans on the seventh day of January 1812.

DAWN CAME like a lamb on January 12, 1812. A clear sky greeted Nicholas Roosevelt as he sat alone on top of the aft cabin. The air was dry, with only occasional small gusts of wind that rippled the placid surface of the river. After all that had transpired, it seemed odd that *New Orleans* would arrive so calmly in the city for which she was named. Nicholas stared to the west. A flock of pelicans, three dozen in all, flew overhead from west to east. The flock was headed for Lake Pontchartrain, some three miles distant. The city of New Orleans was only two miles farther.

"What are you thinking?" Lydia said, as she climbed up onto the roof.

Nicholas smiled and sat quietly for a moment before answering.

"I was wondering what will happen to this old girl in the future," he added.

"*New Orleans* has faced down the devil," Lydia said. "She'll be on this river long after we're gone, dear."

"I hope so," Roosevelt said.

"After all she's been through," Lydia said, "it would really take a lot to hurt her."

Just then Andrew Jack shouted, "New Orleans!"

But Lydia Roosevelt would be proved wrong. *New Orleans* sank thirty months later. After numerous weekly profitable journeys between Natchez and New Orleans and her brief service transporting men and supplies downriver for Andrew Jackson's army during the Battle of New Orleans, the evening of July 14, 1814, found her on the west side of the Mississippi across from Baton Rouge, Louisiana, at a place called Clay's Landing.

John Clay had the wood cut, stacked, and waiting as usual. Ten cords in total; ten dollars would be his payment. Clay waited out of the rain under a nearby tree as *New Orleans* pulled close to the dock leading from shore. He watched as a deckhand tossed a line over one of the poles set deep in the Mississippi River mud. Then he waited until he saw the captain poke his head out of the pilothouse.

"John," the captain shouted. "Got my wood?"

"All cut and stacked." Clay started from under the tree just as a bolt of lightning struck another tree thirty yards upstream. His hair shot out from his scalp at the static electricity, and he huddled back under the tree.

The captain nodded to the deckhands milling around on the deck. "We still have three hours of daylight left. Let's get the wood loaded on board." Then he turned to Clay.

"Come into my cabin," the captain said, "and I'll pay for the wood."

Clay followed the captain to his cabin and waited as he counted out the French gold dauphins. After placing the coins in a leather pouch, John pulled the drawstring tight, then slid the rawhide rope around his head.

"Want a drink?" the captain asked.

"I'm a little chilled," Clay admitted.

So they had a drink and waited together while the wood was loaded.

A short time later, Clay stepped onto the dock and the captain, who followed, stared up at the sky.

"We get your wood on board tonight, we can get an early start in the morning."

"Makes sense," Clay said, as he started up the dock. "The river will be choked with debris from the big rain."

"Good night," the captain shouted after the retreating woodsman.

"Watch for the falling water," Clay shouted back.

But the captain was already inside, and he never heard the warning.

Before the Mississippi River was controlled by dikes and spillways, the water level could quickly drop by feet following a big rain. As the rain-swollen tributaries spilled into the river and the highest point of depth was reached, the water would then race downstream, actually sucking the level lower. After a half-day or so, the level would usually return to normal. The next morning, at first light, the captain ordered *New Orleans* put into reverse to back away from the dock—but she was hung fast on a sunken stump. A few back-and-forth motions and the bottom of her hull was holed.

A passenger on board wrote of the sad event in the *Louisiana Gazette* of July 26, 1814:

> On Sunday 10th July, left New Orleans. On Wednesday the 13th, arrived at Baton Rouge—landed some cargo. And in the evening departed and arrived at Mr. Clay's Landing, two miles above on the opposite shore, the usual place of taking in wood. The night being dark and rainy, the Capt. considered it most prudent to secure the boat for the night . . . Early in the morning, preparations were made for departing, and at daylight the engine was put in motion, but the vessel could only swing around, and could not be forced forward by steam. The water had fallen during the night 16 to 18 inches—the Capt. then concluded she had lodged on a stump, and endeavored to push her off with spars against the bank, but without effect. He immediately satisfied himself it was a stump, and found it by feeling with an oar 15 or 20 feet abaft the wheel on the larboard side. He then ordered the wood thrown overboard, and got an anchor off the starboard quarter, and with the steam capstan hove her off, when she immediately sprung a leak, which increased so rapidly that time was only allowed to make fast again to shore, the passengers to escape with their baggage, and the crew with assistance from the shore,

*saved a great part of the cargo, when she sank
alongside the bank.*

So ended the saga of the first steamboat on the
western rivers.

II

Where Did It Go?

1986, 1995

I CAN'T RECALL WHEN I READ MY FIRST BOOK about steamboats on the Mississippi River, though I suspect it was when I had to give a book report on *Tom Sawyer* in the fifth grade. When my parents went to town on Saturday night, they always parked me at the old Alhambra Public Library. It was there my imagination took hold and I dreamed about floating down the great river with Tom, Huck Finn, and their pals.

For reasons unknown to me, I have always felt a deep attraction to the South. It must sound strange for someone who has no relatives, ancestors, or roots south of the Mason-Dixon line. I arrived in the world in Aurora, Illinois, and grew up in Southern California. My father came from Germany, and my mother's grandfathers were farmers in Iowa who fought in the Union army.

Still, I have to have chicory in my coffee. I insist on grits, redeye gravy, and biscuits for breakfast, and pecan pie for dessert. Maybe we as a people are as much about who we were or who we want to be. It's food for thought, anyway.

There is no more visible symbol of the South than a paddle-wheel steamboat, tooting its whistle as it comes round the bend. Except for a few excursion boats, the image of steamboats belching black smoke, paddle wheels churning the muddy water, and the decks piled high with cotton bales is but a dim memory of the past, like steam locomotives, rumble seats, and running boards.

There are many famous steamboats in American history. One can't help but know about the classic race between the *Natchez* and the *Robert E. Lee*. Then there was Robert Fulton's *Clermont*, the first steamboat in America to go into passenger service on the Hudson River. Another was the *Yellowstone*, the first steamboat to journey far up the Missouri River before heading down the Mississippi to the Gulf, where it evacuated the new president of the Republic of Texas, Sam Houston, and his Congress ahead of the advancing armies of Santa Anna. The first session in the new republic's history was actually held on the *Yellowstone*. The boat then went on to transport a wounded Sam Houston from the battle of San Jacinto to New Orleans for medical care.

I have tried very hard to dig out the final chapter of the *Yellowstone*, but with no success. She was heard of passing through the locks on the Ohio River in 1838. From there she was most likely sold and her name changed, and she may have ended up a derelict tied to a tree along the riverbank, her incredible history ignored and forgotten.

But there was one steamboat whose history no fiction writer could have matched. The saga of the *New Orleans*'s voyage down the Ohio and Mississippi Rivers past the rapids and through the New Madrid earthquake, her escape from hostile Indians, the baby born on board, the comet that streaked above her, all seemed too unbelievable to be true. Yet it was chronicled and her final end described in detail.

During the summer of 1986, unable to resist hunting for such a fabulous boat (any vessel that sails the inland waterways is always called a boat, never a ship), I began researching into a newspaper account of her loss. A passenger on board the morning she hung up on a snag and sank reported the event for a local newspaper. What is most important is that he mentioned almost the exact spot where she came to grief:

Clay's Landing on the west bank of the Mississippi, a short distance above Baton Rouge.

With optimism beating in my heart—my brain too used to failure to be confident—I launched a search for Clay's Landing.

That proved to be tougher than it sounded.

In the meantime, I came across a delightful book by Mary Helen Samoset titled *New Orleans*. I quickly began correspondence with Mrs. Samoset and found her to be a wealth of information about the vessel.

I learned that the owners of the boat salvaged her engines and most of her hardware. Engines were expensive and complicated pieces of machinery for their time. Boilers, however, were seldom salvaged, since prolonged use generally wore them beyond the value of the costly repairs that were usually needed. Any piece of equipment, such as an anchor, a steering mechanism, a helm or hardware, was removed. These were placed in a new vessel, also called *New Orleans*.

This removal of equipment would not leave much for our magnetometer to detect, but we thought there still might be enough iron to detect, and there was always hope that part of the hull might still be visible above the mud and could be picked up on our sidescan sonar.

I began to wonder why no one had ever looked for such a historic ship before.

Fortunately, I was contacted by Keith Sliman, who at the time worked for Seven Seas Dive Shop in Baton Rouge. Keith generously volunteered his time to probe the real-estate records in the Louisiana state capital in Baton Rouge and find the missing part of the puzzle. It wasn't easy. Though ownership of the shore on both sides of the river was reasonably well documented, most records didn't go back to 1814. Until now, no one had found a document recording Clay's Landing. At first it looked as though that part of the west riverbank had been owned by a Dr. Doussan and was now called Anchorage Landing. This item of information did not look encouraging until Keith dug up a deed of transfer of the property from John Clay to Dr. Doussan, which included an 1820 plat map of the site.

Thanks to Keith, we thought we were rounding third and heading for home. Craig Dirgo and I flew down to Louisiana to examine the shoreline and try to get an exact fix on Clay's Landing. Baton Rouge, though a fine capital city, is like the surface of Mars, thanks to the humidity in August. Why is it every time I head south it's August? I never seem to get it through my head to go in the spring, before the bugs and heat are bad.

I am often asked how NUMA schedules shipwreck searches. We use a scientific formula that consists of who is available to go, when necessary permits are in hand, and what the tide and weather conditions are. The main factor, however, centers around whether I have the time to go between writing books.

After landing at the Baton Rouge airport, renting a car, and checking into our motel, we drove to the site above West Baton Rouge across from the state capital on the west side of the Mississippi.

It was not an auspicious beginning.

On what was once the site of Clay's Landing, where the famed *New Orleans* had snagged and sank, was a huge tank facility owned by the Placid Oil Company. On one side of the levee stood the tanks and pumping houses. On the other side, along the bank and out into the water, were the oil-loading platforms, pipelines, and tank barges, all built of steel. With more metal scattered about than what is found in a hundred-acre scrap yard, distinguishing what remained of *New Orleans* with our trusty Schoenstedt gradiometer would be next to impossible.

Though we hadn't planned on conducting an extensive survey on this first exploratory peek at the area, Craig and I decided to give it a try.

That afternoon and most of the next day, we walked a systematic grid across the property we defined as having been Clay's Landing. Other than a few buried pipelines, which are fairly easy to identify because of the narrow readings that stretch in a straight line, we found little of interest. By inspecting the ground in minute detail, we got a pretty good idea of the scope of our task in locating any remains of the steamboat.

Since Sheriff Bergeron and his West Baton Rouge sheriff's department had been so generous with their assistance back in 1981, when Walt Schob and I found the site of the Confederate ironclad *Arkansas*, we asked for their help once again. And they came through again, lending us their aluminum river search boat, which had been beautifully crafted and welded by a trustee who was in jail for murder. A deputy came along as pilot.

We began soon after sunrise. Once Clay's Landing was established from the river side, we began sweeping back and forth. By nine that morning, it was already hot. The Mississippi was as flat as a mirror, and the only wind we enjoyed came from the movement of the boat. For the next few hours we swept, beginning two hundred yards out and working toward the shore. We received no readings of more than a few gamma, certainly no more than what a hammer lying in the mud would record. Closer to shore, we received a strangely consistent mag reading that made no sense to us at the time.

While I ran the gradiometer, Craig killed time perusing the boat's logbook. It made interesting reading, since the little craft was primarily used for retrieving bodies from the river. There wasn't any finesse to it. A large grappling hook on a line was tossed from the stern, and the deputies trolled until they snagged something.

"How do you know if you have a body or a big fish on the line?" Craig asked the deputy.

"A waterlogged body creates a lot of drag," the deputy replied. "It slows down the outboard motor real good."

Craig held the stainless-steel hook in his hands and

examined it. "What do most of the bodies look like when you find them?"

"They can be real ripe," the deputy answered casually. "The skin can slide off like a tangerine."

Craig's face wrinkled as he quickly replaced the hook in its holder and wiped his hands with a rag.

"Sometimes they're gassy and explode like a flesh bomb when they reach the surface," the deputy continued matter-of-factly. "But mostly they've been chewed up by fish and turtles. Sometimes boats go over them, outboard props ripping them up. Once I just hooked a head and part of the shoulders and chest. I ain't got no idea where the rest of the body went."

Craig stared at the grappling hook he'd been handling.

I couldn't resist.

"Lunchtime," I announced. "Want a raw beef and gooey cheese or tainted tuna sandwich?"

Craig shook his head. "Maybe later," he said, finally taking his eyes off the hook.

It was four o'clock when we called it quits. We could not mag close to shore because the steel barges blew the gradiometer off scale. We had gotten no magnetic signature that indicated we had found *New Orleans*. On top of that, we had run out of water two hours earlier.

As we began to cruise back to the boat ramp where the deputy had left the trailer, Craig turned to me and asked, "You sweating?"

I checked and found my skin dry. Strange, I thought, since the atmosphere was like a steam bath. "No," I answered.

"I noticed I'd stopped a half hour ago. I don't think that's good."

"We're dehydrated."

"My thoughts exactly."

By the time we reached the ramp and had helped the deputy load the boat on the trailer, the inside of our mouths felt as if they had been filled with talcum powder. Our faces were sunburned, and our eyes had the vacant look of men dying of thirst in the desert. Climbing into the superheated car that had been left in the sun only made things worse. We were about to stop at a house to ask the owner if we could drink from a garden hose when I gasped and pointed to a Circle K convenience store on the next corner.

"There!"

Craig hurtled the car into the parking lot. We jumped out and ran inside almost before it stopped moving. This being 1989, there was no such thing as cold bottled water as there is today. The only water for sale then was distilled in plastic gallon jugs. We snatched the biggest cups we could find and filled them to the rim at the soda fountain. Downing them in seconds, we again held them under the spigots for seconds. We had become almost completely dehydrated.

"Hey," the clerk yelled at us, "you can't do that."

Craig, a reasonably large man, scowled at him. "When we're done, charge what you will. We're dying here."

The clerk nodded and backed off. He'd probably assumed, judging by our bedraggled appearance, that we couldn't pay. When we'd finished at last, Craig handed him a ten-dollar bill. "Keep the change, and buy the next thirsty travelers a drink."

After a cool shower in our air-conditioned rooms, we met for dinner and discussed the day. Nature and man had thrown every obstacle in our path. We hadn't really expected to find *New Orleans* the first time out. That rarely happens. But we had not expected such a tough project in searching for a ship we knew we could pinpoint within a rectangle the size of a football field.

It was time to head for the old corral and do some homework.

WE NOW WENT back to the basics and overlaid old charts with new ones. The shoreline since the building of the levee seemed vague. From what we could conclude, the bank had receded over the years. But how far?

Then, a few months later, we received a report from the Army Corps of Engineers that came within a hair of halting the search in its tracks. In 1971, during a project to strengthen the levee, they'd laid an articulated concrete mattress along the bottom of the levee just below the waterline. The mattress contained iron rebar inside and hinges made of steel. This is what had given us our continuous mag reading near the west bank. It appeared that the mattress had been laid directly over what was once Clay's Landing.

This dilemma, combined with the steel barges, docks, and pipelines along the shore, made it impossible to detect any remains of *New Orleans*. With a sinking heart, I put the search data in the file marked "Improbable" and turned my thoughts to other lost ships.

THREE YEARS LATER, I was at a cocktail party when I was introduced to a fan of my books. I hate myself for not remembering his name, but we never made contact again. He was an older gentleman with a bald head rimmed with white hair, and deep-blue eyes behind rimless spectacles.

During the course of the conversation, he mentioned that he lived in West Baton Rouge parish. I mentioned our work there on the *Arkansas* and *New Orleans*, and we talked a bit about the history of the Mississippi. He had been diving in the river off and on for many years, a feat most divers from Louisiana or Mississippi don't care to experience. He regaled me with stories of being dragged more than a mile underwater by the four-knot current and of suddenly meeting up with an eight-foot-long, five-hundred-pound catfish in the murky water. He also talked about a strange phenomenon: once you reach a depth of eighty feet, the water visibility suddenly turns from two feet to a hundred feet.

At his urging, I described my search for *New Orleans* in more detail, narrating our failure to find her.

He looked at me and smiled. "You didn't look in the right place."

I hesitated, wondering what he had in mind. "We had Clay's Landing pegged to within a hundred yards," I argued.

"Not the right direction."

"Where would you have us look?"

He leaned back, sipped from his scotch and water, and peered over his glasses. "Certainly not up and down the bank."

"Where else could it be?" I asked, my interest mushrooming.

"Out in the river. Since I was a boy, the west bank has receded anywhere from two to three hundred yards. Clay's Landing must be way out in the river."

I digested that for a few seconds as the revelation

began to build and flood inside my mind. "Then it's beyond the concrete mattresses."

"Way beyond."

Suddenly the siren's call of *New Orleans* began to sound again. Thanks to this chance encounter with a stranger at a Telluride cocktail party, we'd been given a second chance at finding the first steamboat on the river.

IN AUGUST of 1995, we tried again. Why do we always go south in August? After excavating a wreck off Galveston that we hoped would be the Republic of Texas Navy ship *Invincible* but were unable to positively identify, Ralph Wilbanks, Wes Hall, Craig Dirgo, my son Dirk Cussler, and I headed to Baton Rouge with *Diversity* and all the equipment in tow. After arriving and losing a small wad of hard-earned cash on a riverboat casino, we turned in for the night. High rollers that we are, our combined losses came to all of thirty dollars. It might have been more, but I think Ralph actually made a couple of bucks. Interestingly, under Louisiana law, the riverboat cannot dock along the shore but must move along rails attached to the keel in the water. I guess that by using that ploy, the esteemed state legislators can claim that the evils of gambling do not touch sacred Louisiana soil.

Before launching the search, Ralph and I interviewed several of West Baton Rouge parish's senior citizens. They all agreed that during their lifetimes the river had eaten away the west bank, and the present shoreline was three hundred yards west. The next morning, we found a ramp beneath the bridge spanning the Mississippi River and launched *Diversity*.

We began mowing the lawn of the search grid, beginning almost in the center of the Mississippi and working toward the west bank. We ran very tight lines, using both the magnetometer and the sidescan sonar. The day went slowly. Thanks to Ralph and his big ice chest, Craig and I did not become dehydrated again.

Six hours later, we had covered the entire search grid three times. Except for a few minor hits, the mag had recorded nothing worth pursuing. The sonar had found a target at about the right distance from shore, but it was a good two hundred yards downriver from the southern boundary of what had been Clay's property.

Because we were running out of time, and everyone had commitments back home, we decided to return and investigate the target another time. And since none of us was experienced at diving in a muddy river with a four-knot current, we thought it best to line up and work with local divers who were more knowledgeable about the local conditions.

We were in an optimistic mood now that we had a target in the general area. Sadly, we abruptly met with another disappointment.

As we were pulling in the mag and sonar sensors, we watched, stricken, as a huge Army Corps of Engineers dredge came down the river, its buckets digging deep into the mud of the river and depositing it into barges. Though it missed our target by a good hundred yards, we could not help but wonder if this had been the ultimate fate of *New Orleans*.

I once suffered the same discouragement when we arrived hours too late to save the remains of the famous Union ironclad *Carondelet*. A great dredge had gone over the site and ripped it to shreds the day before we launched our search—a hundred and ten years after she had sunk in the Ohio River.

Chances are that the famous old *New Orleans* is gone. But she left a fabulous legacy, and who knows, maybe there is a tiny chance our one-and-only target might just be it. The odds are against us, but hope springs eternal, and someday we'll return and check it out.

PART THREE

The Ironclads *Manassas* and

Louisiana

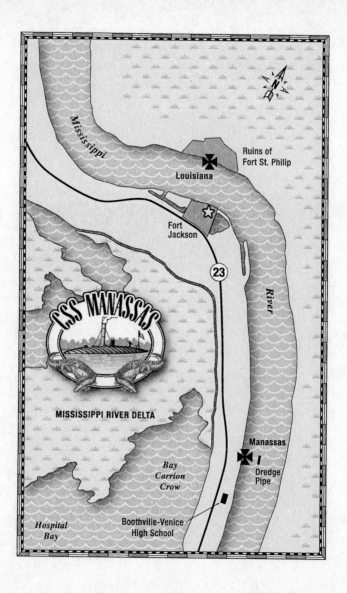

I

Civil War Turtle

1861–1862

"Curse this boat," Lieutenant Alexander Warley said loudly. "I feel like a horse wearing blinders."

His command, the Confederate ironclad *Manassas*, was less than fifty yards downriver of Fort Jackson, some seventy-five miles south of New Orleans. Warley peered through the single bow port into the misty night. The clattering of the machinery, combined with the hissing of the steam boilers, was magnifying the tension Warley already felt. The Confederate ironclad was untested and only weeks from completion. And although the night of October 11, 1861, was unseasonably cool, Warley was sweating.

Fourteen feet of *Manassas* was underwater, with only the top six feet of the convex hull and the twin smokestacks rising into the air. Because of an Indian summer, the temperature of the Mississippi River had remained warm longer than usual. With the shroud of warm water around her hull, combined with the heat from the boilers, *Manassas* was being warmed from without and within. Slipping downstream with the current, Warley wondered how he and his crew had found themselves here.

FARTHER SOUTH, at the Head of the Passes, the area of the Mississippi River Delta where the river forked into three separate channels, Commander Henry French, aboard the ten-gun Union sloop *Preble*, finished writing in his log and prepared to turn in for the night. After waiting for the ink to dry, he closed the logbook, capped his inkwell, and set his quill pen in the holder. Stretching in his chair, he rose to extinguish his whale-oil lamp, then changed his mind. Leaving the lamp burning, he walked through the passageway and up the ladder onto the deck. Saluting the deck sentry, he pulled a leather pouch from his jacket pocket and began to stuff tobacco into the bowl of his newest pipe.

Striking a wooden match, he waited until the strong sulfur smell was carried away by the wind, then touched the match to the bowl and puffed the pipe to life. Then he stared across the water. The night was black, with no moon, and a mist hung low over the water. The scant illumination came from lanterns on the deck of the twenty-two-gun flagship *Richmond*, and the few on the deck of the Union sloop *Joseph H. Toone* that was tied alongside. The sloop was off-loading coal for *Richmond*'s boilers, and French wished the loading operation was finished.

No captain enjoys having the maneuverability of his vessel compromised, and French's feelings were heightened by the fact that he was at the mouth of an inland waterway and not far out to sea, as he preferred. Rivers were for flatboats and barges, not warships,

French thought to himself. He drew in a mouthful of smoke.

"Sights or sounds?" he said to the sentry, after he exhaled.

"No sights, sir," the seaman noted. "With the bunkers being reloaded, it's hard to hear anything from upriver. Nothing indicates it won't be a quiet night, though, sir."

French puffed on his pipe while he smoothed his beard with his hand. "Where are you from, sailor?"

"Maine, sir," the young man answered. "Rockport."

"I imagine you've spent some time on the water, then," French noted.

"Yep," the seaman answered, "family of fishermen and lobstermen."

French finished and tapped the dottle over the side into the water.

"I'm going belowdecks. You keep a sharp eye," he said.

"Aye, sir," the sailor answered.

Just then a small series of waves from far out in the gulf rocked *Richmond* and pressed her and *Toone* together. The sound of the hulls slapping washed across the water like distant thunder.

French climbed back down the ladder and entered his cabin on the *Preble*. Licking his fingertips, he pressed them against the wick of the lamp and climbed into his berth. Making himself comfortable, he settled in to sleep.

LIEUTENANT WARLEY COUGHED, then rubbed his watering eyes. The pair of smokestacks were failing to vent the smoke from the boilers. This was just one more problem to add to the many Warley had noticed with *Manassas*, the first armored warship in North America that would see battle. To begin with, the vessel was proving underpowered, and that was no wonder. The Confederate navy was underbudgeted, and the ironclad's twin engines—one high-pressure, the other low-pressure—were worn out when they were installed. This was a common problem. The Confederates lacked the funds and the foundries to produce new engines themselves. Nor did the Confederates possess the large and modern shipyards of the Union.

The hull of *Manassas* came from a New England icebreaker formerly named *Enoch Train* that had last seen life as a river towboat. A group of enterprising Louisiana businessmen bought *Enoch Train*, then paid to have her razed at a crude shipyard across the river from New Orleans in Algiers. The ship's masts and superstructure were cut off, the hull was lengthened and widened, and her bow was extended and rebuilt with solid wood. Then the worn engines and hardware were installed. Next, a convex iron shield backed by wood was built as the upper deck. In the bow, a rounded shuttered port that flipped up was cut and the hole for the smokestack punched through the top. Last but not least, the shipwrights bolted a cast-iron ram to the bow just below the waterline.

They named her *Manassas* after the site of a recent Confederate army victory.

Then the businessmen applied for a letter of marque and reprisal, a document from the Confederate government giving them the right to sink Union vessels and take their cargoes as prizes.

Their dreams of grandeur above patriotism did not last. Commander George Hollins was in charge of building a fleet of warships to fight the expected fleet of Admiral David Farragut. Needing every vessel he could arm, Hollins sent Warley with a crew from the C.S.S. *McRae* to seize *Manassas* for the Confederacy.

The longshoremen aboard the ironclad defied the navy and shouted that they would kill the first man who attempted to board her. Warley, wielding a revolver, called their bluff. Cowed, the longshoremen abandoned the boat, along with one of the owners, who had tears in his eyes when escorted ashore. It was later reported that the Confederate government paid the businessmen $100,000 as compensation for the ship.

AT THIS INSTANT, Warley was ruing the day he had been assigned her command. To add insult to injury, he was having a great deal of trouble controlling *Manassas*'s direction. To have steering control, Warley needed to exceed the speed of the current by at least a few miles per hour. Right now Warley was barely creeping downriver.

"Get the engineer," Warley shouted to a deckhand standing nearby.

The man scampered down a hatch into the engine room. Warley was well known as a stern disciplinarian, and by the sound of his voice he was none too happy. Crouching down to avoid hitting his head, the deckhand crab-walked to the stern, where William Hardy, the ship's engineer, was applying grease to the shaft leading to the propeller.

"Cap'n wants to see you," the deckhand shouted over the din.

"Be right up," Hardy said, wiping his hands on an already greasy piece of burlap.

Straightening his uniform, Hardy ran a wooden comb through his hair, then climbed up the ladder through the port. Walking forward, he saluted Warley.

"You wanted to see me, sir?" Hardy said.

"Yes," Warley said. "How many inches of steam are we making?"

"About nine, sir," Hardy noted.

Manassas could make nearly thirty before her boilers would blow.

"Why so little?" Warley asked. "I'm having problems with control."

"It's the fuel we loaded," Hardy noted. "We have some seasoned wood and a half-load of coal—but if I burn that, we won't have them when we go into battle."

"So we burn green wood?" Warley said, wiping his nose, which was dripping from the smoke.

"Unless you order me otherwise," Hardy said easily.

Warley nodded. Hardy was a good man and as fine an officer as he had aboard *Manassas*. "You made the right choice, William," he said. "Let's just hope next time we go out, it will be with a full load of prime fuel."

"Yes, sir," Hardy said, "that would be a blessing. For now, however, you have about fifteen more minutes of green wood."

"Then that's the way it is," Warley said, dismissing Hardy with a crisp salute.

Turning the helm over to First Officer Charles Austin, Warley made his way to the bow, where the *Manassas*'s single nine-inch gun sat pointed downriver. He stared out at the blackness as he drew in breaths of clean air.

The Yankees were out there, and, seasoned wood or not, it was time for the rebels to visit.

The fog was growing thicker around the anchored

Union fleet as *Manassas* steamed downriver. The
flotilla was well armed. *Richmond* was armed with a
total of twenty-six guns. The sailing sloop *Preble*
carried seven 32-pound cannon, two 8-inch rifled guns,
and a single 12-pounder. Less heavily armed was the
steamer *Water Witch*, which mounted only four small
guns. More heavily armed was the sloop *Vincennes*,
which carried a complement of fourteen 32-pounders,
twin 9-inch Dahlgren smoothbores, and four 8-inch
rifled guns. Because of the late hour, the decks of the
Union fleet were quiet.

Engineer Hardy popped his head through the hatch
into the pilothouse. "We're into the good wood. You
should feel an improvement."

Charles Austin at the helm shouted. "I felt the speed
pick up a few minutes ago."

"Good," Hardy said. "Fear not—when we attack, I
have a little trick up my sleeve."

"I'll let you know," Austin shouted after the
retreating Hardy.

Manassas was the lead ship of a small Confederate
force.

Just behind and off her port side trailed the small
Confederate tug *Ivy*, which had come downriver a few
days before. *Ivy* mounted a new British-made
Whitworth rifled gun. The Whitworth was a rare and
expensive extravagance for the Confederate navy,
effective and well built. The last few days, *Ivy* had
stayed upriver, harassing the Union blockaders by
shelling the Union fleet from a distance of nearly four
miles.

Calhoun, *Jackson*, and *Tuscarora* also left Fort
Jackson to travel downriver for the attack. *Calhoun* was

an aging vessel equipped with walking beam engines. Her orders called for her to stay away from action and fire her guns from a distance. *Jackson* was a newer high-pressure paddle wheeler, but the Confederates were concerned that the noise from her engines and paddle wheels would alert the Union forces, and she was coming downriver last. *Tuscarora* was a small tug tasked with towing a fire raft the Confederates hoped to use to set the Union fleet ablaze.

Manassas was close to the Union ships. Austin strained to see through the fog.

Frolic, a southern schooner the Union had captured when she tried to run through the blockade with a load of cotton bound for London, was manned by a skeleton crew. She was due to travel north for conversion to a Union vessel in a few more weeks, and only a few men tasked with maintenance were aboard.

The master of *Frolic*, a laconic New Yorker named Sean Riley, was having trouble sleeping. The monotony was wearing on Riley, and after tossing and turning in his berth, he finally decided to try the main deck to see if the fresh air would bring sleep. Carrying a thin wool blanket, he headed for the stern to make himself comfortable.

A sound of tapping reached his ears. Maybe it was a woodpecker, Riley thought. No, not a woodpecker— the tapping had a distinctly metallic tone. Must be from *Richmond*, which was anchored nearby. Riley climbed into the riggings to investigate.

"I SAW a dim outline ahead," Warley said to Austin, after returning from the gun port. "I have no idea if it's a Federal vessel, but she's slightly to port."

Austin adjusted the wheel, then peered from the tiny port into the gloom.

"WHAT IN God's name," Riley blurted aloud.

A blackened leviathan from the depths was quickly approaching. If not for the round smokestack and noise, the unknown object might have been a whale that had lost its bearings and traveled from the Gulf of Mexico upriver. Like a hunter stalking prey, the black object was advancing on *Richmond*.

The time was 3:40 A.M.

Sliding down a line, Riley began ringing *Frolic*'s bell. Then he shouted across the water. "Ahoy, *Richmond*, there's a boat coming down the river."

Over the sound of the bunkers being loaded, no one on *Richmond* heard his pleas.

Riley ran into the pilothouse to find an aerial flare.

"ENEMY DEAD AHEAD," Austin shouted down the hatch to Hardy.

"Now's the time, boys," Hardy yelled to his engine-room crew.

Opening the door to the firebox, the black gang took turns tossing kegs of tar, turpentine, tallow, and sulfur into the flames. Almost immediately, the steam gauge began creeping higher. At the helm, Austin felt *Manassas* surge forward.

ON *PREBLE*, a midshipman saw *Manassas* advancing. He ran to warn Commander French. A few moments later, French appeared on deck in his long underwear. The Confederate ram was only twenty yards from *Richmond*—there was no time to give warning.

The explosive fuel tossed into *Manassas*'s firebox gave the vessel speed but also raised the temperature inside the vessel. The crew of the ram was covered in sweat, and their heads were swimming from the heat. One crewman began to sing *Dixie*. The rest of the sailors quickly followed suit.

Inside *Manassas*, it became chaos. The sailors were singing at the top of their lungs, the Union ships were sounding their warnings, and the vibration of the propeller shaft through the deck was making Austin's feet numb. He peered through the tiny port at the vessel looming above.

They were ten yards from *Richmond* when Riley's flare streaked skyward.

"Fire the gun," Warley shouted to the gun captain.

The shot from the cannon struck the side of *Joseph H. Toone* and exited from the other side. Then *Richmond*'s bell began to ring the call to arms. In the confusion, Austin never hesitated in his advance and never deviated from his course. Hands firmly on the wheel, he steered *Manassas* directly into the side of *Toone*. The cast-iron ram performed as designed. It parted the planks of the frigate like a knife through the belly of a fish. The ram wedged between a pair of thick ribs two feet below the waterline. Water poured into the hull through a six-inch gash.

Fortunately, it was not a fatal blow.

ON BOARD *MANASSAS*, Austin touched the tip of his fingers to his forehead. When he brought them away and into the light, he could see red. At impact his head had slammed into a bulkhead and opened a cut. He dabbed at the wound with his handkerchief. Later he could tend to the wound—right now it was time to make another run at the Union ship.

"Full astern," he shouted down the hatch to Hardy.

In *Manassas*'s engine room, one of the condensers had sprung a leak, and the hold was filled with a thick cloud of steam. A crewman had been badly burned and lay off to one side, moaning. Hardy diverted the steam through one of the side ports on *Manassas*—a device designed to repel boarders by blasting them with a stream of scalding water and steam. Tying a rag over the split condenser pipe, he slammed the controls into full astern.

But *Manassas* did not move.

As soon as the Union officers organized their crews to begin firing, *Manassas* would be taking direct broadsides. Austin wasn't confident that the armor plating could withstand such an attack. He spun the wheel hard to starboard in an attempt to free his command.

Manassas shuddered as the propellers began to find purchase.

"Get us out of here," Warley yelled to Austin.

Austin still had no idea the ram was wedged in *Toone*'s hull.

On *Toone*, a seaman aimed at *Manassas* with a black-powder revolver. He was just about to squeeze off a round when a thin stream of scalding water struck him in the face. Screaming in pain, he flipped over the side into the river. At that instant, *Manassas*'s propeller shaft slowed, then reversed direction. The four-bladed bronze prop began to bite at the muddy water.

Deep inside *Toone*, the iron bolts holding the ram to the solid wood bow began to squeal like a pig stuck by a saber. Something had to give, and it would not be the interwoven layers of hardwood forming the bow. *Manassas* crabbed its way sideways.

And then, like a string of firecrackers being ignited, the nuts began to pop off.

The nuts, with portions of the bolts still attached, shot across the cargo hold of *Toone* and embedded themselves in the far wall. All at once, the ram was pulled from the bow of *Manassas*. With wheel turned to the locks, the Confederate ram had little choice but to respond to the helm. Once free, the vessel slammed full abeam into *Toone*. *Richmond* and *Toone* had been anchored perpendicular to the current, with their anchors upstream. This allowed the Union vessels a margin of safety in case of attack—the cannon were pointing upriver toward the enemy.

Manassas slipped under one of the hawsers holding the anchor.

The thick line slapped against the rounded wooden deck and pulled tight. Deep below the Mississippi River, *Toone*'s anchor was wedged against the hulk of a sunken French schooner. The wreck had lain in the mud for nearly a century and was stuck as fast as if encased in cement.

"Get us out of here," Warley yelled to Austin.

Austin still had no idea the ram was wedged in *Toone*'s hull.

"I'm backing out," he shouted. "We'll come at her again."

Manassas lurched in reverse. The inside of the ship quickly filled with smoke.

"I've got no draft for the fires," Hardy yelled topside, "and one of the condensers is blown. We're now down to a single engine."

Austin backed away to assess the damage.

As soon as *Manassas* engaged *Richmond*, the rest of the Confederate flotilla sprang into action. The tugs *Watson* and *Tuscarora* raced past. Attached to their sterns were a total of five burning fire rafts, and the two ships were looking for a target. Just then, the guns of *Richmond* opened up. The Union gunners were firing blind—shells began raining out from every direction.

Manassas backed away a short distance in the fog, and Warley assumed control. Almost at once, he noticed that the ship was responding sluggishly.

"Something is wrong," he shouted to Austin.

Just then Hardy popped his head through the hatch from the engine room. Hardy's face was covered with soot, and his eyes were as red as a Washington apple. In one hand, he held an ax.

"I can see up through the deck," he shouted. "The stack is attached and dragging."

With Austin supporting him on the slick deck, the two men hacked off the smokestack. It floated a short distance, then sank from sight. Climbing back down into the pilothouse, Hardy addressed Warley.

"Sir, we're damaged," Hardy said. "The ram is gone, and we're down to one engine. Other than our single gun, we're completely defenseless."

Warley nodded and turned his crippled vessel upstream.

"There will be time to fight another day," he said slowly.

When it was all said and done, the battle at the Head of the Passes decided little. The Union navy suffered damage that they repaired, and the blockade was not broken. Even so, the actions of the Confederate fleet gave the citizens of New Orleans a much-needed shot of confidence. The crew of *Manassas* was hailed as heroes, and the vessel was towed to the shipyard for repairs. The vessel, which had entered its first battle as a privateer, officially entered into the roles of the Confederate navy. Engineer Hardy was promoted, and Charles Austin was made her official master.

The repairs necessary on *Manassas* stretched on for months. Her appearance was now changed. Instead of two thin stacks, she now sported a single thick one.

For Union planners, the Mississippi River was a linchpin to winning the war. The river was the artery for shipping and commerce, and it tied together the western Confederate frontier. In 1861, Abraham Lincoln summed it up succinctly: "The Mississippi is the backbone of the Rebellion. It is the key to the whole situation."

The most important city was New Orleans—a hotbed of rebellion and unrest as well as a growing center of shipbuilding and weapons manufacture. By 1861, a total of five shipyards and twelve docks were operating, and the city was second only to Norfolk, Virginia, as a Confederate shipbuilding center. New Orleans had inventors and risk-takers. The first Confederate submarines were tested in Lake Pontchartrain, and newly developed torpedoes (sea mines) were designed there. Equally important, a large number of the cotton traders funding the rebellion lived in the city, and the blockade runners shipping the cotton to London loaded their cargo at the wharves.

Primary defense for the city was provided by Fort St.

Philip on the east side of the river and Fort Jackson on the west. The pair of forts were located some seventy-five miles downstream, near the Head of the Passes. Fort St. Philip was considered to be the stronger of the two. Built of brick and rock and covered with sod, it had originally been constructed by the Spanish. St. Philip had a total of fifty-two guns pointed at the river. To the west, across the expanse of muddy water, Fort Jackson had been built by the Union before the war and bristled with seventy-five guns.

In addition to the pair of forts, a second barrier to the Union navy had been laid in place. Stretched across the river between the two forts was a heavy chain that was supported by the sunken hulks of six sacrificed schooners designed to snag any Union vessels venturing upstream.

At first glance, the Confederacy fielded what appeared to be a formidable defense.

"SHIP ISLAND," David Farragut said quietly.

Folding his brass spyglass, Farragut slid it into the pocket of his uniform jacket. Farragut was one of the Union navy's few flag officers, and his uniform proudly displayed this fact. His epaulets featured the stars denoting his rank. Unlike most of his officers and men, Farragut's uniform had been carefully tailored and fit him perfectly. Farragut was not a tall man, but his erect posture and squared shoulders made him appear larger. A sense of his own importance infused his being and radiated outward to envelop those around him. Farragut was a man comfortable with leading, comfortable with decisions, and comfortable with fate. The fleet he commanded had left Hampton Roads,

Virginia, on February 2. Nine days later, they stopped in Key West, and nine more found him here in the Gulf of Mexico off the Mississippi River.

"Anchor and assemble the flotilla," Farragut said to his second in command.

It was no secret that Farragut's fleet was preparing to attempt a run up the Mississippi River. On April 1, rebel spies reported that all but two of the vessels had crossed the bar and were now in the river. In New Orleans, work proceeded around the clock to finish the Confederate ironclads *Louisiana* and *Mississippi*.

Louisiana was a large vessel, 264 feet in length with a 62-foot beam. Her armament was to consist of a pair of 7-inch rifled guns, a trio of 9-inch shell guns, a quadrant of 8-inch shell guns, and seven 32-pounders. *Mississippi* was no less a vessel. Some 260 feet in length with a beam of 53 feet 8 inches, she was due to carry a battery of twenty guns of various sizes.

The problem was that the two ships were far from final commissioning.

Atop the ramparts of Fort Jackson, Delbert Antoine stared west at the red sunset. The sight was unsettling to the native Louisianian, and he shared his feelings with his partner, Preston Kimble. The date was the eighteenth of April.

"The red of the sky," Antoine said, "looks like blood."

Kimble leaned over to spit off the brick walkway atop the parapet into the moat below. "If our guns don't sink the Yankees," Kimble said, "that gator in the moat will eat them."

Both Kimble and Antoine were early conscripts to the cause. They were dressed in early Confederate gray wool uniforms, now showing wear. Antoine's eyes scanned the fort. It was pentagon-shaped and stood twenty-five feet above the water. The walls were constructed of red brick and were twenty feet thick.

In the area of the sixteen heavy guns that pointed toward the water, the brick had been reinforced with thick granite slabs. Inside the center of the fort was a diagonal-shaped defensive barracks where five hundred men could take shelter during bombardments. The sight of the substantial construction gave Antoine little comfort.

"They're coming for us," Antoine said. "I can feel it."

"We'll blow them out of the water," Kimble said, "like shooting ducks in a pond."

Antoine nodded. But he knew his friend's words were just bluster. If Kimble wasn't afraid, he was just plain stupid—or crazy.

A FEW MILES down the river from Fort Jackson, around a bend and tied to the shore, Franklin Dodd checked the lines holding his barge to the trees. It was dark, and a stiff wind was blowing. Even so, thousands of frogs were croaking, and the sound was making Dodd angry.

"Damn frogs," he said to powder monkey Mark Hallet.

"They'll hush up when we start firing," Hallet noted.

An assignment to one of the numerous mortar boats was not a job relished by a Union sailor. Their job was to soften up the forts before Farragut and his ships made their run upriver. The crews' job was simple. They would load their gun, then stand with mouth agape to avoid having their eardrums blown out. The gun would fire, then they would reload and fire again. Hundreds upon hundreds of times, the exercise would be repeated. By the end of the war, most of the crews would find themselves deaf.

Early on the morning of April 19, the mortar boats opened fire.

The first round slammed into the base of Fort Jackson. For five days the barrage would keep up around the clock. By noon of the first, half the Confederates were trembling.

HALLET POURED a powder charge into the mortar. For the last few days, he had felt a pressure in his head he could not shake. He would yawn and that would relieve the pressure some, but still it always returned. He felt a hand on his arm and stared at Dodd. His friend's mouth was moving, but Hallet could not make out the words. Wiping some powder from his blackened face with a rag, he put his ear next to Dodd's mouth. He could smell Dodd's breath, and it was not pleasant.

"The word is Farragut's making his run tonight," Dodd shouted.

Hallet smiled at the words, but he was worried. He had been unable to stop his body from shaking for the last two days. The only thing that brought him relief was rocking back and forth on the balls of his feet. So he rocked until the gun fired. Then he ran over and set another powder charge.

ON *MANASSAS*, Lieutenant Warley knew the Union was coming. He reasoned that the first order of business for the Federals would be to send a couple of boats upriver to try to breach the chain obstruction stretching across the river. The problem was that *Manassas* was still upriver.

The last few months had reinforced Warley's opinion of *Manassas*. The vessel was underpowered, lightly armored, and poor-handling. Even so, if Warley sighted an enemy ship, he was ready to ram her. For the coming battle, Warley could count on little help. *Louisiana* and *Mississippi* were still not fully operational. Both had been towed down from New Orleans and were now anchored by the forts to be used as floating gun batteries.

The Union gunboats *Pinola* and *Itasca* had been tasked with blowing the Confederate chain obstruction. Sneaking upriver, a crew from *Itasca* rowed a small boat to the obstruction and attached an explosive charge. The charge failed to explode. Luckily, one of the gunboats fouled itself in the chain and, attempting to free itself, pulled the chain apart, creating an opening large enough for the Union fleet to breach.

The Mississippi was open, but the Union navy faced a gauntlet of murderous fire.

ON APRIL 23, *Manassas* and her tender, *Phoenix*, arrived off the forts. Shells were still raining down from the mortar boats as Warley maneuvered into place. So far, Fort Jackson had been the hardest hit. Through the smoke, Warley could see that parts of her outer wall were pocked from the rain of shells. Continuing to scan the fort with his spyglass, he could see the Confederate flag still flying atop the pole.

Just then, one of the Fort Jackson guns returned fire.

*

APRIL 23 melded into April 24. Admiral Farragut rolled his charts and stared at the men around the table in his stateroom aboard his flagship *Hartford*.

"Are there any more questions?" Farragut asked.

The men shook their heads in the negative.

"Then we go at my signal," he said quietly.

The men filtered off to return to their commands and a strange quiet.

Just past 2 A.M., two red lanterns were hoisted atop the mizzen peak of *Hartford*.

From this point forward, there was no turning back.

MANASSAS WAS TIED to the bank just off Fort St. Philip; because of earlier problems, she now sported but a single smokestack, but that had failed to solve all her problems. Earlier, the ship's engineer had reported a balky condenser. Warley ordered it changed before the battle. The pilot was testing the steam power as Warley paced the decks.

"Is the gun crew ready?" he shouted to Lieutenant Reed.

"Yes, sir," Reed said. "I checked with them a half hour ago, as you instructed."

"Fireman and black gang?"

"All in place. The condenser is repaired—they're making steam," Reed noted.

"Are the steam and water ports operational?" Warley asked.

"If we need to repel boarders," Reed said, "they'll be in for a shock."

Just then, the pilot interrupted.

"Sir, we have steam in the boiler and power to the propeller," he said.

"Then cast us off," Warley said.

THE BARRAGE from the mortar boats increased. Delbert Antoine peered through the gloom for signs of the Union navy. The air was thick with the smell of spent powder and brick dust. The temperature was cool, like the inside of a tomb.

"I think I see something," Preston Kimble shouted.

Kimble was fifty feet from Antoine and closer to the water.

Like an evil mourner shrouded in black, the dim outline of *Hartford* slowly materialized on the river. Kimble reached for the pistol lying on the wall of the rampart and fired a minié ball at the approaching wraith. The effect was like trying to use a flyswatter to kill a bird, but Kimble didn't care.

And just then the water batteries of Fort Jackson opened up with a roar.

THE BATTLE BEGAN at 3:40 A.M.

Lieutenant Warley opened the roof hatch on *Manassas* and stared at the sky. Mortar shells arced through the air with a flash of light from their burning fuses. He watched as the shells reached the apex of their trajectory and slowed. Then, looking like spinning Fourth of July sparklers, they accelerated and plunged into the Confederate forts. It was an eerie sight. The air was already clouded with smoke that hung low over the water and billowed and rolled like waves in the ocean.

In the engine room of *Manassas*, Chief Engineer Dearing, who had transferred over from *Tuscarora*, was stoking a hellish fire of his own creation. Dearing knew the Confederate ram would need all the steam he could make, and he took the boilers to the limit just as a Federal ship appeared through the gloom.

"Make for the Yank ship," Warley shouted to the pilot.

The pilot began his course adjustment, but just then the Confederate ram *Resolute*, in full retreat, crossed abeam. *Manassas* struck her around the wheelhouse.

"Back off," Warley shouted.

While still entangled with *Resolute*, the Union vessel slowed and poured shot into the side on *Manassas* before continuing upstream. Once they were free of *Resolute*, Warley ordered a course to midstream, where he had spotted a Union paddle wheeler.

The outline of the familiar ship appeared in the blackness.

"She's the U.S.S. *Mississippi*," Warley shouted.

In a war that pitted brother against brother, there was no time for sentiment. The U.S.S. *Mississippi* was the last ship Warley had served on before resigning his commission in the Union navy. Now Warley was bent on sinking her.

In the foretop of the U.S.S. *Mississippi*, artist William Waud spied the sinister-looking ship approaching. He would later draw her as a lead-colored wet whale, with the smokestack high in the air the only feature that might define it as a ship. At this second, there were pressing matters. Waud shouted to Lieutenant George W. Dewey, later to become famous for his destruction of the Spanish fleet in Manila Bay.

"Here is a queer-looking customer off our port bow," Waud yelled.

Dewey corrected course in an attempt to run down the Confederate vessel, but his paddle wheeler was going upstream against the current and his pilot had little control.

He ordered his guns to fire, but the shots glanced off *Manassas*'s back.

"TAKE HER at the wheelhouse," Warley shouted to the pilot.

Manassas had the current on her side, but the pilot's aim was poor in the blackness.

They came in on *Mississippi*'s quarter.

"Fire the gun," Warley shouted, as they stuck the Union ship.

The single cannon in the bow belched once as *Manassas* rammed into the Union ship. The shell entered through the broken hull planking and lodged in a cabin belowdecks. The U.S.S. *Mississippi* answered the attack with fire of its own. Dewey watched *Manassas* back away into the blackness.

Fear and anger ran through the Confederate fleet as the Union navy steamed upriver. With a few more weeks of preparation, they might have stood a fighting chance. As it was, the saber thrust of the Union navy was cutting through their defenses with indescribable ease. Most Confederate rams were grounded on the side of the river by their captains, and their crews escaped into the swamps. The mighty *Louisiana*, crippled by uncompleted construction and faulty propulsion, lay tied up alongside the shore. She was firing her guns, but the design of her gun ports was faulty, and she had only a limited range in which to fire.

A Union ship came abreast and poured shot into her hull.

Things were no better on *Manassas*. The Mississippi

River had become a boiling inferno. Clouds of smoke rolled across the river, illuminated by bursts of light from muzzle flashes from the passing ships. Shells flew through the air in a rain of lead, and the flames of burning ships made for a macabre scene of destruction. A large orange-tinted moon had risen, but it was hidden behind the thick, choking smoke.

OVER THE NOISE of the engines, Warley could hear the shouts of the Union gunners, and they went through their firing drills. Still, Warley would not back down.

"To port," he shouted to his pilot.

Aboard the Union ship *Pensacola*, Executive Officer F. A. Poe viewed *Manassas* advancing. Ordering a course correction to avoid the ramming, he waited until the last second, then ordered his guns fired into the Confederate ram. The shells exploded on *Manassas*'s back. Only a few inches to starboard and they would have entered the pilothouse through the port.

By now, the majority of the Union fleet had passed, and Warley ordered *Manassas* downstream. He was intent on attacking the mortar boats downstream to take fire off the Confederate forts. His decision would prove deadly. Once *Manassas* came into the range of Fort St. Philip, the batteries, mistaking the Confederate ram for a disabled Union ship, opened fire on their own countrymen.

"Get us out of here!" Warley shouted to the pilot, an order to steer upstream.

Manassas, underpowered to begin with, struggled hard to make headway against the current. And then Warley thought he'd found salvation. A Union vessel appeared in the gloom. Warley thought she was

Farragut's flagship *Hartford*, and he made his way toward her. But salvation would not be his. The vessel was not *Hartford* but *Brooklyn*, a worthy target but not what Warley had hoped for. *Brooklyn* was entangled with part of the remaining chain obstruction and was struggling to free herself. The Union vessel was stuck under the guns of Fort Jackson, and if she didn't free herself soon, the guns now finding their range would turn her into tinder.

"Resin in the boiler," Warley shouted down in the engine room.

The increase in power came seconds later. Warley ordered the pilot to ram *Brooklyn*. Had not the Union navy ordered chain armor mounted to their vessels before the battle, the blow from *Manassas*'s ram would have sunk the Union ship. As it was, the blow was deflected and caused minimal damage. Warley ordered the pilot to back off.

The battle had raged for hours. The sky to the east was beginning to lighten.

Warley noticed the Confederate vessel *McRae* involved in a one-sided fight with several Union ships. *Manassas* came to assist and chased the Union ships upriver. The crew was weary from the hours of battle. *Manassas* had taken numerous hits at close range. Many were injured. But Warley was still game. He ordered the pilot upriver around Quarantine Point, where most of Farragut's fleet was waiting.

"We are losing steam," Dearing shouted up to the pilothouse.

"We're barely making headway," the pilot shouted to Warley, as he stared out the tiny forward port at the approaching Union ships.

Warley stood silently for a moment. They had fought the good fight, but now his ship's systems were failing. His ship was dying, and he was forced to face this fact. From the gun deck, Warley heard the low cries of a wounded sailor. To the front was an advancing enemy he was ill-equipped to fight.

"Run her aground on shore," he said quietly.

The pilot steered for the bank.

"Prepare the men to make shore," Warley shouted.

Manassas was run ashore, and the crew was evacuated. Climbing up the bank, Warley watched as *Mississippi* came abreast and pounded the abandoned ram with all the force of her guns. The rising sun had lightened the sky to a gray half-light. Warley watched as his command was pounded with shot.

Suddenly, a shell from *Mississippi* exploded against the stern just below the waterline, and the lower hold quickly began to flood. With the weight from the water, *Manassas*'s bow became light. She drifted away from shore with the current.

Now a ghost ship, *Manassas* floated a few dozen yards downstream of Warley and the crew. The gunners on *Mississippi* reloaded and fired. Screaming across the water, the shot parted the planks of *Manassas*'s hull.

As *Manassas* drifted downriver, Lieutenant Reed of *McRae* launched a last-ditch effort to save her. Rowing alongside in a small boat, he climbed aboard, only to find that Warley and his crew had cut through the steam pipes with axes. The ship had been rendered unusable. Reed had no choice but to abandon the ship and return to *McRae*.

Captain David Porter, later a distinguished admiral, in command of the mortar fleet, saw *Manassas* coming down the river, seemingly intent on destroying the mortar vessels, but he soon discovered that *Manassas* was never going to harm another ship.

"She was beginning to emit some smoke from her ports of holes," he reported, "and was discovered to be on fire and sinking. Her pipes were all twisted and riddled with shot, and her hull was also well cut-up. She had evidently been used up by the squadron as they passed along. I tried to save her, as a curiosity, by getting a hawser around her and securing her to the bank, but just after doing so, she fairly exploded, her only gun went off, and, emitting flames through her bow port, like some huge animal, she gave a plunge and disappeared under the water."

The career of *Manassas* had been short, but she led the way for armored ships. The first ironclad to do battle, she was soon followed by the *Monitor* and *Merrimac/Virginia*. Thanks to her, naval warfare would never be the same.

II

They Don't
Come Cheaper Than This

1981, 1996

A FEW WEEKS AFTER THE UNSUCCESSFUL conclusion of the 1981 *Hunley* expedition, I was sitting at my desk staring at the NUMA team's graduation picture, a photo of everyone we always take before we head for home. I studied it carefully. The faces of so many dedicated and hardworking people brought back warm memories. Then, for some unknown reason, I counted those staring back at me. There were seventeen, excluding me. Seventeen! I began to wonder if all these bodies were critical to finding a shipwreck lying in no more than thirty feet of water. It seemed to me that three people could have achieved the same results.

The simple fact is—and this has been proven time

and time again by our government—there comes a time when too many people get in one another's way. Bureaucracy breeds bureaucracy. Feeding and housing a large search team require support people. Once breakfast is consumed, a large crew needs at least four rental cars to ferry themselves and their equipment back and forth from the boat dock. And let us not forget the vital use of transportation for the younger members of the expedition team to make whoopee in town after dark.

More and more, it seemed that smaller might be better.

Warming to the idea, I planned the next expedition to the Mississippi River to search for ships sunk during Admiral David Farragut's battle past the forts and his ultimate capture of New Orleans in 1861.

This time, there would be only two of us representing NUMA.

WALTER SCHOB, an old faithful standby of NUMA, arranged to come with me on the expedition. All we brought was our Schonstedt gradiometer to detect ferrous metal and a golfer's rangefinder. Walt met me at the Denver airport, where he had flown from his home in Palmdale, California, and was quite surprised when I rolled up to the gate in a little shuttle with my right ankle sticking out the side in a cast.

The day before I was to meet him, I was jogging behind my house on a path through the woods when I stumbled and twisted my ankle. There was little doubt a bone was broken, because I actually heard the snap. After limping up the path to the house, I found that my wife had gone grocery shopping. With no choice, I drove myself to the doctor, using my left foot for both brake and accelerator.

The ankle, according to orthopedists who have looked at it twenty years later, say the bone didn't mesh right and should have been screwed in place, or whatever it is they do in the twenty-first century to squeeze the parted bones together. As I aged, it developed arthritis. My advice is whatever you do, never get old.

The airline obliged me with a front-row seat facing the bulkhead so I could extend my foot. Incredibly, a fellow with another broken ankle sat across from me. Odd how misery loves company. His break was worse than mine, as his cast ran almost to his knee. Mine came only part way up my calf.

I always recall this flight because Walt had his carry-on bag sitting against the bulkhead at his feet. Now, you have to understand—Walt has a perverse sense of humor. When the flight attendant came along and asked him to move it under the seat or to an overhead bin, he said, "No, thank you, it's fine right where it is."

The flight attendant, with red hair and penetrating dark eyes, was rather attractive except for the fact that her hips brushed both seats as she walked down the aisle. She gave him a stern stare. "I'm sorry, FAA regulations. The bag has to be stowed."

Walt stared back with an innocent expression. "There is no FAA regulation concerning a bag under my feet against the bulkhead needing to be stowed."

"You stow it, sir, or the plane won't take off," she said in a voice filled with crushed ice.

"I'll comply," said Walt, "if you quote me the regulation, the section and paragraph."

I might mention that Walt is an air accident investigator. If anyone knows FAA regulations, it's him.

Now flustered, she said, "Then you leave me no choice but to get the pilot."

This lady was not going to take no for an answer.

Walt smiled politely. "I'll be more than happy to meet our pilot. I'd like to know his experience and flying time before we take off."

Did I mention Walt is a retired air force colonel with several thousand hours' piloting fighters?

She stormed off to the cockpit and returned with an exasperated pilot, who wanted to get the plane off the ground. In the meantime, Walt had stowed his bag and was reading a copy of an air accident investigative report.

"Do we have a problem here?" asked a grandfatherly-looking uniformed man with gray hair.

I looked up with my favorite dumb expression. "Problem?"

"The attendant says you won't stow your bag."

"I did."

"Not you, him!" snapped the frustrated flight attendant, aiming a manicured finger at Walt.

Without looking up from his reading, Walt said calmly, "It's stowed."

As I said: perverse. But you have to like Walt. You can't excite him. I've never seen him mad. With his ready smile and Andy Devine voice, he charms everyone—most of the time.

*

AFTER LANDING at the New Orleans airport, we rented a big station wagon, a model now extinct, and made the seventy-five-mile drive down the river to Venice, Louisiana, the last town at the end of the road in the heart of delta country. From here it's another twenty miles by boat to the Gulf of Mexico.

There's not much to see in Venice: fishermen, boat dealers and part suppliers, a couple of miles of boat docks. We wondered why a huge parking lot was filled with acres of pickup trucks. Our answer came when a Bell Long Ranger helicopter approached, hovered, and settled to the ground. It was emblazoned with the company name, Petroleum Helicopter, Inc. A small army of offshore oil riggers poured to the ground. They had left their trucks parked when they were ferried out for their rig rotation.

We checked into a motel, the only motel at the time. The oil field workers must have had some rather exciting parties, judging from the damage to the place. I have always been amused recalling the Plexiglas sign screwed into the wall above the television. It said:

NO BATTERY CHARGING OR DUCK CLEANING
ALLOWED IN ROOM.

My shoestring expedition was off to a good start.

Our saving grace was a terrific little restaurant called Tom's that was in the town of Buras. Tom's specialty was Gulf oysters, and after shucking them, he'd pile them outside the restaurant. Back then the mound was nearly as high as the restaurant's peaked roof. I still recall with fondness the chili-vinegar sauce his mama made. Nothing ever enhanced an oyster like that sauce.

I was so impressed that when Dirk Pitt was chasing villains through the delta in the book *Deep Six,* I had him stop to eat at Tom's.

We chartered a small fifteen-foot aluminum skiff from a local Cajun fisherman named John who lived in a mobile home near the river with his wife and tribe of kids. John treated Walt and me with great suspicion the first day and never said a word during the search. He was kind enough, though, to provide me with a lawn chair, so I could sit holding the gradiometer's recorder in my lap with my ankle in a cast propped up on the gunwale, sticking over the bow like a battering ram.

The second day, John opened up a little. By the third day, he had opened the floodgates of his personality and begun to regale us with a string of Cajun jokes and stories. I wish I could remember them. Some were semi-jolly.

As we cruised up and down the Mississippi, trailing the gradiometer astern, I watched the needle on the recorder's dial and listened to the sound recorder for any potential ferrous anomaly. With John in the stern of the skiff, steering, Walt sat in the middle, eyeing the shore with his rangefinder and keeping us in relatively straight lines until we neared the shore and he could guide John by eye.

The first day of the expedition, we concentrated on *Manassas*. The Civil War charts of the river were routinely matched to scale with modern charts and showed me that the east and west banks had not changed much over a hundred and twenty years. Only the bend on the east side in front of Fort St. Philip had filled in for a distance of fifty yards or more. I was quite sure *Manassas* had gone down near the west bank, because not only was it reported that the abandoned and burning

ironclad had drifted past the mortar fleet, causing great
concern, but Admiral Porter had tried to put a hawser on
the vessel and save it as a curiosity. Unfortunately, at
just that moment, there had been an internal explosion
and *Manassas* had sunk into the river.

Walt, John, and I began our runs from the east bank
and worked across the river to the west from Venice to
the bend below Fort Jackson. I way overextended the
search grid, because I wasn't going to take any chances
of missing *Manassas*. As I've mentioned before, I've
found that old contemporary reports are not necessarily
the gospel truth.

The hours dragged by as we slowly approached the
west bank, dodging big ocean cargo ships coming and
going to New Orleans. This part of the river was
devoid of any shipwrecks. I failed to receive more than
the occasional one- or two-gamma reading, suggesting
that we were passing over nothing larger than a steel
drum or anchor. We were pretty discouraged as we
made our final run, brushing the edge of the little rock
jetty that ran along the west bank below the levee.

Abruptly, halfway into the last lane about a quarter
of a mile above Boothville-Venice High School, the
recorder screamed and the needle went off the dial, as
we crossed over a massive anomaly. The hit was not in
the river, but alongside and beneath part of the levee.
Normally under a foot of water, the area between the
jetty and levee was dry because the river was low this
time of year. This enabled Walt to jump from the boat
and walk the gradiometer sensor along the base of the
levee as I received a prolonged reading on the recorder.

Obviously, we can't say with certainty this was
Manassas. The fact that this was the only massive target

in the approximate area where she was recorded to have sunk was all we had going for us. I marked the site on my chart, noting the landmarks on the other side of the levee, and called it a day.

The next morning, we headed across the river and began our search of the water just off Fort St. Philip for the Confederate ironclad *Louisiana*. She was a monstrous ship, one of the largest the South built. She was 264 feet long with a beam of 62 feet. Her construction had not been completed before the battle, and she was towed down from New Orleans and moored to the bank slightly above Fort St. Philip as a floating battery. If her engines had been functional, the battle might have taken a different turn. But she could contribute little in keeping the Union fleet from running the gauntlet and taking the city of New Orleans.

After the battle, the Confederates set her on fire. Her mooring lines burned, and she began to drift downriver a short distance before being ripped apart by a massive blast when she was opposite the fort. We found a gigantic anomaly in the first hour of the search: no great feat, since I had studied a sketch of the exploding ironclad, showing a mushroom cloud of smoke erupting from the top of her casemate, done by Alfred Waud, the famous Civil War artist for *Harper's Weekly*. The sketch put her directly off Fort St. Philip. She lies quite deep under the present shoreline in front of Fort St. Philip in a swampy area off the river. Her massive bulk contributed to the buildup of silt at the bend where she originally went down. Chris Goodwin, an archaeologist with an office in New Orleans, conducted an extensive survey over the site and, I believe, actually cored down to her wreck.

The third day, we searched the river for two other boats that went down in the battle: the Confederate gunboat *Governor Moore* and the Union gunboat *Varuna*—fittingly sunk by the *Governor Moore*. *Moore* has the distinction of having fired through her own bow after ramming *Varuna*, because her forward gun would have hurled its shot over the Union boat if she'd fired through her own port. Both ships went ashore within a hundred yards of each other.

We struck a large target to the south on the east bank around where *Varuna* ran aground to keep her from sinking, then continued upriver and found *Governor Moore*. She was easy to identify, because part of her, including the top of her boilers, was protruding from the water along the bank. The local boys often dive off of her boiler.

Walt and I had accomplished all we could. After bidding John farewell, we reluctantly departed our ritzy accommodations and headed for Baton Rouge, where we discovered the final resting place of the Confederate ironclad *Arkansas*.

I HOPE I'm forgiven for not spotting our targets with transits, as a true professional archaeologist would. By simply marking the wreck sites on charts with nearby landmarks, however, we've made it possible for anyone who follows our trail to have little trouble relocating the targets.

Total cost of the expedition?

$3,678.40.

Now, how can you beat that?

The story of *Manassas*, however, does not end here.

*

I TURNED OVER my records to the chief archaeologist for the Army Corps of Engineers, who contracted with Texas A&M University to do a magnetometer study of the site. I returned the following year with my wife, Barbara, and pinpointed the spot where Walt and I had found a huge magnetic anomaly. The investigation was led by Ervan Garrison and James Baker of the university.

The survey was conducted with a magnetometer, sidescan sonar, and subbottom profiler. The project determined that, indeed, a very strong anomaly existed over a large shoal that had formed over the site. The magnetometer readings of 8,000-plus gammas and the hard subbottom reflections indicated that an object the same size as *Manassas* was buried beneath the shoal where contemporary reports put the ironclad. They also found a large mass of steel dredge pipe directly opposite the site and eighteen feet deep in the river. I was surprised at this, since Walt and I recorded no ferrous activity away from the bank.

Everything was fine and dandy, until Garrison and Baker turned over their report to the Corps's chief archaeologist. He blew a fuse, then caused an uproar, when he claimed the report was totally inconclusive and proved nothing. His refusal to accept the report was almost vehement in its condemnation.

The good people at A&M were dumbfounded. These were the nation's leading experts in remote sensing. I read over the report and found it one of the most concise and detailed I've ever read. I was as mystified as Garrison and Baker.

The Corps archaeologist then called in a local marine archaeologist to do another survey of the site. After investigating, he went on television to bemoan the agony of defeat by proclaiming that the magnetic anomaly was not *Manassas* but a pile of old pipe dumped there in the 1920s.

This made absolutely no sense to anyone. Our target was practically under the levee, not eighteen feet deep and thirty-six feet out into the river. That was the pipe, but where had it come from? The Army Corps's rejection of A&M's mag study struck me as strange. The mystery wasn't solved until much later.

FIFTEEN YEARS PASSED before I returned to the *Manassas* site. Ralph Wilbanks, Wes Hall, Craig Dirgo, Dirk Cussler, and I had just finished an expedition to find the Republic of Texas Navy ship *Invincible*, without much luck. Working off Ralph's boat, *Diversity*, we dredged a site off Galveston and identified it as a shipwreck, but nothing more specific, since we couldn't find any artifacts. From Texas, we towed Ralph's boat to the Mississippi River Delta.

My thought was that since mag technology had improved and Ralph and Wes were far more professional than Walt and I, it was time to go back and check out the *Manassas* site again.

We lowered *Diversity* down a boat ramp in Venice and leisurely studied the west bank of the Mississippi with Ralph's state-of-the-art magnetometer. While Ralph steered, Wes ran the mag. Just as it had fifteen years earlier, the recorder's needle showed a steady line that meant the cupboard was bare of wrecks.

I watched the shoreline carefully, keeping a keen eye on the landmarks across the river and the top of a big oak tree that was not far from the site. I also noticed that many huge rocks had been laid against the shore by the Army Corps of Engineers.

Before I could alert the team that we were entering the target zone, Wes let out a gasp as the magnetometer went into hysterics.

"What's your reading?" Ralph asked, turning.

"Eleven thousand gammas," Wes muttered. He'd rarely ever seen a reading that huge.

"We've passed between the pipe and *Manassas*," I explained.

Ralph finished the run almost to Fort Jackson before turning around and making another survey along the bank. This time, by hugging the base of the levee, we got a lower reading, since the sensor was farther from the submerged pipe.

"There's something big running on an angle under the levee," Wes announced, examining his mag records.

We couldn't get ashore, because the river was running too high and the shoal between the bank and the levee was underwater. Returning to Venice, we pulled *Diversity* out of the water and hauled it to the *Manassas* site. There we walked the mag up and down the levee. The signals were still there, but not as strong.

After dinner, a few of us were sitting in the bar of the boat marina in Venice when an older fellow came up and offered to buy us a drink. He was of medium height, with a tanned face and a finely brushed mane of white hair. He said he had retired a few years before from the Army Corps of Engineers and lived just outside Venice.

"You them fellas looking for that old Confederate ironclad?" he inquired.

"We're the ones," I answered.

"I remember some other fellas was looking for her a long time back."

"That was me, about fifteen years back."

"You sure got scammed by the Corps report, didn't you?"

I looked at him. "Scammed?"

"Sure, after you found the *Manassas*, word came down from the chief archaeologist and his boss to drop a load of old dredge pipe on top of it. Boy, was he shook up when that Texas bunch ignored the pipe and concentrated on the wreck under the levee."

"The pipe was dumped there after we found the wreck?" I asked, baffled.

"That's the way it went."

"But why?"

"The Corps had planned a big project to reinforce the west levee. If the state archaeology commission had got wind of an old shipwreck under it, they'd have named it a historic site and stopped the Corps from throwing rock on top of it. That's why the Texas survey was tossed out and another survey contracted that said there was no shipwreck, only a bunch of dredge pipe."

I felt like a man who'd come awake after a hernia operation. I never did understand why a first-class remote-sensing survey was rejected out of hand. I thought it ridiculous then. Now I can see why.

The old guy and I talked long into the night. I shouldn't say "old guy." We must have been about the same age. I can't recall a more satisfying evening.

*

THERE ARE currently plans afoot by John Hunley and a group of interested Louisiana citizens to dig an exploratory hole on the site and see if the *Manassas* is truly there. If so, its removal and restoration would stand alongside that of the Confederate submarine *Hunley*. Not only is she the first armored ship built in America, but she is the first one actually to see combat. The battle between *Monitor* and *Merrimack* did not take place for another five months.

Over the years, the chief archaeologist and I had exchanged Christmas cards. On the back of the last card I sent, I wrote, "You dog." Then I proceeded briefly to relate the story I'd heard from the retired Corps worker.

I never heard from him again.

PART FOUR
U.S.S. *Mississippi*

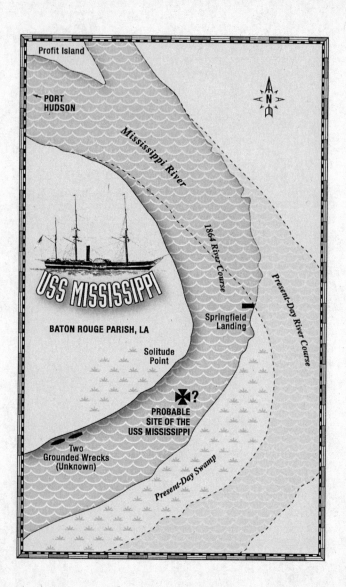

Profit Island

PORT HUDSON

Mississippi River

1864 River Course

Present-Day River Course

USS MISSISSIPPI

BATON ROUGE PARISH, LA

Springfield Landing

Solitude Point

✠?

PROBABLE SITE OF THE USS MISSISSIPPI

Two Grounded Wrecks (Unknown)

Present-Day Swamp

I

A Magnificent End

1863

ON THE HEIGHTS OF PORT HUDSON over-looking the Mississippi River, the Confederate batteries had managed to withstand the daylong bombardment by the Federal fleet, and now the night of March 14, 1863, was curiously quiet. Twenty miles above the state capital at Baton Rouge, Louisiana, the small riverboat landing was perched on a steep eighty-foot-high bluff at a point where the river made a sharp turn to the west. A narrow beach ran along the precipice, overgrown with willows and cottonwoods that provided cover for a two-gun battery.

Major General Franklin Gardner stared through the blackness of night at the stars reflected on the fast-flowing river. A native New Yorker, he had seen service in the Mexican War and fought Indians on the frontier. He had offered his services to the Confederacy because of his love for his wife, the daughter of Louisiana governor Alexandre Mouton, and his affection for his friends and neighbors that had come after many years of living in Baton Rouge.

Port Hudson had great strategic value. The Confederates had fortified the bluffs and thrown up earthworks on the land side because it gave them control of the Red River, as well as the Mississippi. As long as they held the Red River, supplies and troops could be brought into the Confederacy from Texas through Mexico. Gardner's orders were to hold at all cost against the assault by Union General Nathaniel Banks and his troops. He would hold out for forty-eight days before surrendering during the first week of July.

In his early forties, Gardner was of medium height and slender, with sparse reddish hair. He peered into the darkness through a pair of binoculars for a few moments before lowering them. "I have a feeling Farragut will come before dawn."

Lieutenant Wilfred Pratt of Company K, in command of the nearby gun, its muzzle pointed down to fire in the middle of the river, nodded in agreement. "I wouldn't put it past them sneaky Yanks to make a try in the wee hours while it's still dark."

"It should be an interesting battle," murmured Gardner, satisfied that his eighteen guns were well concealed in their emplacements and ready for action.

He and his seven-thousand-man force would soon be surrounded and besieged by a Union army, the same as their comrades at Vicksburg 110 miles upstream. Both positions were of vital importance to the Confederacy. As long as they controlled their positions above the Mississippi, it was too hazardous and costly in ships and men for the Union gunboats and transports to risk passage.

Gardner lifted his glasses again. "What time do you have?"

Lieutenant Pratt pulled a watch from a breast pocket by a gold chain, lit a match, and peered at the dial. "I have three minutes to eleven o'clock, sir."

The words were barely uttered when two red rockets soared into the night sky, breaking the stillness of the air as they burst above the river. Captain Whitfield Youngblood of Gardner's signal corps had ordered the rockets launched upon seeing the red light on the masthead of Farragut's flagship *Hartford*, as the vessel passed his station. The Confederates were neither deceived nor surprised. Their eighteen big guns roared and flashed in a deafening crescendo of thunderclaps that never seemed to end.

Gardner and Pratt watched mesmerized as the Union fleet steadily moved up the river, their black hulls blending in with the dark river. The bedlam mushroomed as the combined 112 guns of the Union fleet, those of the ironclad *Essex*, and the mortar boats tied along the east bank blasted back in reply. The great thirteen-inch mortar shells with their burning fuses rose and fell like meteors within the Confederate fortifications. The sky became a giant fireworks display. The ground shuttered and vibrated as if rolled by an earthquake. The fiery spurts from the gun muzzles blazed and then blinked dark as their crews rammed new charges and shot down their smoking barrels.

Soon the smoke was so thick that gunners on both sides could only sight their guns on the enemy's flashes. Confederate sharpshooters in rifle pits added to the maelstrom clatter as they fired at ships, hoping to bring down the crewmen.

*

"IT WON'T be easy swinging around the bend," said Farragut's pilot on board *Hartford*. George Alder stared down into the black water surging past the frigate's hull. Then he glanced woefully at the gunboat *Albatross* that was lashed along the frigate's port side. "Not with two ships tied side by side against a four-knot current."

"The current is the least of my concern," came the staunch reply. "Just keep us in the center of the river."

Admiral David Glasgow Farragut, a tough Scot with a perennial smile, stood imperturbable. He was as unstirred as a rock assaulted by heavy surf—an image he'd displayed in the battle for New Orleans, as well as one for which he would become famous later, at the battle of Mobile Bay, when he'd ignore the Confederate minefield after losing one of his monitors and shout, "Damn the torpedoes! Full steam ahead!"

The opposite of General Gardner, Farragut came from the South. Though he'd been born in Tennessee, was raised in Louisiana, and lived in Virginia, he was devoted to the United States. After moving his family north, he'd joined the Union and was named flag officer in command of the West Gulf's blockading squadron.

After his great victory at New Orleans, he was determined to run this fleet upriver to Vicksburg to try to aid General Grant in his siege of the city. Farragut turned and surveyed the ships lined up behind *Hartford*. The frigate *Richmond*, with the gunboat *Genesee* alongside, was directly astern. Then came the frigate *Monongahela*, tied to the gunboat *Kineo*. And finally the "old spinning wheel," as the frigate *Mississippi* was affectionately called because of her antiquated paddle wheels.

Bullets whizzed through the riggings as the rebel riflemen aimed high through the smoke, causing few casualties among *Hartford*'s crew. The forty-two-gun sloop of war pushed through the smoke and was almost clear of the worst of the fire when the current caught her and swept her bow toward the Port Hudson batteries.

"The damned current!" shouted Alder. "I can't hold her."

A signal was quickly shouted across the bulwarks to the captain of *Albatross* to reverse his engines while *Hartford*'s engineer poured on the coal full steam ahead. Slowly, the two ships swung on a ninety-degree angle upriver and steamed out of range of the deadly guns.

Farragut was wise enough to know that *Hartford* and *Albatross* were lucky. The Confederates had not depressed their guns low enough to do damage to the Union ships, but they were not about to make the same mistake as the next ships in line came within range.

"I'm afraid the rest of the fleet is in for the worst of it," he said apprehensively, as he saw a fire erupt from an old house on the west bank. The Confederates had obviously ignited it to light up the river and reveal the Union fleet.

Farragut was especially concerned about the last ship in line. *Mississippi* was the oldest steamer in naval service. A hardened battle veteran, she had proved her worth in the run past the forts below New Orleans. By the time it was her turn to run the gauntlet, the Confederate gunners would have had time to zero in on her with deadly accuracy. She was about to find herself in the most exposed position of the entire fleet.

*

THROUGHOUT THE NEARLY 250 years of its existence, the U.S. Navy has been blessed with any number of ships that contributed proud and illustrious service. Some benefit from household names like *Bonhomme Richard*, *Monitor*, *Arizona*, and *Enterprise*. But many others, with careers no less distinguished, are neglected and forgotten by all but a few naval historians. One such ship was the U.S.S. *Mississippi*.

The second to be built of the Navy's oceangoing armed steamships, *Mississippi* was commissioned on December 22, 1841, shortly before her sister ship, *Missouri*. Commodore Matthew C. Perry personally supervised her construction, and she was named after the mighty river that flowed through the heart of the country.

Mississippi was a side-wheel steamer 229 feet in length with a beam of 40 feet and a depth of 19 feet. Her original gun battery consisted of two 10-inch and eight 8-inch guns. She had a respectable top speed of 8 knots, and she carried a crew of 280.

Unlike her virtual twin, *Missouri*, which sailed for only two years before accidentally catching on fire and exploding off of Gibraltar in 1843, *Mississippi* enjoyed a long and glorious existence before she, too, burned and exploded.

She spent her first few years performing research and demonstrations vital to the evolution of steam-powered warships, before sailing to the West Indies, where she became the flagship of her construction overseer, Commodore Perry. In the right place at the right time during the war with Mexico, *Mississippi* engaged in actions against Tampico, Panuco, Alarado, and several other coastal ports, blockading incoming commerce. She was also heavily involved with the amphibious operations at Veracruz, where she landed vital military matériel for Winfield Scott's army. She also supplied heavy guns, and the crews who fought them, all the way to Mexico City, where they bombarded fortifications and helped bring about the city's surrender in only four days. Throughout much of the war, *Mississippi* conducted a series of raids on coastal towns before helping to capture the important town of Tobasco.

After the war, she cruised with the American fleet in the Mediterranean for two years before returning to America in preparation for Commodore Perry's celebrated voyage to Japan. *Mississippi* was his flagship on most of the expedition to open Japan to Western trade. In one of the most studied and admired naval and diplomatic operations in history, Perry negotiated a treaty with the emperor, and the nation that had been utterly opposed to outside influence opened its ports to international trade.

Mississippi sailed for New York and later returned as Commodore Josiah Tatnall's flagship. Commodore Tatnall "went south" at the beginning of the Civil War and was in command of *Merrimac/Virginia* during her lengthy battle with *Monitor*.

From 1857 to 1860, the now-aging ship supported and protected America's booming trade in China and Japan. She was also with the British and French ships during the attack on Taku and landed her marines at Shanghai when the American consul requested Tatnall's help in quelling the rioting in the city.

The veteran steamer sailed back to Boston and was laid up until it was reactivated at the beginning of the

Civil War. Now under the command of Melancthon Smith, she was employed in blockading Pensacola, Florida. After capturing two Confederate blockade runners off Key West in late 1861, she joined Admiral David Farragut for the assault on New Orleans. When she passed over the bar at the South Pass, she became the largest ship ever to enter the Mississippi River.

As previously related, during the battle, as Farragut's fleet ran the gauntlet between Forts St. Philip and Jackson, *Mississippi* battered the Confederate ironclad *Manassas* after it made an unsuccessful attempt to ram and sink her. Surviving the hail of shot and shell from the forts, *Mississippi* triumphantly entered New Orleans with the rest of the fleet and aimed her guns on the buildings along the shore until the city capitulated.

Nearly a year after, Farragut ordered Smith to take *Mississippi* and join the ships that would attempt to pass the Confederate guns of Port Hudson to Vicksburg to help General Grant in his siege of the city. The battle of the bluffs would prove to be her final moment of glory.

JUST AS *RICHMOND,* the second ship in line, was turning the bend and within a hundred yards of safety, a shot ripped into her engine room and shattered her steam valves and pipes. Unable to maintain pressure and make headway with *Genesee* tied to her port side, her captain had no choice but to reverse course and retreat back down the river out of the range of Confederate guns.

Monongahela fared no better. A shell struck the rudderpost of *Kineo*, the gunboat making the run at the frigate's side, and jammed it. Unable to steer against the current while maneuvering both ships, *Monongahela* ran aground. The sudden stop tore away the lines gripping the ships together. While under a devastating fire, *Kineo* struggled valiantly to get a hawser to the big frigate before pulling *Monongahela* free of the bottom mud.

The two ships endeavored to resume their course upriver, but shot incapacitated the frigate's engines, and both ships had to drift helplessly back down the river while sustaining heavy fire from the enemy gun batteries.

Alone and bringing up the rear, *Mississippi* now became the prime target. Concentrating their fire on the lone warship, the Confederates poured shell after shell into the old frigate. She soon became enveloped in a pall of swirling smoke.

Captain Melancthon Smith paced the bridge, calmly smoking a cigar, seemingly oblivious to the hail of shot and shell bursting on and around his ship. *Mississippi*'s paddle wheels were beating the water, propelling her past the bluffs alive with cannon fire. Her top speed of eight knots was cut to four from the equally fast speed of the current, and it seemed to the crew who were working their guns in furious haste that the passage was taking an eternity.

They were moving slowly, the pilot feeling his way through the heavy smoke. Believing that they were safely past the jutting point of the west bank and its shoals, the pilot called out, "Starboard helm! Full speed ahead!"

In the words of the *Mississippi*'s executive officer, George Dewey, "As it turned out, we were anything but past the point. We starboarded the helm right into it and struck just as we developed a powerful momentum. We were hard aground and listing."

Dewey would later become the hero of Manila Bay, where his fleet of warships decimated the Spanish fleet, and he would utter words that have come down through naval history, along with John Paul Jones's "I have not yet begun to fight," Oliver Hazard Perry's "We have met the enemy and they are ours," and James Lawrence's "Don't give up the ship." As the great Spanish-American War sea battle was about to commence, Dewey turned to the captain of his flagship, *Olympia*, and calmly said, "You may fire when ready, Gridley."

Dewey was a handsome man with black straight hair, bushy sideburns, and a great mustache that he kept until his death in 1917.

With guns blasting, engines pounding with every ounce of steam the chief engineer could coax from them, and paddle wheels thrashing the water, old *Mississippi* refused to budge. The Confederates took happy advantage of the stationary target lit up by the nearby burning house, pouring in shells and a swarm of bullets from the rifle pits. As the ship struggled helplessly to back off the shoal, the number of dead and wounded climbed appallingly.

Dewey hunted for Captain Smith and found him lighting a cigar as coolly as if he were standing at a garden party. "Well, it doesn't look as if we could get her off," said Smith, almost indifferently.

"No, it does not," Dewey replied.

At that moment, a fiery hot shot tore into the forward storeroom and set the inflammable supplies and matériel afire. A holocaust soon spread out of control as flames quickly reached the decks above. Looking around at the destruction and his mortally wounded command, Smith had to face the sad prospect of losing his ship.

"Can we save the crew?" he asked Dewey.

"Yes, sir."

Shells had shattered the three boats on the side facing the enemy, but those on the port side were still seaworthy. Dewey directed a crew of able-bodied men to load the worst of the wounded into the first boat and directed the crew to row to one of the ships downstream.

Dewey supervised the loading of the lesser wounded and some that were unhurt. He was frustrated to see how slowly the boats returned. The oarsmen were decidedly unenthusiastic about making the trip back once they reached the temporary safety of the other ships. Unable to speed up the boats' return to the burning ship, Dewey swung a line into a boat just as it was about to push off with a load of crewmen.

Though Dewey was reluctant to desert his ship, his decision turned out to be a wise one. He and the acting master, Joseph Chase, had to use their revolvers to make the men row back. If Dewey hadn't slipped aboard, none of the boats would have been available to rescue the rest of *Mississippi*'s remaining crew.

Upon returning to the main deck, Dewey approached Smith and hastily explained his temporary absence. He motioned to the two empty lifeboats alongside, indicating that they would not be there save for his initiative and fortitude.

"We must make sure none is left aboard alive," Smith said evenly.

What began as a compelling search soon turned into

a grim nightmare. Dewey quickly selected five men to accompany him throughout the disabled warship. Bodies had to be closely examined in the dark and smoke to see if any of the men were still alive. They were very careful to make certain no spark of life remained, or the poor man might lie there, powerless to move, as the flames crept closer and closer.

They moved belowdecks, shouting that there was little time left to abandon the ship. Luckily, they found a young cabin boy who was still breathing despite being buried under a pile of dead bodies that had been cut down by bursting shells. Satisfied that only the dead remained on board, Dewey was then ordered by Smith to make absolutely certain that old *Mississippi* would be totally destroyed before falling into Confederate hands.

Dewey ran to his stateroom, snatched off the mattress from his berth, and dragged it to the wardroom, where he sliced it open with a dress sword, piled chairs and tables on top of it, and then threw an old oil lantern into the debris, igniting a roaring fire almost immediately. Only then did he and the few men left on board join Captain Smith in the last lifeboat.

They pushed off from the hull aft of the paddle wheels and immediately were caught in the powerful current and swept downriver. As they looked back, a giant torrent of flame burst through the skylight of the wardroom that Dewey had set ablaze. The Confederate guns fired away at the lifeboat but fortunately failed to score a hit. At the sight of the flaming ship, the entire bluff above the river broke into a rebel yell. The victory was theirs.

Farragut's fleet had come within an inch of total disaster.

Smith seated himself in the stern of the lifeboat, still

puffing nonchalantly on a cigar while Dewey manned the tiller, and the men rowed through the splashing shells until they reached the safety of the battle-scarred *Richmond,* anchored downriver out of reach of the Confederate guns. During their flight, Smith took off his sword and revolvers and threw them into the river.

"Why did you do that?" Dewey asked him.

"I'm not surrendering them to any rebel," he said haughtily. It was a hasty decision Smith would come to regret.

A humorous episode occurred when the men of *Mississippi* boarded *Richmond.* While Dewey was setting the fire in the wardroom on board the doomed ship, Ensign Dean Batcheller snatched up a dress uniform coat hanging in the cabin he shared with Ensign Francis Shepard. The rest of the crew, including Smith and Dewey, escaped with only the clothes on their backs.

Proudly, Batcheller held up the coat. "At least I'll have something to wear for the ladies in New Orleans."

His cabin mate Ensign Shepard leaned over and eyed the coat. Then he looked up and grinned. "Thanks very much, Batcheller, but that's *my* coat."

And so it was.

Dewey was greeted by a close friend from his Naval Academy days at Annapolis, Winfield Scott Schley, who was destined to command the fleet that would destroy the Spanish fleet off Santiago, Cuba, at almost the same time Dewey was making his mark in the Philippines.

Back at the battered *Mississippi,* the river flowed in through the engine water-delivery pipes that had been cut by the engine-room crew before they abandoned ship. Because the hull was grounded on an angle with the bow slightly raised, the incoming water flowed toward the stern. The added weight lifted the bow, and she slid free off the shoal. The current turned her around so that now she was moving with her bow pointed downstream. The port guns that had been loaded but not fired now faced the Confederates. As the flames reached their primers, they began firing a ragged broadside in a final act of defiance. Dewey solemnly described the sight as "a ship manned by dead men still firing at the enemy."

Engulfed by a sheet of fire that raged through the pummeled ship, *Mississippi* was carried downriver by a four-knot current. The shriek of steam escaping from the ship's safety valve cut through the pandemonium of gunfire. Flames burst from her rigging and erupted into the night sky, casting a flickering orange blaze of light that illuminated both shorelines as bright as day. Looking like a floating, flaming pyramid, *Mississippi* was a funeral pyre for the dead aboard. It was a sight never forgotten by both the Federals and rebels who watched her fiery passage in the night. Her death would later be described as a grand spectacle.

Several reports from both sides in the battle put the frigate sliding off the shoals at 3 A.M. and drifting down around Profit Island, her flaming hull reflecting in the sky until 5:30, when the fire reached the twenty tons of gunpowder in her magazine and she blew up in a tremendous explosion. The ensuing concussion shook the country for miles around and rocked the Union ships from stem to stern. Such was the end of the brave old paddle steamer.

It was somehow fitting that the river she was named

for became her burial shroud.

Perhaps Dewey himself paid *Mississippi* her greatest tribute when he stood on the deck of *Richmond*, stony-faced and deeply saddened as he watched her die. He said, "She goes out magnificently."

II

Nothing Stays the Same

1989

THIS IS ESPECIALLY TRUE OF RIVERS AND THEIR shorelines. Unless it's the Colorado flowing through the Grand Canyon on the same course for thousands of years, most rivers, particularly the Mississippi, change their course on a daily basis. The riverboat *Sultana*, chronicled in the first *Sea Hunters* book, burned and sank a few miles above Memphis in 1865 with a loss of two thousand lives. Our mag search put the remains two miles from the present course of the river, eighteen feet deep in a farmer's soybean field in Arkansas.

The final resting place of the gallant old frigate *Mississippi*, where she has lain ignored and forgotten since that horrendous night in 1863, is not under the present river channel, either. In the approximate area where *Mississippi* was last seen, the river has moved almost a mile to the west and has become an immense bog.

Because I did not feel it was fitting or proper that

"lost in obscurity" be *Mississippi*'s epitaph, I cleared my desk after finishing another Dirk Pitt adventure book and began the research in preparation for the hunt for *Mississippi*.

Relying on researcher Bob Fleming in Washington, who combed the archives, we amassed a mountain of material that we eventually sifted to a ten-inch pile. Then began the investigation to estimate a ballpark for *Mississippi*'s location. One of the first things we had to consider was the possibility that she had been salvaged. Fortunately, a probe through the naval archives revealed no such attempt. Part of the reason was a report that she had exploded in the middle of the channel and sunk in deep water, which would have been between eighty and a hundred feet, a depth that would have made it impractical to undertake a salvage operation 140 years ago.

Since none of the contemporary reports gave a clue to the exact location where she had blasted herself to bits and gone down, and no distances were given to still-existing landmarks, I had to base the search on the time element. With the river running at a known four knots, it didn't take a great strain of my pitifully inadequate talent for mathematics to figure that *Mississippi* drifted a distance of ten to eleven miles before she sank.

There were one or two Confederate reports that put the site of her explosion close to the wrecks of the ironclad *Arkansas*, destroyed by her crew a few months earlier. But we had discovered the ironclad eight years before under a levee sixteen miles below Port Hudson at the bend of the reach before it dropped toward Baton Rouge.

The ten-mile distance was consistent with

contemporary references. Spears's biography of Farragut states that "she reached the foot of Profit Island when the fire reached her magazine and she blew up."

A. J. C. Kerr, a Confederate veteran from Corsicana, Texas, stated later in his memoirs that "the *Mississippi* blew up ten miles below Port Hudson."

The log of the *Richmond* also stated that "the *Mississippi* drifted down the river and blew up ten miles astern of us."

George S. Waterman recounted that "the *Mississippi* floated down the river a short distance below the fleet when the fire reached her magazine."

And finally, there is a sketch of the river and gun emplacements at Port Hudson with a notation by William Waud, a war artist who was on board *Richmond:* "Air very thick with smoke. The *Mississippi* drifting down in flames, exploding near the land pier."

The last was a good reference point, except there were at least six piers along that stretch of river in 1863. Then, to muddy the water, Waud never indicated what he meant by "land pier." Upper Springfield Landing was the closest to the projected site. Also, two contemporary wrecks were marked on the old chart, one on top of the other, on the west bank below the bend in the river. Over the passing of a century or more, the encroaching swamp had covered them and left their remains a good half mile from the present river flow. Since they were unnamed and appeared to have run aground, we eliminated them as *Mississippi*. Also, it seemed likely that if one had been the Union frigate, the chart maker would have labeled her as such.

Next came the important process of overlaying a

new chart showing the present course of the river as compared with an 1868 chart. It quickly became apparent that the approximate spot where we computed *Mississippi* to lie was now nearly a quarter mile west in a huge bog called Solitude Point.

Springfield Bend, as the area that traveled around the point was called, had filled in toward the east. It was encouraging, but we still felt we stood a slim chance.

Having taken it as far as we could go, we decided it was time to gather up the equipment and head for Louisiana to begin our search.

In May of 1989, Craig Dirgo and I arrived in Baton Rouge and arranged with the West Baton Rouge parish sheriff's department to once again borrow their great little aluminum boat for a river survey. Accompanied by a deputy and his son-in-law, we launched the boat on a hot, humid day under a clear sky. Relying on NUMA's EG&G sidescan sonar and the Schonstedt gradiometer to find a promising target, we set out hoping for the best, expecting the worse, and willing to settle for anything in between.

We began surveying the river thirteen miles below Port Hudson and ran north past Profit Island, which has changed very little over the past hundred years, to within six miles of where *Mississippi* grounded and began her drift. I had been told that the Army Corps of Engineers had surveyed part of the river where *Mississippi* had grounded and had recorded several large anomalies on the riverbed, but we found it as barren as the Mojave Desert. Nothing remotely resembling a wreck was discovered, and no targets worth investigating. There was one wreck depicted on an old 1880s chart against the east bank, but we found no trace of it. Not surprising, since the records show that it was likely dredged out of existence many years ago.

The southern tropical heat, shaken and stirred with 100 percent humidity, nearly did in Craig. With no wind to cool the sweat surging from our pores, the atmosphere was agonizingly oppressive. Many people think it is cooler on the water when the weather is hot— not necessarily so. You have little shade on a small boat, and the steaming water can easily raise humidity off the scale when there is no hint of rain from a cloudless sky.

The Solitude Point swamp is not only huge, it's impassable. You couldn't walk, wade, or swim through it, much less penetrate it with a jet ski. Interestingly, the 1836 chart fails to indicate it because it had yet to make its presence known. Oil drilling has since taken place inside the swamp, and pipelines stretch outward like legs on a spider, three of them traveling up the river to the north.

Unable to conduct a mag survey from the surface, I turned to Joe Phillips of World Geoscience, Inc., in Houston, Texas, and arranged for a helicopter geophysical aeromagnetic survey. Using a Bell 206 Ranger equipped with a SCINTREX vapor magnetometer sensor, a Picodaas digital acquisition system, and a GPS navigational system, they launched the survey in August of 1999.

Flying tight ninety-foot lines at an altitude of less than a hundred feet, they found the oil field west of the point without any trouble. Paying special attention to the 1864 course of the river, they easily picked up the magnetic anomalies from the two riverboats aground below the point. Then, almost precisely at the ten-mile drift projection of *Mississippi*, a large anomaly appeared on the magnetometer recording. It was almost directly in the middle of the old river passage. The target was three quarters of a mile inside the swamp from the river's west bank. They also determined that it was very close to the long-gone Springfield Landing pier mentioned by the Civil War artist Waud. Another encouraging indication was the computerized profile of *Mississippi*, showing a large iron mass that would have included guns, shot, anchors, and many tons of ship's hardware.

Was it *Mississippi*? Until we could actually touch a piece of it, there would be no uncorking the champagne.

That was about as far as we could go in our search. We reeled in the sensors, packed the equipment, and headed for a Cajun restaurant. We had done our best and would leave it to future archaeologists, historians, and shipwreck hunters to probe the depths of that loathsome swamp.

Mississippi would be a fascinating wreck to excavate since she hadn't been salvaged, and even despite the damage from the explosion, she had to be relatively intact. Unfortunately, any excavation more than eighty feet deep in the middle of a bog would be extremely difficult, if not impossible.

It seems that *Mississippi* will remain under Point Solitude for a long time to come, perhaps for eternity. You never know if it's best that way.

PART FIVE

The Siege of Charleston:

Keokuk, *Weehawken*, and *Patapsco*

MOUNT
PLEASANT

*Charleston
Harbor*

To
Charleston

Fort
Sumter

Patapsco

Cummings
Point

Fort Wagner

Morris
Island

Weehawken

Keokuk

Lighthouse

*North
Atlantic
Ocean*

Isle of Palms

Sullivans
Island

Fort Moultrie

North Jetty

South Jetty

Housatonic

Hunley

THE SIEGE
OF CHARLESTON

SOUTH CAROLINA COAST

I

Cradle of Secession

1863–1865

Rear Admiral Samuel F. DuPont stared into the distance. The bow of his command, *New Ironsides*, a heavily armed frigate, was pointed in the direction of Charleston. To starboard lay Sullivans Island, to port Morris Island and Cummings Point.

Dead ahead was DuPont's objective, Fort Sumter.

Fort Sumter, a massive brick-and-concrete fortress rising forty feet above the water, was located on a small island off Charleston. Sumter was one of the first Federal installations to be taken by the Confederates. It was also the most visible reminder to the citizens of the United States of the South's defiance. The first shots of the War Between the States had been fired on Sumter.

DuPont swiveled his head and glanced at his assembled fleet.

From west to east they stretched across the water. *Keokuk, Nahant, Nantucket, Catskill*, his own *New Ironsides*, then *Patapsco, Montauk, Passaic*, and

Weehawken. The flotilla was an impressive armada tasked with a difficult mission.

The Union ships were clad in armor—a recent development for the antiquated Union navy—and the fleet was powered by steam, not sail. Still, for all their new technology, their task was as old as sea warfare itself: to bring a concentrated fire of heavy guns to bear, to project force on a distant target.

To achieve this goal, DuPont led the most powerful squadron ever assembled.

Commander A. C. Rhind stared through the forward porthole of his command, *Keokuk*. His ship was farthest to the west and last in the long line of warships. *Keokuk* was an experimental craft commissioned to the Union navy on February 24, 1863.

Her design was different from that of the seven other Passaic-class ironclads. Unlike the razor-edged styling of the monitors, *Keokuk* featured a rounded, whale-like upper deck. A pair of armored, half-conical towers perched on each end of the vessel, separated by a stubby smokestack. Amidships, alongside the slightly taller smokestack, was a davited wooden shore boat. On the stern deck was a wooden staff, where the Stars and Stripes fluttered in the breeze.

The ship looked like a cigar topped by thimbles.

Keokuk was 159 feet 6 inches in length, with a beam of 36 feet and a draft of 8 feet 6 inches. She was propelled by twin screws powered by steam, which gave her greater speed and maneuverability over the monitors. Her armament consisted of a pair of massive 11-inch Dahlgren guns. The guns were designed to pivot to fire through a trio of gun ports. Unlike the monitors, the towers did not rotate to give her a greater field of fire. Her armor was too light for the guns of Sumter, but Rhind did not know this yet. *Keokuk* carried a crew of ninety-two.

Ship engineer N. W. Wheeler approached Rhind. "All is in order," he reported quietly.

"Follow them in," Rhind said to the pilot.

"WE'RE ALMOST in range," Captain John Rodgers shouted. "We'll be hearing from the rebels soon."

Rodgers commanded *Weehawken*, the lead vessel in the line approaching Fort Sumter. While Rodgers was proud of his vessel and crew, he couldn't help but feel anxious. At that moment, he saw a puff of smoke from Sumter, and a shot struck the water twenty feet ahead. The battle was starting.

Weehawken was some 200 feet in length, with a beam of 46 feet. The vessel featured twin gun turrets that packed a wallop. One gun was a standard 11-inch smooth-bore; the second, a 42,000-pound, 15-inch Dahlgren, could hurl a 400-pound shell a mile. On her bow she pushed a torpedo raft to detonate the Confederate mines.

FROM INSIDE the pentagonal-shaped Fort Sumter, the approaching line of warships looked like a corridor of floating death. The commanding officer of Fort Sumter, Major Stephen Elliott Jr., had faith in his ability to ward off the attack. Still, the sight was enough to give pause. Built on an artificial island three and three-eighths miles distant from Charleston, Sumter was a fortress. The fort's base was constructed of chunks of stone from northern quarries. Her walls were solid brick, and concrete masonry stretched sixty feet high. At their thickest point, the walls were twelve feet in width; at the narrowest, a full eight. Guns were arranged on casemates on a pair of decks; the upper deck was open, and the lower deck guns were firing through reinforced ports.

ON BOARD *PATAPSCO*, the fourth Union ship in line, the view ahead was already becoming clouded with smoke. To an untrained eye, *Patapsco* and *Weehawken* looked similar, except for color. *Weehawken* was lead gray and *Patapsco* basic black, but *Patapsco* carried a surprise. She had the massive 15-inch Dahlgren, but her 11-inch smoothbore had been replaced by a 50-pound rifled Parrot gun that had the ability to lob a round over a mile with accuracy.

Slowly, like an old man turning his head, the turret on *Patapsco* rotated. And then the Parrot sang.

MAJOR ELLIOTT was standing on the upper gun deck of Fort Sumter when he heard the high-pitched whine of a rifled round. It slammed into the base of the fort, showering brick dust high into the air. Elliott felt a sting on his cheeks like the bites of many tiny ants. Wiping the lens of his spyglass clean, he ordered the fire returned.

IT WAS 2:41 P.M., some ten minutes after the first shot had been fired from Fort Sumter, and aboard *New Ironsides*, DuPont was seeing his carefully crafted plans unraveling. The line of Union warships was straying out of formation. As he peered through the smoke ahead, it looked as if *Weehawken* was slowing.

New Ironsides was eight hundred yards from Fort Sumter and was inside the curtain of fire from both

Fort Moultrie to the north and Sumter dead ahead. A volley of Confederate shot rang out. DuPont was flung to the deck, as *New Ironsides* took the fourth of the ninety-three hits she would suffer in the next three hours.

Rising from the deck, DuPont trained his spyglass on *Weehawken*.

Captain Rodgers had felt what he thought was a sea mine exploding beneath his hull. The line of sea mines, known as torpedoes, brought more fear to the crews of the Union gunboats than did the guns of Sumter and Moultrie. The forts and their guns could be seen; the torpedoes were hidden assassins lying in wait for the unwary.

"Full astern," Rodgers shouted through the speaking tube to the engine room.

Passaic, second in line, slowed. The Union formation began to deteriorate.

On Sullivans Island, Confederate gunners at Battery Bee and Battery Beauregard added to the fire coming from the parapets of Fort Moultrie. Across the water, the Sumter gunners were hurling several shells a minute in a relentlessly orchestrated symphony of loading and firing. A curtain of smoke blew from the gun decks and was carried by the breezes past the Union fleet. A rain of lead fell from the sky.

"Sir," the pilot of *New Ironsides* said to DuPont, "we are having control problems."

DuPont knew his command was unwieldy. The vessel had been designed and built in a frenzy by a Union navy anxious to meet the threat from Confederate ironclads. Unlike the monitors, she had been designed on the old tried-and-true hull of sail and steamships, and her hybrid design of steam, sails, and armor had never truly worked efficiently.

"We've been struck forty times," DuPont noted. "I don't doubt there are problems."

"I fear we might run down one of the monitors," the pilot noted.

DuPont turned to the signalman. "Make the signal to disregard motions of commander-in-chief." The man scampered away. Next DuPont turned to the pilot.

"Take us out," he said quietly. "I'll be damned if I'll sink one of my own."

From last in line to first. As the formation broke apart, *Keokuk* bravely steamed to the front of the line. For her brave actions, she would pay a stern price.

"Sir," *Keokuk*'s signalman reported, "*New Ironsides* asks we disregard her movement."

Commander Rhind nodded absently. He had more important things to contend with. In the last thirty minutes, *Keokuk* had taken eighty-seven hits. The ironclad was holed in nineteen places above and below the waterline. Her gun towers and smokestack were riddled with holes through which one could see the fading daylight, and his aft gun had been disabled before it could ever fire a round.

The forward gun had gotten off five shots—then it, too, was disabled. Rhind was in command of a vessel that was now completely defenseless. Then the engines stopped.

Weehawken had been struck nearly fifty times by the Confederate guns. One cannonball had jammed the turret, making the gun unusable. The pilot backed away, then turned to starboard to retreat. The ship's engineers ran to the turret. After great effort, they managed to get it to rotate. *Weehawken* withdrew from the battle with the dangerous torpedo raft, which was left to drift ashore.

Patapsco was taking a drubbing. The guns of Fort Moultrie were pounding her starboard side. The pilot was doing his best to position his ironclad so the guns could not find their range, but he could barely see through the smoke, and Union ships were everywhere. With the line of attack in deterioration and fully half the Union ironclads in retreat, only the chaos of an action gone wrong was visible out of the viewing port.

Smoke rolled across the water. Plumes of water shot into the air like just-spouted fountains, as missed shots plunged into the water. The few Union ironclads still engaged were trying to return fire to the forts, but that merely added to the noise and confusion. Along with the scream of shells flying seaward and back to the forts was the din of steam engines, boilers, and chains. There was no quiet on an ironclad. The metal hulls reverberated with the smallest sound and echoed like the tolling gates of hell. When the hull or deck armor was struck by Confederate shot, the sound for the crew was akin to having their head inside a church bell being rung.

Along with constant noise was constant heat. Even though the temperature outside was mild, in battle all ports were closed and battened down. With no breeze coming inside, the air became superheated.

Then the smells. Gunpowder, fuses, metal, and grease. Paint and cotton batting. Food from the galley, odors from the head compartment, unwashed sailors. Fear. It was a cacophony of sights and sounds, a sensory overload for the captain and crew.

Disabled and battered, the pilot steered *Patapsco* from the line.

On the deck of *New Ironsides*, Rear Admiral DuPont could see that it was hopeless. The battle was three hours old, and the Union fleet had not managed to accomplish much. *Keokuk* was battered and barely moving.

Weehawken and *Patapsco* had been hit many times.

The Union monitors *Nahant*, *Nantucket*, *Montauk*, *Passaic*, and *Catskill* had all taken numerous blows. DuPont's flotilla was in disarray and deteriorating minute by minute.

DuPont gave the order to withdraw.

The Union fleet retreated the way they arrived, south down the ship channel past Morris Island. But it was a different picture from when they had steamed north to engage the rebels. The monitors showed spots where the paint had been jarred loose, and their armor was dented like a tin can hit by a golf club. Uneven streams of smoke trailed from their stacks as engineers struggled to keep the battered boilers operating. Two of the seven monitors were leaking. For now, the flow of the water into the hulls was being dissipated overboard by the pumps. Still, the weight of the water before it was discharged was causing both to list slightly. The armada came crawling back past Morris Island resembling a boxer after a losing match. Later, it would be learned that the fleet had suffered a total of 493 hits.

The powerful Union force had been beaten like a borrowed mule. *Keokuk* had gone from last in line to first and back to last again.

Commander Rhind climbed through the hatch into

one of the towers. He could use only one arm—the other was peppered with wooden shards that went inches into his flesh.

Keokuk's experimental armor had proved a failure. Designed with alternating horizontal rows of wood interspersed with metal strips, the mishmash failed to provide adequate protection. The truth was that the design of the armor was as practical as making a bulletproof vest without sides. When a cannonball struck the iron straps on the hull, it was repelled. But what of the wood hull inches away? That usually exploded in a hail of splinters and wood chips. Rhind's arm was proof of that.

Staring fore and aft, Rhind assessed *Keokuk*'s damage.

The forward tower was pounded to pulp—it looked as if a giant had beaten it with a sledgehammer. The crew inside the forward tower were all wounded. The aft tower, where Rhind was standing, was not much better. The gun had been disabled after only five shots, but the crew had fared better. Only a little more than half had been wounded.

Between the two towers stood the remains of *Keokuk*'s smokestack.

The stack was riddled with so many holes, it looked like a tin shed hit by a shotgun blast. Smoke rose along the outline of the pipe until reaching a hole. Then it puffed out of the holes in rings, like those from the lips of an accomplished smoker.

While Rhind watched, *Keokuk* rolled over a wave. Just then, part of the ornamental top of the stack broke loose. It struck the deck before being washed overboard.

Rhind's ship was coming apart.

Nineteen shells had penetrated *Keokuk*'s armor. Several of those were below the waterline. Rhind knew that the engineering crew was hard at work just keeping the vessel afloat. Thirty-two of his crew were wounded, but thankfully no one had died.

Rhind opened the hatch and climbed back to the main deck. *Keokuk* was out of range of the Confederate guns; his crew was now concentrating on keeping afloat.

Thirty-two wounded, but no dead. Soon there would be a death, but it would be the death of *Keokuk*. As the sun set in the west, the cigar-shaped craft limped toward her anchorage off Morris Island. Commander Rhind had no illusions about the battle. He and the rest of the Union fleet had been savagely pummeled, and his ship had suffered the worst. Climbing down into the hold, he shouted to Engineer Wheeler, who was near the bow supervising the plugging of a leak.

"How bad is it?" Rhind asked.

Wheeler was covered in grease and sopping wet. Wiping his hands on a grimy rag, he walked closer. "It's not good, Commander," Wheeler said. "I count nineteen holes in the hull, and more than half are below waterline. The pumps are keeping up, but just barely. The engines keep cutting out, and the forward turret is useless. To make matters worse, half my engine-room crew is wounded, so we are having trouble keeping up with all of the problems that are cropping up."

"I'll send down some of the gun crew and deckhands to help," Rhind offered.

At that instant, *Keokuk* rolled over a wave and the hull flexed. A bolt that held the planking to the ribs shot across the hold like a minié ball and stuck in the far wall.

"We need to anchor," Wheeler shouted, as he ran to inspect the damage.

An hour later, four miles from Fort Sumter and two miles off Morris Island, Rhind ordered the anchor dropped. The engineers mounted a brave defense, but *Keokuk*'s short life was over. Throughout the night, the weather was calm with fair seas. And for a time it seemed that Wheeler and his crew might save the battered vessel.

Fate, however, had another plan. The winds kicked up at 5 A.M. It was nothing that a healthy ship would even notice, but *Keokuk* was far from healthy. As the vessel flexed, the cotton batting that Wheeler's crew had stuffed between the planking became saturated, then worked loose. *Keokuk* began sinking farther into the water.

Rhind reacted by ordering parts of the damaged towers and smokestack cut loose, but the action did little to stop the inevitable. It was a battle that could not be won.

The sun broke on April 8, and with it came stronger winds.

"Signal for assistance," Rhind said. "We need tugs to evacuate the wounded."

Wheeler climbed the ladder to the main deck. From shoes to belt line, he was soaked. He had gone twenty-four hours without sleep, and his face was etched with exhaustion.

"Sir," he said, saluting Rhind, "the water's rising faster than we can handle."

Rhind pointed to a trio of approaching tugs.

"Help is here, just keep her afloat until we off-load the wounded," he said.

"It will be an honor, sir," Wheeler said, as he made his way back to the ladder, "but I estimate we have twenty minutes and little more."

It was 7:20 A.M. when Rhind and Wheeler stepped from the deck of *Keokuk*. As soon as the tug cast off, the ironclad began her death spasms. First she shifted bow-down, as water borne by the wind entered through her hawse pipe. Then the ironclad shuddered as the immense weight of the water settled in the lower hold and sprang the already battered planking. The second the water filled the hold, *Keokuk* burped a cloud of coal dust like the last gasp of a diseased smoker.

Then she settled to the seafloor in fifteen feet of water.

Her battered smokestack was partially visible. *Keokuk* had lived but six weeks.

PHILO T. HACKETT spit tobacco juice at a nearby anthill and watched the tiny insects struggle to free themselves from the sticky mess. At fourteen, he was too young to be chewing, but he was also too young to be hiding on Morris Island under a makeshift covering of brush and limbs. Hackett had been hiding since yesterday evening. First, he had watched the battle, then he had observed the Union ironclad struggle to stay afloat before dying.

Hackett's father was stationed on Fort Sumter, and his mother was home, worried sick about her missing son. Crawling from his hiding place, Hackett made his way to his rowboat hidden on the lee side of the island.

Then he quietly rowed across the water to report to General Beauregard.

*

"I want those guns," Beauregard said.

Adolphus La Coste nodded.

La Coste was a civil engineer. However, in a war where all were called, he was not one to shirk responsibility. He stared at the aging lightship at the dock in Charleston.

"I think we can do it, sir," La Coste said, "but it is not without peril. We will be operating right under the nose of the Yankees."

"How long will it take, Adolphus?" Beauregard asked.

"With the right help, a couple of weeks," La Coste answered.

"Whatever you need," Beauregard said, walking away. "I want those guns."

Outfitting the lightship with tackle and hoist required a week. True to his word, Beauregard had given La Coste all he needed. The tackle was new, the ropes unused. A half-dozen divers sat on the deck amid a pile of freshly oiled saws, pry bars, and levers. Now it was time to do the impossible.

A driving rain was making visibility nonexistent.

Diver Angus Smith climbed up a Jacob's ladder onto the deck of the lightship. His leather gloves were in tatters and his hands cut from his labors. Smith barely felt the pain, because the cold from being immersed in the chilled water had permeated his very being. For seven nights now, Smith and the other divers had rowed out on small boats to labor a fathom below the water. To avoid being seen, they used no lights. To avoid being heard, they were careful not to bang tools against the metal. Before first light, the divers retreated; each evening they came anew. Four days into the operation, they reported to La Coste that the guns were free from their mounts and that openings in the turrets had been hewn. Tonight was the first time the modified lightship had visited the site.

"We're doing this all by feel, sir," Smith said. "It's as black as night down there, but I think we have everything attached as ordered."

La Coste nodded, then stepped into the pilothouse near a single burning candle and stared at his pocket watch. It was nearly 4 A.M. Attaching the lines had taken longer than expected. Soon it would be light, and the minute the Yankees saw the lightship on station above *Keokuk*, they were sure to come. He stepped back out of the pilothouse.

"Are all your divers out of the water, Smith?" La Coste asked.

Smith did a quick count of the men on deck. Four were sleeping, still in their diving gear; one other had disrobed and stood in his long johns, peeing over the railing on the lee side.

"They're all accounted for, sir," Smith said laconically.

"Power to the turnstile," La Coste ordered.

Four Confederate sailors began walking in a circle. Their hands were gripping the oak arms of the turnstile. Slowly the thick lines were tightened until the 15,700-pound weight of the first gun was being supported only by cable and rope and chain.

The cannon rose slowly through the water. Inch by inch by inch.

La Coste stared at the wooden derrick on the bow. The wood creaked in protest as the joints rubbed, but it held fast. "Grease the fair ends," he whispered to a sailor, who slathered animal fat on the lines. Then he staggered as the deck of the lightship settled from the immense weight being transferred. Almost imperceptibly, the cannon rose.

Wiping water from his beard, La Coste peered into the depths of *Keokuk*'s grave.

And then he saw it. The merest edge of the outer tube of the cannon.

"Harder, boys," he said a little too loudly.

The cannon was almost at the top edge of the tower—a few more inches and it would be free. Then it stopped.

"Mr. La Coste," a deckhand whispered, "the tackle's together. We can't go farther."

Inches from salvation and miles from success. And the sky was becoming lighter.

"Damn," La Coste said. Soon they would be visible. Once they were spotted, this operation would be finished for good. "We need to move all the weight we can to the stern. That should raise the bow enough to give us the small space we need."

A little more—but not enough. The dangling gun muzzle clung stubbornly to the wreck. La Coste stared east—it was growing lighter. A few more minutes and he would need to abort the mission to escape detection. A span thinner than a slice of bread.

Then the sea came to the rescue.

Perhaps there was a storm a hundred miles offshore. Maybe somewhere the earth had trembled. Whatever the case, a large wave came from nowhere. It rolled across the placid surface of the water like a bedsheet being straightened.

Into the trough in advance of the wave, the lightship

dropped. Then, all at once, the hull of the ship rose, and the gun came free and hung on the cable.

"Can you steer with the gun weight off your bow?" La Coste asked the captain.

"I can sure as hell try," the captain said.

Three nights later, they came back and raised the second gun.

It was not until much later that the Union found out that *Keokuk* had been salvaged.

A FEW MONTHS after the debacle off Fort Sumter, Captain Rodgers was sleeping in his cabin on *Weehawken*. He had been reassigned farther south, and the ironclad was riding at anchor in the Wassaw Sound off Georgia. *Nehant*, a second Union monitor, lay a league away. It was hot, four degrees over eighty, and the air was still. Wispy Spanish moss hung from the trees nearby, and the croak of thousands of frogs filled the air. The Union ships were waiting to intercept the newest Confederate ram.

THE PILOT of the Confederate ironclad *Atlanta* was groping his way down the Savannah River. The channel was narrow, and to escape detection he had ordered no lights lit. *Atlanta* was unwieldy, underpowered, and deeply drafted, all the things that made a ship hard to handle. Converted from the fast blockade runner *Fingal*, *Atlanta* had been armored and a cast-iron ram mounted to her bow. Her firepower consisted of four Brooke-rifled guns and a lethal spar-torpedo stretching ahead of the ram. Slowly, she went downriver.

Atop *Atlanta*'s casement, ordinary seaman Jesse

Merrill was standing watch. Even in the darkness, he could see the difference in the river astern. *Atlanta* was dragging her keel and churning up the river mud. The ship was dragging bottom.

Peering forward, Merrill strained to see through the mist on the river. He thought he caught the outline of another ship, but just as he trained his eyes on the spot, *Atlanta* ran aground and he was pitched forward.

"Back her up," he heard the pilot whisper.

Spinning her prop in the mud, the big ironclad struggled to break free.

After a few minutes of rocking the ship back and forth, she was freed.

TWO HUNDRED yards away, *Weehawken* was closest to the Confederate ram. Her lookout was struggling to stay awake and losing the battle. Time after time as he peered through the port upriver, his head nodded as sleep overtook him.

It was warm, and there was little fresh air. His head bobbed up and down.

ATLANTA BACKED UP and started downriver again. Jesse Merrill continued to peer into the distance. There it was again. Low to the water and dark in color, he might have missed it except for the rounded sweep of the gun turret.

Climbing down from the nest, he alerted the captain.

"Take it slow," the captain ordered. "The lookout sees a Yankee ironclad."

Seconds later, the pilot ran *Atlanta* hard aground again.

First light poked through the view port and stabbed

the lookout in the eye like a saber. Shaking his head, he wiped the slobber from his mustache, then scanned the water. Like a ghostly apparition some two hundred yards distant, *Atlanta* came into view. The lookout stared for a second, then sounded the alarm.

He continued ringing the bell for a full three minutes.

At the sound of the bell, Captain Rodgers leapt from his bed and ran to the pilothouse, still in his nightclothes. His second in command, Lieutenant Pyle, was already at his station.

"She hasn't moved, sir."

Rodgers scanned the water with his spyglass. "The crew is scurrying on deck," Rodgers said. "If I had to guess, I'd say she's run aground."

"I took the liberty of signaling *Nehant*," the lieutenant said, "and ordered a full head of steam from the engine room."

"Head straight at her," Rodgers ordered.

"Guns at ready," Lieutenant Pyle said.

"Commence firing," Rodgers said.

It was impossible to miss. The first shot from *Weehawken*'s fifteen-inch gun scored a hit. It tore apart *Atlanta*'s casement like a fireman's ax through a flimsy front door. And the rebel ironclad was powerless to reply. The grounding had keeled her over. Even with her guns depressed as far as they would go, when she tried to return fire, her shells sailed over the treetops along the riverbank. *Weehawken*'s second volley bashed in ten square feet of *Atlanta*'s armor and blew the gun crew off their feet.

Number three tore off the top of the pilothouse. That was all it took.

The captain hauled down the flag and surrendered.

Later, *Atlanta* was taken to the Philadelphia Naval Yard, where she was refitted and returned to service as a Union navy vessel. Rodgers was hailed as a hero and promoted to commodore. As captain of the first monitor to defeat an ironclad in individual combat, he returned to Charleston to continue the fight against Fort Sumter.

EIGHT MONTHS after capturing *Atlanta,* *Weehawken* was a seasoned veteran. Her crew was honed by combat and their onboard routine entrenched. Day after day, she lobbed shells toward Sumter. So it was nothing unusual when she anchored off Morris Island to refill her magazine.

Harold McKenzie was an ordinary seaman. And ordinary seamen followed orders. Even so, McKenzie could not help but mention his apprehensions to his friend Pat Wicks.

"The weight is not being distributed correctly," he whispered, as the two men carried a wooden crate filled with shells. "We're putting too much forward."

But Wicks had other matters on his mind.

"We're taking on a full load. The officers must be planning another run at the forts."

Wicks had been wounded by shrapnel in the first attack on Sumter, and ever since he had been more than a little gun-shy. By contrast, McKenzie had just transferred to *Weehawken*. He was still itching to see combat.

"Good," McKenzie said. "It's high time we taught the rebels a lesson."

But that was not to be, for McKenzie's worst fears would soon be realized.

That evening, as the sailors slept in their berths, a stiff wind came from land. The misplaced load of fresh munitions was making *Weehawken* ride low in the bow, and it took only a matter of moments for serious trouble to arise. As the first series of waves washed over the bow, the water flooded into an unsecured hatch. As the bow dropped a few inches lower, water raced into the anchor chain hawse pipe. As the water filled the lower hold, the bow quickly settled lower. Now the bilge pumps in the stern were of no use, and the ones forward could not handle the volume of water.

A simple mistake, but it doomed *Weehawken* to an early grave.

Wicks was in the top bunk, and he felt it first. A sharp jolt as the bow slipped down made his head strike the deck above, jarring him awake.

"Mac," Wicks shouted, "wake up."

McKenzie struggled to free himself from his berth, but Wicks's warning would come a moment too late for either man. *Weehawken* was already going through her death throes. As the flow of water increased, her trim was upset. The water flowed into the lower hold, then quickly to one side. Like a toy ship in a bathtub, *Weehawken* rolled onto her starboard beam. Within seconds, the sea flooded in through the open turret ports and deck hatches and made contact with the boilers with a burst of steam.

Then *Weehawken* slipped beneath the waves, taking thirty-one souls to their graves.

IT WAS January 15, 1865, and the long and bloody war was drawing to a close. On board the monitor

Patapsco, Commander Stephen Quackenbush looked forward to going home. His vessel had seen nearly constant action since the first assault on Fort Sumter, and he and his crew were weary from war. While similar in design to the rest of the monitor class, *Patapsco* had heavier armament that kept her constantly utilized. With the only big Parrot gun in the fleet, *Patapsco* could lie out of reach of the forts' guns and fire without fear of damage. Because of this fact, *Patapsco* had fired more shells at the rebel defenders than any other vessel.

With her record of accomplishments well recognized, it was little surprise that in early 1865 *Patapsco* was assigned the dangerous task of picket duty. Picket duty was no picnic; it was a dangerous combination of nightly scouting sorties and minesweeping in the outer harbor. Captain and crew hated it soundly.

"We have a strong flood tide," executive officer Ensign William Sampson said to Quackenbush, as the two men stood on the top of the turret, staring through the moonless night.

"We'll escort the launches and minesweeping boats inside the channel before we drift back out and provide fire support," Quackenbush said quietly.

"Shall I go below and give the order to the helmsman and chief engineer for slow speed?" Sampson asked.

"Do that. I'll remain here and keep watch."

It was a choice that would save Quackenbush's life.

Patapsco steamed closer to the Confederate forts. Behind came the small, steam-powered launches equipped with grapnels and drags. Slowly, they passed the monitor and began the tedious task of sweeping for mines.

Sampson reappeared topside. "I've ordered the guns run out, sir."

Quackenbush nodded. His command was now ready to provide fire support.

The night passed with agonizing slowness as the Union ironclad drifted in and out of the channel. It is said the third time is a charm, but this did not ring true with *Patapsco* and her crew. As the tidal current carried the ship out of the harbor entrance for the third time after midnight, the hull struck a floating mine set only a day before.

The device was a wooden barrel torpedo carrying a hundred pounds of gunpowder.

Igniting when jarred, the torpedo ripped a huge hole on the port side aft of the bow. The explosion lifted *Patapsco*'s bow up in the air. Quackenbush and Sampson were thrown to the deck as a giant column of water rose into the air before slamming down on the gun turret.

"Man the boats!" Quackenbush shouted.

But it was too late. *Patapsco* dove beneath the waves in less than a minute and a half, down forty feet to the seabed. Sixty-two of the officers and crew went with her. Only the tip of the smokestack remained above water at low tide.

Quackenbush and Sampson barely escaped being sucked under by the doomed monitor and were rescued by a launch.

It was a fortunate rescue for the U.S. Navy.

William Sampson later became superintendent of the Naval Academy and was named commander of the Atlantic squadron during the Spanish-American War. When the Spanish fleet attempted to escape Santiago,

Cuba, Sampson's fleet, utilizing his battle plans and temporarily under the command of Winfield Scott Schley, destroyed it.

Honed by their combat experience in the Civil War, Sampson, Schley, and Dewey all died as heroes with the rank of admiral.

II

Three for the Price of One

1981, 2001

WHEN POSSIBLE, I ALWAYS TRY TO PIGGYBACK expeditions. It makes perfect sense on an obtuse level. If NUMA is searching for a certain ship, it becomes cost- and time-efficient to look for other wrecks in the same general area.

Charleston is a case in point. During the 1981 expedition to find the Confederate submarine *Hunley*, we used two boats, one to mow the search grid line with a magnetometer and the other to carry a gradiometer and divers to investigate any interesting targets.

You might want to scan over this paragraph, since I think it's a good time to differentiate between a magnetometer and a gradiometer. The Schonstedt gradiometer, which we have used over the years with great success, reads the difference in magnetic intensity of a ferrous object between two sensors placed twenty inches apart and can be towed at speeds up to twenty-five knots. By comparison, a magnetometer reads differences in the earth's magnetic field, which, because of various atmospheric conditions, may often cause bogus readings. It must be towed at relatively slow speeds.

While the survey boat went about its business hunting the sub, the dive boat drifted around with nothing to do, waiting for a call that rarely came. Having learned that time is money, I sent the dive boat prowling after other shipwrecks that sank during the siege of Charleston in the Civil War.

The waters in and around Charleston Harbor are a veritable salvage yard of old shipwrecks. From the late 1600s until the eve of the twentieth century, hundreds of ships of every size and rig have gone to the bottom within sight of the city. Nearly forty New England whalers were scuttled in a vain attempt to barricade the channels to keep the Confederate blockade runners from entering and leaving. Twenty or more greyhounds of the sea were sunk by Union navy gunfire attempting to run the blockade.

Union ships went on the bottom too: *Housatonic* was torpedoed by *Hunley*. *Weehawken* sank accidentally in a squall. *Patapsco* was sunk by a mine. And *Keokuk* sank after being struck nearly a hundred times by Confederate cannon shells. They all lay in the silt in a common burial ground.

At first it appeared as if finding them would be a kindergarten hide-and-seek operation. We had a chart drawn by a Union navy officer in 1864 that showed the approximate position of ten blockade runners and the Union ironclads that had been lost. It seemed a simple matter to transpose them onto a modern chart. The only catch, as I discovered quite by chance, was that the longitude meridians sometime prior to 1890 ran four hundred yards farther west than later projections. I caught this when I noticed that the fifty-second meridian appeared much closer to Fort Sumter on an 1870 chart than on a 1980 chart. The revelation seemed to be confirmed by the fact that every wreck we found was a quarter of a mile west of where it should have been, which goes to show that you can never do enough homework.

WALT SCHOB acted as our advance man, arriving in town with his wife, Lee, to charter a boat and arrange quarters for a crew whose eventual size could have fielded three hockey teams. The house he rented was a large two-story affair on Sullivans Island with a long boardwalk that stretched over the dunes to the beach and ended in a comfortable little gazebo. Walt hired a lady named Doris to cook for the guys. Doris turned out excellent meals, but for a reason she would never explain, she refused to fix me grits for breakfast. She also had a strange habit of making only baloney sandwiches for our afternoon picnics at sea. No cheese, tuna, or peanut butter. Not until much later did I find out that it was at Walt's insistence. He laid out the afternoon one-course menu because he liked baloney sandwiches. I still become drowned in nostalgia whenever I see baloney in a delicatessen showcase.

Sadly, during Hurricane Hugo, the house was completely swept away and destroyed. The same is true of the motel we all stayed in during the 1980 expedition. All that was left were the concrete slabs where the cottages once sat.

*

A BRIEF detour here: No historical saga of the Civil War ships lost in Charleston can be written without a mention of Benjamin Mallifert, a former Union officer of engineers, who became the most renowned salvage specialist of his time. One of his descendants sent me a photo of him in the uniform of a Union army major. The ladies would have considered him an attractive man; his eyes burned with a humorous twinkle, and he sported a neatly trimmed thick beard. He was energetic, and no slouch when it came to stripping a shipwreck of anything that was valuable, including scrap metal.

Mallifert ruled over an operation that salvaged more than fifty Civil War shipwrecks in the years after the war. In Charleston alone, he raised millions of pounds of iron, brass, and copper from the sunken warships, Union and Confederate alike.

His diving operations are recorded in his diaries that rest in the Charleston Fireproof Building archives, and they make interesting reading. He must have been a congenial man with a droll wit. One of his entries reads, "My divers reported bringing up five hundred pounds of iron today, more or less . . . probably less."

His description of each wreck, and his accounting of the metal removed, was valuable in determining how much wreckage remained after he moved on.

Ten years ago, I ran across him again. Not in Charleston, but on the James River of Virginia. My NUMA team and I were searching for *Virginia II*, *Richmond*, and *Fredericksburg*, three Confederate iron-clads that made up the James River fleet. When General Grant took Petersburg near the end of the war, the commander of the fleet, Admiral Raphael Semmes, former captain of the famed Confederate raider *Alabama*, ordered the fleet blown up and scuttled.

There was a crude drawing of the ships exploding below Drewry's Bluff on the river below Richmond. We found nothing on the sidescan sonar. The magnetometer registered large targets, but they seemed indistinct and scattered. Since they were all buried in the river's mud, Doc Harold Edgerton, renowned inventor of the sidescan sonar and strobe light, came along with his subbottom profiler—or penetrator, as he called it.

Doc tried hard but had no luck. His penetrator could not see through the gas pockets under the mud formed over the decades by decomposing leaves from trees along the banks. We were about to throw in the towel when I decided to take a day off from the search to comb through the Army Corps of Engineers archives in Portsmouth, Virginia. I was determined to study every drawer and cabinet in the place if it took me all week.

At two o'clock in the afternoon, I pulled open a drawer labeled *Survey of the Pamunkey River, 1931.* One by one, I went through a stack of old photographs, survey drawings, and sheets of statistics. Then, out of the blue, I ran across a sheet of thick transparent paper 28 inches by 18 inches, with a scale of ¾ of an inch equaling 50 feet, and pulled it from the drawer. At first glance, it appeared to be a drawing of the banks along a section of the James River. It clearly didn't belong in the Pamunkey River drawer. How it got there, and for how long it had been there, was anybody's guess.

I stood spellbound as I examined the artwork that was uniquely tinted from the back of the transparent paper. The wording at the top in front read, "Disposition of wrecks below Drewry's Bluff, 1881."

The illustrator signed his name Benjamin Mallifert.

I felt as though I'd stepped into the Twilight Zone. This had to be more than mere luck. It could only come under the heading of fate. Researchers spend half their lives stalking the mother lode. I found it after only four hours of looking in what should have been the wrong place.

Benjamin Mallifert. I couldn't believe we had met up again, three hundred miles away in Virginia and ten years after his salvage efforts in Charleston. There before my eyes was his illustration that interpreted detailed locations of the ships of the James River fleet scuttled by Admiral Semmes.

A comparative analysis showed why we had missed the wreckage of the ironclads. The warships had been moored along shore when they were destroyed. As the years passed, they had built up a huge shoal of sedimentation that covered them over and moved the main channel of the river below Drewry's Bluff 150 feet toward the opposite bank on the south.

The team from Underwater Archaeological Joint Ventures that I hired probed the mud and discovered that Mallifert had called the right plays. Some wrecks were in bits and pieces. Most were pretty well scattered. But they were all there: the steamer *Northampton;* steamer *Curtis Peck;* pilot boat *Marcus;* steamer *Jamestown;* steamer *Beaufort;* ironclad *Fredericksburg;* and ironclad *Virginia II.* The third ironclad, *Richmond,* we found around the bend off Chaffin's Bluff. It appeared that only five feet of sediment had covered the ironclads over the past 120 years.

I owe a considerable debt to old Ben for Charleston and the James River. A fascinating man. I wish I could have known him. A great pity no one has written a biography on his life and the colorful salvage projects he directed.

BACK TO CHARLESTON: *Keokuk* was the first warship on my list to be found and surveyed. A chart drawn by a Union navy officer by the name of Boutelle showed her almost in a direct line east of the old Morris Island lighthouse, which had once stood on land. Morris Island had eroded since the Civil War, and now the lighthouse rose out of the water nearly five hundred yards from the beach.

Cussler's Law: Riverbanks and coastal shorelines are very restless and are in a constant state of motion. They are never where they were when the target you're looking for came to rest.

I chartered a reliable thirty-two-foot wooden boat owned by a big German, Harold Stauber, a quiet man, dependable as a rock and completely unshakable. He knew the waters off Charleston, having fished them for many years. His boat was called *Sweet Sue*, after his wife. One cup of his coffee and you'd never have worms again.

Ralph Wilbanks came on board. Those were the days when he worked for the South Carolina Institute of Archaeology. He was sent by the director of the institute, Alan Albright, to monitor our operation, along with a terrific guy named Rodney Warren who acted as Ralph's assistant. Ralph and Alan didn't quite know what to make of us. Shipwreck hunters who were interested purely in history and not treasure did not just drop out of the trees. In short, they didn't trust us. Oh, ye of little faith.

As we neared Morris Island and the lighthouse, I became cocky. I turned to Ralph and pointed to the lighthouse. "Bet you ten bucks I can find *Keokuk* on the first lap, and ten bucks a lap until we find her." I was that sure of myself.

Ralph gave me his best *this guy must be a jerk* stare and nodded. "You're on."

I told Harold to aim the bow for the lighthouse and run a straight course until he was about a half-mile from shore before making a 180-degree turn for another try. Then I sat back and waited for the Schonstedt gradiometer to sing as it detected *Keokuk*'s iron hull.

We reached the end of the lane. The needle on the instrument dial hadn't so much as twitched, and the sound recorder had remained as silent as a tomb. Woe is me.

As we worked north, the next ten search lanes refused to cooperate, and I began to feel like a fox that had found a coyote with indigestion sitting alone in an empty henhouse. I was out a hundred bucks, and my blood pressure had risen twenty points. Where was that dirty *Keokuk?*

I looked at Ralph. Now he was blatantly smirking. "I'm going out tonight, and I'm going to have a blast."

"I'll bet you are," I muttered under my breath. I put my arm on Harold's shoulder as he stood at the helm. "Run south of our first lane, and don't turn until I give word."

"Will do," Harold acknowledged, blissfully unaware of the silent skirmish between Wilbanks and Cussler.

As we closed the distance to the lighthouse, Stauber kept one eye on the fathometer as we went beyond our normal turn mark. The depth began to rise beneath the keel from thirty feet to twenty, then ten. Another few minutes and the keel would scrape the sand. The lighthouse looked close enough to hit with a tossed rock. Yet, judging the distance by eye, it seemed to me that the beach was still too far from where I estimated *Keokuk*'s site to be.

One hundred yards, two hundred. Everyone on board wondered when I was going to give the order to turn. The tension began to build.

"Now?" asked Harold, apprehensively. I didn't doubt that he would throw me overboard before he ran his boat aground in the surf.

The waves could be heard curling onto the sandy beach of Morris Island back of the lighthouse. "Give it another fifty yards," I said, standing like Captain Kirk holding his fire on the Klingons.

After a few minutes, Harold was sure that gray matter was leaking out of my ears, yet he stood firm.

"Okay, now!" I burst out, looking up at the looming lighthouse.

He swung the wheel to port. At almost the same instant, the gradiometer sound recorder squawked loudly. He had struck *Keokuk* in the turn.

Only then did a happy Ralph do his Charleston jig on the stern deck.

Divers Wilson West, Bob Browning, Tim Firme, and Rodney went over the side and probed the bottom. They found the wreck buried four to six feet deep in the silt. She lies north to south, almost under the shadow of the lighthouse. Without dredging, there is no way to tell how much of her hulk is still intact.

Good old Ralph. He wouldn't take my money and settled for a bottle of Bombay gin instead.

It's times like this that I take an almost sensual pleasure from shipwreck hunting.

WEEHAWKEN IS BURIED deep, more than ten feet, a mile or so north of *Keokuk*. Her bow points on an angle toward Morris Island, not far from where Fort Wagner once stood. The remains of the fort, famous for the attack against it by black soldiers from a Massachusetts fighting regiment, depicted in the movie *Glory*, now lie a hundred feet out into the water. This vast erosion came after the long rock jetties were laid along the channel into Charleston Harbor shortly before the twentieth century.

Because of *Weehawken*'s fame as the only ironclad to capture another ironclad in battle, I hope that someday archaeologists will excavate her as a historic treasure.

We spent half a day dragging the gradiometer all around the seascape before we passed her tomb in the silt. Hers was a tale so gripping, it shocked the world. Unfortunately, the crew slept through most of it.

It was a hot, humid, miserable day without a breath of wind on the water, a day that made me wonder what the local temperature would be in the next life. Then a voice came over the boat's radio and announced that the temperature was 96 degrees and the humidity pegged at 100 percent. I gazed up into a totally cloudless sky. Dumb westerner that I was, I couldn't fathom how the humidity could be 100 percent when it wasn't raining.

To pass time during the search, I asked Ralph, "Did

you know Shakespeare wrote Hamlet and Macbeth?"

Ralph looked thoughtful for a moment, then replied, "Oh really, did they ever answer his letters?"

This business requires patience sometimes—a whole lot of patience.

FINDING *PATAPSCO* came as a surprise. Unlike the other vessels that rest under a thick blanket of silt, she rests upright and exposed on the bottom of the channel off Fort Moultrie. We gambled that part of her might be protruding from the bottom and engaged the sidescan sonar. The search took less than twenty minutes, and we found her on the first pass.

Harold anchored the boat. No one wanted to remain on board when we had an honest-to-gosh wreck to investigate—especially one standing up proud out of the mud. The whole crew went over and swam down forty feet to the hulk. There were artifacts galore, from ship's hardware to cannonballs. None was retrieved. We had to maintain our squeaky-clean NUMA image of searching for history and leaving salvage to others. Besides, the U.S. Navy considers *Patapsco* a tomb, since the bones of sixty-two of her crew remain inside. Still, she is a historical treasure that should be studied in the future.

Though she was extensively salvaged by Mallifert's divers, he made no mention in his diaries of finding any remains of the crew.

WE WENT on that summer to find several blockade runners that had been run ashore and destroyed. We also looked for the Confederate ironclads *Chicora, Palmetto State,* and *Charleston,* destroyed when

Sherman marched into Charleston, but found no sign of wreckage. Benjamin Mallifert also salvaged these wrecks, and whatever was left when he finished was dredged out of existence by the Army Corps of Engineers when they deepened the ship's channel to the navy base up the Cooper River. Some people just don't have a love for history.

I am reminded of personal loss in my past. I hate to belittle my poor old mother, but I find it hard to forgive her for throwing my comic book collection in the trash after I enlisted in the air force. Many years later, I found a list of my comics in my old Boy Scout manual. I asked an expert to appraise the first *Superman*, *Batman*, *Torch*, and a hundred others I'd owned. The results hurt badly. According to the appraisal, if I still owned them today, they would be worth three million dollars to collectors.

My mother also sneaked stamps out of my collection and mailed letters with them. I wish I could have seen the face of the postal worker when he handed over a letter with a two hundred-year-old stamp worth $500. I suppose most men have the same stories about their mothers.

IN FEBRUARY 2001, I asked Ralph to go back and correct the positions of the wrecks we had located with the Motorola Mini Ranger system using the newer differential global positioning system. He also completed a magnetic contour map of the wreck sites. All neat and tidy.

Keokuk was relocated and now found to have 6 feet of silt covering her. The water depth was only 16 feet, and her contour indicated a mass at least 130 feet long, so much of her lower hull had to be intact.

Weehawken was also pinpointed and found to be resting northwest to southeast in twenty-two feet of water under twelve feet of silt. Ralph also located a magnetic target about a hundred feet from the suspected bow. This could well be *Weehawken*'s anchor and chain, since the mag contour runs in a straight line.

Ralph's report brought down the curtain on the Siege of Charleston shipwreck hunt. My fondest wish is that once the *Hunley* is finally conserved and mounted for public viewing, the museum building will be large enough to accept and display hundreds, perhaps thousands, of artifacts from Charleston's glorious maritime history that wait in the silt to be retrieved and preserved.

PART SIX

The Cannon of San Jacinto

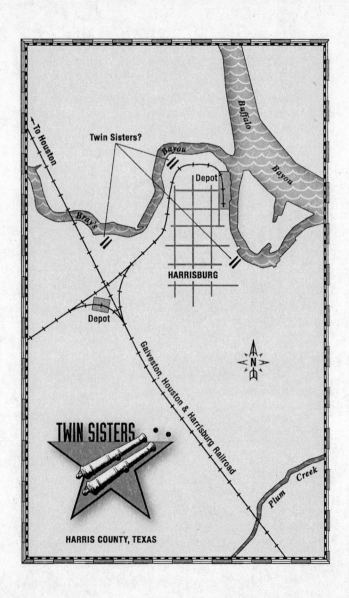

Twin Sisters?

Buffalo
Bayou

Bayou
Depot

Brays

Bayou

HARRISBURG

Depot

→ To Houston

Galveston, Houston & Harrisburg Railroad

N

TWIN SISTERS

Plum Creek

HARRIS COUNTY, TEXAS

I

The Twin Sisters

1835, 1865, 1905

"DAMN THEM," HENRY GRAVES SAID, "DAMN them straight to hell."

"What is it, Hank?" Sol Thomas asked.

Graves wiped the sweat from his brow and motioned with his head for Thomas and the others in their party to follow. The afternoon was sweltering, the land covered with a blanket of wet, oppressive heat. August in Houston is never temperate, and this, the fifteenth day of August 1865, was no exception. Climbing off the Galveston, Houston & Harrisburg Railroad platform, Graves led his party around the back of the wood-framed whitewashed building until they were out of earshot of any Union sympathizers.

"You see that pile of cannon?" Graves whispered.

"Sure," Jack Taylor noted, "damn Yankees are probably shipping them north to the smelter."

"Well," Graves said, "two of them are the Twin Sisters."

"You sure?" Ira Pruitt asked. "You sure those are Sam Houston's San Jacinto guns?"

"Positive," Graves said. "I read the plaques mounted on the carriages."

Sick with measles, John Barnett crouched in the dirt before he fell over. "Lord," he said.

The men were standing in a semicircle on the packed dirt. Off to the side was Dan, Henry Graves's friend and servant. It was four months after Lee's surrender at Appomattox, and other than a few skirmishes in Texas, the long War Between the States was finally over. The five soldiers were dressed in the Confederate butternut-colored wool uniforms used in the last years of the war. The uniforms were tattered, dirty, and soaked with sweat. The men didn't look much better.

Thomas had a swollen jaw, the result of a rotting rear molar he had been unable to have extracted. Pruitt looked like a walking skeleton. The scant rations available to a common soldier on the losing side of the war had caused him to shed nearly fifteen pounds. His uniform hung on his frame like coveralls on a scarecrow. Taylor was limping. The soles of his boots had worn through in several places, and he had stepped on the bent end of a rusty nail while aboard the railroad cattle car.

And then there was Barnett, a proud citizen of Gonzales, Texas. Barnett had emerged from the war relatively unscathed, only to be infected with measles upon mustering out. His face was splotchy and covered with tiny spots. The skin that was unaffected was a pale white. Barnett had a temperature of 101 degrees—not much higher than the temperature outdoors. Only Graves looked reasonably healthy.

Graves stared to the west at the sun, a glowing red orb clouded in haze hanging low near the horizon.

"Be dark in a few hours," he noted, "and the train north doesn't leave tomorrow until midmorning."

Thomas reached into his pocket and removed a tattered piece of paper. "My commanding officer said there was a hotel here that was supportive of Confederate soldiers." He handed the paper to Graves, the de facto leader of the defeated soldiers.

"Harris House," Graves read. "Let's make our way there and talk this over."

The Confederates walked down Magnolia and into the town of Harrisburg. Dan followed a short distance behind.

1835: THIRTY YEARS BEFORE

"You need to sign that you are accepting," the clerk said.

Inside the shipping office along the levee in New Orleans, Dr. C. C. Rice checked the receipt and initialed. Then he walked up the gangplank and joined his family on the deck of the steamboat. The United States had a policy of neutrality concerning the war between Texas and Mexico, so the two cannon in his control had been listed on the manifest as Hollow Ware.

The pair of cannon had been forged at the Cincinnati foundry of Greenwood & Webb in secrecy, paid for by funds donated by the citizens of Ohio who were sympathetic to the Texas cause. Lacking foundry marks, ammunition, caissons, or limber chests, they weighed around 350 pounds each.

Two metal tubes——700 pounds aggregate weight——
were destined to free a nation.

"They're raising that big board," Eleanor Rice said.

"That's called the gangplank," Mrs. Rice said
sweetly. "It means the trip has started."

Eleanor's twin sister, Elizabeth, smiled. "That means
we'll soon be in Texas," she said to her father, who
clutched her hand, "and then me and Ellie get our
horses, right?"

"Yes, dear," Dr. Rice said, "soon we'll be at our new
home."

The trip of 100 miles down the Mississippi River to
the Gulf of Mexico, combined with the 350 miles across
the Gulf to Galveston, took ten full days. It was just
past 9 P.M. when the boilers were stoked and the boat
made her way into the Mississippi River current.

"IT TOOK US longer than scheduled," Mrs. Rice
said, as the steamboat passed over the bar into
Galveston Harbor. "Will there be someone to meet
us?"

"I don't know," Dr. Rice said. "We'll just have to
see."

"There she is," Josh Bartlett shouted.

The ship was several hours overdue, and his hastily
assembled band had grown more and more drunk as
each minute had passed. Bartlett reached over to support a tuba player as he struggled into his instrument.
The fife player was laughing hysterically.

"Get ready, girls," Dr. Rice said, as the ship was tied
fast to the pier.

The crate carrying the cannon was rolled out of the
hold and down the plank, followed by Dr. Rice, his

wife, and the twin girls. The makeshift band was playing a crude medley of Texas revolution songs as Dr. Rice set foot on the wood-planked pier. Bartlett, dressed in an ill-fitting suit covered by a red sash denoting his largely ceremonial position in the Republic of Texas government, walked forward and shook Rice's hand.

"Welcome to Texas," he said, over the noise from the band.

"Thank you," Dr. Rice said.

Rice opened the top of the crate to show off the two guns, then nodded to his twin daughters, who stood next to him on the pier.

"On behalf of the citizens of Cincinnati," Eleanor said.

"We present you these two cannon," Elizabeth finished.

The drunken fife player stopped playing for a moment and yelled over the heads of the small crowd of people assembled. "Looks like we have two sets of twins here."

"Twin sisters for freedom," Bartlett said, laughing.

A STRAW-HAIRED LAD of sixteen climbed from a mare flecked with sweat.

"Mr. Houston," he said breathlessly, "the guns have arrived."

Houston was crouching in front of his tent, sketching out battle plans on the dirt with a stick. He smiled broadly, then turned to his aide.

"Make sure they are brought forward immediately," he said to the aide, Tommy Kent.

"Right away," Kent said.

"This changes everything," Houston said, rubbing the dirt clear with his boot.

The odds were against the Texans. Houston commanded an army of 783 troops. The invading Mexican forces, capably led by General Santa Anna, numbered 7,500. The Mexican soldiers had uniforms, regular rations, and numerous field pieces to lend them support. The Texan troops were ill equipped, underfed, and, until now, lacking even a single cannon. Most of the Texans had little or no combat experience. The Mexican troops had been drilled and honed into a cohesive fighting force.

Until now, Houston had been content to retreat. Three months prior, when Santa Anna's troops had poured across the Rio Grande, the Texan army consisted of a small garrison located at the Alamo at San Antonio, another at the fort at Goliad, and a small contingent of troops that had assembled at Gonzales.

The Texans were outnumbered and outgunned.

"SIR," KENT REPORTED, "we have no shot for the guns."

"I was afraid that might happen," Houston said. "I've had the men scrounge around. We managed to locate enough scrap metal and broken glass to give Santa Anna something to think about."

"Scrap metal?" Kent said in surprise.

"Nails, broken horseshoes, and metal chain," Houston said.

Kent smiled. "I'd hate to be hit by that," he said quietly.

"In that case, Mr. Kent," Houston said, "I'd stay to the rear of the sisters."

*

When the sun rose on the morning of April 21, 1836, it was tinged a blood red. Afternoon brought with it a haze, making the light dim and the mood sleepy. The temperature was in the low seventies, and a light breeze blew the smoke from the fires at the Mexican encampment at San Jacinto toward Houston, who was camped less than a mile away. There had been a few small skirmishes earlier in the day, but for the most part it was quiet.

"The smoke has lessened," Houston noted. "They have finished their afternoon meal."

"Is that what you have been waiting for?" Kent asked.

"No, Mr. Kent," Houston said, "I'm waiting for them to bed down. We will attack at siesta time."

"Make sure guards are posted, then relieve the men," Santa Anna ordered.

Santa Anna waved his hand at a horsefly, then opened the flap of his tent and walked inside. The heavy noon meal and three glasses of wine had made him sleepy. His quartermasters had liberated several pigs from the Texas countryside, and he and the troops had enjoyed fresh meat for the first time in a week.

Standing by his cot, he removed his uniform and folded it over a wooden chair. Dressed in slightly dingy long underwear, he scratched a bug bite under his arm, then climbed under his smooth silk sheets and embraced his mistress.

Sam Houston was walking along a line of troops. "This is for Texas, men," he said. "Move quietly forward, flanking the twin sisters. When you hear the sisters sing, we go straight to the center."

Houston stared at his men. They were a ragtag group dressed in fringed buckskin, dirty work clothes, even a few old uniforms left over from the Revolutionary War. For weapons they carried their personal black powder guns, knives, and swords. They were farmers, ranchers, prospectors, and blacksmiths.

But they burned with the fervor of the righteous.

"Yes, sir," the troops said as one, "for Texas."

"And let every man remember the Alamo," Houston added.

The sister to the right sang first. A second later, her sibling cried out as well.

Yelling at the top of their lungs, the Texans lunged into the fray, urged on by a soldier with a flute playing "In the Bower."

"Remember the Alamo—remember Goliad!" they shouted.

It was three-thirty in the afternoon when the first load of nails shredded two Mexican tents on the far edge of the battlefield. The guns continued to fire until their barrels were cherry-red. Then a swarming horde of screaming Texans charged the Mexicans' crude barricade. Black powder smoke filled the air, while bayonets and swords flashed through the haze. The Mexican troops tried to rouse themselves from their slumber, but they were unable to assemble before they were inundated by the determined Texans.

"Into the center," Houston screamed.

As soon as he heard the first cannon fire, Santa Anna stumbled from his tent. All he could see were smoke and chaos. The element of surprise proved a strong equalizer. Eighteen minutes after the first shot was fired, the battle was over. The Mexicans suffered 630 dead, 208 wounded, and the rest were taken prisoner. Nine Texans died that day. Twenty-eight others, including Houston, were wounded.

Santa Anna surrendered his army and any claim to Texas at San Jacinto, thanks in large part to the Twin Sisters.

1 8 6 5

"Lemonade or whiskey," Rob Harris, the proprietor of the Harris House, said.

"Whiskey, but we're a little short," Graves said. "How much for the bottle?"

Harris lifted the square glass bottle and made sure the cork was loose, then handed it over the front desk to Graves. "It's on me, soldier."

"You're a true Southern gentleman," Harris said.

"There's some tin cups in the sideboard," Harris said. "You boys make yourself comfortable on the porch. You can usually find some breeze there."

Graves collected the cups, then walked out onto the porch. Barnett was upstairs in his room, felled by the measles. Thomas, Pruitt, and Taylor were out back at the well pump, washing off the dust from the journey. Dan was dozing under the shade of an alder tree.

Graves poured a tin cup of whiskey, then sat in a rocking chair. Taking a sip, he stared at the town and began to plan. Harrisburg was a thriving hamlet. Along with the Harris House were two other hotels, several stores, and a steam mill to hew raw lumber. The railroad depot, located at Magnolia and Manchester, consisted of the station, a machine shop, and yards where a few locomotives were stored. All told, there were a few hundred souls—some friendly, some not.

A whistle from a steamer on Buffalo Bayou broke the silence, and Graves turned his head to the east. Buildings blocked his view, but he could see the trail of smoke from the stack. He watched the smoke travel north, then start east. The vessel was starting up Bray's Bayou, the smaller stream directly in front of the hotel. She was on her way to Houston.

Graves sipped the burning liquid. His eyes watered, and he wiped them on his sleeve. A skinny dog, little more than bones and fur, rolled in the dirt of Kellogg Street in front of the hotel. At the sound of an approaching wagon, the dog jumped to its feet and ran north along Nueces Street. The sun was down, and the sky was growing darker. To the east, Graves could just make out the first star of the coming night.

"Henry," Pruitt said, "you seem lost in your own world." Pruitt was wiping his face with a threadbare cotton hand towel.

"Just thinking," Graves said, "about the sisters."

"While you were cleaning up, I reconnoitered," Pruitt said. "There's a wooded area north of the train station near Bray's Bayou."

"What's the land like?" Graves asked.

"It's rough," Pruitt admitted, "but there's a crude wagon path."

Sol Thomas climbed up the front steps. His face was fresh-scrubbed, and that made his swollen jaw more visible. "No dentist in town, but the blacksmith offered to help," he said. "I declined."

"Here," Graves said, pouring a cup of whiskey, "this should help."

Thomas took the cup and downed it in a single gulp.

Jack Taylor limped out of the front door onto the porch. "So how's this going to work?" he asked.

"Let me explain," Graves said.

JUST PAST MIDNIGHT, with a crescent moon overhead, the men slipped one at a time from the hotel and met up at the stables. John Barnett had rustled himself out of bed, but he did not look good. In the dim light, he glowed a blotchy pale white. He and Dan were the only two not to partake of the whiskey, and it showed. The others seemed filled with an alcohol-fueled fervor. Dan just looked scared.

"Matches?" Graves asked.

"Got them," Thomas said, "and the tools."

"I was just up at the station," Taylor said. "It's quiet."

"I walked the path an hour ago," Graves said. "There's nobody to the north of the train station—it's clear all the way to Bray's."

They moved through the town like silent wraiths. Two blocks west, they turned. Two more west to Manchester Street, passing a few houses that were blissfully quiet. Turning north, they passed a few blocks of empty fields until they reached the station and found the Twin Sisters, still on their carriages amid a jumbled mass of other, larger cannon. The air smelled of gunpowder and grease, swamp soil and sweat. Graves stared for a second at the pair of famous cannon, then turned to Thomas.

"I hear something," Thomas whispered.

"Get down," Graves ordered.

The men crouched alongside the landing.

Two Union soldiers were stumbling along the tracks from east to west. They were safely in their cups after a night of liberty and oblivious to their surroundings. Singing an Irish ditty, they cut across a field outside the station, making their way northwest to their encampment three-quarters of a mile distant. Had they turned to the south, they might have been able to make out the men crouched along the platform. Instead, they stumbled toward home. Graves waited until they were out of sight before speaking.

"That was close," he said. "Let's drag the guns from the pile and get out of here."

Feverishly, they began moving the cannon and their carriages into the darkness, Graves and Dan pulling on one, Pruitt, Thomas, and Taylor dragging the other. Barnett stumbled along in the rear, keeping watch.

After moving a few hundred yards into the trees and bushes, they stopped not far from the bayou.

"Gather some tinder," Graves ordered Dan.

Thomas removed the matches from a round metal container, then began to arrange the twigs and leaves Dan retrieved. Barnett was leaning against a tree, unable to be of help.

"Henry, the wood of the carriages is good and dry," he said slowly. "Won't smoke much."

Graves nodded. "You just take it easy, John. We'll handle the work."

Taylor removed one of the shovels from the wagon and limped a short distance away. He started poking the ground, seeking soft earth. Thomas broke a few more twigs into smaller pieces, then struck a match. It sputtered, then fizzled out. Removing a knife from his pocket, he shaved the sulfur from a half-dozen matches and piled them on some dried leaves. Positioning himself on his knees, he bent his head down next to the tinder.

"Come on, now," he whispered, as he struck another match.

The match sparked, and he thrust it into the pile of sulfur, which burst into flames. The leaves ignited, and the small tinder began to burn. Thomas waited a few minutes, then began to fan the flames with his hat.

Graves stared at the crescent moon. A few clouds passed in front, and then it was clear again. "Hotter than a smitty's forge," he noted.

The whiskey the men had consumed was wearing off, and with it went the false bravado. If the nearby Union troops stumbled across their little operation, it could mean imprisonment, even death. It was time to move this along.

"You find a spot?" he said to Taylor, who stepped into the light from the fire.

"Got one, Henry," Thomas whispered. "It's near those pines over there."

"Light those cattails in the fire for torches," Graves said. "Dan, you go with Jack and get the hole started."

Dan followed Taylor a short distance into the woods.

"I have a good fire," Thomas noted.

"Then let's start lifting these carriage pieces onto the flame," Graves said.

Taylor was soaked in sweat. The first few feet had been easy. Sandy soil and loose loam. Then the pair had struck a layer of solid soil. Now they were going down inch by inch.

"Wish we had a pick," Dan said easily. "Make this go quicker."

Graves poked in the fire with a stick. Dragging out a metal fitting, he waited until Pruitt poured water over the blackened metal, then reached down and tossed it aside. There was already a pile of metal plates and bolts, enough to fill a bucket.

"Fill that empty bucket with what metal will fit," Graves said to Pruitt, "then dump it in the bayou. Bring back a full bucket of water."

Pruitt bent down and began tossing the warm metal pieces into the bucket.

Graves walked over to where the digging was progressing and whispered to Taylor, "How far you down?"

"About three feet," Taylor noted.

"That's deep enough. Help pull the twins over here and drop them in their grave."

Dan climbed from the hole. The cattails were almost out, and the light had grown dim. "Ain't much of a hole, Mr. Taylor."

"No, it ain't, Dan," he said, "but it'll have to do."

As if on cue, Graves, Pruitt, and Thomas appeared, dragging one of the cannon.

"Jack," Graves whispered, "you and Dan on one side, me and Sol on the other."

Walking the few feet to the hole, they tossed it in, then walked back and repeated the procedure with the second gun.

"Ain't much of a hole, Jack," Graves said, grinning.

"That soil was a damn shade harder than it looked, Henry," Taylor said.

Dan began to shovel dirt over the guns, as Graves

stepped back and wiped his hands on his pants. "Let me have your pocketknife, Sol," he said quietly.

Sol reached into his pocket, removed the knife, and flipped it open. He handed it to Graves, who pricked his finger and handed it back. Thomas did the same, then handed it to Taylor, who reached up and handed it to Barnett.

"Now, men," Graves said, "this is a blood pact that we tell no one about any of this until such time as the Confederacy rises again."

The men touched fingers together.

"The Twin Sisters stay hidden," Taylor said, "until they are safe."

The men repeated the mantra.

"Mark a few trees with the ax," Graves said, "and spread leaves over the hole."

Taylor grabbed the ax and hacked marks into several nearby trees, while Pruitt and Thomas covered the area with leaves and branches. Graves walked a few yards to the east and stared into the distance. He could just make out a light inside a top-floor room of a three-story house in Harrisburg. Taking his bearings from all points on the compass, he walked back. Barnett had turned the wagon around and was pointed back toward the tracks.

"Let's get on out of here," Graves said quietly.

1905: FORTY YEARS LATER

"We're here, John," Graves said easily.

Barnett was staring out the window. "Seems so long ago, Henry," he said, "like it was a dream."

Graves and Barnett stepped off the train in Harrisburg into a vastly different world. Harrisburg was slowly being absorbed into Houston, and the area had been greatly built up in the last four decades. Graves had become a doctor, while Barnett was now a successful businessman in Gonzales. The men had aged and were no longer the wild-eyed youthful soldiers of 1865. Graves's hair was more white than blond. Barnett, for his part, sported salt-and-pepper hair and a middle-aged paunch. Over the years, the pair had lost touch with Taylor and Thomas. It was rumored that Taylor had settled in Oklahoma in the land rush of 1889. It was said Sol Thomas had gone north to the Dakota Territories when gold was discovered, then died when he stepped out in the street in Deadwood during a bank robbery and caught a stray bullet. No one really knew. Dan had chosen to remain in Graves's employment after he was freed. He had passed away in 1878 when an outbreak of yellow fever swept through the South.

"Let's start back at the Harris House," Graves said, staring up as a Ford Model C backfired on the street outside, then puttered away.

The two men walked the short distance to Myrtle Street, then looked around in surprise. The block where the hotel had been located had been razed. To the north was a new building with a sign that said "Harrisburg Electrical Cooperative."

"Let's ask in there," Graves said.

Barnett nodded and followed Graves inside.

The clerk at the counter looked up as the two men entered. "Can I help you?"

"There used to be a hotel named the Harris House," Graves said, smiling. "You familiar with that?"

"No," the clerk said, "but hold on. Jeff," he shouted in back.

An older man walked out carrying a rag. He wiped his hands. The man was tall and lean. His hair was going to gray, and he had a neatly trimmed beard.

"Jeff's been around these parts forever," the clerk said.

"Do you know where the Harris House Hotel was located?" Graves asked.

"I haven't heard that name in thirty years," Jeff said, "since just after the War of Northern Aggression."

"We stayed there just after the war," Barnett offered.

"After the war," Jeff said. "You boys Yankees?"

"No, sir," Graves said, "rebels. I'm Dr. Henry Graves from Lometa, this here's John Barnett of Gonzales."

Jeff nodded. "Good. I don't trust Yankees."

"About the hotel," Barnett said.

"You men are two blocks south of where the old hotel was located," Jeff said. "The streets were all changed 'bout ten years after the war when they relaid the railroad tracks. It's all different around here now."

"The tracks were moved?" Graves said anxiously.

"Sure enough," Jeff said. "This city's been all changed around since you was last here."

"There used to be a three-story house near the bayou," Graves said quickly. "You know the house I mean?"

"The old Valentine place," Jeff said. "That's still there. Three blocks north and two blocks west."

"Thanks a lot," Barnett said.

"No problem," Jeff said. "If you need some more help finding something, you just give me a shout."

That day, Graves and Barnett searched for where the cannon were buried.

But that, and all subsequent searches, turned up nothing.

II

Dr. Graves,
What Have You Done?

1987–1997

EVERY TIME WE RETURN FROM SEARCHING FOR the Twin Sisters cannon in Harrisburg, we swear we'll never go back. It's the only sane thing to do. I don't wish to demean the good citizens of Harrisburg, but I can envision more exotic locales to spend a holiday. Why we've come four times to torture ourselves, I'll never know. That we go again and again borders on psychosis, which means we have definitely lost contact with reality.

Like other searchers who have become addicted to the Twin Sisters, some of whom have looked half a lifetime, I believe that, despite the fragmentary and incoherent evidence, they are buried somewhere around Harrisburg. This isn't all that inconceivable when you consider that I believed in the tooth fairy, Santa Claus, and virgins until my fortieth birthday.

No one really knows what happened to the famed Twin Sisters cannon that were put to good use by Sam Houston at the battle of San Jacinto. Stories circulated that they were dumped in Galveston Bay to keep them out of the hands of Union soldiers, or sent north after the war where they were melted down, or—the most fabulous tale of all—buried after the war in Harrisburg. The truth is probably lost in the mists of time.

The only good source is the eyewitness account of a Union soldier stationed in Houston who found the cannon lying in a pile with several others near his barracks. Corporal M. A. Sweetman, who was about to be mustered out of the army, wrote in his diary, on July 30, 1865:

> I saw a number of old cannon, one and perhaps more of large size, and all of them dismounted. There were no caissons, limbers nor ammunition boxes, and the guns had the appearance of having been picked up somewhere, hauled in and dumped temporarily to await removal to some other place. Among these guns were two short and very common-looking iron 24-pounders.

Sweetman also found another pair of guns that he thought interesting:

> On brass plates attached to the wooden carriages of each of the two guns, iron six-pounders, much more symmetrical in shape and appearance, was the following, the first line in old English.

TWIN SISTERS
THIS GUN WAS USED WITH TERRIBLE EFFECT
AT THE BATTLE OF SAN JACINTO.
PRESENTED TO THE STATE OF TEXAS
BY THE STATE OF LOUISIANA
MARCH 4, 1861
HENRY W. ALLEN
CHARLES C. BRUSLE
WILLIAM G. AUSTIN
COMMITTEE OF PRESENTATION

From the condition of the guns at the time I saw them, it was evident that no person there at the time took very much interest in them, and if the only object was to get rid of them it is more likely they would be thrown into Buffalo Bayou than shipped.

Sweetman then exits stage left while Dr. H. N. Graves enters stage right.

ON THEIR WAY home after the end of the war, Dr. Graves and his buddies step off the train at Harrisburg six miles south of Houston on August 15, 1865. In Graves's own words:

Arriving at Harrisburg, when alighted from the train we saw a number of cannon of various sizes dumped by the side of the railroad track. Looking over the pile, I was surprised to note that the famous Twin Sisters were among them and felt that they, at least, should be protected from vandalism or confiscation by the Federal Troops, then preparing

to take possession of Texas. Therefore, to my
messmates, Sol Thomas, Ira Pruitt, Jack Taylor,
and John Barnett of Gonzales, I suggested that we
bury the Twin Sisters. One of them responded,
"That's right—we'll bury them so deep no damned
Yankee will ever find them."

He goes on to say:

Before burying the cannon, we took the woodwork
apart and burned it. The carriages themselves, we
threw in the bayou, after which we rolled the cannon
some 300 or 400 yards into the woods.

I have a problem with this statement. Number one,
what woodwork? An entire gun carriage was built of
wood. Number two, a fire would have caused suspicion.
Union soldiers were camped within a mile and often
walked to Harrisburg for food and drink. Number
three, what was left of the carriages to throw in the river
if they were burned? And number four, why roll the
cannon 400 yards into the woods when you could have
rolled them on carriages? Besides, you can't roll cannon
because of the trunnions, the pins opposite each other
on a gun so it can be pivoted up and down. This
scenario doesn't make sense. Also, it was a hot, sultry
night. These guys were toughened by war, but they
weren't at their physical peak, and one of them had
measles. So I don't believe they hauled the guns as far
as Graves claimed, certainly not through a forest at
night. They must have used a road or path most of the
way before turning into the woods.

Graves went on:

> It developed that the earth at the spot selected for
> burial was more compact than anticipated, as a result
> of which we dug only about two and a half or three
> feet. Then we buried the little Twins in a single
> shallow grave, marking the spot as best we could by
> hacking a number of nearby trees. The earth was
> tamped down as firmly as could be done with our feet,
> and dried leaves and brush were heaped over the spot.

This is the only detailed account Graves gave. If
only he had said which direction he and his buddies
took when they stole the cannon and pushed them off
into the night. Regrettably, he left more questions than
answers.

Before leaving, the men all took a solemn oath that
none of them would ever reveal the secret of their
hiding place until all possibility of their cannons'
capture and confiscation by enemy hands was removed.

In 1905, forty years later, Dr. Graves, Sol Thomas,
and John Barnett returned to Harrisburg and attempted
to relocate the site where they buried the guns. They
drew maps separately, according to their memories of
the landmarks, and compared sketches. The maps all
coincided; however, the men were not successful in
finding the exact spot, since the terrain had undergone
marked changes—a situation I find all too often on
NUMA searches.

The three men actually found three of the original
marked trees and two of the stones they had placed in
the general area. This would indicate that they must
have been within a dozen feet of the Twin Sisters.

Another fifteen years passed, and then, in 1920, a reporter with the *Houston Chronicle* by the name of Mamie Cox persuaded Dr. Graves to come back to Harrisburg for another try at finding the Twin Sisters. In her story, Graves was driven around Harrisburg before stopping in the general location of the guns' burial. Unfortunately, no record was left as to where the car stopped for the search or to whom the property belonged. Supposedly, Graves found two of the landmarks he left in 1865.

So ends an intriguing tale of a mystery filled with bafflement.

Texans have been drawn to search for their heritage over the decades. Many individuals and groups have probed the landscape around Harrisburg looking for the guns. They're probably the only tourists who go there. Despite their efforts in analyzing clues and pursuing tantalizing leads that never pan out, they still search. And so does NUMA.

WE FIRST BEAT the bushes in the fall of 1987. Wayne Gronquist, Austin attorney and then president of NUMA, assembled a group of ten or so Texans who owned metal detectors and were fired up for the hunt. The first probe concentrated on the area west of the railroad tracks that run north across Bray's Bayou into Houston. We spread out in a line and worked inland from Bray's Bayou.

It was like trying to pick up confetti with a nail on a stick during a windstorm. Over the years, industrial manufacturers had used this location to dump everything from scrap metal to steel fifty-five-gallon drums to old refrigerators. There was so much iron that the metal detectors and magnetometers almost burned up.

I made the only discovery of the day. When sweeping through a field of high grass, I was startled down to my socks when two illegal immigrants leaped up and took off across the field. They must have been either hiding or sleeping when I almost walked on top of them. I shouted after them, "It's okay, enjoy your day!" But they never turned or looked back before vanishing in the woods.

IN 1988, Gronquist met up with another group of Texans looking for the cannon, led by Richard Harper and Randy Wiseman, who agreed to join forces with NUMA. Our people consisted of Bob Esbenson, Dana Larson, Tony Bell, and the Ross family. We all gathered in Harrisburg in March to begin the sweep. While we searched along the bayou, Harper and Wiseman hired a huge backhoe to dig a hundred-foot trench twenty feet wide and fifteen feet deep, but found nothing of interest.

The next day, using the Schonstedt gradiometer, I found an iron rim that came off an old wagon wheel and dug it up along with several old bottles. I felt the rim was too narrow for a cannon carriage, more in keeping with the size of a buggy wheel. But Harper and Wiseman became enthused, and they felt sure the rim came from the Twin Sisters gun carriage. They later dated the bottles to sometime in the 1860s.

The next day, there was a conflict between the two groups. Harper and Wiseman became angry because one of the people who had volunteered to bring his metal detector was a known treasure hunter. Why this bothered them, I'll never know. If found, there was no way the guns were going anywhere but to the state capital in Austin, and from there to the conservation labs at Texas A&M. They were also disappointed that we had not rented a bigger backhoe, even though we had excavated along the railroad tracks where they requested. Then there was a problem of proprietary rights. I got the idea that they thought the Twin Sisters belonged to them and that we were interlopers cutting into their territory.

I figured this was the perfect time to steal off into the night and head to the nearest saloon for a tequila on the rocks.

For the next safari through the tick-infested Harrisburg bush country, I called on the services of Connie Young, the noted psychic from Enid, Oklahoma. Along with Craig Dirgo, on his first expedition with NUMA, we drove through Harrisburg while Connie worked her magic. She sensed a pair of hot spots between the Southern Pacific railroad tracks and Bray's Bayou. We then continued to Galveston, where Wayne Gronquist and a group of volunteers were searching for the Republic of Texas warship *Invincible*. Connie thought there was a possibility that *Invincible* might be under the sand on the beach, since the shoreline had worked out nearly half a mile after the long rock jetties were built around the turn of the century. A Texas rancher, who had volunteered his services, drove up and down the beach in his SUV while I dragged a gradiometer out the rear end. Connie, Craig, and a Boy Scout came along for the ride.

We were passing time waiting for a target to make itself known on the recorders, when I turned to Connie and said, "Time sure flies when you're having fun."

The words were barely out of my mouth when the rancher drove over a ditch in the beach without slowing. Craig and I both tumbled from where we were sitting on the tailgate. He rolled on the sand and back to his feet. I went straight up into the air and down onto my head. The blow crushed two of the discs in my spine. Anguish and torment can't describe the pain. I could only gasp, unable to utter a word. Everyone stood around in a daze, thinking I had broken my back, until Craig walked over, picking sand from his ear, then looked down at me on the ground.

"You don't look so good," he said tilting his head to allow the sand to run from his ear.

Over time Dirgo has proved to be a master of the obvious.

"Move your leg for me," he said.

I did, though in much pain. He reached down to help me to my feet.

"I think you'll live to write another day," he said, as I slowly rose to my feet, "but we might want to take a side trip to the hospital."

A trip to the hospital and an X ray told the story. I've lost half an inch in height due to age and another inch and a half to a pair of mashed discs. I had compressed from six feet three to six feet one in two seconds and was no longer as tall as Dirk Pitt, the hero in my books. A year and six months would pass before the pain slowly receded.

I think Craig said it best that day after we left the hospital and were driving back to the motel in the rental car. "I thought we killed the goose that laid the golden egg."

"I'll make it," I said through gritted teeth.

Craig steered along the road running down Galveston's seawall. "You know the good thing about motels?"

"What's that," I asked.

"Ice machines."

Craig, who over the years has proven to be a more than an adequate scrounger, continued. "I'm going to get a trash bag and fill it with ice," he said, "then I'll take some duct tape and wrap it around your body to hold it in place."

It worked, but I looked like a hunchback.

UNABLE TO GO out on the search boat the following day, I instructed Gronquist to begin running search lanes at the outer edge of the grid and work in while hunting for *Invincible* with the gradiometer. Not wishing to sit around, I thought I could take my mind off the pain with a side expedition. So Connie, Craig, and I took a little handheld magnetometer and drove the short distance to Harrisburg and looked for the Twin Sisters.

Craig ran the mag over the area while Connie experienced vibes. There was a low reading, perhaps suggesting a buried target. Craig then drove into town and rented a backhoe and operator. I was still in the throes of anguish when Connie, bless her heart, bought me a lawn chair to sit on and relax my aching back during the dig.

As soon as the operator with the backhoe arrived, it began to rain. We sat there under newspapers, teeth clenched, as Craig crammed into the scoop, went down in the trench every few feet, and swept the mag around the bottom, which was now rapidly filling with water.

The mag target petered out as we went deeper.

I paid off the patient backhoe operator, and we drove back to the motel where we stay in Galveston, Gaidos Motor Lodge. No sooner did we walk in, Connie drenched, Craig looking like a snowman built from mud, and me sloped over like the Hunchback of Notre Dame, than we find Gronquist and crew packing and almost ready to depart.

I said, "What's going on? We have another four days scheduled for the project."

Gronquist snapped his bag shut and began walking out the door. "We overturned the boat in the surf, and the gradiometer was immersed and shorted out in the salt water. So we're calling it quits and going home."

I was somewhere between enraged and infuriated. "But you finished the search grid."

"Nope," muttered Gronquist. "We were running the first lane when a wave spilled over the side."

"I told you to begin out where it's calm before working toward the surf."

Gronquist merely shrugged. "I though it best to start in close where I thought the ship might be."

I thought it was a pity it wasn't Sunday and Gronquist could have stayed in bed.

Craig wiped some mud from under his eye and looked at me. "I might be able to fix the mag," he said, "but do you mind if I take a shower first?"

Later that night, he repaired the damage with a hair dryer borrowed from the front desk, along with some WD-40, solder, and a soldering gun from the hardware store. By that time the volunteers had already given up, but Connie, Craig, and I managed to spend the remaining days in a fruitless search for the cannon.

So ended the great calamity of 1989.

I should have scratched the Twin Sisters off my list of things to do, but I was swept away in an orgy of obstinacy. We'd be back.

THE NEXT few rounds of battle were fought by Craig and me, along with my son Dirk. When Craig was running the NUMA office, he would drive up to my house on Lookout Mountain outside Denver a couple of times a week to report on what was happening, and we'd spend hours talking. One of the topics was the Twin Sisters. He didn't want to give up and neither did I, so we would occasionally reread the tale and format strategies. Our flights of fancy could become quite elaborate and detailed.

My personal favorite was the time we waited until dark and then set off into the woods near my home with a pedometer. After walking four hundred yards in a random direction, we marked several trees with dabs of spray paint and returned by a different route. We then waited a week and set out to find them. We never did. Not only that, when we later checked the distance once again with the pedometer, we found that the area where we had searched for the marked trees was more like two hundred or two hundred and fifty yards from my house. That showed that, without accurate aids, estimating distances in a forest at night is at best a hit-or-miss proposition.

Next we tried carrying a bag of Portland cement, which weighs a lot less than a heavy iron cannon, a distance into the woods. I think I can now tell you that if they were carrying the guns, they didn't go four hundred yards. More like a hundred and forty yards.

*

IN 1989 AND 1994, Craig stopped in Harrisburg for a day here and a day there while going to or returning from other searches, but to no avail. In 1995, when NUMA returned to search for the Texas Navy ship *Invincible*, Craig and I had a go at it again. I still laugh about this. My son Dirk was due to arrive from Phoenix to lend a hand that afternoon, and since Harrisburg is close to Hobby Airport, where Dirk was arriving, Craig and I figured we could search almost right up until his plane was due to arrive and then rush over and pick him up.

Over the years, we had moved around our search area and were now concentrating in an area north of the old railroad station and east of the current north-to-south running line. This area is heavily wooded and brushy. Long sleeves and a machete are good things to have. Craig and I marked off a grid and began methodically covering the area. Every chirp from the detector needed to be dug, and we'd brought along a pick and shovel for that purpose.

My first big find was a bum that was living in the woods—I scared him awake by nearly stepping on him as I walked along, head down. He ran off into the woods like a deer frightened by a bear. He even left his cardboard box behind. I moved it to the side I'd already searched and checked under it—nothing.

By now it was getting hot, and Craig and I were sweating. We continued to search. An hour or so later, Craig discovered a fifty-five-gallon drum that had been buried, not too long after I discovered an old engine block that had been buried. So went the next few hours until early afternoon. We had decided to wait and eat lunch until after we picked up Dirk, since we figured they probably wouldn't have fed him on the plane.

Leaving markers to show the area we'd covered, we grabbed our pick, shovel, and detector and walked back to the rental car. I looked at Craig. His T-shirt was wet enough to wring out, and his face was covered with dirt. He opened up the trunk of the rental car and tossed in the tools while removing two cans of warm soda. "Tom Clancy's drinking fine champagne right now," he said, as he handed one over.

"Thanks," I said, as I popped the top.

Craig walked around and opened the car door—and a wave of heat erupted from inside that dried out my eyeballs. He slid into the driver's seat and twisted the ignition. A few minutes later, we were cruising toward the airport. I looked at my watch. "We should have just enough time to park and walk inside," I said.

Craig slid the rental car into a short-term parking spot, and we walked across the asphalt toward the terminal. Oh, was it ever hot! Then the doors to the terminal slid open, and we walked into the baggage claim area. It must have been forty degrees in there; Craig still swears he could see his breath.

And then there were the stares coming from the deplaning passengers. Craig seemed oblivious as he walked along, searching for Dirk, but the sight was comical, to say the least. His boots were coated with dirt and mud, his pants and shirt wet with sweat. That wasn't the funny thing, however—as soon as he'd walked inside, the cold had instantly chilled him, and he was twitching like a Georgia farmer going ice-fishing for the first time. Both his shoulders were pumping up and down, and he was rubbing his hands together like a maniacal scientist intent on destruction. As he walked along, the crowd parted like a tank going through a crystal shop. Then Dirk approached from the other direction, headed for the baggage carousel.

At first glimpse, he actually stopped and broke out laughing.

"What in the hell," he said between laughs, "happened to you two?"

"It's those damn Twin Sisters," I said. "We'll tell you about it outside."

THOSE DAMN Twin Sisters. Dirk and Craig did more work in 1997 when NUMA was in Galveston searching for the *Invincible*. This time, they moved outside the prime search area and scanned around some of the nearby homes. When Dirk and Craig work together, it often resembles a bad Abbott and Costello routine. The two feed off each other, passing the time doing poor comedy skits and worse impersonations. It usually starts with an innocuous comment and goes downhill from there.

And the Twin Sisters send both men into a frenzy.

"HOT ENOUGH for you?" Dirk began, as the pair unloaded the equipment from the trunk of the rental car.

"All we need is water and some good people," said Craig.

"Of course," replied Dirk, "that's all that hell needs, as well."

Craig hefted a pickax. "Volunteers," he said. "We need volunteers."

Dirk removed the last of the equipment and shut the

trunk. "We could run an ad," he said, as the pair began walking toward the search area.

"Looking for a few people who enjoy intense boredom interspersed with moments of extreme discomfort. Masochists welcome," Craig said.

"Are your hobbies magnetometry, sweating, and digging holes? NUMA needs you."

"Did you ever hide stuff from yourself just for the thrill of finding it later? You may be our type."

"Will you work for free?" said Dirk.

Craig laughed. "Will you *pay* us to suffer?"

Dirk pointed to a ditch in front of an old frame house. The men began swiping the gradiometer back and forth. Craig watched the readout.

"Have you ever been so hot that your tongue was sweating?" Dirk said.

"Ever had to wash your clothes in a motel-room sink?"

"Because the Laundromat turned you away?" Dirk said.

"Stop," said Craig. "Back about a foot."

Dirk scanned the area.

"It's small," said Craig. "Continue."

"Do you like greasy diner food?" Dirk resumed.

"Can you exist on a diet of taco chips and warm soda?"

Dirk looked over at Craig. "This area is magnetically deserted. Let's move on."

"As barren as a whore's heart."

"As deserted as a Vanilla Ice concert," said Dirk.

This gives you a pretty good idea of what the first thirty minutes of the search went like. You can expand it for eight hours or so to understand the verbal barrage I'm faced with. When possible, I send the two off alone. If not, Ralph and I banish them to the rear deck of the search boat.

LATER THAT DAY, Dirk received a good reading inside a horse corral. Craig, and the gift of a case of cold Miller Lite, convinced the owner to let them dig. After digging through the packed soil for most of one hot afternoon, the pair located an old anvil buried six feet deep. So they moved on to the next target. Such is the nature of what we do.

IN EARLY 2001, Craig flew to Phoenix so we could go over progress on this book. We spent a couple hours going over the Twin Sisters file and have come up with yet another hypothesis. Time will tell on this.

Both Dirk and Craig did make one request, however: When NUMA returns, they want to schedule it for some month besides August. Wimps.

PART SEVEN
Mary Celeste

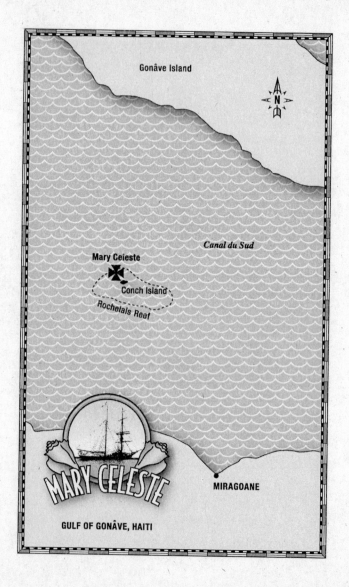

I

Mystery Ship

1872

WHEN *MARY CELESTE* EDGED AWAY FROM PIER 50 in the East River, there was no reason to think this voyage would be any different from others she had made. Tuesday, the fifth day of November 1872, was cold and gray, but not insufferably so. Just an early-winter New York day like hundreds before and hundreds since. Coats were worn, to be sure, but it was not so cold that a person would turn away from the wind. It was a normal day, with winter fast approaching.

Captain Benjamin Spooner Briggs tugged at his thick goatee, then adjusted the wheel slightly. The current in the East River was running strong and trying to push him back against the dock. He shouted to Albert Richardson of Stockton Springs, Maine, the first mate.

"Furl the main staysail," Briggs shouted.

The wind caught in the fabric and pulled the ship farther into the river.

Briggs nodded slightly, as if he approved of *Mary Celeste*'s motion. Briggs was the son of a sea captain from Wareham, Massachusetts. Benjamin was the second of five sons, and all but one of his brothers would make their careers on the sea. His was a childhood of sea tales and letters from faraway ports. In Sippican Village, where the Briggs clan eventually settled, it is said that if you cut a Briggs boy, salt water would flow from the veins. Captain Briggs was as at home on the sea as he was sitting in front of a fireplace in a fine mansion. As part owner of the *Mary Celeste*, he was anxious to start the voyage.

He sniffed the air and twisted the wheel slightly.

Belowdecks in the captain's quarters, Sarah Elizabeth Briggs, Benjamin's wife, was tending to their two-year-old daughter, Sophia Matilda. After feeding her and placing her in a small wood-framed playpen in the room, Sarah played a quiet tune on her melodeon until the child fell asleep.

This was not Mrs. Briggs's first trip with her husband—but it would be her last.

The winds were not favorable.

Mary Celeste was a mile off Staten Island when Briggs gave the order.

"Heave to," he shouted to the sailors. "We'll anchor and await a change in winds."

Once his ship was stationary, Briggs went belowdecks to check his cargo. Other than a few crates full of personal items going to a New York art student studying in Italy, his hold was filled with a single cargo: barrels of alcohol bound for Genoa, 1,700 in total, being shipped by Meisser, Ackerman & Company, of 48 Beaver Street, New York City.

Befitting his Yankee upbringing, Briggs was a cautious man. And although the barrels were tightly plugged and appeared intact, he worried about the possibility of fumes. More than one ship had exploded and burned when carrying such dangerous goods. With both his wife and baby daughter aboard, he wanted to be sure he averted an accident before it happened.

Satisfied that the cargo was safe, he climbed from the hold and made his way to his cabin. Sarah sat in front of her foot-operated sewing machine, hemming a baby dress. To one side, in a folding playpen made of lathe-turned walnut, Sophia was standing quietly. When Briggs entered, she cocked her head and stared quizzically.

"Da," she squealed.

Captain Briggs made his way over to the playpen and rubbed his daughter's hair. Then he turned to Sarah and smiled.

"The winds are against us," he said. "We'll wait here until they turn."

"Any idea how long?" Sarah asked easily.

"The barometer shows changes," Briggs admitted, "but there is really no way to know for sure."

Early on the morning of Thursday, November 7, the winds began to cooperate.

A pilot guided *Mary Celeste* from her anchorage into deeper water. Once clear of the shallows and in the Atlantic Ocean, a pilot boat came alongside to retrieve the pilot and take him back to New York City. As was the custom, when the pilot boarded his boat to shore, he carried letters from the ship to post.

The last communications from the captain and crew of *Mary Celeste*.

Benjamin Briggs stood behind the wheel and steered his ship east. There was an inky blackness to the sea that day, combined with an unyielding roughness. It was as if the water consisted of shards of black marble like that used to build a mausoleum. *Mary Celeste* was on a roller-coaster ride. In front of the bow, the waves rose in a building flood of righteous indignation; then, as the bow broke over the top, the ship headed down with such force that the captain could feel his stomach rising in protest. It was as if they were on a rocking chair that was hitting the wall.

Two thousand feet down was the bottom. Two thousand miles ahead was the Azores.

Briggs had faced harsh seas before and was not concerned. His ship was stout and strong, his crew handpicked and checked. There was First Mate Albert Richardson, twenty-eight years old, with a light complexion and brown hair. Richardson had served in the Maine Volunteers during the Civil War, so Briggs knew he was used to hardship. His pay was $50 a month. Second mate Andrew Gilling, a twenty-five-year-old from New York City, was fair of skin and hair, a seasoned sailor from Denmark. His wages were $35 a month. The cook and steward, Edward William Head, was twenty-three and newly married. His pay was $40 a month.

And the deckhands and ordinary sailors received $30 monthly.

Brothers Boz and Volkert Lorenzen, ages twenty-five and twenty-nine, respectively. Thirty-five-year-old Arian Martens. Gottlieb Goodschaad, the youngest at twenty-three. All were from Germany—all were experienced. All of these men, along with Gilling, listed their address as 19 Thames Street, New York. The Seaman's Hall.

Edward Head carefully made his way across the deck to Captain Briggs.

"Captain," he shouted over the wind, "can I get you anything?"

"I'll eat when the watch changes," Briggs said, "in an hour and a half."

"Coffee?" Head asked as he turned to leave.

"Hot tea with molasses," Briggs said, "to settle my stomach."

"I'll bring it out shortly," Head agreed.

At that instant, at the docks in New York City, another ship was being loaded.

Dei Gratia was a British brigantine of 295 tons that hailed from Nova Scotia. Her captain, David Reed Moorhouse, was supervising the loading of oil from the fields of Pennsylvania. His first mate, Oliver Deveau, stood alongside as the casks were lowered by ropes into the hold.

"We are scheduled to leave on the fifteenth," Moorhouse said. "Do you have any recommendations for the rest of the crew?"

"I talked to Augustus Anderson and John Johnson about coming aboard as ordinary seamen. I've worked with them before."

"What do you think about John Wright as the second mate?"

"He's a good hand," Deveau agreed.

"I'll make him an offer, then," Moorhouse said.

"The wind is turning," Deveau noted.

"Then we should leave on time," Moorhouse said easily.

MOST GREAT CIVILIZATIONS have one thing in common: seapower. The Vikings, the Spanish, the British—all could trace their power and prestige to the fact that they ruled the oceans. And in the days before corporations, a captain of a ship at sea was a powerful man. Along with being the representative of the ship owners and his country of flag, he was tasked with a fiduciary duty to the owners of the cargo that his ship carried. But his duties were insured.

The hull of *Mary Celeste* was insured by four companies: Maine Lloyds, in the amount of $6,000; Orient Mutual Company, for $4,000; Mercantile Mutual Company, $2,500; and New England Mutual Insurance Company, with the smallest coverage at $1,500. The total coverage was $14,000, not an insignificant sum in 1872. The cargo was insured separately through Atlantic Mutual Insurance Company for $3,400. The companies were careful about the ships they insured— they insisted that they were fit to sail and properly crewed. *Mary Celeste* fit all the criteria.

Halfway to the Azores, Captain Briggs was guiding *Mary Celeste* over the Rehoboth Seamount, an underwater plateau along the sixty-degree-longitude line. Turning the helm over to Richardson, he opened a polished cherrywood box, then carefully removed a sextant from a soft deerskin bag. Shooting a fix of the horizon, he determined their location.

Mary Celeste was on the proper course.

"Same heading," he said to Richardson. "I'll be below if you need me."

"Very good, sir," Richardson said.

The hatch leading below was halfway open, folded back on itself, and the ladder leading down was firmly secured to the bulkhead. Briggs had learned through experience to check such things, as early in his career he had descended a loose ladder and tumbled into the hold, badly wrenching his ankle. Nowadays he left nothing to chance.

Briggs was happy with his crew so far. The Lorenzen brothers spoke halting English with a thick German accent, but they seemed to understand his directions and complied quickly. Not only that, the brothers were hard workers. Every time Briggs looked around, they were tending to sails, swabbing the deck, or finding some other task to occupy their time. Good sailors.

Martens and Goodschaad seemed quiet and studious compared to the Lorenzens, but they worked hard and followed directions. Richardson was skilled enough to captain his own ship, and Gilling would be there soon. Only Edward Head worried Briggs. While he performed his duties with skill, he seemed sad.

Reaching the lower deck, Briggs headed down a companionway to the galley.

"Captain," Head said, looking up from peeling potatoes.

"How are things, Edward?" Briggs asked.

"Salt beef, potatoes, and beets for dinner."

"I'd say that sounds good," Briggs said, smiling, "but I would be lying."

"I have a barrel of dried apples," Head offered, "and shall try to bake a pie."

"Are you missing your wife?" Briggs asked.

"Very much so, sir," Head offered. "After this trip, I may stay on shore."

"The return has already been arranged," Briggs said easily. "A load of fruit, so we should have only a short layover for loading. A month or so, and you will be back home and can decide."

"I'm glad, sir," Head said easily.

But in less than a month, *Mary Celeste* would be in Gibraltar, and the people now aboard would be gone.

CAPTAIN MOORHOUSE stood on the upper deck of *Dei Gratia*. His cargo was secured, and the last of the supplies were being loaded.

"Once the stores are secured, give the men a ration of rum," Moorhouse said to Deveau.

"Yes, sir," Deveau said.

The date was November 14, 1872. *Dei Gratia* would leave New York the following morning. Moorhouse headed below to check his charts—a large expanse of ocean lay ahead, and he needed to be prepared for anything.

Far to the north, near the Arctic Circle, a storm was building. As the sky faded to black, the wind grew in intensity. Dry snow began forming, and it grew until it was a blinding blanket. A herd of musk ox knew the signs and formed into a protective circle, their faces to the outside and the young and sick on the interior. Huddled together to conserve heat, they began to wait out the storm.

NO REST for the weary. *Mary Celeste* was facing rougher seas. Briggs knew that November was always fickle, but this trip was proving to be the exception, not the rule. He had thought that once they crossed the sixty-degree mark, the seas would be calm, but in fact they were building. The temperature had risen, so cold was no longer a problem, but the increasing battering to the hull worried Briggs. One of the barrels of alcohol had already split, spilling its contents into the bilge—a few more and Briggs would have a problem.

"How's the baby?" Briggs asked, entering the captain's cabin.

"She's fine if she's in the crib," Sarah answered. "It rocks with the ship and comforts her. If she's in the playpen, she's tossed around."

Briggs looked at his wife. Her skin had a grayish-green tinge.

"And you?"

"I've been sick," Sarah admitted.

"I'll get a few crackers from the cook," Briggs said. "They usually comfort the stomach."

"Thank you, dear."

"We're making good time," Briggs said. "If this continues, we will pass into the Mediterranean within the week. It's usually calmer there."

"I hope," Sarah said quietly.

CAPTAIN MOORHOUSE was dressed in a full leather raincoat and matching hat. Under his eyes were bags from lack of sleep, and he had not eaten a full meal since the morning they left New York. From day one of the trip, they had faced ugly weather. First it was snow and wind—now rain and wind. A nor'easter was sweeping *Dei Gratia* toward a date with destiny. Whatever else was happening, they were making good time.

*

BRIGGS MADE an entry into the captain's log. The log was a feature on every ship at sea. Notes on weather, location, ship's condition, and unusual events were constantly recorded with date and time. The log went with the captain when he reached port; to new owners when a ship was sold. It was a record of triumph and tragedy, a visible sign of the passage of a journey.

> *November 23, 1872. Eight evening sea time. Two more barrels split, hull leaking some, but pumps adequate. Weather still rough. Location 40 degrees 22 minutes North by 19 degrees 17 minutes West. Should see the first of the Azores tomorrow.*

Handing the helm to Gilling, who had late watch, he climbed below, shook the water from his hat and coat, then made his way to his cabin to try to sleep. Astern of the captain's cabin, divided by the storage hold, were the berths for the ordinary seamen. Boz Lorenzen whispered across the space in German to his brother Volkert.

"Volkie," he said.

"Yes, Boz."

"Are the fumes giving you a headache?"

"Not so much a headache," Volkert said, "but I was dreaming a vivid dream."

"What was it?"

"We were home in Germany and mother was still alive."

"A good dream."

"Not really," Volkert said. "It was her head, but her body was a potato."

"Mother did love the spatzel."

"Why don't you crack the porthole?" Volkert asked.

"Because water comes in," Boz said, before turning over to try to sleep.

DEI GRATIA's second mate, Oliver Deveau, stared up at the mainsail. The sail had been rigged six months before, on a layover in London, and while slightly weathered by time, it appeared unfrayed. The bass grommets, where the lines attached, showed no wear, and the hemmed edges had yet to unravel. That was a good thing. Since the start of the voyage from New York, *Dei Gratia* had faced strong winds. And while the temperature had warmed as the ship had dropped into lower latitudes, the winds had not diminished.

Twin wakes flowed from the bow as *Dei Gratia* made way, and the wind buffeted Deveau's hair. To port, Deveau caught sight of a trio of bottlenose porpoises jumping the wake, and he smiled. The ship was making good time, and if it continued, there might be a bonus from the grateful owners upon completion.

Deveau did not know his bonus would come from an unexpected source.

On *MARY CELESTE*, First Mate Albert Richardson was straining his eyes to catch a glimpse of Santa Cruz das Flores Island. The landmass and its sister island, Corvo, would be the first land to be passed since leaving New York. The date was November 24, 1872. The wind continued to blow.

Belowdecks in the captain's cabin, Benjamin Briggs and his wife, Sarah, were enjoying the last of the fresh eggs. Captain Briggs liked his fried, Sarah poached; baby Sophia just liked them. Sarah slid an egg onto a piece of thick-sliced bread, then spoke to her husband.

"I saw a rat," she said easily. "We should have a cat aboard."

"I'll have the men clean the hull when we off-load the alcohol," Briggs said, "before the fruit is loaded."

"Won't the fruit have insects?" Sarah asked. "Scorpions and roaches?"

"Possibly, dear," Briggs admitted, "but they won't last once we reach the colder climates."

"I think the fumes are affecting Sophia," Sarah said.

"She seems fine," Briggs said, reaching over and tickling Sophia, who sat in her mother's lap.

"Well, they're affecting me," Sarah said. "I feel like I've been embalmed."

"Two more barrels are leaking," Briggs said. "I'm afraid since they were filled when it was cold that as we pass farther into warmer water they will expand more."

"That wouldn't be good," Sarah said.

"No," Briggs admitted, "it wouldn't."

DEI GRATIA sailed east, and the sailors began a ritual as old as time. There was cleaning and tending to the sails. Scrubbing and soapstone on the decks. Brightwork needed to be attended to—rust had to be dealt with harshly. The weather was lifting, allowing more time on the open upper deck. The sun shone through the clouds on the faces of the sailors.

So far the voyage had been like many others, but that was about to change.

Off-course from the fickle winds. This was not an unusual thing aboard a sailing ship, but one that did require an adjustment in plans. During the night, *Mary Celeste* had passed north of St. Mary's Island, not south, as caution and ease would have indicated. For one thing, the Gibraltar Strait now lay south and east of their position and was more easily accessed by passing south of the Azores. For another, just twenty-one miles north of St. Mary's, not many miles from where *Mary Celeste* was now passing, lay the dangerous group of rocks known as the Dollabarat Shoals. In bad weather, waves broke over the area with great force. In calm seas, they lay just below the surface, ready to rip the hull out from under unsuspecting vessels.

A good navigator could thread the needle through the danger, but most avoided the area. In the first place, there was little reason to pass to the north. St. Mary's Island had no usable anchorages. No fresh water, towns, or help available.

SHIP'S LOG—Mary Celeste
November 25, 1872 Eight bells.
At 8, Eastern Point bore SSW, 6 miles distant.

This was to be the last entry in the log under "Captain Benjamin Briggs."

The ship was passing the last of the Azores, and the eastern point was Ponta Castello, a high peak on the southeastern shore of the island.

Andrew Gilling wiped the back of his neck with a handkerchief.

"Six hundred miles to Gibraltar," he whispered to himself.

His watch was almost over, and Gilling was glad. All night he had felt a foreboding, a sense of unease without definition. It was strange. *Mary Celeste* was currently out of the clouds, but in the early-morning light Gilling had seen them to the south and east—a black wall that ebbed and flowed like a living organism. Twice during the night, waterspouts had sprung up near the ship but dissolved before fully forming. And squalls had come and gone quickly and mysteriously, like a knock on the door with no one there.

Albert Richardson walked along the deck unsteadily.

"Watch change," he said when he reached Gilling.

Gilling stared at the first mate—his eyes were red and bloodshot and his words were slightly slurred. There was a palpable order of alcohol saturating his skin. If the Dane was to hazard a guess, he'd have to conclude that Richardson was drunk.

"Where's Captain Briggs?" Gilling asked.

"Sick belowdecks," Richardson said, "as is most of the crew. The fumes are wreaking havoc with everyone. Just before sunrise, I could hear Mrs. Briggs playing her melodeon and singing. The noise woke everyone."

"Sir," Gilling said slowly, "I've been in fresh air all night. Perhaps I should continue my watch."

"I'll be okay," Richardson said, "once I air out."

"Very good, sir," Gilling said. "Just be careful—the area ahead is uncharted and might contain a few unrecorded shoals."

"I will, Andrew," Richardson said, as he assumed control of the helm.

Baby Sophia smiled at the black spot in front of her eyes. She rubbed her eyes with the back of her hand, but the little dots remained. Benjamin Briggs was singing the Stephen Foster song "Beautiful Dreamer." He and Sarah, who sat at the melodeon playing like a woman possessed, had slept little.

"More baritone," she shouted.

Forward in the seaman's cabin, the Germans were playing cards. Arian Harbens had dealt the hand nearly an hour ago—no one had yet screamed gin. Gottlieb Goodschaad tried to concentrate on the cards in his hand. The joker seemed to be talking. The nine looked like a six.

In the galley, Edward Head was trying to start the stove. Finally, after much effort, he gave up. Removing a side of preserved meat from storage, he reached for a knife to slice off chunks, but his hand refused to answer the signal from his brain. It was as if his brain were coated in molasses. But he didn't care. A rat walked along a high shelf, and Head tried to communicate with the rodent telepathically. Strangely, he thought, he received no answer.

Volkert Lorenzen was packing tobacco in a pipe. Once filled, he handed it to his brother Boz and then packed another for himself. Maybe a smoke up on deck would clear their heads. Their heads needed clearing— Boz had just told him for the tenth time how much he loved him. Volkert knew Boz loved him—they were brothers. Even so, the two had never found the need to say it out loud.

Mary Celeste was a ship of fools under the influence of an invisible vapor.

TWELVE FEET below the surface of the water dead ahead was an underwater seamount, uncharted and without a name. A series of rocky plateaus with scattered pieces of volcanic rock formed hundreds of thousands of years in the past.

Mary Celeste might have barely passed over the hazard—she drew but eleven feet, seven inches—but the waves were ebbing and flowing, and the ship was pitching up and down a full four feet.

Wood was about to meet stone with disastrous result.

ALBERT RICHARDSON stared to the south. The ship was passing lee of St. Mary's, and only time and six hundred miles of water lay between them and Gibraltar. And then it happened. A lurch, a crash, a scraping along the length of the hull. *Mary Celeste* slowed as the keel ran along the rocks, but in seconds the forward momentum carried her free.

"Aground!" Richardson shouted.

Even in his befuddled state, Captain Benjamin Briggs knew that sound.

Racing from his cabin, he climbed the ladder on deck and ran to the helm. Staring astern, he could see that the sea in their wake was dirty from where the ship had scraped. He stared ahead and was reassured with what appeared to be deep water. Looking starboard, he could see St. Mary's Island.

"Why are we north of the island?" he shouted to Richardson.

"The storm," Richardson said, "carried us north in the night."

The Lorenzen brothers, Goodschaad, and Harbens ran on deck, along with Gilling and even a slow-moving Edward Head. They all knew the sound, and they all feared the result.

"Stay at the wheel," Briggs shouted. "Come with me," he said to the sailors.

Water flooded into the hold between the spaces in the planking. Two feet lay inside the hull, and the depth was rising. Several more barrels of alcohol had burst, mixing with the sea mist into a toxic vapor.

Briggs surveyed the situation quickly.

"Volkie, Boz, man the pumps," he shouted. "Arian, you and Gottlieb bring me the barrel of caulking."

As the men ran off, he got on his knees and felt around—a steady flow of water pressure. He dipped his head under the water. The alcohol burned his eyes, but he could see through the dirty water. No broken planks, just a fast seepage through planks that had been dislodged. Pulling his head from the water, he tasted the alcohol. His head was spinning, and he was unable to restore his equilibrium. A churning grew in his stomach, and he vomited.

"Here you go, sir," Harbens said, handing the cask filled with waxed rope to Briggs.

"Go to my cabin," he said, taking the cask of rope. "Tell my wife to prepare to abandon ship if necessary."

Harbens sloshed over to the ladder and climbed up a deck.

"Mrs. Briggs," he shouted to the closed door, "the captain asks that you prepare to abandon ship."

The door opened, and Sarah stood there, smiling. Her eyes were beet-red and her cheeks were flushed, as if she had spent the morning ice-skating on a windswept Kansas lake. Peering inside, Harbens could see baby Sophia. She was sitting listlessly in her playpen, a thin trickle of drool hanging from her chin.

"What about Sophia?" Sarah asked.

"Make her ready," Harbens said quickly. "She's coming with us."

A tainted layer of vomit floated on top of the water, but Briggs did not care. He plunged his head below the surface and began to stuff the waxed rope into any crack he could feel. Pausing to take breaths of air, he went under the water time and time again.

"Pumps are going," Boz shouted, once when his head was above water.

"Gottlieb," Briggs said, "tell Harbens to make sure he packs my chronometer, sextant, and navigation book, as well as the ship's register. Then you and Arian launch the shore boat."

Briggs looked at a mark on the side wall of the hull. The water was not receding, but neither was it quickly rising. They might have a chance. Briggs stood upright; his head was spinning, and he fought to regain control. The air at head level was thick with the fumes. He shouted down the length of the ship to the Lorenzen brothers. Just then, a sudden squall hit the boat.

"Come topside," he said. "We'll take to the boat and ride this out."

At the wheel of *Mary Celeste*, Richardson watched in amazement as a pair of waterspouts formed to each side of the vessel. Seconds before, it had been relatively clear, a light mist, a few random gusts, a sprinkling of rain. Then, all at once, the fury had descended like a slap from an angry lover.

"Use the main peak halyard to tie to the painter," he shouted to Harbens and Goodschaad, who were preparing to lower the boat over the side. "It's already out."

The line, three hundred feet in length and three inches in diameter, remained on deck at all times; to take out another line would require the men to go forward to the lazeret where the spares were stored.

"Okay," Harbens shouted.

Goodschaad tied the line to the boat's painter, then he and Martens hoisted the boat over the rail and into the water. They played out the line around a deck stanchion and let the boat float back to the stern.

Briggs appeared on deck, just as Sarah, who was carrying Sophia in her arms like a football, made her way to the ladder topside.

"Furl the main sails," Briggs shouted to Harbens and Goodschaad, as Sarah stepped on deck.

"Honey, what is it?" Sarah asked.

"We scraped bottom," Briggs said. "I think I have the flow stanched, but just to be safe, I want to take to the shore boat for a time."

"I'm scared," Sarah said, as Sophia began to whimper.

Just then a wall of rain washed across the deck and disappeared just as quickly. Briggs stared aft; a wooden box with the items he had ordered Harbens to secure sat on the deck awaiting loading.

"Open the main and lazeret hatches," he shouted to Harbens, "then make your way aft to the stern."

The Lorenzen brothers appeared on deck.

"Help Sarah and Sophia aboard the boat, then board yourself," he told the brothers.

"Should I lash the wheel?" Richardson asked.

"Leave it free," Briggs ordered.

In the last few minutes, Gilling had remained out of the fray—his mind was clearer than the others, and he

believed that Briggs was overreacting. Even so, he was
in no place to question the captain's decisions, so he
had gone to the galley and, along with Edward Head,
had prepared food and water to load on the boat.
Steadying the boat alongside the stern ladder, he
waited until Head loaded the stores. Next, steadied by
the Lorenzen brothers on each side, Sarah and Sophia
boarded.

"Go ahead and board," he told the brothers, who
entered and took a seat.

The loading was going quickly. Harbens and
Goodschaad, then Head and Richardson. Briggs came
alongside and tapped him on the shoulder.

"Climb on in," Briggs told him. "I enter last."

Ten people total, on a small boat attached to the
mother by a thin line.

A WHALE BREACHED near *Dei Gratia* and blew
water from its blowhole.

"Whale a port," Deveau shouted.

Moorhouse made a note in the ship's log, then shot
the horizon with the sextant. They were on a true
course and making time. The weather had moderated,
and the sun was peeking through the clouds. All in all,
it was an ordinary day at sea.

He had no way to know of the drama unfolding five
hundred miles distant.

PULLED LIKE the last child in a game of crack-the-
whip, Briggs stared at *Mary Celeste* in the distance
ahead. An hour had passed, and the ship was riding the
same—his caulking job must have worked. By now,
with the hatches off the hold would be vented. The

fresh air had cleared his head, and now he was doubting his decision.

"I think it's safe to pull in the line and board," he said to the others on the boat.

The men nodded; their heads, too, had cleared. Although they were at home on the water, being crowded on a small boat far from land was disconcerting, to say the least. Everyone wanted to board *Mary Celeste* and return to their normal duties. It had been a scare and nothing more—a tale to tell their children. A lesson to be learned.

"Do you want me and Gilling to start pulling?" Richardson asked.

Right then, before Briggs could answer, another squall descended. Two hundred and seventy-five yards ahead, *Mary Celeste* surged forward like a greyhound leaving the starting gate. The line connecting them to their home at sea went slack, then pulled hard against the stanchion and snapped. Almost instantly, the small boat began to slow, as the brigantine loaded with alcohol continued on. Richardson raised the now-limp line and stared back at Briggs.

"Row, men, row," he shouted.

TEN DAYS ADRIFT and they were dying. They lost sight of *Mary Celeste* the first day, and all efforts to row back to St. Mary's Island had been in vain. There had been no food and water for a week, and now when they most needed it, there was no rain.

Baby Sophia was gone, committed to the sea with Sarah soon after.

Harbens, Gilling, and Richardson were gone as well. Goodschaad had died quietly in the night and lay in the bottom of the boat, while Head had died of a heart attack but three days adrift. A broken heart, Briggs had thought to himself as soon as he realized he would never again see his bride.

"Help me with Goodschaad," Briggs said near 10 A.M. when some strength returned.

Boz and Volkert helped him over the side.

Briggs stared at the Germans—it gave him an idea of his own condition. The skin on both men's faces was peeling off in sheets. Their cracked and dried lips were as plump as sausages. Dried blood was below Volkert's nose, while greenish pus was visible at the corner of Boz's eyes.

"Kill me," he said to the brothers quietly.

Boz looked at his brother and nodded. They were trained not to question orders from their captain. Volkert took one stiff wooden paddle, his brother another. Then, with what little strength they had left, they complied.

Two hours passed before enough strength returned to put Briggs over the side.

They died within minutes of each other the following morning.

DECEMBER 4, 1872, was a sunny day. Captain Moorhouse was at the wheel of *Dei Gratia*. The British brigantine had passed far north of the Azores out of sight of the islands and was now tacking southeast by south on a course to drop down into the Gibraltar Straits. Moorhouse had just taken his position, recording it as 38 degrees 20 minutes north by 17 degrees 15 minutes west, when he spotted another ship approaching six miles distant off the port bow. The time was 1:52 P.M.

"Hand me the spyglass," Moorhouse said to Second Officer Wright.

Wright reached into a drawer and handed Moorhouse the telescoping spyglass.

With a flick of the wrist, Moorhouse opened the telescope and stared at the vessel. The main sails were furled, and no one was visible on deck. Strange, but not overly so.

"She seems to be laden, but just plodding along," Moorhouse noted.

"Our course will converge with her shortly," Wright noted. "Should I signal her and find out the sea conditions?"

"All right," Moorhouse said easily.

But the first and all subsequent signals went unanswered.

A few hundred yards ahead, the ghost ship continued west at a speed of one and a half to two knots. Moorhouse had yet to see anyone come on deck, and he was beginning to worry that the entire crew of the vessel had taken ill.

He stared at the vessel through the spyglass, then made a decision.

"Down with the mainsails," he shouted to Seamen Anderson and Johnson.

Dei Gratia slowed until she was barely bobbing on the water.

"What should we do?" Deveau, who had now come on deck, asked.

"Ready the boat," Moorhouse ordered. "I want you and Wright to board. Take Johnson with you to man the boat."

"Ahoy," he shouted over a megaphone to *Mary Celeste*.

There was no answer.

Once in the shore boat with Johnson at the oars, the trio of men watched the hull of the ship as they rowed closer. Not a single sailor was on deck; not a single sound could be heard save the slap of water against the hull. The men felt an eerie gloom, a sense of foreboding. They read the name on the stern as they approached: *Mary Celeste*.

"Stay here," Deveau said to Johnson, as the shore boat came alongside. "Mr. Wright and I will investigate."

Tossing a hooked ladder over the gunwale, Deveau and Wright climbed aboard.

"Ahoy," Deveau shouted once he was on the main deck.

No answer.

He and Wright walked forward. The main and lazeret hatches were lying on deck, the forward one upside down—a bad sign. Sailors are superstitious, and an upside-down hatch spelled trouble. The main staysail lay across the forward hatch across the chimney for the galley cookstove. No sailor in his right mind would allow that. The jib and the fore topmast staysail were set on a starboard tack, while the foresail and upper foretopsail had been blow away. The lower foretopsail was hanging by threads at four corners. No shore boat was visible on deck.

"Let's go below," Deveau said.

Climbing down the ladder, Deveau reached the lower deck. He began to open the cabin doors but found not a single soul. He and Wright searched through the cabins. In the captain's cabin, Deveau noted that the chronometer, sextant, ship's register, and navigation book were missing. In the mate's cabin, Wright found the logbook and log slate. In the galley, where both men converged, there was no prepared food nor was there any food or drink on the crew's table.

"I'll check the stores," Wright said.

"I'm going to check the hold," Deveau said.

Wright found a six-month supply of food and water; Deveau a strong odor of alcohol and almost four feet of water in the hold. He began to pump the hold dry, and that was where Wright found him a few moments later.

"No one aboard," Deveau said, "but no major problems, save this water."

"I don't know if you noticed it earlier when we were on deck," Wright said, "but the binnacle was knocked loose and the compass destroyed."

"That is most odd," Deveau agreed. "Let's pump out the hold, then report back to Mr. Moorhouse."

After lowering the remaining sails and tossing out the sea anchor, they did.

"Sir," Deveau reported, "she's a ghost ship."

He and Wright had just explained what they had found, and now Moorhouse was puffing on his pipe and thinking. Less than a hundred yards away, *Mary Celeste*, the ship without a crew, sat awaiting a decision.

"My first duty is to my ship and cargo," Moorhouse said slowly.

"I understand," Deveau said, "and the choice is yours. However, if you give me two seamen and some food, I think we can make Gibraltar and claim salvage rights."

"Do you have your own navigation tools?"

Deveau had been a commanding captain in the past.

"Yes, sir," Deveau said. "If you could spare a

barometer, watch, another compass, and some food, I think we can make port."

Sparing three men from *Dei Gratia* would leave Moorhouse seriously shorthanded.

"Let's try it," Moorhouse said at last, "but if we run into trouble we cast *Mary Celeste* adrift, transfer your men back, and report the loss upon reaching port."

"Thank you, sir," Deveau said.

"Take Lund and Anderson," Moorhouse said. "We'll wait here until you have the ship seaworthy."

At 8:26 that evening, the hold was pumped and the spare sails set in place. They set off for the six-hundred-mile journey to Gibraltar just as the moon rose over the horizon. A fool's moon lit the ghostly journey.

The weather stayed fair until the Straits of Gibraltar. Then, for the first time since taking command of *Mary Celeste*, Deveau lost sight of *Dei Gratia* in the rough seas. On Friday the thirteenth, nine days since the ghost ship had first been spotted, Deveau entered the port of Gibraltar. *Dei Gratia* was already there.

"HERE'S YOUR CHANGE," the telegraph clerk said to Captain Moorhouse.

On Saturday the fourteenth of December, the disaster clerk at the New York offices of Atlantic Mutual Insurance Company received the following cablegram from Gibraltar:

FOUND FOURTH AND BROUGHT HERE "MARY CELESTE." ABANDONED SEAWORTHY. ADMIRALTY IMPOST. NOTIFY ALL PARTIES TELEGRAPH OFFER OF SALVAGE. MOORHOUSE.

The cable was the first notice in the United States that something had gone terribly wrong on *Mary Celeste*.

Of its crew and passengers, nothing would ever be found. The *Mary Celeste* itself would be put back into service, but a little over twelve years later, on January 3, 1885, the ship would be wrecked on the Reefs of the Rochelais near Miragoane, Haiti.

And while the ship was gone, the legend continued to grow.

II

Paradise Gone

2001

THE TALE OF THE *MARY CELESTE* MAKES THE hair rise on the nape of the neck. She is enshrined as the most famous ghost ship in the history of the sea. There are other accounts of ships being found abandoned, their crews having vanished, but none has the fascination and the intrigue that fire the imagination like *Mary Celeste*. She still wears the crown of haunted ships.

I was drawn into her web at least twenty years ago when I asked Bob Fleming, NUMA's researcher in Washington, D.C., to probe the archives for her ultimate end. Had she sunk during a storm while on a voyage, or had she simply outlived her usefulness and ended up a derelict in the mudflats of some port's backwater, along with so many of her sister ships? Only a few records, and fewer yet of more than a hundred books written since her tragedy, held the answer.

Mary Celeste was sailed for another twelve years and

two months after being abandoned in the Azores in 1872. During this time, she went through a number of different owners. She set sail on her final passage from New York to Port-au-Prince, Haiti, in December of 1884, under the command of Captain Gilman Parker of Winthrop, Massachusetts. On January 3, 1885, she was sailing on a southeasterly course through a narrow channel between the Haitian southern peninsula and Gonâve Island. The sky was empty of clouds, and the seas no higher than a man's knee.

Rising ominously in the middle of the channel was Rochelais Reef, a small rocky mountain rising from the seafloor, its peak capped with thick coral. The reef was plainly marked on the chart and sharply visible to the helmsman. He set a new course around the reef and was beginning to turn the spokes of the wheel when Captain Parker gripped him roughly by the arm.

"Belay that! Stay on course."

"But, sir, we'll run onto the reef for sure," protested the helmsman.

"Damn you!" Parker snapped. "Do as you're ordered."

Knowing the ship was headed for certain disaster, the helmsman, out of fear of punishment, steered for the reef dead ahead. At high tide, the menacing Rochelais Reef barely rose above the surface of the water, as the once-beautiful ship came closer to what would be her grave. The helmsman gave the captain one last desperate look, but Parker remained resolute and nodded straight ahead where the waves were rolling over the reef.

Mary Celeste struck dead center of Rochelais Reef. Her keel and hull planking cut a gouge through the coral, but the sharp spines cut through her copper-sheathed bottom and ripped into her bowels, sending tons of water inside her lower decks. Her bow drove up onto the reef as her stern settled beneath the water. In her death throes, *Mary Celeste* groaned horribly, as her hull and timbers were crushed by her momentum into the unyielding coral. At last, the agonized sounds died across the water and the ship became silent.

Calmly, Captain Parker sent his crew into the boats and ordered them to row to the nearby port of Miragoane, Haiti, not more than twelve miles to the south. Unfortunately for Captain Parker, *Mary Celeste* did not immediately sink. It would not be long before an inspection of the wrecked hulk and its cargo revealed that it carried little more than fish and rubber shoes, which were not the expensive cargo listed in the manifest. The vessel, as it turned out, was exorbitantly insured to the tune of $25,000, far above the value of the ship and its cargo. Today, we call it an insurance scam. Back then, it was referred to as barratry, and was an offense punishable under U.S. law and carried the death penalty.

It seemed that Parker's bad luck had no end. Kingman Putnam, a New York surveyor, happened to be in Haiti at the time and was hired by the insurance underwriters to conduct an examination. His examination of the waterlogged cargo was instrumental in Parker's arrest when he returned to New York. Parker was tried in court, but the jury hung, and another trial was immediately ordered by the court. True to form, Parker died before a new trial could be held.

Mary Celeste soon disappeared into the coral that grew over her timbers and buried her decks. Despite her previous notoriety, she died neglected and forgotten, her drama played out on a barren reef in Haiti, perhaps in revenge by the ghosts of her vanished crew.

ARMED WITH enough research data to give it a good shot, I began making plans to charter a boat and sail to Rochelais Reef. I contacted Mr. Mark Sheldon, who had purchased my favorite old search boat, *Arvor III*. This was the vessel I had sailed on when searching for the *Bonhomme Richard* in 1980. I charted her again in 1984, when my team and I encountered all sorts of wild adventures in the North Sea, finding sixteen shipwrecks while losing a war of words with the French navy in Cherbourg, France, who refused to allow us to search for the Confederate raider *Alabama*.

I had planned to meet the boat in Kingston, Jamaica, and then run across the Jamaica Channel and around Cape Dame Marie to Rochelais Reef, about a two-day trip. Unfortunately, Sheldon became ill and was not available for charter until the following year.

John Davis of ECO-NOVA Productions then stepped in and offered to set up an expedition to conduct the search. Since John and his team are from Nova Scotia and *Mary Celeste* was built in Nova Scotia, they had a strong incentive to find the wreck. They were also enthusiastic about making a *Sea Hunters* documentary about the ship.

In April of 2001, John set up the logistics, chartered a boat, and sent me round-trip airline tickets to Haiti. I arrived in Fort Lauderdale in the evening and was mildly surprised to see no one there to meet me. I hailed a shuttle van and headed for the Sheraton Hotel, then walked alone into the lobby, to the surprise of Davis. He had sent a friend to meet me, who had somehow missed picking me out of the deplaning crowd.

With a face like mine, I wondered how I could be lost in the crowd. I began to wonder if this was the start of an ordeal. I was sure my guardian angel had gone on vacation and an evil demon taken his place, especially when I found I'd forgotten my passport. How's that for dementia?

John didn't give it a thought. "You'll be all right," he said cheerfully. "The Haitians won't care."

Images of being thrown into a Haitian jail streamed through my mind. I called my wife, Barbara, and asked her to send the passport through the airline's courier service. Just to play it safe, she faxed the pertinent pages to the hotel, at least so I had some kind of identification for Haitian immigration if for some reason the passport did not arrive.

Naturally, the airplane with my passport was late, which wasn't too disastrous. I still had almost an hour before our scheduled departure. Exotic Lynx Airlines, our air carrier to Haiti, had other plans. Unexpectedly, the clerk at the counter announced that because all passengers were present, the plane would be taking off an hour early. I do believe Lynx belongs in the *Guinness Book of World Records*. When I bemoaned my lack of passport, the clerk laughed it off and said, "They won't care."

Where had I heard *that* before?

Somehow I didn't relish the idea of entering into a third world country that had revolutionaries stalking the hills, without proper credentials. Left with no choice, I arranged with Craig Dirgo, who was living in

Fort Lauderdale at the time, to pick up my passport when it finally arrived.

The flight was on a nineteen-passenger DeHavilland prop plane. It was uneventful except for a huge black man who resembled Mike Tyson seated in back of me. He was terrified of flying and clutched the back of my seat every time we hit turbulence. As I looked down on the islands surrounded by turquoise waters, I had dreams of arriving at a sun-drenched tropical paradise with local natives playing marimbas and steel drums while passing around piña coladas. The bubble was burst as the plane touched down at a weed-infested airstrip and I was jolted back to reality. There was no terminal, only a bunch of dilapidated shacks strung around a dusty parking lot filled with battered old French and Japanese autos.

We disembarked and headed for the immigration shack. Thankfully, my perceptive eye noted that my suitcase and John's bag had been stowed in the nose section of the plane when we left Fort Lauderdale. I turned and saw that the Haitian baggage handler, after removing the passengers' luggage from the rear of the plane, was pushing his load, minus our bags, on a cart across the field. With John following, I returned to the airplane, unlatched the locks on the nose section, lifted it up, and removed our bags. No one interfered. If we hadn't snagged our luggage from the plane's nose, they'd have been on their way back to Fort Lauderdale in another twenty minutes.

I smiled my best smile, and the immigration official graciously stamped my fax copy passport and waved me through.

"See," said Davis, "didn't I tell you? A piece of cake."

"Now the trick is to get out," I muttered, wondering what I was getting myself into.

Davis had arranged for us to stay at the Cormier Plage Hotel, a tropical paradise in a cove farther up the coast not far from the border with the Dominican Republic. The resort is owned by Jean Claude and Kathy Dicquemare, who had lived in Haiti over twenty-five years. The plan was for Davis and me to stay overnight until the boat containing the rest of the team arrived from Fort Lauderdale by sea. After clearing customs, we were met by Jean Claude's nephew, whose name unfortunately escapes me. We came out into a mob scene stomping up a cloud of dust. There were hundreds of Haitians milling about the airport—doing what, I have no idea.

We were stormed by little boys demanding a dollar. Considering the poverty of the nation, these kids don't mess around. In most countries I've visited, the little beggar boys and girls usually ask for coins.

After throwing our bags in the back of a little Honda SUV, we drove through the port city of Cape Haitian. I've seen squalor before, but nothing I've ever seen compared to this. The worst slums in the hills above Rio de Janeiro looked like Beverly Hills compared to this place. The streets were in total disrepair, with battered old cars, some moving, some parked and stripped, cluttering the landscape. Buildings were crumbling like they were rotting from within. Any place else, they would have been condemned years before. Mobs of people wandered the streets and sidewalks, as if searching for something that didn't exist. We passed a huge ten-acre dump, where hordes of people were shoveling garbage and trash into plastic bags and carting it home in wheelbarrows. It was not a pretty sight.

We finally left the self-destructing town and traveled over the mountain on a road that had not been graded in ten years—no, make that twenty. We passed shanties with scrawny chickens pecking barren ground, long lines of people at a single water faucet, waiting to fill their plastic jugs, staring at us as if we'd just flown down from the moon. At seeing their thin bodies, I began to feel self-conscious about being twenty pounds overweight.

The potholes looked like the size of meteor craters, and the ruts were as deep as the trenches in World War I. Yet the landscape was scenic and quite beautiful. The few areas on the mountain where the trees had not been cut down were quite picturesque. I have found it easy to imagine Haiti as a beautiful nation in the years that have passed.

We finally dropped down into a delightful cove with hundreds of palm trees. Village shacks lined one side of the road, and the children were playing happily while their mothers washed clothes in a stream flowing down from the mountains. Jean Claude's nephew turned the truck through the gate of the resort and we met Jean Claude and Kathy, a quiet lady who obviously ran the show behind the scenes. Jean Claude is a genuine character—someone that everyone should have as a friend. Though we were both pushing seventy, he was twice as active as I was. He dove at least once every day, and often two or three times. He kept a record that revealed he had already slipped beneath the waves 165 times. The term *half man/half fish* applied to Jean Claude.

The hotel was very charming, with neatly cut lawns, a long sandy beach, and white buildings with a restaurant and a bar under a beautifully crafted thatched roof of palm fronds. The only drawback is that the coral comes up to within a few feet of the beach, and though it makes for great snorkeling, you'd scrape your chest off if you tried to swim in it. The food was gourmet quality. Seven different lobster dishes cooked in different ways and tinged in exotic sauces were only a small part of the menu. Then on to the bar for after-dinner drinks and hours of telling tales of shipwrecks and the people who search for them.

The boat showed up the next day. Owned by Allan Gardner of Highland Beach, Florida, *Ella Warley II* is a fifty-four-foot steel-hulled vessel specially designed by Allan for underwater research. She carries the latest dive and detection gear with state-of-the-art electronics. Allan is a very successful businessman who owns a large computer technology company. When not directing his corporate empire, he spends his time searching for shipwrecks in the Caribbean. My kind of guy.

Allan is a truly nice guy with the patience of Job who smiles constantly and, after a few shots of scotch, laughs continuously. Joining him on the voyage from Fort Lauderdale was the team from ECO-NOVA, including Mike Fletcher, master diver, and underwater photographers Robert Guertin and Lawrence Taylor—all friendly and good-hearted guys with enough *esprit de corps* to turn a grueling expedition into a proud moment of achievement and success.

John and I boarded a boat from a dock in a lagoon used by Carnival Cruise Lines ships to send their passengers to a tropical cove to enjoy a day of sun and surf. Like Allan, Jean Claude generously gave his time to come along, because he knew Haiti and could converse with the natives in Creole—a handy arrangement, as it turned out.

The voyage to Rochelais Reef began early the next morning. The seas were very rough, but I fortified myself with a bottle of Porfido tequila I had brought along for just such an occasion. Though a fairly stable boat, *Ella Warley II* rolled with the punches. With her flat bottom, she makes the perfect dive platform for underwater survey, but she's not exactly what you'd call a luxury yacht. She was built for a purpose without the niceties of plush furnishings, a deep keel, or stabilizers. Plus she suffered from heads that always clogged when you flushed them.

Sleeping accommodations were austere. Allan, as owner, had the only stateroom. Two of the team slept in bunks in the wheelhouse. Two slept on the deck outside. Jean Claude and I shared the main cabin, me on a small foldout couch, he on the bench of the dining table.

We were both outcasts from the others because we snored. Jean Claude began from ten to two, while I took up the trumpet calls from two to six. Now I know what my poor wife goes through.

But our seven-man crew was tough. No one ever suffered seasickness or complained, except me.

We anchored for the night on the northwest tip of Haiti. The next morning, we sailed around Gonâve Island and reached Rochelais Reef by midmorning. As we approached, I was peering through binoculars into the distance where the reef was supposed to rise. An image materialized, and I adjusted the focus.

I turned to Allan and John and said, "If I didn't know better, I'd say there is a village with huts sitting on the reef."

Forty-five minutes later, we reached Rochelais Reef and anchored a hundred yards offshore. This place was an anthropologist's dream. The story is that about eighty years ago, two brothers decided to take up residence on the reef to hunt conch. Over the decades, more native Haitians moved onto the reef, until now it is an island four feet above the water, built from more than a million conch shells. There are about fifty shacks erected from every scrap of flotsam you can imagine. We estimated the population at about two hundred. There wasn't a tree or a bush to be seen. The sun beat down unmercifully on the conch-shell landscape. The nearest land was twelve miles away, and all the food and water had to be brought in by dugout canoes. We could not believe human beings could survive in such harsh conditions, much less spend their entire lives there.

John and his film crew, along with Jean Claude, took the thirteen-foot Boston Whaler over to the man-made island sitting atop the shallow reef. Naturally, the natives were curious about our presence. Jean Claude did not tell them we were looking for a shipwreck. They might have mistaken our intent and thought we were after treasure, which could have caused problems. He simply told them we were making a movie and pacified them about our intrusion by giving them ten gallons of gas for their outboard motors and a case of Coca-Cola.

We had studied the oldest accurate chart of the reef dating to 1910 and laid it over a modern chart. The reef had not changed. According to both charts, there was a pinnacle labeled "Vandalia Rock" on the southern end of the reef, but the natives assured us that no such rock existed. This would cause extra time in research later, exploring the possibility that a ship named *Vandalia* had also grounded on the reef.

The wind picked up, and Allan took the boat into a small bay on Gonâve Island, where we settled in for the night. With an early start the next morning, Allan dropped his cesium marine magnetometer over the side and began circling the reef for any magnetic anomalies. From fifty yards offshore, only one ten-gamma reading showed on his computer monitor. It came from the dead center of Rochelais Reef, where *Mary Celeste* was reported to have crushed her hull on the coral. The site also perfectly matched the direction a ship sailing from the southwest would have met the reef.

My demon must have taken a break.

Mike Fletcher suited up and dropped over the side, followed by Robert Guertin with his underwater video camera. The rest of us set on the stern of the boat, soaking up the tropical breeze, wondering if Mike had found anything. Half an hour later, he returned to the boat and threw some copper sheathing, ballast rocks, and old wood with brass spikes driven through them onto the deck.

We had a shipwreck right where *Mary Celeste* was supposed to lie. But without finding the bell, which was no doubt salvaged, with the ship's name in raised letters in bronze or inscribed ceramics, or some other artifact to identify her, we could only speculate. Everyone dove and retrieved what pitifully few artifacts we could find. The coral was some of the most beautiful I've seen in fifty years of diving, but I wished I weren't there. What remained of the ship's timbers was deeply buried in the calcareous growth that had rapidly buried the ship. After 116 years, the ship was entombed in an impenetrable burial shroud.

We found part of the anchor chain and an anchor. I tried to remove a bar from the coral, but it was stuck fast. Jean Claude and Mike brought up enough wood to fill a fair-sized bucket. And we removed some loose artifacts that were embedded in the sand. Every item was videotaped in position, tagged, and catalogued. Once the team returned home, the wood would be sent to laboratories to determine a date and source. It's incredible how science and technology can tell you how old the wood is within years, as well as what part of the world it originally came from.

The ballast stones would also show characteristic mineralogy and texture that can identify the location from which they were extracted. They had to come from either the Palisades above the Hudson River, when *Mary Celeste* was rebuilt during the summer of 1872 in New York, or the mountains or shores of Nova Scotia, where she was originally constructed and then launched under the name *Amazon*. The brass spikes might give only an approximate age, but a clue might come from the copper sheathing. Whatever the case, it would take time to find the answers we sought.

Satisfied we could do no more, the anchor was pulled, and we bid a fond farewell to Rochelais Reef, now affectionately known as Conch Island, then set a course back to the Cormier Plage Hotel. We had a few rough hours battling choppy seas, but it actually became relaxing after a while. I was transfixed, staring at the color of the water in this part of the Caribbean. It was not the blue-green turquoise of shallow water around the reefs and islands. This was deep water, the fathometer showing three thousand feet to the bottom, and the color was a deep violet, almost purple.

Two days later, we docked near the hotel, amused at having the land seeming to sway around us after seven days without stepping foot off the boat. Everyone relaxed on the beach and in the hotel bar and talked long into the night about what we had found. The following morning, the whole team departed for Fort Lauderdale by boat while I made arrangements to fly out later that afternoon. We said our good-byes and I took a shower, packed my bags, and breathed a sigh of relief that I was escaping Haiti without being bitten by a ring-necked fuzzwort or infected with Haitian jungle fever.

I sallied forth, expecting a car to carry me to the airport, but the local police thought Jean Claude had failed to pay his license fee and confiscated his Land Rover. I was pointed to a battered, dust-laden little Nissan pickup.

Any port in a storm.

One of the workers at Jean Claude's hotel drove me over the obstacle course road to Cape Haitian, picking up hitchhikers along the way and then throwing them all around the bed of the truck before they would pound on the roof to be let out. Once we reached the city, I noticed it was the same filthy mess, with nonexistent pavement, traffic surging nowhere, and pollution that would have sent an environmentalist into cardiac arrest. My only apprehension now was whether my fax passport would get me passed through immigration.

We arrived at the Lynx Airlines boarding shack. If I've ever made a wise move in my life, it was when I told the driver to wait just in case the flight was canceled. I entered the shack, counting the minutes until I would be in the wild blue yonder to the U.S. of A.

"You're too late," said the attendant behind a counter I didn't dare lean on or touch with my bare hands.

"What do you mean I'm late?" I replied indignantly, naively thinking she was kidding me. I pointed at the time printed on my ticket. "This says departure time is twelve-thirty. It is now only eleven-twenty. I have an hour and ten minutes."

She glanced at the ticket and shrugged. "That's Miami time."

"You don't print your tickets with local arrival or departure time?" I was beginning to panic.

"No, you should have been here an hour ago. Now it's too late. The plane is taking off in five minutes."

"Let me talk to the pilots," I pleaded in desperation.

She nodded and accompanied me out through a weed-covered field to the airplane, where the pilots were standing with hands in their pockets. I pleaded my case to no avail.

The chief pilot shrugged. "You'll never get through immigration in time."

"Let me try?" I begged.

Then the pilot and copilot grinned like the Artful Dodger and Oliver, after having adroitly picked a pocket. "Not a chance. We're about to take off."

There I stood, like a kid who'd had his bicycle stolen. My only salvation came from the airline attendant, who promised me a seat on the next day's flight. "You get here two hours early," she admonished me. "You hear?"

I heard.

Never in my life have I felt so miserable. Thank God I had the foresight to ask the driver to wait for me. If he had driven off and left me stranded in the mob at the airport, I'd probably have been torn limb from limb for my Nike sneakers.

Now it was time for another ride through the wretchedness and over the road to hell. I felt like Roy Scheider transporting nitroglycerin through the jungles in the movie *Wages of Fear*. Distress turned into rage at having been abandoned in the poorest country in the Western Hemisphere. If I had known that while I was in Haiti an American businessman had been shot and killed and two others taken hostage, I would have really been depressed.

Back to my room, where I lay in bed that afternoon, staring at the whirling blades of the overhead fans. A lonely meal, and then I headed for the bar, where I was lucky enough to join the company of some young Americans who worked for Carnival Cruise Lines over in the cove where the big ships docked. I enjoyed the conversation and several beers before retiring for the night with visions of my own bed dancing in my head.

No fooling around this time. I hauled the driver, who spoke almost no English, to the truck and gestured at the steering wheel. He got the drift from the devil expression on my face. By now you know the routine to reach the airport. This time, however, there was no stopping and picking up hitchhikers. If the driver even thought about stopping, I stomped my foot on his foot and mashed the gas pedal to the floor. We jolted over the road like a race car in an endurance rally.

By now, with lots of practice, I was immune to the

misery and poverty. Watching people taking home garbage no longer offended me. That was simply their life and the way they had to live it. Perhaps someday, when their internal struggles are over, the country will return to the lovely paradise it once was.

I burst into the Lynx shack two hours early. The attendant smiled and gave me a boarding pass. One hurdle down, immigration to go. There I sat in an unventilated shack in the middle of the day with eighteen Haitians, mostly women and children. They do like perfume and cologne. I passed the time reading a book on the battle of Gettysburg and realized I didn't have it so bad after all.

The scary part was coming up. I had been told the night before that if you didn't have a valid passport, the airline pilots would not allow you to board. It seems they're none too happy if American immigration officials won't let you into the country. Not only were they liable for a hefty fine, but they had to transport you back to Haiti at their expense. I began to hope that being a hotshot author might carry an ounce of weight.

At twelve noon on the dot, the plane's engines could be heard through the cracks in the walls as it landed and taxied toward the shack. After a few minutes, a blond-haired pilot opened the door and stepped into the waiting room. He walked right up to me and handed me an envelope.

"I hope to enjoy your book," he said, smiling.

I stared at the envelope and looked up questioningly. "Book?"

"Yes, your friend gave me one of your books in Fort Lauderdale. He figured I'd know you by the author's photo on the book jacket."

Craig Dirgo, bless his heart, had driven to the airport and given my passport to the pilot to give to me. The sun burst through the clouds. Then came the sound of trumpets, a drumroll, and harp music. Home was just over the horizon at last.

Haitian immigration whisked me through, and I ran, not walked, out to the airplane. Then there was a wait, while an official riffled through every passenger's luggage. I'm sure he wished he had a different job when it came to my bag. It was filled with two-week-old laundry. We guys are like that. Why do laundry when you have someone waiting to do it at home?

I don't know if I was ever happier than when the wheels left the ground. For the next hour, I listened to the beat of the engines, making sure they were hitting on all cylinders. I couldn't conceive of a mechanical problem that would force us to return to the bedlam of Cape Haitian.

After a short hop, we landed on Caicos Island to refuel and were asked to leave the airplane and wait in the terminal as a safety precaution. Simple Simon Cussler, of course, walks through the wrong door into the heart of the terminal, finds the bar, and has a cold beer. Figuring it's time to go back, I walked toward the exit door and was promptly stopped by a security guard the size of a redwood tree.

"Can't go out there," he said sternly.

"I have to get back to my airplane."

"You'll have to go through immigration and customs."

The bile rose in my throat. Things just couldn't go wrong now. Not after I'd been over the streets and roads of hell. My demon was a stubborn rascal. I was considering making a break for it, when the blond pilot walked by. A few words and he talked the guard into letting me accompany him to the plane. I wondered if my ordeal would ever end.

I feel sorry for the people who never know the feeling of joy and bliss that comes from returning to the United States. You truly have to travel outside our borders to appreciate the advantages we all too often take for granted. We landed, and I smiled.

Slapping my passport down with glee at the immigration booth, I was given a green light. "Welcome back to the United States, Mr. Cussler," said the agent, with a friendly smile. "I read all your books."

It sure was nice to be home.

Upon reaching the lobby of the terminal, I was surprised to see no Craig. A German like me, he prides himself on following schedules. I was sure he was supposed to meet me. I was looking around for a telephone when he strolled by, sipping a cup of coffee. He looked at me queerly.

"You're an hour early," he said, taking a sip.

I actually hugged him, I was so glad to see someone I knew.

"Lynx Air has a fetish for departing and arriving early," I explained.

Craig stared at me. "Good God, boss," he said slowly, "you look like you've seen a ghost. What in the hell did they do to you?"

"I'll explain it to you someday," I said. "Right now, why don't you take me to the hotel?"

Craig grabbed my bags and started walking to his car. "We'll go get you checked in," he said slyly, "then there's a Haitian restaurant I've been wanting to try—they say the jerked goat is tasty."

After checking into the hotel, we went to a good old American steak house. Craig had a sirloin, I had a chopped steak. Chopped steak just like my mother used to make.

In a parting shot, before my guardian angel returned, the demon took away my first-class seat on the flight to Phoenix because I was a day late. I couldn't have cared less. I was finally going home to my lovely wife and adobe home. That was all that mattered. Besides, coach was only partially full, and I had three seats to myself.

We may never be able to prove 100 percent that the shipwreck we found was *Mary Celeste*. In a court of law, our evidence would be labeled circumstantial. Still, we are confident the shipwreck found in the coral is she, for a number of reasons.

Alan Guffman of Geomarine Associates in Nova Scotia coordinated the scientific testing of the wood and ballast stones. The process of rock geochemistry and radiometric dating is complicated, but the results proved that the ballast showed the characteristic mineralogy and texture of the North Mountains basalt of Nova Scotia.

The wood was identified as southern pine, often used in shipbuilding in New York, where *Mary Celeste* was rebuilt and enlarged. Some was white pine, which comes from the northeast United States and Canada. One piece of wood made everyone happy. It was yellow birch, which comes from the maritime provinces, including Nova Scotia.

It was all coming together.

James Delgado, noted marine archaeologist and

director of the Vancouver Maritime Museum, identified the copper sheathing as Muntz metal, a yellow alloy of three parts copper, two parts zinc, a substance that came into general use as hull protection against shipworms after 1860.

We were getting closer.

While the artifacts were being analyzed, I tackled the job of researching other potential wrecks that might have run onto the coral of Rochelais Reef. We had to prove we hadn't found the wrong wreck. I hired researchers here and in Europe to scour the archives. Insurance companies cooperated, particularly Lloyd's of London. No stone was left unturned. No records of shipwrecks were ignored. The results came back positive.

A ship named *Vandalia* had indeed met her end in Haiti a hundred years ago. But she had run aground at Port-de-Paix, a bay sixty miles from Rochelais Reef, and she was later pulled off and scrapped. The only other wreck that was recorded in the same time zone was a steamship that burned in the port of Miragoane twelve miles away. The extensive research project proved conclusively that *Mary Celeste* was the only ship known to have run aground on Rochelais Reef and stayed there.

Allan Gardner, John Davis and his ECO-NOVA team, and I could now say with a great measure of confidence that the grave of *Mary Celeste* had been found. The ghost ship's story has been drawn to a fitting end.

PART EIGHT
The Steamboat *General Slocum*

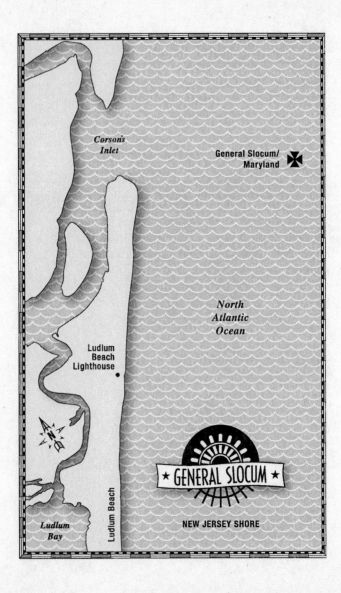

I

Never Again

1904

"THESE DAMN CORPORATIONS," PRESIDENT Theodore Roosevelt thundered, "are just a means of hiding."

Attorney General Philander Knox contentedly puffed on his pipe while Roosevelt raged. He was used to the president's mercurial temperament—in time he would calm and come to the point.

"They have all the benefits of man without the guidance of a conscience," Roosevelt noted. "Trusts and corporations—they'll bring this country down."

Knox stared at the president. He was not a large man—five feet nine, 165 pounds—but he carried himself like a giant. At this instant, his face was flushed with anger, and the eyes behind his wire-framed spectacles were blazing. Roosevelt's hair was dark and short and formed a small point near the center of his forehead. His hand was tugging the right side of his bushy mustache.

"I agree, sir," Knox said.

"The Knickerbocker Steamboat Company," Roosevelt said, "are just organized murderers."

"Uh-huh," Knox said.

"I want you and the secretary of commerce and labor to travel up to New York," Roosevelt said, "and find the parties responsible for this disaster—then prosecute them."

Knox glanced at the president. The color was seeping from his cheeks as he calmed down. He watched as Roosevelt sipped from a glass of water.

"Mr. President," Knox said evenly, "I think that would fall under New York State jurisdiction."

Roosevelt spit a partial mouthful of water across the desk. "We are the federal government," he said loudly. "We're in charge here."

"Very good," Knox said, rising from his seat in the Oval Office. "I'll contact the secretary and make arrangements to leave tomorrow."

"Philander?" Roosevelt said, as the attorney general opened the door to the office.

"Yes, sir," Knox said easily.

"Knock some heads up there for me," Roosevelt said, smiling.

"As you wish, sir," Knox said.

June 15, 1904, the Prior Day

Captain William Van Schaick leaned against the chart desk and scratched the date into *General Slocum*'s log. Thursday came with overcast skies and light rain, with the temperature hovering around eighty degrees.

Toward Long Island, Van Schaick noticed the sun peering from the clouds—once the haze burned off, it should be a fine day.

Van Schaick was tall and lanky, six feet tall, 170 pounds. His blue uniform was clean and pressed but faded some. The gold braid around his armpits was showing signs of tarnish. The fresh white flower stuck in his lapel appeared slightly out of place—like a new saddle on an aged horse.

His employer, the Knickerbocker Steamboat Company, continued to cut costs, and lately Van Schaick had been thinking more and more about transferring to another line. Few, if any, of his deckhands had experience—in fact, their primary skill seemed to be the ability to work for slave wages—and *General Slocum* itself needed work that the company seemed unwilling or unable to afford.

Turning on his heel to glance from the window, Van Schaick felt a softness in the deck that signified rot. He turned back and noted this in the log.

REVEREND GEORGE HAAS stood on the Third Street Pier and stared up at the ship. The graceful twin-decked excursion boat was finished in white both above and below and seemed easily capable of carrying the thousand plus passengers that had signed up for the trip. As pastor of St. Mark's Lutheran Church, Haas presided over a congregation of mainly German immigrants that numbered nearly two thousand. Today was to be an outing for the Sunday school students and whatever parents could attend. The trip was scheduled to take them from the Third Street Pier to Locust Grove on Long Island for a day of picnicking and fun.

Haas smiled as the band began to play Martin Luther's "A Mighty Fortress Is Our God."

Haas had no way to know the horror he would soon experience.

THIRTEEN-YEAR-OLD John Tischner stared at the coins in his hand as he stood in the line at the refreshment stand aboard ship. The fried clams smelled good, but Tischner's mother had packed him a tin pail with a pair of liverwurst-and-onion sandwiches for the noon meal along with a slice of chocolate cake for dessert. The pulled taffy held his interest for a time, but by the time he reached the head of the line, he had settled on a scoop of strawberry ice cream. It was a strange choice at 9:25 in the morning, but it was a day of celebration. He handed the man at the counter a few coins, then received his change and the ice cream. Enough for another scoop on the return trip.

Things were looking up.

VAN SCHAICK ORDERED the whistle to blow, signaling five minutes until they shoved off, then called down to the engine room to order steam. *General Slocum* was built in Brooklyn in 1891 and measured 263 feet with a 38-foot beam.

Powered by a single vertical-beam engine constructed by W. A. Fletcher Company, she was supplied steam by a pair of boilers fueled with coal. A pair of sidewheel paddles with the name of the vessel in ornamental letters on the outside propelled her. Twin stacks vented the smoke into the air. Strung along the upper deck on each side were a half-dozen lifeboats on davits. The paint on the lifeboats was chipped and flaking. Originally finished with a white hull and a hardwood finish on the upper decks, the ship had been repainted with a white-on-white motif that was now showing stains from hard use. Still, all in all, she was a graceful vessel.

"HURRY," HENRY IDA said to his sweetheart, Amelia Swartz, "they're leaving."

Swartz increased her pace along the pier, but it was difficult—her dress boots were laced tight, and the boned corset pinching her waist made deep breaths almost impossible. Twirling her parasol, she made her way to the gangplank. Ida was overdressed for summer, but he had little choice—he owned only two suits, both wool. His only concession to the heat had been to leave the vest at home. Pushing the straw boater back on his forehead, he switched the wicker lunch hamper to his other hand and started up the ramp. In three minutes, *General Slocum* would pull from the pier. Forging through the crowd, he found a spot for them on deck.

DARRELL MILLET pried the top off a wooden barrel containing glasses packed in straw. The head steward needed the glassware at the aft refreshment stand immediately. Filling his fingers with the glasses, he made his way aft. Six trips later, the barrel was empty, and he dragged it to the forward storeroom. Finding a spot amid the paint pots and oil lamps, he balanced it on a couple of overturned pails, then shut the door. The straw was dry and smelled of the prairie.

Captain Van Schaick blew the whistle one last time, then ordered the gangplank retracted. Calling down to the engine room for steam, he placed the drives in forward and steered *General Slocum* from the pier. More than one thousand passengers were now under his care. The band began to play "Nearer My God to Thee."

PORTER WALTER PAYNE entered the crowded storeroom. Making his way to a workbench, he began to fill a pair of oil lamps. Suddenly the ship rolled from side to side from the wake of a passing barge. Payne spilled some of the fuel onto the floor. After finishing the fueling, he twisted the metal caps back on the lamps. Carrying them over near the door, he paused to light a match out of the wind. Touching the match to the wicks, he tossed the match over his shoulder, then adjusted the flames. With a lit lamp in each hand, he walked onto the deck, then aft.

Paint fumes and spilled fuel were the recipe for disaster. The burning ember from the tossed match was little more than the size of a pencil lead, but it was enough. The fumes from the paint hung low over the floor, mixing with the smell from the spilled fuel. The gas ignited with a fuzzy blue flame. At just that instant, *General Slocum* hit the second set of wakes from the barge. As the ship rocked from side to side, the precariously placed barrel tipped forward and spilled the straw into the almost extinguished fire. Red and yellow points of fire streaked skyward.

CAPTAIN VAN SCHAICK was staring forward when he saw a puff of smoke from a porthole in the forward storeroom.

"Fire," he shouted.

Then he ordered his second in command, Marcus Anthony, to round up a few sailors to man the hoses.

They were five minutes from Hell's Gate.

Reverend Haas was ladling clam chowder into bowls for his young parishioners when a sailor ran past, tugging a rubber fire hose. He prayed the man was just going forward to wash the deck, but deep in his heart he knew different. Turning his head from side to side, he tried to locate where the life jackets were stored.

"My command for an experienced sailor," Van Schaick shouted.

His employer had saddled him with a crew consisting of untrained day laborers and general miscreants, and it was little wonder. The economy was in high gear, and unemployment was at its lowest level in twenty years. To compound the problem, just two months before, the United States had taken possession of Panama, and many able-bodied seamen had headed south for the higher wages. Workers were hard to come by, and the Knickerbocker Steamboat Company was not noted for paying high wages. Van Schaick looked down to the deck—it was chaos. He watched as one of his deckhands strapped on a life vest and jumped over the side.

"Turn on the water," Anthony yelled back.

The forward storeroom was completely ablaze. At that precise instant, the cans of paint exploded and blew the door to splinters. Deckhand Brad Creighton twisted the brass knob that fed water from the pumps in the lower hold to the fire hoses. He watched as the rubber hose expanded and filled. Halfway down the deck, along the outer walkway, the aged rubber burst. The broken end of the hose began to flail around the deck like the body of a severed snake.

Henry Ida broke the rusted lock off the locker

containing the life jackets and began to hand them out to the passengers. The canvas on the vests was old and moth-eaten, and several of the jackets burst open as soon as he grabbed them. Rotted cork littered the floor. Helping Amelia into a jacket, Ida tried to tie the straps to hold it tight. The straps broke off in his hands.

"If we have to go into the water," Ida shouted amid the growing pandemonium, "you will have to hold the vest on."

Amelia Swartz nodded. Her face plainly showed the fear she was feeling.

"If we become separated," Ida said, "just swim for shore. I'll meet you there."

"Form a bucket brigade," Marcus Anthony shouted, "and hook another hose to the spigot."

This was day laborer Paul Endicott's first day on the water. His trade was that of an apprentice cobbler, but times were so good that people were purchasing new shoes instead of having the old ones repaired. His work was slow and he needed money, so he'd signed on for a day of work.

"Where are the buckets?" Endicott asked Anthony.

"Damn," Anthony said loudly, "they're in the forward storeroom."

"What should I do?" Endicott asked.

"Climb up to the pilothouse and explain our problems to the captain," Anthony said. "Ask him to make his way to shore."

It was bad, and Reverend Haas knew this. The fire had spread to the bow deck, and with the ship still moving forward, the flames were being fanned backward onto the mid and rear decks. All around him there was confusion—he watched as another hose was hooked to the spigot. This one burst only feet from the knob. The life vests Haas had been able to secure were rotted and deteriorating. Even so, with help from a few of the other adults, he strapped in the children and tried to line them up on the rear deck.

"We'll try to make North Brother Island," Van Schaick said, after Endicott's report, "and run her aground."

North Brother Island was three miles away.

"Full steam," Van Schaick shouted down to the engine room.

With smoke and embers flying from her bow, *General Slocum* raced upriver.

CAPTAIN McGOVERN was on his dredge boat *Chelsea*. He looked up as *General Slocum* steamed past at full speed, trailing smoke. He watched the decks as a mass of people ran aft. They piled up along the wooden railing until it gave way and nearly a hundred passengers were pitched into the water. Making his way down to his steam-powered launch *Mosquito*, McGovern headed to the site to try to rescue those swimming.

AT THE BATHHOUSE at 134th Street and the East River, Helmut Gilbey had just settled into a wooden Andirondack chair for a day of fresh air and sunshine. Seeing the burning steamer running upriver, he ran out to the street and flagged down the first police officer who happened past.

"There's a steamer burning on the river," he said breathlessly.

Michael O'Shaunassey looked between the buildings

and caught a glimpse of *General Slocum*. Racing down the street to the precinct house, he sounded the alarm.

The precinct house emptied as the police fanned out in search of boats.

Boats were dispatched from the Seawanhaka Boat Club and the Knickerbocker Yacht Club while the police boats of the Twelfth Street substation were readied. Within minutes, the fireboat *Zophar Mills* and the Health Department's tug *Franklin Edson* pulled from their docks and chased after the burning steamer. At the same time, two nearby ferryboats diverted from their runs to comb the waters for survivors.

VAN SCHAICK was captain of a dying ship. His crew's inexperience, combined with the shoddy fire hoses and a myriad of other problems, had proved to be *General Slocum*'s undoing. His decision to run at full speed for North Brother Island had not helped matters any—the winds had fanned the flames into a near maelstrom. Followed by two dozen boats, Van Schaick ran his command hard aground.

JOHN TISCHNER was trembling. His day of fun and frivolity had turned into a horror that his young mind could not comprehend. Tears streaked down his face as he tugged at the straps on his rotting life vest. At that instant the ship's keel struck earth, and Tischner was tossed to the deck. Peering up, he could see that the paddle wheels were still spinning wildly. Crawling through the legs of the panic-stricken adults, he made his way to where the railing had broken away and rolled into the water. As soon as the life vest met water, it became waterlogged and pulled him under.

*

THE SHOCK of running aground collapsed part of the hurricane deck, spilling nearly a hundred passengers directly into the center of the fire. Their screams grew loud as their flesh was burned from their bones. Several passengers were tossed directly atop the spinning paddle wheels, where their bodies were battered, then pulled under.

Reverend Haas managed to toss nearly eighty of the younger children into the water before a burning timber from the upper deck slammed into his shoulder and brought him to his knees. Hair on fire, he tried to roll off the deck but was sucked under by the paddle wheels.

"Amelia," Ida shouted, "Amelia."

But there was no answer.

Ida had no way to know this, but Amelia Swartz had leapt from the burning ship a mile back. At this instant, Captain McGovern on *Mosquito* was fishing her from the water, more dead than alive. Racing aft while shouting her name, Ida stepped upon a section of smoldering deck that gave way underfoot. Falling through up to his shoulders, Ida struggled to climb back out again.

Nurse Agnes Livingston paused just outside the main doors to the Municipal Hospital on North Brother Island. She watched as a man, his hat ablaze, crept from the small house at the highest point of the burning ship. The man climbed over the railing, then dived into the water. Livingston had no way to know that Captain Van Schaick had abandoned ship.

"Let's go," Dr. Todd Kacynski shouted, as he raced out of the hospital.

Livingston followed Kacynski to the shoreline. A nurse hardened by years of service, she was conditioned to blood and gore. Still, the sight of blackened and burned bodies washing up on shore sickened her. Walking a few feet away, she vomited into a bush, then tidied her white hat and headed back into the fray.

Big Jim Wade steered his tug *Easy Times* toward the burning excursion boat. What he saw was a horrific sight. The top deck had collapsed into the center of the vessel, and the additional fuel stoked the fires. Flames shot skyward with a column of dirty black smoke. The paddle wheels had stopped spinning, and several people were clutching the wooden paddles in an effort to stay clear of the flames. Wade approached along the starboard side. He could see large sections of railing that had given way under the crush of passengers, and pockets of people clustered fore and aft.

Without thought of the danger, he eased *Easy Times* alongside the burning hull.

Back in the city, a reporter with the *Tribune* called his office from police headquarters. "The excursion boat *General Slocum*, carrying a Sunday school group, is ablaze in the East River. Casualties will be high," he finished.

The *Tribune* editor arranged for photographers and reporters to be sent to the scene.

Mayor McClellan paced the floors of his office in City Hall.

"The police commissioner reports that he has sent all his available men to the scene," he said to his aide. "Make sure the fire chief is pulling out all the stops, as well."

The man started for the door.

"What's the number for City Hospital?" McClellan shouted at the retreating man.

"Gotham 621," the man shouted back.

McClellan reached for the telephone.

"This is the mayor," he shouted into the phone. "Give me the head of operations."

"Pull them across," Wade shouted to his deckhands out of the window of the pilothouse, "then send them aft."

Glancing toward the transom, Wade could see several blackened bodies floating close to his propellers. There was nothing he could do—he needed propulsion to stay close to the steamer and to be ready to back away at a moment's notice. He watched as a corpse swirled in the propellers' whirlpool, then was sucked under and shredded.

He turned back to the bow.

"Get them off there," he screamed.

Little Germany on the Lower East Side was in chaos. Relatives of the passengers on *General Slocum* jammed the elevated train platforms from Fourteenth Street to First Street in an effort to board an uptown train. Rumors ran through the crowd as the tension grew. Outside St. Mark's Church, a crowd grew large. Parents with tearstained faces awaited word of a miracle that would never come.

The captain of *Zophar Mills* was directing a stream of water at the burning center of *General Slocum*. The visible flames were gone, but the wreckage was still smoldering. The water around his fireboat was littered with the corpses of adults and children. His crew had managed to pluck nearly thirty people from the water, and they huddled on the stern deck like refugees from a violent war.

At that instant, a rumbling was heard from *General Slocum,* and the ship rolled to one side.

NURSE LIVINGSTON had grown numb to the suffering. The shore of North Brother Island looked like a battlefield. She no longer heard the moans of the dying—the screams of the burned and injured were much louder. Dr. Kacynski had administered the fifty doses of morphine he had brought along.

"Nurse Livingston," he shouted over the screams, "return to the pharmacy. I need all the stores of pain medication we have available."

"Yes, Doctor," Livingston said.

She began jogging toward the hospital, momentarily free from the horrors.

WADE HAD DONE all he could. *General Slocum* was awash, only one side of the paddle wheel and a portion of the fore deck above water. Backing away from the wreckage, he turned *Easy Times* ninety degrees and set off for New York City with his load of sick and injured.

The hospital on North Brother Island was filled to overflowing.

"At least five hundred, maybe a thousand," Alderman John Dougherty reported over the telephone to Mayor McClellan.

"Good Lord," McClellan exclaimed, "maybe there will be more survivors."

"I don't think so, sir," Dougherty said. "The steamer is awash."

"I want you to find the commander of Engine Company 35," McClellan said.

"The fire on board is out, sir," Dougherty said.

"I know, John," McClellan said wearily. "I want the firemen to help the coroner to identify the bodies."

"Yes, sir," Dougherty said.

"I'll send some boats across to bring the bodies back to the pier at East Twenty-sixth Street," McClellan said. "The families of the deceased can retrieve the bodies there."

ON THE EAST RIVER, New York City police boats were dragging the river for bodies. By seven that evening, they had retrieved more than two hundred. It was dark when the coroner stood over another blackened body.

"Check the pockets," he said to a fireman.

The man rolled the body over and removed a soggy leather wallet from the pocket.

"George Pullman," the fireman said, as he stared at the name on a library card, "and there's a check here for $300 made out to the Knickerbocker Steamboat Company."

The coroner nodded. "I knew George," he said quietly. "He was the treasurer of the St. Mark's Sunday School."

The fireman nodded.

"At least these bastards never got paid," the coroner said angrily.

GENERAL SLOCUM's hold still held some air, and the ship was drifting on the current. After traveling a short distance, the hulk grounded off Hunt's Point. A diver was sent down into the hull. He found nearly a dozen bodies trapped in the wreckage. He brought them to the surface one by one.

The last was a lad nine years old who was clutching a prayer book in his hands.

As soon as the heavy dive helmet was removed, the diver burst into sobs. As his boat made its way back to the city, the diver sat on the stern deck, alone with his thoughts. *General Slocum* was his last dive ever.

JOE FLARETHY, a lieutenant with the New York City Police Department, stared at the man on the stretcher at the hospital on North Brother Island with barely concealed disgust. The man's leg had been fractured when he'd leapt from *General Slocum*.

"I understand you're Captain Van Schaick," Flarethy spat.

"I am," Van Schaick said.

"You're under arrest by order of the mayor," Flarethy said. "Now, why don't you make it easy on us and point out the rest of your crew?"

Van Schaick raised himself up on his elbows. "I'm the captain," he said. "I'm responsible. You want to identify the crew, you do it yourself."

Flarethy turned to the sergeant at his side. "Go bed to bed and ask the patients for identification. The seamen should have papers. Anyone that doesn't—tag their toe and we'll sort through them later."

He turned back to Van Schaick.

"A real hero, aren't you? Trying to protect your crew." Flarethy pointed out the window toward the river. "The time to be a hero was out there."

Van Schaick said nothing.

"Cuff this son of a bitch," Flarethy said to a patrolman standing nearby.

"THE TWENTY-SIXTH STREET morgue is full," Mayor McClellan said over the telephone to Dougherty. "We can't take any more bodies."

"Hold on," Dougherty said.

McClellan heard snippets of conversation as Dougherty spoke to someone nearby.

"Okay, sir," he said after a few moments, "there's an abandoned coal shed just to the side of the hospital we can use as a makeshift morgue."

"Excellent," McClellan said.

"There's just one thing," Dougherty said.

"What's that?" McClellan asked.

"We'll need another boatload of ice to chill the bodies."

"I'll have it sent over immediately."

THERE WAS a dim electric light illuminating the Twenty-sixth Street Pier as the first load of coffins was unloaded from the boats. Ice had been placed in the coffins to keep the bodies from decomposing, and as it melted it ran through the cracks in the wood and stained the street. Hundreds of ashen-faced parents had gathered to see if they could locate their missing children. A few survivors straggled off the boats. Most were half-dressed or slightly injured in some way. Almost all were adults. They hung their heads in shame.

Halfway up a ladder, in the center of the crowd, was a fireman from Engine Company Number 35. As the 432 caskets were carried past, he shouted out the names of the dead that had been identified. The wails from mourning parents filled the area around the pier. Those that had not been identified were stacked in neat rows waiting for space to open up at the morgue.

THE MORNING following the disaster dawned clear and warm. Throughout New York City, flags flew at half-mast. At City Hall, Mayor McClellan learned that bodies were still washing up on the banks of the East River. He made the arrangements for collection and burial, then turned his attention to preventing another such disaster. First, he instituted a free "Learn to Swim" program. Second, he ordered all excursion boats in New York Harbor to cease operations until the vessels were checked and approved. Third, he began a full-scale investigation into the *General Slocum* tragedy.

When the final count was tallied, 1,021 passengers had perished.

But *General Slocum* was not finished.

DIVER JACKSON HALL stood on the side of the hull above water and shouted across the water to the captain of the salvage ship *Francis Ann*. He had spent the last hour inspecting the hull, which was resting on the bottom of the East River off Hunt's Point.

"You can pick me up now," Hall shouted across the water.

"How's she look?" the captain shouted back.

"She can be raised," Hall said. "The lower hull is intact—it's the upper decks that sustained the most damage."

"What's she look like inside?" the captain questioned.

"Lots of blackened wood is piled in the center," Hall said. "I was nearly hung up twice. The boilers appeared intact but bent. The port paddle wheel is shredded from the weight of the hulk pressing down."

"What's the surface like below the hulk?"

"It felt like soft mud," Hall noted.

"Then we can get straps under the hull," the captain said.

"Yes, sir," Hall said.

"Then we'll come alongside to pick you up," the captain said, as he walked back toward the pilothouse.

"Good," Hall muttered under his breath.

His inspection of *General Slocum* had made him uneasy. Ghosts of a thousand souls seemed to inhabit the inner sanctum he had entered. Twice he had thought he felt arms grab for him. Once he had caught sight of what he thought was an apparition out of the corner of his faceplate. When he turned his head and glanced through the murky water, he'd realized that it was part of a canvas top covering flapping in the current. Still, Hall had been spooked. He finished his inspection in record time.

THREE WEEKS LATER, *General Slocum* was above water once again. The burned hulk was towed to a shipyard in New Jersey, where the top decks were razed and the wreckage in the hull removed and scrapped. Over the next few weeks, the hull was converted into a barge and rechristened *Maryland*.

She, too, would meet with an inglorious end.

THE COAST off the eastern seaboard of the United States can be a dangerous place when the winds of

winter whip the surface of the sea. Captain Tebo
Mallick of the towboat *Gestimaine* was a salty dog.
Thirty-seven of his fifty years on the planet had been
spent at sea, and he'd learned to read the signs on the
water like they were lit with spotlights. Tonight, the sea
off Atlantic City, New Jersey, was no place for man nor
ship. Towering waves were rolling from east to west,
the tops frosted with foamy white. Sheets of cold rain
rattled the pilothouse windows like sand shot from a
cannon. He stared toward land.

"I can barely see the lighthouse," he said to a cat that
lay atop the chart desk.

Then he swiveled and tried to look astern. Somewhere in the fog, a hundred yards to the rear and
attached to his ship by a thick hemp line, was a barge
loaded with furnace coke named *Maryland*. At just that
second, a wave broke over his bow as the door to the
pilothouse opened. The light from the brass fuel oil
lamp hanging from the ceiling flickered and almost
went out.

"I think the barge is taking on water," deckhand
Frank Terbill shouted.

Mallick twisted the wheel of *Francis Ann* as the
weight from the barge pulled his stern toward the
waves.

"She's been porpoising for the last half hour,"
Mallick said. "I was hoping the seas would calm some."

Mallick felt his engine surge as the line connecting
Maryland to his stern slackened.

"She's going to whipsaw," Mallick managed to shout
to Terbill, before a wave hit *Francis Ann* broadside and
threw them both against the bulkhead.

Then one of the lines connecting them to *Maryland*

parted. It whipped over the pilothouse like an angry snake and snapped against the windshield. *Francis Ann* was pulled to port as the weight shifted and Mallick struggled to keep her from facing abeam to the mounting waves. Grabbing an ax mounted on the wall, he handed it to Terbill.

"Cut that bitch loose," he shouted, "or we're going in."

Terbill raced to the stern deck and raised the ax over his head. Then he swung with all the force he possessed. The blade parted the line and embedded itself in the gunwale. In the fog, no one witnessed *Maryland* go under.

II

Coke Isn't Necessarily a Soft Drink

1994, 2000

IN 1987, BOB FLEMING, MY OLD FRIEND AND researcher, sent me a report from the Army Corps of Engineers on the sinking and later demolition of a barge called the *Maryland*. At first I failed to see the significance of a lost barge, but then he called me on the phone and explained that Maryland was the ill-fated excursion steamboat *General Slocum* that had burned in New York's East River in the summer of 1904 with horrible loss of life.

Sometime after the burned-out hulk had grounded on Brother's Island in the East River, she was raised and towed to a shipyard. With her hull still sound below the waterline, *General Slocum* was sold for $70,000 by the Knickerbocker Steamship Company for use as a coal barge and renamed *Maryland*.

Six years later, while hauling a cargo of furnace coke

and being pulled by the tug *Asher J. Hudson* from Camden to Newark, New Jersey, her hull began to leak. With a gale blowing and seas rising, the tug captain, Robert Moon, knew *Maryland* could not stay afloat. He removed his crew from the barge and cut her loose.

For the final time, *General Slocum/Maryland* slipped into the sea.

Upon hearing of her sinking, *Maryland*'s owner, Peter Hagen, celebrated. Not only would marine insurance cover the loss, but he was glad she was off his hands. In his mind, the vessel was cursed. She was always tied up for repairs, and before she made her last trip he was forced to add to her expense by replacing her rudder.

"Ill fortune always followed the *Slocum*," said Hagen. "She was always getting into trouble. I'm glad she's gone."

The 1912 annual report of the Chief of Engineers of the Army Corps stated:

The wreck of barge "Maryland" lying sunk in Atlantic Ocean off Corson's Inlet, N.J. Under date at December 15, 1911, an allotment of $75.00 was made for an examination of the wreck for its removal. On January 29, 1912, a further allotment of $150 was made. The wreck was originally the steamer "Slocum," which was burned to the water's edge and sank in New York Harbor a number of years ago. An examination showed the wreck to be lying about 1 mile offshore, in the path of frequent coast traffic. It was a wooden hull vessel, 210 feet long, 37 feet wide and 13 feet deep. It was wrecked during a storm and sank

December 4, 1911, while in tow in route from Philadelphia to New York. After due advertisement an emergency contract was made with Eugene Boehm, of Atlantic City, the lowest bidder at $1,442. Work was begun February 12 and completed February 18, 1912. The wreck was broken up with dynamite. Upon completion of the operations the late site was carefully swept over an area of about 500 square feet and found to be clear of wreckage.

Another Corps report stated that the wreck was standing fifteen feet off the bottom in a water depth of twenty-four feet—thus the concern over her endangering other passing ships.

FINDING *GENERAL SLOCUM*, a.k.a. *Maryland*, sounded like a piece of cake, right? The initial thinking was that the wreck would lie exposed on the bottom and that a sidescan sonar would have a relatively easy time locating it. Thus all we had to do was merely sail a mile off Corson's Inlet, cruise around for twenty minutes, and shout "Eureka!" Right?

Ho, ho, ho.

In September of 1994, Ralph Wilbanks and Wes Hall had finished a survey job in New York, so I asked them to try for *General Slocum* on their way home to the Carolinas. They launched Ralph's survey boat *Diversity* and spent two days mowing the lawn outside Corson's Inlet with a sidescan sonar.

A thorough search of the seafloor turned up nothing. The sonar read only a flat sandy bottom.

Now it was time to get back to the archival research. Different pieces of information began filtering in. One mention of the wreck put it two miles off the Ludlum Beach Lifeguard Station. Divers up and down the Jersey coast claimed to have dived on *Maryland*, but they all described intact remains that looked to them like a barge.

Two different targets were provided by Gene Patterson of Atlantic Divers at Egg Harbor Township. One turned out to be an old steamship, and another was probably the anchor and chain of the wreck, since the anomaly was spread out in the same vicinity. Gene also offered another target, but it was more than five miles off Corson's Inlet.

Steve Nagiweiz, executive director of the Explorers Club, sent a set of coordinates he thought was *General Slocum*. Steve's target was also too far off the inlet to be the wreck. Both Gene's and Steve's wrecks were found at a water depth between forty and fifty feet. According to the Army Corps's indicated depth of twenty-four feet off Corson's Inlet, they were both too deep.

Local divers who were interviewed all said they were expecting the remains of the wreck to be intact and have the appearance of a barge. None was aware of the Army Corps reports, nor did it occur to them that the wreck might be buried.

IN LATE SEPTEMBER of 2000, Ralph and Shea McLean set up headquarters in Sea Isle, New Jersey, for the second attempt to find *General Slocum/Maryland*. Not taking any chances, they expanded the search grid from the old Ludlum Beach Lighthouse beyond Corson's Inlet. They began a mile and a half from the shore and worked in, running search lanes parallel to the beach. Ralph expected that the target, when they passed over it, would have the characteristics of a shattered wreck with scattered remains. This would be in keeping with the Army Corps account of the *General Slocum/Maryland* being blasted nearly level to the seabed.

The search now turned to targets that did not protrude or reach to the surface. It stood to reason that, if the barge was flattened by explosives as a menace to navigation, there was a better-than-even chance she had worked her way into the bottom silt.

The survey was conducted by towing the sensor of a Geometrics cesium magnetometer. Ralph was looking for a magnetic signature that would indicate iron hardware and pins in the original hull. There would be no huge mass, because the engine and boilers had been removed after the tragic fire. The clincher would be the fragments of the coke she was carrying when she sank.

Several small targets were located, but none had the criteria that fit the barge. Eventually, one magnetic anomaly looked promising. Just to be certain, Ralph and Shea continued running their hundred-foot search lanes until they were satisfied there were no other targets that matched the predicted signature. Satisfied that their main target filled the bill, they spent the next three days dredging in the sand, exposing large timbers, many splintered as if ripped apart, and many scattered fragments that resembled coke.

The last day was spent in performing a magnetic contour of the site. This contour process gave them a rough measurement of the wreckage that worked out to 217 feet by 38 feet, nearly the same known dimensions of *General Slocum* after she was refitted as the barge *Maryland*. The site was three miles north of the Ludlum

Beach Lighthouse and one mile off Corson's Inlet, right where the Army Corps of Engineers said it would be.

After returning to Charleston, Ralph took the pieces of what he'd recovered and believed was coke to a gemologist and four professors from the local college. They all agreed that it was indeed coke.

The curtain was drawn on the final act of *General Slocum*. It was almost as if she'd served penance for that horrible holocaust on a warm summer day in June 1904. Perhaps it was fitting that the once-beautiful ship, the pride of the New York excursion lines, with her glory days far behind her, became a stripped-down barge that was banished to roam the seas for another six years, carrying residue from steel furnaces.

She is still remembered in New York City when descendants of the victims gather at the memorial services held on the anniversary of the disaster at the Trinity Lutheran Church in Middle Village, Queens. Sixty-one victims are buried in the nearby church cemetery near a beautiful twenty-foot-high memorial statue.

At the last service, two of the only known survivors still living were present.

PART NINE
S.S. *Waratah*

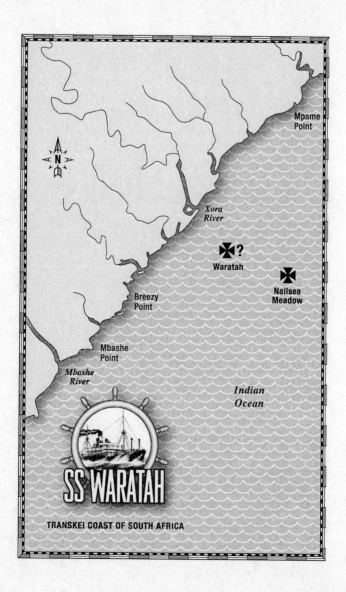

Mpame
Point

N

*Xora
River*

✠?
Waratah

✠
Nailsea
Meadow

Breezy
Point

Mbashe
Point

*Mbashe
River*

*Indian
Ocean*

SS WARATAH

TRANSKEI COAST OF SOUTH AFRICA

I

Disappearing Act

1909

"THERE IS A STRANGE FEELING AFOOT," Captain Joshua Ilbery said. "Vibrations in the winds."

The date was July 23, 1909. *Waratah* was less than an hour from her scheduled stop in Durban, and the trip had not been without incident. As soon as the ship left London on her maiden voyage to Australia via South Africa, Ilbery had noticed her tendency to roll to starboard. The first such twitch had happened on maiden day in the English Channel off Guernsey. It had been a clear day, with fair seas and winds from the west. A series of three waves, each larger than the last, borne from an underwater disturbance far out in the Atlantic Ocean, had rocked the ship. The waves were nothing really—eight-, ten-, and twelve-foot rollers against seas of six—but *Waratah* had immediately reacted with displeasure. Like a punch-drunk fighter, she had bobbed far to starboard as though she were going to drop. Then, as the waves passed, she shrugged off the seas and settled into a rolling pitching that lasted for close to a quarter hour. Ilbery had thought that the incident was a result of improper loading in the cargo hold and ordered the stores balanced, but the stability was not improved.

"Strange feelings on *Waratah*?" Second Officer Charles Cheatum joked. "Will wonders never cease."

Ilbery turned to Cheatum and smiled. If nothing else, his right-hand man had tried to maintain his spirits on the long journey. When *Waratah* had shuttered off the Azores on the way south, Cheatum had commented that they must have struck a whale. Off Cape Hope, it was a rogue wave. Far in the Indian Ocean, two days from Sydney, the ship had suddenly shook as if she were going to come apart. Cheatum had joked that it was a sudden gust of gravity.

Even so, for all the strange occurrences, *Waratah* was still steaming.

From Sydney, the ship had called on Melbourne, then Adelaide. There she was reloaded with cargo and passengers for the return to London. All told, the voyage had lasted for eighteen months and should show a profit for the owners of *Waratah*, the Lund Blue Anchor Line. Profit or not, this would be Ilbery's last voyage as captain of the vessel. He would be turning over the ship to Cheatum as soon as they reached London. Ilbery believed he had cheated fate one too many times.

CLAUD SAWYER was in the grips of another nightmare. The apparition had returned. In one hand, the wraith held a medieval sword, in the other hand a bloodstained sheet.

"Away," Sawyer screamed in his sleep, awakening himself.

Sitting upright in his berth, he struggled to calm himself. Swiveling in the berth, he placed his bare feet on the deck, then reached across to a small table. Grasping a hand towel, he dried the icy sweat from his brow, then sipped from a half-full glass of water. Rising to his feet, he took a few steps to the brass porthole and stared through the circle.

"Land," he said to himself, staring at the cliffs near the port of Durban. "God, I miss you so."

Reaching for his shirt and pants, he quickly dressed and walked toward the door to the outer deck. Once he opened the door, he stared back at his berth. An outline of his body in sweat, thick torso and twin lines where his legs had lain, was evident on the cotton-padded berth cushion. The design resembled the bloody outline on the sheet clutched by the apparition. Sawyer grabbed his single suitcase and hurried from his cabin. He would watch the docking from deck. Durban was to be his final stop.

CAPTAIN CHARLES DEROOT stared at the approaching ship from the pilothouse of his tugboat *Transkei*.

"Ugly spud," he said to his deckhand.

"Lines like a bread box on a gravy boat," the deckhand agreed.

The tides were pulling *Transkei* out to sea. DeRoot pushed his throttles forward to remain on station, then resumed his viewing. Some ships have a grace and elegance you can see from afar. The ship coming into view had all the style of a square dancer with a clubfoot.

DeRoot knew the history of *Waratah*—it was a hobby of his to know the pedigree of the ships he serviced—and this vessel was far from a thoroughbred.

Built by the British firm Barclay, Curle & Company as a sistership to *Geelong*, she came into being under two dark clouds. The first strike was the most basic, her design. *Geelong* had proven to suffer stability problems, and the construction specifications for *Waratah* were drafted to address that problem. To cover themselves, the builders had inserted two words, *if possible*, into the contract. Apparently, it was not. The ships had a flawed design, and there was little that could be done to correct the problem.

The second strike was her very name. Of the three other ships since 1848 to be named *Waratah*, all had so far vanished or wrecked. Most men of the sea are superstitious, and DeRoot was no different. A cursed name atop a bad design was an omen he could not ignore.

"Backing down," DeRoot shouted to the deckhands, as he spun *Transkei* around and checked the transmissions in reverse.

All was in order, so he stared back to *Waratah*.

NEARLY FIVE HUNDRED FEET in length, with a displacement of 9,339 tons, *Waratah* was a large vessel for her day. Her hull was jet black, now showing some streaks of rust from the year and a half she had been at sea. Her upper decks were a pale yellow. The ship's single funnel, which vented the smoke from the steam boilers that fed power to the twin screws, was painted a tricolor scheme of black at the base, a middle band of white, then black again at the top. Twin masts pierced the air—one on the forward deck, the other aft—but the masts did little to subtract from the vessel's squat appearance.

In DeRoot's view, *Waratah* was an ugly duckling dancing on the sea.

"SLOW AND SIGNAL the pilot boat," Ilbery ordered Cheatum.

Cheatum turned to the signalman, who semaphored the instructions to a nearby boat.

A few minutes later, the pilot boat came alongside and dropped off the pilot, who climbed a stairway to the main deck, then walked across to the pilothouse stairway. Climbing the stairs, he stopped at the door to the wheelhouse and knocked.

"Durban pilots," he said loudly.

"Permission to enter," Ilbery said, motioning for the door to be opened.

The pilot entered the pilothouse and walked over to Ilbery with his hand outstretched. "Peter Vandermeer," he said. "I'll be taking you inside."

"Welcome aboard *Waratah*, Captain Vandermeer," Ilbery said.

"Thank you, Captain. Anything I should know," Vandermeer asked, "before we start inside?"

"She's a little sluggish," Ilbery noted.

"Full of cargo, eh," Vandermeer said pleasantly.

"Not really," Ilbery said quietly, "just a sluggish gal."

Vandermeer stared at Ilbery. It was slightly odd for a captain to speak any ill of his command—perhaps Ilbery was just jesting. "So noted," he said.

"Pilot's in command," Ilbery said loudly, handing the command to Vandermeer.

Twenty minutes later, with help from the tug *Transkei*, Vandermeer steered *Waratah* up to the dock. By then, he knew exactly what Ilbery had meant.

Vandermeer had piloted canoes with more stability.

CLAUD SAWYER STOOD on the deck near the gangplank and willed it to lower. He stepped from one foot to the other as if the deck were on fire. He kept switching the suitcase from hand to hand. Just then, *Waratah*'s steam whistle pierced the air, signaling that they were secure. Five minutes later, the gangplank was lowered. Sawyer muscled his way to the front of the line. As soon as the chain was withdrawn, he ran down the gangplank to the dock. Moving off to the side, he kneeled down and kissed the wooden dock. Six feet away, a sandy-haired lad on a bicycle sat watching.

"Mister," he said, "you're still on the dock and over water. If you want to kiss land—it's about twenty feet over there," he said, pointing his finger.

Sawyer looked up and smiled. Then he grabbed his suitcase, walked over to land, and kneeled down again. He stayed on the ground a full ten minutes.

CAPTAIN ILBERY STARED at the manifest. Wheat from the farms to the north. Tallow and hides from the vast cattle ranches in the interior of South Africa. Lead concentrates on their way to Capetown for processing. And more passengers, some bound for Capetown, others going through to London, 211 in total.

It was the massive shipment of raw lead that bothered Ilbery.

The weight would be concentrated in a small area, and with the shipments already on board from

Australia, there would be no way for the porters to secure the load exactly amidship. Any way you sliced it, *Waratah* had proved unstable. The addition of more weight, to either side, was something of concern. The weather was another.

Ilbery had steamed these waters enough years to know the signs. The Indian Ocean was a deceptive mistress. Days like today, with clear blue sides and an ocean of flat-slabbed waves surging to shore like a screen door flapping in the wind, hid a dark secret. Offshore, some disturbance was creating the surging tides. Ilbery knew that next the waves would begin to fragment and turn choppy. Sometime soon, it might turn ugly.

"Secure the cargo," Ilbery ordered Cheatum. "I'm going ashore."

"Very good, sir," Cheatum said.

THE DATE WAS July 25, 1909. The time just past 4 P.M. *Waratah* was scheduled to steam from port at first light in the morning. Ilbery walked along the dock, then climbed the stairs leading to the port office. A hot dry wind was blowing from the Kalahari Desert far to the north, and Ilbery could taste the grit on his teeth. Wiping a few drops of sweat from his brow, he opened the door to the office and entered.

"Afternoon, sir," the clerk said.

"I'm Captain Ilbery of *Waratah*. Do you have an updated weather forecast?"

The clerk shuffled some papers on the desk, then removed a single sheet. "There's not much," he admitted. "Ministry in Pretoria warns of dust storms and thunderstorms in the interior continuing through the twenty-eighth."

Ilbery nodded.

"We've had two ships make port since your arrival. The clipper *Tangerine* crossed from Madagascar midday, and she reported rough conditions in the Mozambique Channel. Her mainsail was shredded and her decks raked with hail."

"Hail?" Ilbery said in surprise.

"I know," the clerk said. "Most odd."

"What of the other ship?" Ilbery asked.

The clerk consulted the sheet again.

"The cargo ship *Keltic Castle* out of Port Elizabeth. She makes a regular run from Cape Town to Durban. The captain noted rough seas between the Xora and Mbashe rivers." He stared at the sheet again. "Said there were choppy conditions and much debris in the water. That's about it."

"Appreciate it," Ilbery said, touching the brim of his cap. "Do you have the tugs scheduled for seven A.M., as ordered?"

The clerk removed a clipboard from under a pile of papers on the desk and glanced.

"*Waratah,* seven A.M."

"Thank you," Ilbery said, as he turned to leave.

"Captain," the clerk said, as Ilbery opened the door, "good luck and fair seas."

Ilbery smiled a grim smile, nodded, then walked out the door.

SIX HOURS, six pints of ale, and six shots of whiskey later, Claud Sawyer was seeing stars. The Royal Hotel was plush by frontier standards. Electric lights and ceiling fans, indoor plumbing on each floor. As soon as Sawyer had checked in, he'd made his way to his room.

A large wooden, four-poster bed draped in mosquito netting. Cotton sheets and hand towels for the bathroom down the hall. Sawyer had washed up, changed into clean clothes, and lain on the bed, but sleep would not come. After a few hours, he had given up and walked downstairs to the bar. He'd been there ever since.

The ornate bar was nearly twenty feet long and carved from zebra wood. To the rear, the back bar had several panes of stained glass lit from behind by lightbulbs. The floors were made of a sandstone-colored tile. Carved chairs sat in front, and Sawyer had parked there for the first few hours. Once the night had cooled some, he had made his way outside.

"Sir," the bartender said, walking out to the patio, "we'll be closing soon."

Sawyer was staring skyward at the Milky Way. He looked down and smiled at the man. "Nothing else, thank you," he said.

The bartender walked back inside.

Sawyer had failed to eat since lunch, and he had vomited his lunch into the toilet in the lobby bathroom upon arriving. His head was not swimming, but it was far from placid. The alcohol had failed to have the desired effect. *Waratah* was never far from his mind. Rising unsteadily to his feet, he made his way to the stairs in the lobby and climbed them to his floor. After several tries, he managed to unlock his door and enter his room. He prayed he would pass out soon.

CAPTAIN ILBERY STOOD on the foredeck of *Waratah*. He was smoking a pipe and staring at the sea. Even over the smell of his cherry-tinted tobacco, he could smell the ocean. A bitter, acrid odor like that of a copper coin cooked in a cast-iron skillet. Knocking the dottle from the pipe, he made his way to his cabin.

THE SHEETS WERE bathed in sweat, and Sawyer's feet were entangled in the mosquito netting. He had passed into a stupor, a feather pillow pressed against his mouth making breathing difficult. Sawyer shook his head from side to side for air.

Waratah was steaming into a storm. Sawyer could see it as clear as if he were standing only a short distance away. Then, in Sawyer's mind, the ship became small, as if he were watching it from the heavens. He watched as a rogue wave far out to sea made its way toward the vessel, then slammed into the side. Then the image faded, and a knight in medieval armor appeared. "Stay clear of *Waratah*," the knight said ominously.

Sawyer bolted upright, the pillow flying to the side.

The rest of the night he tried to sleep, but sleep never came.

CAPTAIN DEROOT MANEUVERED *Transkei* alongside *Waratah* and began the push away from the dock. The Lund Blue Anchor Line ship was responding differently than he remembered. If possible, the ship seemed stiffer and more ungainly than before.

Captain Ilbery stood alongside the chief pilot, Hugh Lindsay, as he guided *Waratah* out of the harbor and past the outer bar. After a celebratory drink with Lindsay, then his transfer off, Ilbery assumed control of *Waratah*. Ordering a course along the coast, he tried to shake his feelings of impending doom.

*

CORPORAL EDWARD "Joe" Conquer stepped from his tent along the Xora River mouth. His unit, the Cape Mounted Rifles, was on field maneuvers. For the last hour, a warm rain had been falling. It leaked through the crude canvas and soaked the crude wood-planked floor. Conquer had waited for the storm to abate before venturing outside. Staring over the cliff to the ocean, he could see that the skies were temporarily clear. Farther out, Conquer could see another storm building. A black wall of clouds had formed. At that instant, gusts of wind raked the camp. The temperature, which had been hovering around ninety degrees, dropped into the seventies as if by magic.

Conquer reached up and smashed his hat down on his head before it blew away.

Then he reentered his tent to strap on his side arm.

"MERCIFUL ALLAH," the African said, "protect me."

She came with a fury on a wind of destruction, with no name or number to mark her passage. Formed of hot wet winds far in the Indian Ocean, she moved on a westward course like a relentless marching army. The leading edge of the hurricane packed winds of nearly a hundred miles an hour. Lightning streaked from water to heavens, and booms of thunder racked across the tossing seas. Waterspouts fanned out from the center, sucking fish and marine life high into the air.

Urbuki Mali was in the wrong spot at the wrong time.

His cargo dhow *Khalia* was carrying a load of cinnamon and pearls, enough for Mali to retire at last. A trader in East London had agreed to buy the load—all

Mali needed to do was bring it home. It was greed that made Mali tempt the weather, and avarice that would end his life.

Twelve miles from land, Mali might have seen the shoreline had the weather been better; as it was, he was surrounded by a tempest that refused to release him. A strong gust carried his foremast away.

"My fortune for fair winds," Mali shouted.

And then the sky rained fish, and *Khalia* turned turtle.

ON *WARATAH*, Captain Ilbery was fighting a losing battle. The leading edge of the storm was still miles offshore, but the effects were being felt in the pilothouse. Choppy waves raked against the hull, and twice already his vessel had dropped into troughs, as if the seawater had been sucked out to sea. All at once, *Waratah* listed hard to starboard and hung suspended at a forty-five-degree angle. Fully three minutes passed before she righted herself.

"Mother of God," Ilbery said.

Second Officer Charles Cheatum could no longer contain his anxiety. His face was ashen white, and moments earlier he had nearly vomited onto the floor.

"Captain, this is bad," Cheatum said loudly.

"Hell, I know," Ilbery said. "Go below and check the cargo hold. I feel it's shifted."

Cheatum tried to move, but the muscles in his legs were knotted with tension. Pounding his upper legs with his fist, he made a few steps toward the door before he had a stomach spasm and vomited onto the pilothouse floor.

"Swab that down," Ilbery shouted to a deckhand.

Cheatum wiped his mouth with his handkerchief and walked woodenly out the door.

FULLY HALF of the passengers were clustered in the dining room. Each time the ship listed, they were tossed from one side of the great room to the other. Most were bruised and bloodied from slamming into tables and flipping from their chairs. Fear was palatable—chaos was reigning. Carl Childers, a robust Australian cattle baron on his first trip to London, did his best to quell the increasing pandemonium.

"I peered out the port," he shouted. "I can see land."

Sydney diamond merchant Magness Abernathy found no solace in Childers's words.

"Well, it best be close enough to swim to," Abernathy yelled, "because that's what we'll soon be doing."

A deckhand made his way into the dining room with an armful of cork life vests. The children were outfitted first, the women and elderly second.

"She's pitching and wallowing," Ilbery shouted, as he spun the wheel in an attempt to bring *Waratah* back on a solid heading.

DEEP IN THE ENGINE ROOM, Chief Engineer Hampton Brody could sense things were not right. Every time *Waratah* heeled over, one of the two propellers was wrenched from the water into the air. Without the drag of water, the shaft would spin rapidly, taxing the steam boiler providing power. At just that instant, a pressure valve on the starboard boiler exploded, and the engine room was filled with clouds of scalding steam.

Cheatum made it down to the cargo hold. He raced amidships to where the container carrying the unprocessed lead had been stowed. Three of the massive wooden crates had tumbled from the top row and broken apart. Several tons of rock lay scattered on the starboard side. There was nothing he could do but report his findings. Turning on his heel, he started for the ladder.

"Engine room," Captain Ilbery shouted into the speaking tube, "I've lost starboard propulsion."

He repeated his pleas, but no one answered.

TWELVE DEAD, including Brody. Their bodies were boiled—their skin cooked from their bones. Three African shovelers had been spared, but they did not understand the words that came out of the copper tube. They held their shovels in their hands, frozen in horror.

JOE CONQUER PEERED through his telescope as the cargo vessel came into view. Wiping water from the lens, he stared again. She was an ungainly vessel, with a squat black superstructure and yellow decks. Her single stack was black, with a band of white in the center.

As Conquer watched, she heeled to one side and hung there for a few moments.

FATE CAN COME in many packages. For *Waratah*, it would arrive on a rogue wave.

His ship was already wounded, and Ilbery knew this. The best he might hope for was to ground her on shore or limp back to Durban on a single engine. He waited for a clear spot, then spun the wheel to the stops.

A mile distant from the struggling ship, the rogue wave was gathering force. Fifteen, then twenty feet in height, and she kept growing. A half-mile away, the surface tension of the water should have broken, but it did not. The thousands of gallons of seawater that should be sliding down the leading edge of the wave rose higher and higher, as if stuck together with glue. A single object lay between the wave and shore.

"Mother of God," Ilbery managed to say.

Waratah was struggling to turn on a single engine and was just past the halfway point of the arc. Captain Ilbery looked out the side window. He saw death and he knew it. The seconds ticked past as he awaited the arrival of fate.

From where he stood on the cliff, Conquer could see the cargo ship and the sea behind. He watched in horror as a giant curled wave raced toward the stricken vessel. He held his breath as it slammed into the vessel.

Clinging to the metal ladder leading from the cargo hold, Cheatum felt *Waratah* lurch hard to starboard. Farther and farther she heeled over, until she passed the point of no return. The upper decks went awash, and thousands of gallons of water flooded into the holds. Cheatum lost his grip on the wet metal rung and fell the twenty feet to what had moments before been the inside of the upper deck. His neck snapped like a twig, and then there was only blackness with a tiny pinpoint of growing light.

No one had time to react. Not the frightened passengers in the dining room, not the passengers in their cabins. The few crewmen lucky enough to have been on deck were tossed into the water and not trapped in the ship. Their deaths would take longer.

Captain Joshua Ilbery was shaking his fist at the wave when *Waratah* flipped on its end beams. His head struck the ship's binnacle, shattering the glass and removing his scalp from his skull. He drowned minus his hair. *Waratah* filled with water and plunged down. Flipping upright as she sank, she settled on the bottom on her keel.

JOE CONQUER COULD NOT believe his eyes. Three minutes had elapsed from the time the wave had struck the ship to the time the last part of her hull had slipped beneath the waves. It was as if a hole in the sea had opened and swallowed the ship whole. Wiping the lens again, he scanned the water. A few pieces of debris, a shiny spot where oil had spilled. Then the storm increased, and the surface of the sea was swept clean. Folding up the telescope, he made his way back to his tent a few minutes ahead of the approaching wall of rain. Using a quill pen, he wrote a report of what he had witnessed.

WHEN THE SHIP failed to reach Cape Town, authorities hoped for the best but feared the worst. *Waratah* was known to be unstable, and the hurricane that had raked the coast at the same time was one of the worst in the last decade. The 211 passengers were mourned, and at Lloyd's of London the bell was rung. The mystery of what became of *Waratah* remained unsolved.

SIXTEEN YEARS LATER

Lieutenant D. J. Roos talked to himself when flying. He found comfort in uttering his motions aloud, as if he were verifying his actions with heaven's copilot.

"Richer fuel mixture," he said, twisting the knob.

The throbbing from the engine evened out.

Roos was piloting an experimental South African air force plane on a mail run from Durban to East London, and the aircraft was performing almost flawlessly.

"I think I'll take her out to sea a bit," Roos said aloud.

It was a glorious day, and Roos was happy. The skies were clear, with unlimited visibility, and the sea below showed nary a wave. Days like today happened maybe once a year—crystal-clear skies and the Indian Ocean appearing as a pond. Roos stared at the water out of the side window. A dozen T-shaped images appeared in the water below.

"Hammerheads," Roos said quietly, as he continued along the coast.

Lighting a cigarette, Roos puffed contentedly.

"Fuel three-quarters, manifold temperature dead on," he said.

A whale, a small sailboat, and ten minutes passed. Roos pushed the yoke forward and descended two hundred feet. He smiled to himself and watched the water again.

"Whoa," he said.

A ship came into view—two hundred feet below the water. It looked close enough to touch. The ship sat upright, as if it were steaming for a port it would never reach. This was a sea mirage, and Roos knew it. He turned the plane and circled around.

"Damn," he said.

Sure enough, it was a ship, and a big one. Must be close to five hundred feet, Roos thought, and the smokestack is still attached. He adjusted course and passed down one side. The decks must be yellow, he thought, that's why it looked like the sandy bottom. Must have sunk in a storm, he thought. Marking the position on his chart, he turned the plane around and continued to New London. Then he reported his findings.

The next day on his return trip, the seas were rougher and the bottom not visible.

He passed over the area three times, but he couldn't find the phantom ship.

II

Is It Here or Is It There?

1987–2001

THE QUESTION THAT HAS BEEN ASKED FOR more than ninety years is what happened to *Waratah* and the 211 people she had on board. From the time she sailed into oblivion during a storm off the east coast of South Africa, her ultimate fate has never been far from the minds of dedicated marine historians. And yet, since the day she vanished in 1909, no one seemed interested in launching a search for her until Emlyn Brown and I met up during my book tour in South Africa in 1985.

I was speaking at a book conference in Cape Town when Emlyn came up to me and asked if I was familiar with *Waratah*. He seemed mildly surprised that I had researched the ship's disappearance in the hope that someday I might go out and search for it. We later met at the Mount Nelson Hotel and discussed the possibility of joining forces for a search. The meeting led to a friendship that remains strong to this day. Emlyn is one of the nicest men I've ever met. I couldn't have been luckier in finding someone like him to run the show. Courteous, determined, and dedicated to finding the legendary ship, he formed a branch of NUMA as a closed South African corporation in 1990.

Emlyn believed the freak wave phenomenon—that a tremendous wave smashed over *Waratah* and took her to the bottom. He theorized that the rapidly sloping continental shelf and the power of the Agulhas Current, combined with a severe gale, caused a series of gigantic waves that engulfed *Waratah* and drove her to the bottom. That she wasn't a stable ship must not have helped during her struggle with a sea gone berserk.

Over many years, Brown pieced together every scrap of data pertaining to *Waratah*, with an emphasis on the reports surrounding her loss. Although maritime historians believed she went down much farther north due to sightings by other ships that survived the tempest, Brown bet his cards on the observations of Joe Conquer and D. J. Roos. Both men met not long after Roos claimed to have seen a ship lying on the bottom off the mouth of the Xora River, and they compared notes. They agreed on a location, and Roos drew a map with an X marking the spot.

They put the final resting place of *Waratah* four miles off the Xora River where its waters met the sea off Transkei Coast. This area is known as the Wild Coast, an inhospitable shoreline where severe ocean conditions prevail.

Roos followed up with several flights over the next few years but never again found the sea visibly clear enough to reveal a shipwreck on the bottom. Engine trouble and poor weather conditions also worked against him. Unfortunately, he was killed in a car accident, and his map was missing for several years before his family found it in the back of a desk drawer.

In 1977, a routine sidescan sonar survey by a South African university recorded an unknown wreck 360 feet deep several miles off the Xora River. The contact caused much speculation, but most historians ruled it out as *Waratah*.

After an unsuccessful sonar survey in the southern area preferred by historians, Brown became more certain than ever that the reports by Conquer and Roos of a wreck they swore they saw off the Transkei Coast pointed to the *Waratah*.

Believing wholeheartedly that the legendary ship could be found, I funded Emlyn's searches, beginning in 1987, when he conducted an intense sidescan survey of the area surrounding the wreck six miles offshore. Making several passes, Emlyn's crew estimated that the vessel's dimensions were quite similar to those of the long-missing ship.

Emlyn came back early in 1989 and attempted to lower cameras over the wreck. But little was accomplished, because the powerful five-knot Agulhas Current swept the cameras past the wreck and left him with only blurred images of the seafloor.

Later that year, he returned aboard the survey vessel *Deep Salvage I*. Using a sophisticated diving bell, Captain Peter Wilmot, master of the vessel, descended to the wreck and captured vague video footage of the hull. But again, the current was too much for the bell, and Wilmot's video images fell far short of making a positive identification.

This was proving one tough mystery to solve.

Not one to give up against the odds of a Las Vegas

keno game, Emlyn plunged forward. In 1991, he was on site with *Deep Salvage I* again, only this time he was accompanied by the world-famous scientist Professor Hans Fricke and his sophisticated submersible *Jago*, which was capable of diving to depths of nine hundred feet. It was inside *Jago* that Professor Fricke became the first person to observe and film living coelacanths in the ocean.

History repeated itself. The current again bedeviled operations during the ten-day mission, and *Jago* was never even launched.

Back to the drawing board.

In 1995, Emlyn was approached by Rehan Bouwer, a professional technical diver who believed he could reach the wreck during a carefully calculated Trimix dive, using a combination of three different breathing mixtures.

The first attempt was defeated by foul weather, and not until January 1997 did Emlyn and Bouwer's expert divers make another attempt. Pushing mixed-gas decompression tables to the limits, Bouwer and Steve Minne, the two-man team that had successfully dived on the cruise liner *Oceanos* that sank almost within sight of Emlyn's wreck, dropped deep into the restless sea.

They were unable to reach the bottom, the unrelenting current sweeping them thirty-six feet over the wreck. At that depth there was little light from above, and they had to rely on dive lights. They didn't see much, but there was no doubt in their minds that the vessel they'd drifted over was the size of *Waratah*. She was lying upright with a slight list. Most of her forward superstructure appeared gone, as if destroyed by a monstrous wave. During the thirty-five-second fly-by,

Minne was certain that the upper bulwark of the stern could have been that of *Waratah*.

The dive plan allowed a descent time of only three minutes to reach the seafloor at 340 feet, where they spent twelve minutes. This was followed by a complicated decompression ascent lasting two hours. During the drift-decompression stops, the five-knot current dragged the divers far downstream from the wreck site before they could be retrieved. Rarely had technical deep diving been so severely tested without the slightest mishap.

Over the next two days, the dive team conducted three more descents but could not come close enough to positively identify the elusive ship on the bottom.

Sadly, Rehan Bouwer was later lost in a diving accident in June of 1998.

Undaunted, Emlyn teamed up in 1999 with Dr. Ramsey and his crew from the Marine Geoscience Unit to conduct a high-resolution sidescan sonar image of the wreck off the Xora River. Everyone was certain their highly sophisticated equipment would produce the final proof that the wreck was indeed *Waratah*. The expedition members set sail in June, which in the Southern Hemisphere is wintertime.

Astounding imagery was captured by the Marine Geoscience team, and all the early indications pointed to a high probability that the wreck was indeed *Waratah*. Closer inspection of the sonar imagery suggested that the dimensions and various features of the wreck seemed quite similar to those contained in the *Waratah*'s shipbuilder plans.

A black-and-white camera was mounted on the sidescan and towed seven meters above the wreck. This seemed to be the only plausible way of beating the strong current. For fear of losing an expensive sensor and camera, the gear was not swept as close as Emlyn might have liked. Yet Emlyn found good images that matched portholes, deck machinery, and winches, as the camera flew over the stern section like a kite.

Confident that the wreck was indeed *Waratah*, and dogged in his stubbornness to prove once and for all that the lost ship was within his grasp, Emlyn initiated what he thought would be the final expedition. For this mission, he hired the services of Delta Oceanographic and their two-man submersible, which flew from the United States especially to close the final chapter on *Waratah*.

Excitement began to mount when the team arrived over the wreck site. All systems were tested and okayed, the weather was clear without more than a four-knot wind, and the sea was calm. Since all attempts over the past eighteen years had been plagued by technical problems and adverse weather conditions, Emlyn could not believe his luck. Incredibly, even the notorious current seemed to have slackened. Seeing the flat sea, Emlyn thought it might be a sign. Conditions were too good not to have been touched by the wand of good fortune.

He and Dave Slater, the submersible pilot, slipped through the hatch and settled into their cramped positions. The crane lowered them into the water, and divers unhooked the lift cable. Once free, Slater took the sub down to the seafloor. Visibility was more than one hundred feet as the upright image of the ship's superstructure came into view. Elation began to cool and was replaced by concern as they moved closer to the wreck. What they saw did not square with what they thought they should have been seeing.

Through the submersible's ports they recognized a military armored tank standing on the bottom. Their mood quickly became one of shock and disbelief.

"It is not the *Waratah*—I repeat, not the *Waratah*," came the voice of Slater over the radio to the stunned team above on the survey ship.

They moved alongside the hull and rose even with the main deck. Tanks, with their guns pointed into the gloom, and rubber tires could be seen still secured where they had been tied down when the ship left port. At first Emlyn naively wondered how *Waratah* could have been carrying tanks when World War I was still six years away when she sank. Surely this was not possible. It was difficult to accept the hard fact that this was not the 1909 British mail ship *Waratah*.

It proved the eye sees what it wants to see. The general characteristics and dimensions of the two ships were very similar. The diver accounts and sidescan sonar recordings had all been misinterpreted. What Emlyn had discovered after all this adversity was most likely a World War II cargo ship that had been torpedoed by a German U-boat. As it turned out, that is exactly what she was.

Eleven tanks were counted, and scattered dumps of small arms. Emlyn and Slater searched for a name or some identifying clue that would reveal the identity of the sunken cargo ship, but none was found.

Disheartened, Emlyn and his team returned to Cape Town. His later research showed that the name of the ship he had thought was *Waratah* was actually the 4,926-ton *Nailsea Meadow*. She was transporting a cargo of tanks and other military hardware for General Montgomery's Eighth Army on a voyage north toward the Suez Canal to Egypt when she was torpedoed by the *U-196* in 1942. Like so many ships found by NUMA, she was not where she was supposed to be. Documented records put her four miles north of her actual watery grave.

So where was *Waratah*? Why has all the evidence gathered over years of intense research pointed to this location? The thinking now is that the old liner lies much closer to shore, a theory I've always held because it seemed unlikely to me that Roos could have seen *Waratah* from the air through 350 feet of water—150 to 200 feet maybe, but not beyond the length of a football field, plus the yardage of the goalpost and then some.

There is little doubt that Joe Conquer witnessed a ship with a black hull and khaki-colored upper deck superstructure roll over and sink in a violent storm. If he and Roos are correct, then *Waratah* lies much closer to shore than where Emlyn found *Nailsea Meadow*.

Emlyn's efforts have not been abandoned. He remains focused, and we are both more determined than ever to get to the bottom of the mystery. Early in 2001, Emlyn conducted a helicopter surveillance survey over the waters off the Xora River where we think *Waratah* is most likely to be found. His primary objective was to establish boundaries for an extensive sidescan sonar search to be held later in the year when the weather settled down.

I still have great confidence in Emlyn and his NUMA team. The search will continue, but, for now, *Waratah* retains her secrets, and the mystery lives on.

PART TEN
R.M.S. *Carpathia*

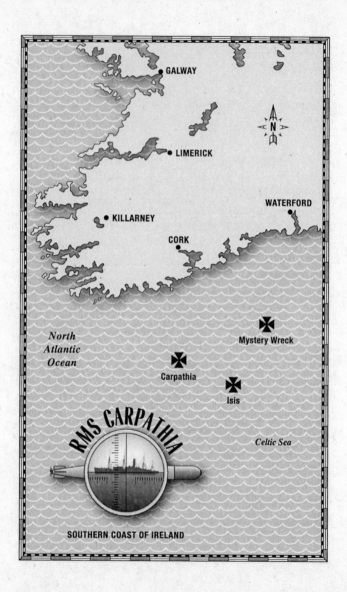

GALWAY

LIMERICK

N

WATERFORD

KILLARNEY

CORK

North
Atlantic
Ocean

Mystery Wreck

Carpathia

Isis

RMS CARPATHIA

Celtic Sea

SOUTHERN COAST OF IRELAND

I

Savior of the Seas

1912, 1918

"BRIDGE!" WIRELESS OPERATOR HAROLD Cottam shouted into the speaking tube.

A few seconds passed before the booming voice of *Carpathia*'s second in command, Miles Dean, answered.

"Bridge, go ahead," Dean said.

"I have received a QCD," the operator said.

"QCD," Dean boomed, "from what vessel?"

"Let me adjust the radio," Cottam said. "Hold one second, please."

Straining to hear through the speaking tube, Dean could just make out the faint wavering sounds of the radio. The radio shack was less than a hundred yards aft, but as Dean waited, the source of the noise seemed miles distant. Keeping his ear close to the speaking tube, Dean scanned the water with a pair of binoculars. A full moon was reflecting off the water, which allowed night visibility, and Dean was concerned with ice floes. Twice already tonight, Dean had ordered course corrections, and he wanted to be alert in case another was necessary.

"Sir," Cottam said, "I have a complete message now."

"Go ahead, then," Dean said.

"It's *Titanic*, sir," the operator said slowly.

"What about her?" Dean said.

"She's struck an iceberg, sir," the operator said, "and reports she's sinking."

"What's her location?"

"Latitude 41 degrees, 46 minutes north," the operator read from his pad, "50 degrees, 41 minutes west."

"Stand by," Dean said.

Racing over to the chart table, he plotted out the location on a chart.

"Telegraph *Titanic* that we are forty-eight miles distant," Dean said. "Explain that with all the ice floes in the area, we cannot steam at full speed."

"How long, sir?" the operator said quickly. "How long should I tell them?"

"Tell them we're at most four hours away," Dean said.

"Yes, sir," the operator said.

Dean turned to the watch officer. "Awake Captain Rostron. Tell him we have received a distress call from *Titanic* and I've set a course north."

The man sprinted from the wheelhouse and raced down the deck.

"Helmsman," Dean said, "Starboard one-half, increase speed one-quarter."

The helmsman repeated the commands while Dean once again scanned the surface of the water with his binoculars.

"God in heaven," he muttered to himself, "take us through in safety and speed."

As *TITANIC* FILLED WITH WATER, First Operator John George Phillips continued transmitting as long as possible. QCD followed by MGY, the call sign for *Titanic*.

"Have you tried the new sign?" Second Operator Harold Bride asked.

"SOS?" Phillips asked, as the carpet under his feet became soaked.

"Yes," Bride said.

"No," Phillips said, "but I will now."

Phillips began tapping the keys. It was the first SOS ever sent.

FROM THE DECK of *Titanic*, seamen began firing rockets into the air.

After streaking skyward, they exploded in a crescendo of white.

From a floating palace of heat and light to a dreary place of haze and cold—the shock must have been incredible for the passengers of *Titanic*.

In a lifeboat two hundred yards south of *Titanic*, Molly Brown watched the scene unfold in horror. The lights on the great liner remained burning as she groaned and creaked while the thousands of gallons of water filled her breached hull. From a distance, it seemed like a horrible joke, only the screams of the dying intruding.

Then, all at once, *Titanic*'s giant stern rose in the air as if to wave good-bye.

She slipped below the surface with one final burp.

*

TEN MILES and a thousand lives from *Titanic,* the vessel *Californian* was dead in the water. Just to be safe, her captain was awaiting the light of dawn to try to pick her way through the ice field. *Californian* was an awkward six-thousand-ton vessel owned by the Leyland Lines and was designed more for cargo than passengers. Though she had cabin space for forty-seven passengers, tonight she carried none. Her route for this journey was London to Boston, but at this instant she was surrounded by an ice field that allowed for no safe movement.

Second Officer Harold Stone waited for morning in the bridge. He watched the ship in the distance through binoculars. Whatever vessel it was had also stopped. Stone did not know *Titanic* had struck an iceberg. *Californian*'s wireless operator had shut the set off for the night before the distress call had been sent, so those on watch just assumed the ship on the horizon was waiting for first light to continue on.

CAPTAIN ROSTRON burst into the wheelhouse, still buttoning the top few buttons on his starched white shirt.

"Captain on the bridge," Dean shouted.

"How far away do you place us?" Rostron said without preamble.

"Forty-six miles and just under four hours, sir," Dean said quickly.

"Watch?" Rostron shouted.

A seaman stood next to the window with a pair of binoculars trained on the sea.

"Sir, I have bergs to both sides," the seaman

answered. "Seems like a field ahead."

Rostron turned to Dean. "What speed have you ordered?"

"Three-quarters ahead, sir," Dean noted.

"Roger," Rostron said. "Sound the alarm to awake the crew, Mr. Dean, then alert the galley to start as much soup and other hot liquids as they possibly can."

"Yes, sir," Dean said.

"Then place two sailors on the bow and one in the crow's nest as lookouts."

"Yes, sir," Dean said.

Rostron turned to another brass speaking tube. "Engine room."

"This is Engineer Sullivan," a sleepy sounding voice answered.

"Sullivan," Rostron shouted, "*Titanic* has struck an iceberg forty-five miles distant and we've been called to help with the rescue."

"Yes, sir," Sullivan said quickly.

"I'm going to need every ounce of steam you can give me, Sullivan," Rostron said. "The crew is being wakened now."

"I understand, sir," Sullivan said. "You can count on us."

"Full steam ahead, then, Mr. Sullivan," Rostron said.

"Full steam ahead," Sullivan answered.

Carpathia's top speed was rated at fourteen knots.

Within a quarter hour, Sullivan had her flying through the water at just over seventeen.

Carpathia was a buzz of activity. She was flying across the water like a winning thoroughbred. From her stack, a thick stream of smoke and ash trailed off the stern. At 560 feet in length, with a breadth of 64 feet

3 inches, she could not be called a nimble ship. Still, Rostron was steering her through the ice fields as if she were a pleasure yacht. With a gross tonnage of 13,555 tons, *Carpathia* threw a large wake as she raced north. To the front, her bow parted the icy water like a razor through a hair. Twice already Captain Rostron had felt his keel scrape across underwater ice as his command had come close to icebergs. Even with that, he refused to back off the pace.

"Signal from the bow lookout," the helmsman shouted, "ice to port."

"Starboard an eight," Rostron ordered.

SHIP'S ENGINEER Patrick Sullivan wiped his forehead with a rag, then stared again at the wall of gauges. Sullivan loved *Carpathia* and her inner workings, loved the feeling of power that was now surging through her hull. Built by C. S. Swan & Hunter with engineering by Wallsend Slipway Company for the Cunard Line, *Carpathia* featured a stack that rose a full 130 feet above the bottom of the vessel, and for Sullivan this was a blessing. The immense height of the stack created a great draft for the fires that supplied her power, and at this exact instant the fires were raging.

Sullivan stared aft, where teams of firemen were singing a ditty while shoveling ton after ton of coal into the fireboxes. At each of the seven scotch boilers, a pair of men with loaded shovels would approach the open doors and heave their fuel into the flames. After stepping to the side to refill their shovels at a bunker port, another pair with loaded shovels would step forward and fling their contents into the inferno, only to be followed by another pair of men. There were three pairs of shovelers per boiler, forty-two men in all. The chanting men were stripped to the waist, covered with sweat and coal dust and constantly in motion.

COLD AND FEAR. A stabbing cold from frozen water and frigid air. A palpable fear from witnessing death. The screams of the dying surrounded the few lifeboats that had been launched. To mark *Titanic's* grave, the sea was littered with chunks of cork, floating deck chairs, and lifeless bodies bound in life belts. High overhead, a hoar frost framed the moon. Down at sea level, puffs of steam from the lungs of the survivors marked the presence of those who were lucky.

ON *CARPATHIA*, Captain Rostron never wavered, never faltered.

He kept his command running at full speed through a field of ice floes that could spell the same doom for him that *Titanic* had met. On April 11, *Carpathia* had left New York bound for Gibraltar, Genoa, Trieste, and Fiume. She carried a total of 725 passengers in first and second class. The passengers were seeking warmth and sun, so it came as a surprise when the few that began awaking that night did so from the chill. As soon as *Carpathia* had turned north, the temperature began falling. It was cold—bitterly cold.

TEN MILES from *Titanic's* last position, Second Officer Stone had watched the rockets light the night sky. He alerted Captain Lord, who was sleeping on the couch in the chart room. Lord inquired as to whether the rockets had all been white. After receiving a yes from Stone, Lord had gone back to sleep.

Then the lights of the liner had sunk lower in the water, as if she were steaming away.

The time was 2:45 A.M.

At 4 A.M., Stone was relieved by Chief Officer Frederick Stewart. He related the strange events to Stewart, then went belowdecks to sleep.

SMOKE TRAILING from her towering stack and rockets blasting from her decks, *Carpathia* arrived at the reported coordinates at 4 A.M. Captain Rostron expected to see the *Titanic* still afloat.

After ordering the engines stopped, he ordered the lookouts to scan the surrounding area.

There was nothing.

Eight hundred and eighty-two feet of the finest ship yet constructed had vanished.

To the north, Rostron could see an unbroken line of ice. At the spot where *Carpathia* was stopped, the sea was littered with chunks of ice and several large bergs. Minute by minute, the sky began to lighten. The flickering stars overhead began to disappear as the coming light fought the darkness. Slowly, the scene came into focus.

At that instant, a green flare streaked skyward.

"Starboard a quarter," Rostron ordered.

Carefully maneuvering through the chunks of ice, *Carpathia* pulled abreast of a lifeboat.

Mrs. Walter Douglas in Lifeboat 2 was hysterical. "*Titanic* has gone down with all hands," she screamed up at those on the deck of *Carpathia*.

As deckhands secured Lifeboat 2 and began to unload the passengers, Rostron scanned the sea in the growing light. He could make out lifeboats on all sides now, along with the flotsam from a ship now dead.

A thick fur coat rolled on the light waves. A swamped steamer trunk was just barely above water. Wooden deck chairs, planks, and empty life vests. To add to the chaotic scene were chunks of ice and a pair of nearby bergs, which towered nearly two hundred feet over *Carpathia*'s highest point. Seat cushions and ornate rugs floated past. Hundreds of sheets of paper formed a floating parquet of a story never to be read. A case of champagne, another filled with tins of snails. Bottles and casks and wooden slats ripped from *Titanic* on her plunge to the depths.

A Bible, a hatbox, several pair of shoes. A single body dead for hours.

"Get the survivors off the boats and into the salon," Rostron ordered.

One by one, the lifeboats rowed closer.

THE NAGGING DOUBTS that had plagued Chief Officer Stewart finally proved too much.

At 5:40 A.M., he woke the *Californian*'s wireless operator, Cyril Evans, and related what Stone had told him. Evans struggled to awake, then warmed up his wireless set and adjusted the dial. Seconds later, he heard the news.

"*Titanic* has sunk," he shouted to Stewart.

Stewart immediately raced back to the bridge with the news and woke Captain Lord.

Within minutes, Lord began to steer a course for *Titanic*'s last position.

THE SUN WAS ABOVE the horizon, and the temperature had warmed some.

Carpathia was a blur of activity, as more lifeboats arrived and the passengers were off-loaded. The passengers stumbled onto the deck in a daze. Most were dressed in a haphazard fashion—some in formal attire, others in everything from silk kimonos to velvet smoking jackets. Most were wearing hats, as was the fashion: the men in fedoras and bowlers with a sprinkling of tall top hats and a few snap-brim tweed caps; the women in a variety of headgear, from Russian fur caps to formal black boaters. The survivors' shoes were a study in contrasts as well—an eclectic collection from silk opera slippers to rubber boots to polished black evening shoes to high-heeled pumps.

All the passengers were wet, and all were cold.

The passengers on *Carpathia* raided their trunks for dry clothes that were passed out by the crew. The kitchen kept vats of soup, coffee, and cocoa filled, along with large silver platters piled with sandwiches of ham, turkey, and roast beef, but few of the survivors could muster an appetite.

The shock, cold, and horror they had witnessed rendered many mute, their senses numb.

At 8:30 A.M., Lifeboat 12, the last still afloat, was secured and the survivors unloaded. Harold Bride, the brave wireless operator from *Titanic,* had stayed on his station until the last possible instant, radioing the distress calls to sea. Ordered into a lifeboat, he had survived the ordeal.

Crewmen from *Carpathia* pulled him from the last lifeboat as much dead as alive. As soon as he reached the deck, Bride collapsed. The surgeon on *Carpathia* would need to administer stimulants to revive him enough to tell his story.

Captain Rostron had the 705 survivors safely on board—now what would he do with them? The *Olympic*, *Titanic*'s sister ship, was drawing nearer. She radioed *Carpathia* and offered to take survivors on board.

"Absolutely not," Rostron told Second Officer Dean. "Can you imagine the shock to the survivors if they saw a near mirror image of their sunken vessel come alongside and ask them to come aboard? These people have suffered enough."

"What, then, Captain?" Dean asked.

"New York," Rostron said quietly. "We turn around and take them home."

"Very good, sir," Dean said.

"But first have the clergy aboard come to the bridge," Rostron said.

THE SUN WAS BURNING brightly over the scene of the disaster at 8:50 A.M.

After a brief multidenominational ceremony to honor the dead, there was nothing more *Carpathia* could do. Captain Rostron ordered a course set for New York City.

At full steam, *Carpathia* was four days away.

A CROWD NUMBERING ten thousand milled around the Battery in New York City as *Carpathia* steamed past the Statue of Liberty, carrying the *Titanic* survivors. Captain Rostron had no way of knowing how much the story of the sinking of the great liner had captivated the public's attention.

"Look at the crowds," Rostron said to Dean, who stood alongside him on the bridge.

"That's the last thing the survivors need," Dean said quietly.

Rostron nodded. The last few days had given him an opportunity to observe some of the survivors firsthand. Most were still suffering from a deep shock. Captain Rostron had noted two distinct feelings. The first was surprise. Surprise at how quickly they had been thrown from a floating palace into a freezing hell. The second was grief, tinged with remorse. Grief that others had died; remorse that they had somehow survived.

"I want you to take charge of boarding at Quarantine," Rostron said to Dean, "and keep the reporters from boarding."

"Yes, sir," Dean said.

Rostron knew this was but a stopgap. Once *Carpathia* was moored along the White Star Pier on the East River and the survivors had disembarked, there was nothing he would be able to do to protect them from the hordes. Still, he wanted to give them as much time as possible to collect their thoughts.

UNSINKABLE MOLLY BROWN had fared better than most. Her hardscrabble existence in the mining camps of Colorado had given her an inner strength on which she could call in times of trouble. Even so, as *Carpathia* left Quarantine and steamed up the East River, surrounded by tugboats and pleasure craft, she realized she was party to an event that defined an era. The great industrial age of which she was a part had shown its rotting underbelly. The ship that "God himself could not sink" lay far below the frigid waters of the North Atlantic, and people would no longer place their faith blindly in the creations of man.

Spitting into the water alongside, she turned to a crewman nearby.

"From this day forward," she said, "I shall always be defined by what happened."

"What do you mean, Mrs. Brown?" the crewman asked.

"Whatever I do in the future will pale," Brown said, "and when I die, the first sentence they write will be that I was a survivor of *Titanic*."

"You and the others," the crewman agreed.

"I wonder why I lived when others died?" Brown said.

"I think," the crewman said quietly, "that that is a question only God can answer."

AT 8:37, *Carpathia* began unloading the *Titanic*'s lifeboats so she could moor. At 9:35 Thursday evening, she was finally tied fast, and the journey was at an end. Captain Rostron had done all he could. He and the entire crew of *Carpathia* had performed their jobs with honor.

"Lower the gangplank," Rostron ordered.

Three minutes later, the first survivors struggled onto land.

Not one of the survivors imagined their savior would meet a similar fate.

SIX YEARS LATER

A pair of tugs began pushing *Carpathia* from the pier in Liverpool. July 15, 1918, was a typical summer day in Great Britain—it was raining. But it was not the type of rain that plagued the island in the North Sea in winter, spring, and fall. This sprinkle was a halfhearted affair, lacking purpose and strength. At first it came from the north, then switched directions from east to west. It ebbed and flowed like a dying tide, at times opening to pockets of sunlight and dry air.

Captain William Prothero stood on the bridge as the tugs pushed his ship from port.

The Great War that now enveloped Europe had begun nearly four years before, yet it was only some fifteen months since the United States had entered the conflict. The prowling German submarines had finally wrested the country from neutrality. The *Lusitania* had been sunk in 1915, scores of other ships since. At first the German submarines were an annoyance, now they were threatening the very concept of open seas. Losses of 100,000 tons a month had now grown to nearly a million, with no end in sight. Cargo ships, passenger carriers, war ships—all were fair game for the fleet of German U-boats.

Captain Prothero was a stout man with a black mustache that perched on his upper lip like a bristle brush. Those who served under him found him to be a consummate professional, firm but fair. While Prothero believed in protocol, he was not without a sense of humor.

"I hear there's a chance of rain later," he said to his second officer, John Smyth.

"In England?" Smyth said, smiling. "In summer? I find that hard to believe."

Prothero thanked a steward who entered the bridge with a silver pot of tea, then poured himself a cup and added milk and sugar. "Would you check with the wireless shack," he said to Smyth, "and see if they have received the latest warnings?"

"Very good, sir," Smyth said.

Prothero sipped the tea and stared at his chart. The thought of German submarines was never far from his mind. They hid in wait off the ports until the ships had cleared and were in deep enough water to make salvage impossible. To reduce their losses, the Allies had taken to traveling in convoys with gunboat escorts, zig-zagging through the water like snakes and running their vessels at the fastest possible speed so they might outrun any torpedoes that were fired. Even so, hardly a day went by when a ship was not sunk or fired at. The battle in the North Atlantic was a watery war of attrition.

A BEAM OF LIGHT pierced the clouds and lit a patch of water directly ahead of *U-55*. Commander Gerhart Werner stared at the patch of sea through his binoculars. *U-Boat 55*, like most in the German fleet, spent a great deal of time above water—in fact, as much as was safely possible. Batteries could be recharged while it surfaced, fresh air allowed into the always foul-smelling hull.

No matter what Werner and his crew tried, there was no way to wash away the smell of diesel fuel, sweaty bodies, and fear that permeated every square inch of the inside of *U-55*. The smell was part of the duty, and the duty was hazardous at best.

Werner turned his binoculars from the spot of light and scanned the horizon. Five days before, *U-55* had managed to board a small cargo ship at sea off Cork, and he was hoping for another. Before scuttling the vessel, the Germans had raided the stores for fresh food. Ham and bacon, potatoes, and some dairy. The confiscated food was a welcome change for his crew. For the most part, they survived off tins of meat and cans of vegetables from their pantry. At times the cook could make fresh bread, but it was not often—flour soon went bad in the galley, and yeast grew a strange fungus that looked like fur.

Submarine duty was not for a budding gourmet.

Swiveling in the conning tower, he turned to the stern. There a seaman was reeling in a perforated barrel they had been dragging behind on a line. The crew's clothes were inside, along with a measure of powdered soap. After being agitated by the current and rinsed by the seawater, the barrel was being brought back on deck so the clothes could be unloaded and hung from a line running from the conning tower to a stern support.

Werner stared to the west, where the sky was clearing. Hopefully, the weather would hold and no ships would approach. Then the clothes would have a chance to dry some before they needed to dive once again. Just then, Second Officer Franz Dieter climbed through the hatch in the conning tower with a folded slip of paper in his hands. Saluting Werner, he handed him the paper.

"There is a convoy assembling off Liverpool," Werner said.

"Yes, sir," Dieter said.

"That means they are still several hours away," Werner noted. "Have the men check the torpedoes and the batteries, and mop the inner deck. Then allow them to rotate topside four at a time. Provided no ships pass by, each group will be allowed to spend ten minutes in the fresh air."

"Yes, sir," Dieter said, climbing below.

CARPATHIA STEAMED through the Irish Sea approaching Carmel Head. In the next few hours, she would enter St. George's Channel, then follow the curve of Ireland along her southern shore. Once past Fastnet Rock on the southeast tip, the convoy would set a course west for Boston.

Captain Prothero stepped from the bridge and glanced back at the stern. Now that they had reached cruising speed, the powerful twin-screws of his command whipped the water into a foamy froth that trailed behind the vessel for nearly a mile. Far to the rear, past six other ships of the convoy, was a trailing British destroyer. Far to the front, nearly a half-mile distant, was the leading destroyer. The destroyers would stay with them through St. George's before turning back.

After that, the convoy of seven needed to rely on themselves.

Carpathia had been selected as commodore ship for the trip across the Atlantic Ocean, and with good reason—Prothero was a skilled captain who had made the crossing many times before. Last year, while captain of *Carpathia,* he'd had the honor of transporting the first American troops to Great Britain to join the Great War. After safely dropping off the soldiers, *Carpathia* had been on her way to London to replenish her stores when a torpedo had fired off Star Point. Prothero had ordered an evasive action and the torpedo had run past *Carpathia,* instead striking a U.S. oil tanker running nearby.

Another incident bears noting. Not long after the near miss by the torpedo, Prothero saw what he thought was a lifeboat on the water. Watching through his glasses, he was surprised to see a German U-boat surface nearby to retrieve the object. Prothero reported that the Germans were using decoys, thus saving a few more ships.

In short, there were few captains with the breadth of experience possessed by Prothero.

COMMANDER WERNER had yet to leave the conning tower. His people were farmers, and his ancestral genes were used to open spaces. The cramped inner hull of a U-boat was as foreign to him as Chinese fireworks, so he spent as much time abovedecks as possible. Even with his dislike of confined spaces, Werner was a competent leader.

He and the crew of *U-55* had more than a handful of kills under their belt.

"That's the last of the rotation," Dieter said. "The men are now being fed in shifts."

"What's our location?" Werner inquired.

"Still approximately a hundred miles off Fastnet Rock," Dieter noted.

"It will be night soon," Werner said, "so we might as well remain above water. Why don't you take the first watch?"

"Yes, sir," Dieter said.

"Unless we see something that makes me change my mind," Werner said, "we'll just wait for the next convoy to happen along."

Werner began climbing down the ladder in the center of the conning tower.

"Sir?" Dieter said.

"Yes, Dieter," Werner said, pausing.

"We're down to four torpedoes."

"Duly noted," Werner said.

WHEN *CARPATHIA* PASSED Fastnet Rock, it was 11 P.M. and pitch black.

Already, there had been trouble. One of the ships in the convoy was having problems maintaining speed. She could make the prescribed ten knots, but when she did, the huge volumes of smoke from her funnels could be seen nearly twenty miles away.

Prothero knew that at sunrise they would be sixty miles into the Atlantic Ocean, and if the skies were clear, the plume of smoke would be a beacon to any nearby U-boats. The captain of the vessel reported that his engineers were working on the problem with little result, and Prothero knew it was a lost cause. Most likely the ship's bunkers were filled with bad coal. There was no way to change that while at sea.

Prothero walked *Carpathia*'s passageways toward his cabin.

He would deal with the problem in the morning.

IT SMELLED like feet. Werner's pillow smelled like feet. Rolling over on his back, he stared at the deck above his hammock bunk. As soon as these last four torpedoes were expended, *U-55* could make her way back to the submarine base at Bremerhaven for a long-needed cleaning and refit. Hopefully, he would receive enough liberty time to go home and see his wife. His wife was a fine cook and housekeeper—her house never smelled of feet—and she had yet to serve Werner meat from a can.

On the conning tower above, it was as dark as a madman's moods. Franz Dieter stared skyward, waiting for the stars to appear. Tonight they were hiding behind the clouds. Some nights the air was playful and fresh, but tonight it had all the comfort of a lead blanket. Dieter reached into the tin pail by his side and removed a slab of slightly moldy cheese and a hunk of blood sausage. Taking his pocketknife out of his uniform pants, he sliced the food, then nibbled it slowly.

It was going to be a long night.

As though in a maze with no barriers, the convoy zigged and zagged as it made its way west. So many minutes at this heading, then a change. So many minutes at that heading, then a turn. To a plane passing overhead, the wakes of the convoy looked like the jagged steps from lightning flashes. To those on board, however, the constant changes meant safety.

Carpathia carried a total of 215 passengers and crew. At this instant, half of the crew and most of the passengers were asleep in their berths.

"Captain," Dieter whispered.

Werner bolted upright, rubbing his eyes. Dieter's breath smelled of sausage.

"Yes, Dieter."

"Destroyers in the distance."

Werner stared at his watch; it was just past 1:30 in the morning.

"Have you ordered a dive?" he asked.

"No, sir," Dieter said. "They're still far in the distance."

"What's our position?" Werner asked.

"Approximately a hundred and ten miles from Fastnet," Dieter said.

"The destroyers will be turning back soon," Werner said. "Stay above water and maintain a safe distance. Stalk the prey until the time is right."

Then Werner rolled over and went back to sleep. The hunt would take hours.

BREAKFAST WAS SERVED on *Carpathia* at 8 A.M. Oatmeal porridge and milk, fried fish and onions, bread and butter and marmalade. Tea or coffee to drink. The passengers and crew ate their meal in leisure, never knowing a wraith from below was slowly stalking them.

Captain Prothero stared back at the smoking vessel. The repairs had made little difference in the emissions from the stacks. A black rope trailed in the sky far behind the ship.

"Mark," he said.

The helmsman changed course and began a zag to the north.

ON *U-55*, breakfast was powdered eggs and coffee that tasted like diesel fuel.

"The lead vessel has a single stack and ample beam," Werner said. "If I was to hazard a guess, I'd say she might be *Carpathia*."

"The Cunarder?" Dieter asked.

"Yes," Werner said.

"Is she your intended target?" Dieter asked.

"She's the lead vessel," Werner said, "and the largest. We might as well try for the best."

A crewman handed Dieter a slip of paper.

"The latest position, as you requested, Captain," he said.

"What is it?" Werner asked.

"Forty-nine degrees, 41 minutes north," Dieter said. "10 degrees, 45 minutes west."

"Good. Sound the alarm and have the torpedoes readied," Werner said. "It'll be a twin shot from the surface."

"Yes, sir," Dieter said.

Werner scanned the ship in the distance with binoculars.

"Fire two," he shouted into the speaking tube a few seconds later.

NINE-FIFTEEN in the morning. Captain Prothero was scanning the water with a pair of binoculars, but he didn't see the wake of the first torpedo until it was almost upon them. He sounded the alarm only seconds before the first torpedo struck *Carpathia* just below the bridge. This was followed a minute later by a second explosion directly in the engine room. The second torpedo would be the one that claimed five lives.

"Sound the alert," Captain Prothero said loudly, "and get me a damage report."

"Yes, sir," Second Officer Smyth said.

Five minutes passed before the voice of Smyth called from the engine room.

"Sir," Smyth said into the speaking tube, "we have five dead—three firemen and two trimmers."

"Damage?"

"It's bad," Smyth said, "but it might be contained. The engineer has the pumps operating, and he's attempting to fill the hole below the waterline so we might have a chance at port."

"Good," Prothero said, "keep me posted."

Scanning the water with his binoculars, he caught a glimpse of the German U-boat in the distance. One of the new types, five hundred feet in length.

Prothero considered firing the deck guns, but the U-boat was too faraway to hit.

"THEY CAN SEE us," Werner said. "Dive."

U-55 slipped beneath the waves and moved closer to *Carpathia*.

Raising the periscope, Werner studied his prey.

The torpedoes had run true. One had struck below the bridge, the other where Werner felt the engine room was located. Even with the fine shooting, the steamer was still afloat. Through the periscope, he could see the pumps below dispelling water over the sides in ever-increasing amounts. If this continued and they could get another ship alongside *Carpathia* for a tow, they might be able to push her back to port.

"Prepare to fire another," Werner ordered.

"That will leave us only one for the trip home," Dieter noted.

"Then you'd better hope that puts her down," Werner said, "or I'll fire that one, too, and we'll have none."

"Yes, sir," Dieter said.

"Loose it as soon as ready," Werner shouted.

*

"I THINK we're gaining," Smyth shouted through the speaking tube.

"A ship will be alongside in minutes," Prothero said. "We'll try to make Ireland."

"I could use a few more seamen down here," Smyth said.

"They'll be down directly," Prothero said.

Then he scanned the sea again.

To see it coming is sometimes worse. A bulge on the top of the water as the torpedo raced toward them just below the surface. Lines like a bullwhip, with a sting that went far deeper. A visible death with nowhere to hide.

"STRAIGHT AND TRUE," Werner said. "That should finish the job."

He held his breath as the torpedo drew closer to *Carpathia*. Time seemed to slow to a crawl. The twin propellers of the torpedo bit at the seawater and moved the weapon forward. Her nose cone was packed with explosives, and her fuselage was filled with fuel that would burn. Yards, then feet, then inches. Slamming into the hull at the gunner's room, the charge exploded and shredded the iron like a paper bag blown full of air and ruptured.

The explosion ignited the powder and shells in the hold. It made the hole in the hull larger, and much more water than the pumps could ever handle flooded into the hull. *Carpathia* settled lower in the water.

NO ONE needed to tell Captain Prothero the seriousness of the situation, but they did.

The order was given to abandon ship.

Those still alive aboard *Carpathia* were rescued, and at just past 11 A.M., she slipped below the waves for the final time.

II

It's Never Easy

2000

I'VE ALWAYS BEEN AMAZED AT HOW THE obituaries of ships of historic significance end up lost and forgotten. No curiosity seems to exist over what happened to them after their moment of tragedy or triumph. *Mary Celeste* was like that, and the ship that performed what is perhaps the greatest rescue in the annals of the sea, *Carpathia*, was another. Few of the marine enthusiasts whom I contacted knew what had happened to *Carpathia* after her intrepid dash to save *Titanic*'s survivors. Most simply thought she had outlived her time and was sent to the scrappers like so many of her ocean liner sisters.

Intrigued by a ship whose story has never been fully told, I decided to delve into her epilogue, along with that of the *Californian*, the cargo ship that has come down through legend as the ship that stood by, silent and unresponsive in the ice floes, as more than fifteen hundred souls perished in the icy Atlantic water a few miles away. Her failure to come to *Titanic*'s rescue has all the makings of a classic mystery.

Both ships are irrevocably linked with the most famous ocean liner in history. No story of *Titanic* is complete without *Carpathia* and *Californian*. Unlike Captain Smith of *Titanic*, Captain Lord Stanley of *Californian* was more cautious. Rather than navigate through the huge ice floes at night, he prudently stopped and drifted among the bergs until daylight. After midnight, members of his crew saw flares rising across the ice pack to the south. Tragically, the ship's radio operator had gone to bed and did not receive *Titantic*'s frantic SOS. Alerted by his crew, Captain Lord ignored the flares and chose to believe they were simply fireworks fired during festivities on the passenger liner and lamentably failed to see a calamity in the making.

The questions without hard answers still persist.

Could the *Californian* have responded in time and saved the poor souls of *Titanic*? Or was she too distant to reach the stricken liner before she sank? The controversy rages. There are revisionists who believe the lights seen by *Titanic*'s officers during the sinking came from a sailing ship, called *Samson*, that was engaged in illegal seal-fishing. Mistaking the flares for a government patrol boat out of Halifax, the crew of *Samson* fled the scene out of fear of being arrested. They didn't find out about their part in the tragedy until almost a month later.

What became of *Carpathia* and *Californian*, the two ships forever linked together in one of the sea's great disasters? Were they scrapped at the end of their shipping careers? Or do they lie in solitude beneath the sea?

In a strange historical coincidence, they were both torpedoed by German U-boats in World War I. One lies in the Mediterranean, the other in the Atlantic, but exactly where?

To find keys to their final resting places, I went directly to the most knowledgeable source, Ed Kamuda of the *Titanic* Historical Society in Indian Orchard, Massachusetts. Ed sent me not only charts showing the approximate positions of the wrecks but also reports of the sinkings.

The S.S. *Californian* was torpedoed on November 11, 1915, off Cape Matapan in the Mediterranean Sea, thirty miles from the coast of Greece. She slipped under the sea at 7:45 in the morning while on a voyage from Saloniki to Marseilles. She had been sailing as a troopship, but fortunately she was empty when she was struck by a single torpedo. Most of the crew escaped, and a French patrol boat took her under tow. But later in the afternoon, the persistent captain of the U-boat threw another torpedo at her, and she sank in thirteen thousand feet of water.

I scratched *Californian* off my wish list. The reported position of the sinking given by the ship's officers, the patrol boat, and the U-boat captain was not a good match. The site was quite vague. This is understandable, though. It's hard to take a sun sighting with a sextant—these were the days before LORAN and GPS—while a disaster is going on around you. You can't operate on luck alone, however, and searching the seafloor for a shipwreck lying over two and a half miles deep within a two-hundred-mile search grid, and operating strictly on guesswork, is certain folly.

So I left the *Californian*, along with her legacy of what-might-have-been, alone in the depths.

The *Carpathia* was a different story. Here we stood a fighting chance of finding her. That's all I ever ask. If the odds are a hundred or fifty to one, forget it. But I'm a sucker for a ten-to-one bet. Perhaps that's why the red carpet is always out for Cussler in Las Vegas and at Indian casinos. I simply give my money to the croupier and dealer, then walk away. Why waste time suffering the agony of losing? It's much simpler doing it my way.

I learned that *Carpathia* had been torpedoed by *U-55* on the morning of July 17, 1918, while sailing as part of a convoy carrying 225 military passengers and crew. The U-boat pumped two torpedoes into her, instantly killing five men in the engine room. Amazingly, *Carpathia* remained afloat. Captain William Prothero gave the order to abandon ship and lower the lifeboats. Impatient to finish the job, the U-boat's commander sent a third torpedo into the battered liner. Ten minutes later, she went down. Interestingly, *Lusitania* sank in eighteen minutes after a single torpedo strike and lies just forty miles west of *Carpathia*.

Again we were confronted with conflicting position reports of the *Carpathia*'s sinking. The H.M.S. *Snowdrop*, the ship that rescued the 225 survivors, gave one position while the officer from *Carpathia* gave another one 4 miles away. The U-boat's commander put the sinking 6 miles north of the others. Admiralty charts showed a wreck in the general vicinity, about 4 miles from *Carpathia*'s last visual sighting, but it failed to coincide with the other sightings. The search grid now worked out to a lengthy area 12 miles by 12 miles, or a box covering 144 square miles.

The dilemma never ends. This wasn't going to be as easy as I thought.

About this time, Keith Jessup contacted me. He is the legendary British diver who found and directed the salvage operations of the H.M.S. *Edinburgh*, the British cruiser sunk in the Baltic Sea during World War II with millions in Russian gold aboard. More than ninety percent of the gold was brought up by divers living in a decompression tank eight hundred feet deep.

During our conversation, I asked Keith if he knew anybody with a boat that I might charter to search for *Carpathia*. He replied that his son Graham was in the shipwreck survey business and would be delighted to join in and oversee the search. Graham and I hit it off, and plans were under way to form an expedition, funded by me and directed by Graham through his company, Argosy International. I would have given my left arm to lead it myself, but I was buried in work, my wife Barbara was suffering serious health problems, and negotiations were under way to sell my books to Hollywood. As much as I would have enjoyed participating, there was simply too much hanging over my head to leave the homestead in search of an old shipwreck.

Graham chartered a survey boat called *Ocean Venture*, skippered by an experienced seaman named Gary Goodyear. After loading the remote operating vehicle (ROV) on board to take underwater video and photos, the ship and crew cast off during the middle of April from Penzance, England, the town made famous by Gilbert and Sullivan.

The weather was not kind, and it was a rough trip to the search area in the North Atlantic off southern

Ireland. Once on-site, they began to run survey lines in a box between the positions given by *Carpathia*, *Snowdrop*, and *U-55*, using a forward-seeking sonar that sent out sweeping arcs ahead of the ship and a sidescan sonar that threw out signals to both sides of the boat to detect any objects rising from the seafloor. The sonar units were backed up with a magnetometer to detect magnetic anomalies.

On the second day, the forward sonar turned up a target. They had a wreck with the approximate dimensions of *Carpathia* located almost seven miles from her last reported position. The sidescan sonar showed a sunken vessel that appeared to be lying upside down with scattered debris along her hull, a common situation with ships that invert on the way down.

With great anticipation and excitement, the crew prepared to explore the wreck. At 550 feet, the depth was too great for divers, so the crew prepared to deploy the ROV and its cameras to examine the wrecks. There were high hopes that it was indeed *Carpathia*. The weather was choppy and the waves high for such an operation. With the forecast calling for storms, they rushed to shoot the video and head for harbor before the seas turned uglier.

Captain Goodyear positioned *Ocean Venture* over the wreck site. To minimize the length of cable between the ship and the ROV and to reduce the effects of a strong current, they employed a tether management system. Along with the ROV, a cage is lowered near the wreck with a winch that reels out a shorter length of cable to prevent the vehicle from bouncing around and becoming entangled in the wreckage.

Unfortunately, at this point, Graham jumped the

gun and made the announcement over the radio that *Carpathia* had been found.

Not so.

The video cameras revealed a large wreck similar to *Carpathia* lying atop her crushed superstructure, rudder and propellers rising toward the surface like grotesque fingered hands. The first tip-off came from the propellers. They were four-bladed, and *Carpathia*'s were known to have been three-bladed. Her length was also a hundred feet short.

This was not looking good.

It proved impossible to make a positive identification. The only hope was to stumble onto something in the extensive debris field around the wreck. The ROV and its cameras were sent over to videotape the objects lying like trash along a freeway.

Then came a gruesome find. The cameras revealed a human bone protruding from the silt, a visible reminder of those who had gone down with the ship. Although NUMA is not in the artifact-removal business, the team decided to bring up for identification a piece of the ship's china that was found resting in the silt not far from the bone. Rigging a wire, the ROV operator maneuvered his joystick and managed to hook the wire into the handle of what was soon seen as a soup tureen. Once the tureen was on board and delicately cleaned, the script on the base could be read: *H.A.L.*

This was definitely not *Carpathia*. But what was this wreck, and how had it come to be here?

With time now run out, *Ocean Venture* set a course for home, and I went back to the archives.

Research identified the wreck as the Hamburg American Lines ship *Isis*, a cargo/passenger ship of

4,454 tons built in Hamburg, Germany, and launched in 1922. Newspaper accounts reported that she had gone down in a raging storm on November 8, 1936. Thirty-five died. Only the cabin boy that tied himself under the seat of a lifeboat survived. One can only imagine the horror in the ship's final moments as a huge wave crushed her superstructure and rolled her upside down before sending her to the bottom.

It might be said that some wreck is better than no wreck at all. But that's no compensation when we had our hearts set on finding *Carpathia*.

Return to Go and wish for luckier dice.

For the next try, Graham was joined by John Davis and his film crew from ECO-NOVA, along with master diver Mike Fletcher. Setting out from Penzance for the second attempt, *Ocean Venture* stopped in the fishing town of Baltimore, Ireland, where Graham and John talked to the local fishermen. Ocean fishermen are a great source for locating shipwrecks. They take great pains to carefully mark hangers or snags on their charts—any objects protruding from the bottom that cause them to tear or lose their expensive nets and trawl gear.

They were kind enough to provide a list of eighteen spots where they had hooked their nets. One of them might be *Carpathia*. One trawler belonged to a Spanish fisherman who had programmed snags in and around the *Carpathia* search area. The boat's new owner was helpful in supplying the GPS coordinates that revealed the exact locations. There was one snag he thought had a high potential, and he suggested we search it first.

But it was not to be. The famous old liner was still

not ready to be found. Fate in the form of nasty weather set in, and a near disaster dropped on our doorstep.

When we reached the first prime target, the *Ocean Venture*'s ROV was dropped into the deep and moved around a wreck that proved to be a large trawler that had sunk in a storm in 1996. If nothing else, our position was right on the money. The fix couldn't have been more accurate. Then came a break in the umbilical cable, and cold salt water began causing electrical shorts in the delicate wiring. There would be no more underwater images this trip. The cable could not be repaired, only replaced, and there was no spare on board. With disappointment written in everyone's eyes, the ship turned for port.

There are times I'd like to strangle the guy who wrote, "If at first you don't succeed, try, try again." Not that I haven't taken his advice on occasion. It's just that I have this feeling that he never succeeded in anything he ever attempted.

We decided that next time, provided my hand wasn't tired of writing checks to pay for the madness, it would be pointless to continue search grids because of the vagaries of the sea and weather.

Given the accuracy of the fishermen's positions, it seemed more expedient and less time-consuming to simply check out each individual hanger. Running search lanes was like looking for the proverbial needle in the haystack, one straw at a time. But now the stormy season was coming on. We would have to hang tough before making another effort.

Graham Jessup fitted out a new ship and headed for the *Titanic* site to bring up artifacts, but luckily, John Davis of ECO-NOVA, who had involved me in the

Sea Hunters documentaries, offered to joint-venture the third *Carpathia* expedition. John would direct operations, as well as bring along a film crew to videotape the seafloor using a newer and larger ROV—with better capabilities—than the one used previously.

In December, during a lull in the weather and restocked with food, water, and fuel, *Ocean Venture*, with reliable Gary Goodyear at the helm, set out once again. During the voyage to the search area, the remaining seventeen snag positions provided by the fishermen were plotted into the ship's computer. The plan was to start at the north end and zigzag down south, hitting the marked snags as they went.

The first target was a mystery we still haven't solved. The sonar readings showed what is most definitely a destroyer, with the aft hundred feet totally missing—almost as if a giant hand had sliced it off with a knife. The stern could not be found on either forward or sidescan sonar. The best guess is that the ship was torpedoed but did not sink right away. The stern pulled free and sank, but the rest of the ship floated long enough to be towed until it sank, too. There were no records of a warship going down in this area. Hopefully, someday we'll be able to identify her.

The following days passed without a solid strike on which we could hang our hat. Operating twenty-four hours a day, the ship and crew began to show signs of frustration and fatigue. Still, anxiety ran high as *Ocean Venture* neared the seventeenth and last target in the extreme end of the southern search area.

Then, at last, the gods smiled, and the sonar reading began revealing what looked like a large ship on the bottom. Everyone in the wheelhouse stood in silent anticipation as the target began to increase in size, until Goodyear pointed and said, "There's your ship."

Optimism was high, but failure is always standing behind those who look for sunken ships. Despite the advances in equipment technology and computer projections, shipwreck-searching is not an exact science. The lesson of *Isis,* and at least two other wrecks that NUMA misidentified over twenty years, came back to haunt everyone. Several more passes were made over the remains of the ship far below. The dimensions checked out. So far, so good. Now it was the turn of the robotic vehicle and its cameras to probe the carcass.

While Goodyear's first mate jockeyed *Ocean Venture*'s thrusters, fighting the current and waves to keep the ship stabilized above the wreck, the ROV was lowered over the stern. As the deck crane swung it over, the winch slowly played out the umbilical cord, sending the little unmanned craft into a sea turned gray from the dark, menacing clouds above. Inside the wheelhouse, Goodyear sat in front of a video monitor with a remote-control unit perched in his lap, moving the joysticks and switches that maneuvered the underwater vehicle's motors and cameras.

Now every eye was locked on the monitor, waiting for the ROV to drop through the gloomy void to the bottom. After what seemed a millennium, we could see the drab, sunless silt spread across the sea bottom.

"I think we're about fifty feet north of her," said Davis.

"Turning south," acknowledged Goodyear.

Plankton and sediment swirled like chaff in a

windstorm, kicked up by a strong current. Visibility on the seafloor was poor, no more than six or seven feet. It was like looking through a lace curtain on a window as it swayed in the breeze.

Then a huge, dark shape began to loom in the murk before materializing into the hull of the ship. Unlike *Isis*, which had turned turtle on its descent, this wreck was sitting upright. She looked for all the world like a haunted castle or, better yet, the ominous house that belonged to Norman Bates and his mother in *Psycho*. Her black paint no longer showed, and her steel hull and remaining bulkheads had long been covered with marine incrustations and silt.

"Come around to the stern so we can count the prop blades," said Davis.

"Heading toward the stern," replied Goodyear, as he manipulated the ROV controls.

Large openings in the hull appeared, their steel borders disjointed and jagged, with debris spilling out from them.

"Could be where the torpedoes struck," observed Fletcher.

Soon, a massive rudder and bronze propellers came into view.

"She's got three blades," Davis noted excitedly.

"The number of spindles holding the rudder look right," added Goodyear.

"She's got to be *Carpathia*," Fletcher said, in growing excitement.

"What's that lying in the sand off to the side of the hull?" Davis said, pointing.

Everyone stared intently at the monitor's screen and the object half-buried in the silt.

"By God, a ship's bell," muttered Goodyear. "It's *Carpathia*'s bell!"

He zoomed in with the ROV's cameras, but the raised letters identifying the ship were too encrusted to read. The ravages of time and sea life had laid a blanket over them. Unable to make a positive identification from the bell or the bow proved irritating to the men in the wheelhouse.

The ROV rose from the bottom and moved along the dead hull, past rows of portholes, some still with glass in them, past the hatches through which *Titanic*'s survivors had entered that cold dawn six years before *Carpathia* went down. The *Ocean Venture*'s crew could almost envision the slightly more than seven hundred people—pitifully few men, heartbroken wives, fatherless children—who had either climbed the ladders or been hoisted aboard *Carpathia*'s decks.

Dozens of trawl nets were entangled in the wreckage, making Goodyear's job very tricky indeed. The upper superstructure and funnel were gone, collapsed into a great tangle of shattered wreckage. A huge conger eel came out of a jumbled mess to stare at the intruder to its domain. The ROV sailed over the forecastle, focusing on the deck winches, finding the fallen forward mast.

Suddenly, the cable became snagged, wedged in the twisted metal on the main deck.

It seemed as though, after eighty years in black solitude, *Carpathia* didn't want to be left alone again. With a sensitive touch, Goodyear feathered the joysticks on the remote, retracing the ROV's path until the umbilical cord finally pulled free. With a sigh of relief, he brought up the ROV and the first images of *Carpathia* since 1918.

With nothing more to be accomplished, the weary but exhilarated crew reluctantly stowed the ROV and the sonar and magnetometer gear and set a course back to Penzance, England. The disappointment over the *Isis* hung heavily on their minds. The big question was whether they had truly discovered *Carpathia*, or some other ship of the same design.

The absolute proof came in Halifax a few weeks later, when the renowned marine archaeologist James Delgado sat down and systematically compared the video images with the original blueprints of *Carpathia*. The rudder, the propellers, the sternpost, the position of the portholes all matched. Delgado made the final pronouncement.

"*Carpathia* has been found!"

Thanks to the crew of the *Ocean Venture* and John Davis, the search is over. Here at last was the ship forever tied to that fateful day in April 1912. I can't help but wonder who will be the next to see her bones. She has no treasure on board, certainly not in the usual sense. However, in the glass case in the purser's office are the many medals, cups, plaques, and mementos commemorating her gallant role in rescuing the *Titanic* survivors. But I doubt they can be recovered, so deep are they within the collapsed superstructure. *Carpathia*'s trophies will probably rest with her forever.

She lies in five hundred feet of water about three miles from the original *Carpathia* coordinates and a hundred and twenty miles off Fastnet, Ireland. Somehow, it almost seems fitting that she joined the White Star liner in the depths of the cruel sea.

NUMA and ECO-NOVA are proud to have recaptured a celebrated piece of history. *Carpathia* left us all with an inspiring legend that will be cherished by all who love the sea and her rich history.

PART ELEVEN

L'Oiseau Blanc

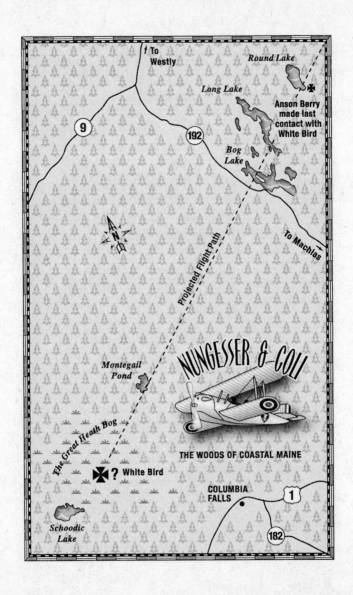

I

The White Bird

1927

"Seems like it's a fifty-fifty proposition," Charles Nungesser noted.

"And how do you figure that?" François Coli asked.

The men were standing on the packed dirt at La Bourget Airfield outside Paris. Nungesser was a handsome man with a rakish air. His chin sported a scar from one of his many crashes during World War I, but his eyes still burned with an intensity that showed no fear. Coli was more compact, with a jaded air about him. His upper lip was covered with a bushy black mustache. A black patch covered the eye he had lost in the Great War, and his cheeks were becoming jowls. Coli's double chin was resting on a silk flight scarf.

"Either we take off in this fuel-laden beast," Nungesser said, "or we crash."

"Flip of the coin," Coli said.

"Soar into greatness," Nungesser said, "or burn into history."

"You make it sound so fun," Coli said wearily.

To attempt the risky Paris–to–New York flight, Nungesser and Coli were inspired by glory, not money. The money due the winner of the Orteig Prize had awaited a claimant since 1919. Raymond Orteig, owner of the fashionable Brevoort and Lafayette Hotels in Paris, offered $25,000 to the first airplane that completed a Paris-to-New York or New York-to-Paris nonstop flight. While $25,000 was not an inconsequential sum, the acclaim that would be garnered by the winners was priceless.

Whoever won the Orteig Prize would be the world's most famous living person.

THE PRIOR YEAR, fellow Frenchman Rene Fonck, the leading Allied fighter pilot in World War I, made an attempt. The flight had ended in disaster. Fonck's Sikorsky S-35 crashed on takeoff from Roosevelt Field in New York with a crew of four. Fonck and his copilot lived, but the radio operator and the mechanic aboard perished in the flames.

Commander Richard Byrd, famed for his exploration of the North Pole, assembled a crack team to make an attempt. A modified Fokker trimotor, similar to the plane Byrd had used for his North Pole journey, was selected. On April 16, Anthony Fokker, Byrd, pilot Floyd Bennett, and a radio man crashed while landing on a final test flight. No one was killed, but three of the four aboard were injured.

Ten days later, another group mounted an effort. With sponsorship from a U.S. group of war veterans named the American Legion, Lieutenant Commander Noel Davis bought a Keystone Aircraft Corporation

Pathfinder. When performing the final tests at Langley Field in Virginia, the Pathfinder went down, killing both Davis and his copilot, Stanton Wooster.

Next to tempt fate was Clarence Chamberlin in a Wright-Bellanca WB-2. Chamberlin and copilot Bert Acosta tested the plane, named *Columbia*, by staying aloft for a little over fifty-one hours, a new world's record and more than enough time to reach Paris. On one of their last test flights, they lost their left wheel after takeoff. Chamberlin managed to land, but the damage to the plane would require time to fix.

AT THE SAME TIME, in San Diego, at the Ryan Aircraft Company, a former mail pilot named Charles Lindbergh was waiting for a low-pressure area to lift over the Rockies so he could fly east to make a solo attempt. He was sitting on a wooden folding chair in the hangar next to his plane, *Spirit of St. Louis*, studying the current weather reports, when the news reached him that Nungesser and Coli would soon take off from Paris.

The date was May 8, 1927.

"MONSIEUR," THE MECHANIC said quietly, "the time is here."

It was 3 A.M., the darkest part of night. Nungesser and Coli were lying on wooden pallets covered by thick horsehair mattresses in a corner of the hangar at La Bourget Airfield. Nungesser was clutching his favorite war medal; Coli had removed his eye patch. They awoke immediately. Nungesser reached for the steaming cup of Viennese coffee the mechanic offered, while Coli sat upright and stared at the plane that would carry them into the history books.

L'Oiseau Blanc (*The White Bird*) was a French-built Levasseur PL-8. The white biplane had detachable wheels that would be jettisoned after takeoff and a watertight belly made of treated plywood that allowed it to land on water like a seaplane. Powered by a sophisticated water-cooled, twelve-cylinder Lorraine-Dietrich engine that produced 450 horsepower, spinning a massive propeller designed to fold away for landing, the plane had the smooth good looks of a dove in flight.

"She's a beautiful mistress," Coli said, as he pulled the eye patch over his socket.

"So much more so," Nungesser said, "with the emblem attached."

Coli simply smiled.

Nungesser's ego was exceeded only by his flying ability. When he had insisted on attaching his personal emblem, Coli had readily agreed. The emblem was a black heart with drawings of twin candelabra holding lighted candles pointing toward the round humps at the top. Between the candles was a drawing of a casket with a cross on the top. Below that was the ancient skull-and-crossbones symbol. The emblem was positioned directly below and slightly to the rear of the open cockpit where Nungesser would fly the plane.

Coli rose from the mattress and pulled on his leather flight suit. "We should make ready," he said. "The president will be here soon."

"He'll wait," Nungesser said, as he leisurely sipped his coffee.

OUTSIDE THE HANGAR, the sky was dotted with millions of stars. A rare wind flowing east washed across the ground, and if they were lucky it would carry *White Bird* across the Atlantic. André Melain was not staring at the stars or worrying about the wind. Instead, he was carefully smoothing the packed-dirt, two-mile-long runway with a small diesel tractor that featured a crude spotlight hooked to the battery. Placing the tractor in neutral, he climbed from the seat, then lifted some twigs from the dirt. After placing them in a metal box at the rear of the tractor, he climbed back aboard and resumed his meticulous work.

THE PRESIDENT OF FRANCE, Gaston Doumergue, had heard the rumors that Chamberlin had taken off in the now-repaired *Columbia*. After waiting to receive word from the French ambassador in New York City that the report was erroneous, he set off for the airfield.

The Orteig Prize had been funded by a Frenchman, and it was a matter of national pride that it also be claimed by a French team of flyers. Right this instant, however, Doumergue was cursing French engineers. The 1925 Renault 40CV carrying the president was stopped on the side of the road three miles distant from La Bouret. The driver had the hood of the car, emblazoned with the diamond-shaped Renault emblem, raised and was staring into the engine compartment. He fiddled with some wires, then returned to his spot behind the wheel and turned the engine over.

The engine fired and settled into a quiet purr.

"My apologies, Monsieur," the driver mumbled, as he placed the Renault in gear and pulled away from the curb.

Just under ten minutes later, they arrived outside the hangar.

FRANÇOIS COLI WAS SIPPING from a glass of Merlot and nibbling on his breakfast of crusty bread smeared with runny Brie. Charles Nungesser had spurned the offer of wine for another cup of coffee rich with heavy cream and sugar. He was alternating between a chunk of bread heavy with pâté and a hard-boiled egg in his left hand.

"Is the mailbag safely aboard?" he inquired of a mechanic who walked past.

"Stowed forward, as you requested," the man noted.

Nungesser nodded. The special postcards would be postmarked after their arrival in New York and later sold as souvenirs for a handsome profit. He stared over at his navigator. Dressed in his full-leather flight suit, Coli looked like a sausage with a meaty head attached. Still, in spite of their differences, Nungesser trusted Coli's ability completely. Coli came from a family of seafarers based in Marseilles, and navigation was in his genes. Shortly after the war, he had piloted the first nonstop flight from Paris to Casablanca across the Mediterranean. He was originally slated to make his own attempt for the Orteig Prize, but Coli's plane had been destroyed in a crash.

For all his quiet demeanor, Coli wanted the honor as much as Nungesser.

THE RENAULT STEERED past the crowds and made its way to the side of the hangar. The driver shut off the engine and climbed out, stepped back to the rear door, and opened it for Doumergue. The French president walked to the hangar's side door, waited for the driver to open that, too, then walked inside.

Glancing to the right, nearest the overhead doors, he saw the white Levasseur. The tail of the plane was painted with a vertical stripe of blue nearest the cockpit, then an open stripe of white, then a stripe of red at the end of the tail. The colors of the French flag. Horizontally, above the stabilizer, were black block letters that read: P. LEVASSEUR TYPE 8. Just below the stabilizer was a painted anchor. The sheet metal surrounding the engine was also white and was rounded, like the end of a bullet. The nose of the plane was peppered with access panels, four round air intakes per side and a single exhaust pipe to port and starboard.

The light from the few electric lights in the hangar was dim, but Doumergue could make out Nungesser and Coli standing off to one side. He walked over and shook the men's hands.

"This is the first I've seen the plane up close," Doumergue said.

"And what do you think, Monsieur President?" Nungesser asked.

"The cockpit is farther to the rear than I thought it would be," Doumergue admitted.

"Three aluminum fuel tanks that can carry 886 gallons are mounted just under the wings, just aft of the engines," Coli said, grinning. "We wouldn't want to run short of fuel before reaching New York."

"An excellent idea," Doumergue said.

Nungesser looked over to the French president. "Have we heard word of Chamberlin?"

"The rumors were false," Doumergue noted. "At last report, he was still in New York."

"Then the winds are against him and favoring us," Coli said.

"So it would seem," Doumergue said.

Nungesser turned and shouted to a mechanic. "Hook *White Bird* to a tractor and pull her onto the runway. Monsieur Coli and I have a date in New York City."

The dozen workers in the hangar broke into cheers.

THE EASTERN SKY was paling with the first light of the coming dawn, as Nungesser and Coli climbed into *White Bird* and started the engine. A cacophony of noises washed across the hundreds that had gathered to watch the historic journey. Popping noises sounded as the engine belched and wheezed and then settled into a loud roar. Puffs of smoke billowed from the exhaust ports.

Nungesser engaged the propeller for a test.

A loud thumping noise came as the massive wooden blades began to beat at the air. Next, a screech, as Nungesser powered up and moved *White Bird* a short distance.

"Manifold pressure and temperature okay," Nungesser shouted to Coli.

"Check," Coli said.

"Control surfaces responding—fuel shows full."

"Check," said Coli.

"I say it's a go," Nungesser said.

"Confirm the go," Coli shouted. "Next stop, New York City."

Nungesser steered *White Bird* into an arc at the far end of the runway, then stopped and ran up the engines while holding the brake. The crowd had followed the plane downfield, and hundreds of people stood watching. Nungesser raised his arm over his head and as far out of the cockpit as he could, then waved to the crowd.

"*Au revoir*," he shouted.

He pushed the throttles forward and started down the runway. It was 5:17 A.M.

ANDRÉ MELAIN WATCHED *White Bird* roll past, then followed with the tractor. From his perch atop the tractor, he had a better view than most of the crowd. *White Bird* was gaining speed and passed the one-mile marker. Slowly, the plane inched skyward, then sagged back onto the runway. A collective sigh ran through the crowd. A hundred yards farther and the tail wheel was far off the ground. Suddenly, Melain could see under the belly of *White Bird* as she climbed foot by foot from the runway. A mile past the end of the runway and the plane was only seventy feet in the air. Then he saw what he was watching for—Nungesser dropped the landing gear, which fell through the dim light to the ground below.

Melain set off in the tractor to retrieve the prize.

"COAST AHEAD," Nungesser shouted.

Coli marked it on a chart. "You are right on course."

White Bird passed over the English Channel at 6:47 A.M.

NUNGESSER STARED at the gauges. All seemed in order. He headed toward Ireland as he thought of his past. His had been a life of challenges and adventure. As a teenager, he had favored boxing, fencing, and swimming—all individual sports. As a young man, he'd found school oppressive and his desire to be outdoors almost overwhelming. At sixteen, he had quit school and convinced his parents to allow him to visit an uncle in Brazil. The uncle had resettled in Argentina, and it would be nearly five years before Nungesser found him, but in Brazil Nungesser indulged in his love of mechanical things. He began to race motorcycles, and later automobiles, supporting himself with his increasing skills as a mechanic. He gambled, boxed for money, and lived the life of a bon vivant, but still something was lacking. He began to feel bored with his life and bound to the earth.

A few years later, he traveled to Argentina to locate his uncle. There he found the passion he had sought so long. Visiting an airfield one day, he approached a pilot who had just landed. He explained to the man that he was an accomplished automobile racer and thus felt qualified to fly—and the man laughed him off as if he were the village idiot. The man went inside, and Nungesser climbed into the cockpit, roared down the runway, and lifted off. After a short flight, he approached the runway and touched down. The owner of the plane was not so much angered as amazed.

In that instant, Nungesser became completely enamored with flying.

After a few weeks of flying lessons and a stint barnstorming in Argentina, he returned to France just as the winds of war began to howl. After a brief time in the cavalry, he wrangled a transfer to the air service and began a distinguished, if dangerous, career. Nungesser loved aerial combat and approached it with a passion that bordered on foolhardiness. After crashing many times, shooting down forty-five German planes and getting wounded seventeen times, he ended the war with a chest covered with medals, a plate in his head, and a silver ankle.

But after the thrill of war, his civilian life seemed sedate and ordinary.

He suffered financial setbacks and failed endeavors. After traveling to the United States, he barnstormed and starred in an early silent movie, but the fame and adoration he sought were slow in coming. All that was soon to change.

As soon as he and Coli made New York City, it would all be his.

"WE SHOULD SEE Ireland in the next few minutes," Coli shouted.

Coli, too, had felt the tug of flight. After switching from sea to air, he had been commander of an aircraft squadron during the war. Where Nungesser was fool-hardy, Coli was persistent and methodical. As soon as he agreed to attempt the flight, he had insisted that they rigorously train and plan for the event. The men began a program of physical fitness using barbells, medicine balls, and light running. They practiced staying awake for long periods so they could better understand the effects of sleep deprivation. Their record was sixty hours. To ensure that he could keep them on course, Coli studied charts of sea and land. He checked and rechecked currents, wind patterns, and meteorological informa-tion. On test flights aboard *White Bird*, he noted speeds and elevations so he could better plan the route. And he studied Nungesser and his flying style. His partner on the flight seemed much more comfortable over land than water, and Coli had figured that into the plans. Once they reached North America, he would keep them over land as much as possible. Reaching into a picnic hamper, he twisted the top off a ceramic container of hot tea and poured himself a cup.

After he had finished, he poured one for Nungesser and handed it forward.

"SHOO," THE WHITE-HAIRED man said quietly.

Shamus McDermott sat on a rocking chair just outside the door of the net maker's shop at the port of Castletown Bearhaven, Ireland. A few moments before, he had fed the fat, yellow tabby cat at his feet a sardine, and now the animal would not leave him alone. A lifetime of cod fishing had taken its toll on McDermott. The cold, hard work had given him arthritis, and the hand pain and phantom aches from the missing ring finger on his left hand never seemed to leave him nowadays. He would turn seventy years old this fall, and his days of working were eight years past.

These days, most of his time was spent watching and waiting.

In the mornings, he would head to the port and see the ships off. At night, he would wait for their return, then share a pint with the working fishermen. After a few tall tales and the dispensing of mostly unwanted advice, he would return to his small stone cottage to make dinner over his peat-fired stove. By 9 P.M., he would be asleep.

"That's a strange sight," McDermott said to himself and the cat.

Two thousand feet overhead, a stark white plane approached from the east. It continued over the town and out to sea in a relentless pursuit of some faraway location. McDermott watched it recede into the distance.

"Like a fine white arctic plover," he noted happily.

Then he rose from the chair to walk inside the shop to notify the others.

The time was five minutes before noon.

"RESET TO ELEVEN A.M. local time," Coli shouted at the moment the chart showed they had crossed the time line.

"Affirmative," Nungesser said.

The Irish isle was no longer in sight. For the next thirteen hours, their only companion would be an endless expanse of open water. Coli stared at the sea below. From his vantage point thousands of feet above, he could make out small whitecaps on the ocean. The sea was breaking east. The predicted tailwinds had shifted.

"What's she feel like?" he shouted to Nungesser.

"By the engine revolutions and indicated airspeed, I think we have about a twenty-five-knot head wind," Nungesser said quietly.

"What happened to the predicted tailwinds?" Coli said.

"The weather is an unpredictable mistress," Nungesser said easily.

Coli took a pencil and slide rule and calculated. On takeoff, *White Bird* had carried fuel sufficient for forty-four hours of flight. With the head winds, their speed would be reduced to closer to eighty miles an hour. The current rate of fuel burn would leave them nearly four hundred miles short of New York City. He performed the calculations again.

*

"THE LOW PRESSURE has lifted," the designer of *Spirit of St. Louis*, Don Hall, said.

"I'm planning to take off shortly," Lindbergh said.

"No word yet on Nungesser and Coli," Hall admitted.

"I pray they make it safely," Lindbergh said.

"Then why fly to New York?" Hall asked.

"If they are successful," Lindbergh said, "I can still claim the prize for the first solo flight."

"The Ryan is gassed and ready to go," Hall said.

"Let me just fill this thermos with milk," Lindbergh said, "and I'll be on my way."

An hour later, he was high above the earth following the railroad tracks east.

THE PHOSPHORESCENCE of the ocean and the stars overhead were their only companion. They were twenty-eight hours into the flight and an hour away from Newfoundland when the first pangs of doubt and fear crept into Nungesser's mind. He was tired and hungry, and aching from sitting so long. The vibrations had made his arms cramp and his bottom numb, and the loud roar from the engines was giving him a splitting headache.

Coli was not faring much better. He was seated to the rear of Nungesser, farther back in the cockpit. Here there was less fresh air, and the fumes from the massive aluminum fuel tanks gathered in the fuselage. This, combined with the light rocking as *White Bird* made its way west, was giving him a mild case of seasickness. He opened a tin of crackers and nibbled a few.

"François," Nungesser said, "open the flask of brandy and pour me a measure."

"Very well," Coli said.

He unsnapped a leather satchel and dug around in the bottom until he located the flask. After filling a tin cup, he tapped Nungesser on the shoulder and handed it forward.

"*Merci,*" Nungesser said, after taking a sip.

Coli stared at his pocket timer. "It's time to switch tanks," he noted.

Nungesser switched the brass lever. He watched as the fuel gauge reset to full.

"How long until we should see Newfoundland?" he asked.

"Within the hour," Coli said.

ABOARD *SPIRIT OF ST. LOUIS*, Lindbergh was approaching the western end of the Rocky Mountains. The moon was giving him some light. He could just make out strips of snow still atop the highest peaks. Climbing to thirteen thousand feet, he followed his course through New Mexico. And then the engine started to sputter. Below were jagged peaks and rocky ravines that offered little chance for a safe landing.

Lindbergh enriched the fuel mixture, and the engine smoothed some.

Most worthwhile pursuits are defined by moments of decision. He could either turn away from the string of mountains ahead and seek a safe place to land or he could press on. Lindbergh coaxed the balky engine to climb slowly. Altitude spelled safety if the engine conked out.

TWO A.M. and Venus was at her zenith.

"To starboard," Coli said, shaking Nungesser's shoulder.

Nungesser concentrated on the water below. His head was reeling from lack of sleep and the incessant roar from the engines. It was cold at that elevation, and his nose was dripping. Wiping it with the sleeve of his flight jacket, he stared into the darkness below.

AT THE AIRFIELD just outside St. John's, Newfoundland, it was six minutes before 2 A.M. Two dozen small fires had been lit on each side of the packed dirt runway, and every available electric light had been turned on and pointed skyward. The fires formed twin lines and the main offices a giant dot—from the sky, the display looked like a giant letter *i*. The manager of the airfield, Douglas McClure, stared at his watch. The French flyers were a little overdue. They might be having trouble finding land.

"Go ahead and light the fuel pits," McClure said to several of his helpers.

Yesterday they had dug a dozen holes in the earth with a tractor, then lined them with sand. Thirty minutes ago, McClure had driven past each hole and poured the contents of five-gallon diesel fuel containers into each hole. There were now pools of standing fuel and saturated sand spaced ten feet apart. He watched by the office as one of his helpers threw a lit torch into the first pit. The fuel flared twenty feet in the air, then began to burn with clouds of black smoke.

"FLARE TO STARBOARD," Nungesser shouted happily.

Coli strained his neck to get a better view. "There's another."

"I see lights," Nungesser said.

"That's St. John's," Coli said. "They promised they'd light the way for us."

"North America," Nungesser said.

"If all continues to go well," Coli said, "we should reach Maine around seven A.M."

AT THAT SAME INSTANT, Charles Lindbergh was looking down on the eastern plains of Kansas. Once he had dropped past the mountains, the air had warmed some and his engine smoothed out. Deciding the problem had been carburetor icing, he made a mental note to watch for it when he crossed the Atlantic.

NUNGESSER AND COLI were exhausted. The vibrations, the relentless roar of the engines, and the lack of sleep had reduced them to automatons. An hour earlier, they had passed over Nova Scotia, but little had been said. They were thirty-four hours into the flight and 550 miles from New York City. Far below *White Bird* was the Bay of Fundy. The water was being whipped into whitecaps by a stiff wind. François Coli poked his head out the side of the cockpit and stared at the wall of clouds approaching to port. The sight was not reassuring. He scrawled equations on a sheet of paper and stared at his results.

"We are still nearly six hundred miles from New York," he shouted. "How's the fuel holding up?"

"I estimate six more hours of flight time," Nungesser stated. "The head winds have changed and are now blowing north to south."

"Then we have just enough to make it," Coli said, "if nothing happens."

"Then I should stay the course of forty-five degrees latitude?" Nungesser asked.

"Affirmative," Coli said. "We'll enter the United States just north of Perry, Maine."

Nungesser stared at the wall of clouds only minutes away. "What then?"

"Once we enter the cloud bank, I'll be unable to take a fix," Coli said. "Our only chance will be to follow the coastline until the clouds break or we reach New York."

"So we pray the winds push us south before we run out of fuel," Nungesser said.

"That's the idea," Coli said wearily.

ANSON BERRY was in a small wooden rowboat on the south end of Round Lake, a dozen miles north of Machias, Maine. Berry was part owner of an icehouse. The coming months were, of course, his busy season, but his passion for fishing had got the best of him today. He had left work in early afternoon. After catching a few fat pickerel for tonight's meal, he was due to spend the night at his camp on the shores of the lake. Casting a plug fifty feet away, he slowly reeled it back.

FIVE HUNDRED MILES from fame—five miles from infamy. *White Bird* was flying through a spring storm. On the ground, the storm was wind-whipped rain; at two thousand feet, it was a freezing hell. Hail and sleet pelted the small curved windshield to the front of the cockpit, and Nungesser's goggles were fogged.

At just that instant, a bolt of lightning shot up and passed through *White Bird*.

Coli stared forward to the radium-coated instrument

needles. The shock had shorted out the instrument panel, and the needles lay useless on the left side. Then the Lorraine-Dietrich started to sputter. They were above Gardner Lake, Maine. Nungesser twisted the knob to enrich the fuel mixture, and the engine smoothed some.

"We're flying blind," he shouted.

"What do you want to do, Captain?" Coli asked.

It was the first time in the entire flight that Coli had called Nungesser by rank.

"I'll try to remain over water," Nungesser shouted. "If the engine quits we can attempt a water landing."

"Otherwise?" Coli asked.

"Otherwise we keep pushing on," Nungesser said. "There is nothing else."

BERRY WAS SWATTING at a black fly at the same second his bobber was pulled under the water. Yanking the rod up in the air, he set the hook. Passing the rod to his left hand, he led the fish around the stern of the rowboat.

"Gotcha," he said.

INSIDE THE BULLET-SHAPED housing protecting the Lorraine-Dietrich engine of *White Bird*, all was not well. The sleet being sucked into the air intake had iced the carburetor slide. Condensation in the low fuel tanks was magnifying the problem. The engine sputtered and popped as more of the chilled fuel was introduced. With the uneven running failing to burn off all the fuel, the engine began to flood.

"The engine is icing," Nungesser shouted. "I'm

going to take her down and see if we can find some
warm air."

BERRY FOUGHT THE PICKEREL to exhaustion and
then slowly reeled in his catch. When the plump silver
fish was alongside the rowboat, Berry glanced down
into the water. The fish was sucking in water past her
gills and flicking her tail in an attempt to find freedom.
Reaching into the water, Berry grabbed the fish behind
the gills and hoisted her into the boat. Removing the
hook with a pair of pliers, he set the fish on the floor of
the boat and held her back. Taking a wooden fish club
in his other hand, he swung the club at a spot just behind
the eyes. There was a loud thump, then the fish quit
twitching.

Thump, thump, thump.

Berry stared at the fish.

Pop, pop, pop.

"Damn," Berry said aloud, "it's coming from
above."

Squinting through the mist, he scanned the sky for
the source of the noise.

"WE MUST MAKE A DECISION," Nungesser said.
"To the south the clouds seem thicker, but looking
north and east I can see light."

"Without the airspeed indicator," Coli said, "it's
difficult to calculate fuel burn."

"We fought the good fight," Nungesser said, "but
I believe the Orteig Prize is going to elude us this
trip."

"If we continue on for New York, we will arrive on
fumes," Coli said.

"But the Paris-to-Quebec prize is within reach," Nungesser noted.

"Quebec is only two hundred miles away," Coli said easily. "We could make it with two hours of fuel remaining."

"Then it is decided," Nungesser said. "We make Quebec today, refuel, and make New York tomorrow. As soon as the weather cooperates, we fly home west to east."

"Not quite as we'd planned," Coli said, "but whatever is."

"I'll make the turn," Nungesser said wearily.

If all went as planned, they could still beat Chamberlin and Lindbergh across the pond. And they would make the return flight with the benefit of experience. The Frenchmen were not giving up—at least not yet.

ANSON BERRY STARED up at the clouds. The noise was closer now and becoming more defined. What had first sounded like a faraway locomotive now sounded like a logging truck in the air. Berry now knew it was a plane, a rarity in these parts, but where was it? The sound was coming from the south and growing in volume. He craned his neck around. For a second, he saw a flash of white. Then only clouds once again. He followed the sound as it passed over the lake from south to north. The sound diminished, then he heard it sputter, then go quiet.

"*MERDE*," Nungesser shouted.

Though Nungesser had no way of knowing it, the slide in the carburetor had frozen open. Raw fuel had poured into the float bowl and was choking the engine. Inside each of the twelve cylinders, the spark plugs were becoming wet. A strong spark might have helped matters, but the lightning strike had weakened the alternator and wreaked havoc with the voltage regulator. Just then the engine fired up and raced.

"Buy us as much altitude as you can, Captain," Coli shouted. "I'll seek out a lake for landing."

Nungesser pushed the throttles forward. *White Bird* clawed at the air.

ANSON BERRY WAITED until the plane was out of earshot, then resumed his fishing. Two more pickerel and he would call it a night. He had an hour, maybe two, of light, and he wanted to be inside his cabin with dinner on the table before night fell.

THE ENGINE SPUTTERED and died once again. The clouds were thinning, and Nungesser knew there were clear skies only a few hundred feet above. *White Bird* continued to climb, powered only by the force from the last burst of speed until she exhausted her forward momentum. For a brief second, Nungesser could see the bank of clouds from above. To his left there was a hole in the layer, and he glimpsed the blue-green hue of water. Flaring his propellers, he pitched *White Bird* over in a dive.

"Hold on, François," he shouted.

Mountains and bogs and wilderness below. *White Bird* floated down, slow at first, then gaining in speed. The landing angle was all wrong. Instead of a gradual descent, *White Bird* was plunging down like an albino fish hawk after prey.

Nungesser jammed an unlit cigar into his mouth and clenched his teeth as they fell downward, just on the edge of control. Coli knew it was bad—in the last hour his emotions had gone from exhaustion to disappointment to euphoria to acceptance. He was no longer mourning the end of his dreams but praying instead that he might somehow live. The hell with New York City or even Quebec—just to land safely once again would be enough. He removed a rosary from his leather flight bag and clutched it in his hand. Nungesser struggled with the yoke to pull *White Bird* from the steep dive, but the controls were sluggish and his arms weak from the long hours without sleep. *White Bird* slowly began to flare out of the dive. Nungesser could see the water below.

"François," he shouted, "we're going to make it."

A moose stood in water up to his belly. He was chewing a mouthful of plants. A shadow passed over his head, followed a second later by *White Bird*. The sound of the wind whipping against the fabric wings less than twenty feet overhead spooked the beast. He beat a hasty retreat out of the water toward shore. Nungesser had managed to level out the plane, but he had no way to slow the forward movement. He slowly lowered the plane down to water level. *White Bird* was now ten feet above the water. He stared forward out of the cockpit.

The lake ended less than two hundred yards ahead. A rocky ridge rising eight hundred feet in the air lined the shore. If the engine would fire one last time, he might be able to force the plane into a 180-degree turn. He tried the starter, but the engine was dead. Nungesser pushed the yoke all the way down. They would not have a soft landing.

White Bird struck hard.

The bottom of the stationary propeller cut into the lower fuselage. The top broke off and shot rearward like a razor-sharp boomerang. It severed the top of Nungesser's head just above the eyebrow.

The brain matter splattered Coli, who screamed in horror.

White Bird continued forward on momentum, the ripped lower fuselage dragging while the left wing dipped over and struck a rock. *White Bird* spun counterclockwise as the wing was ripped off the side. Coli fell out and was hit in the chest by the horizontal tail wing. It crushed his ribs and broke his back. He was alive when he slipped from the wreckage, but he had no feeling in his arms and legs.

And then it was quiet, save for a small fire that the rain quickly extinguished.

II

Rain, Black Flies, and Bogs

1984, 1997, 1998

ONE OF THE GREAT MYSTERIES OF HISTORY IS
one that is little known nor long remembered. The tale
of the *White Bird* and Nungesser and Coli could be a
story by Stephen King, all the more so since the plane
probably lies within a hundred miles of his house in
Bangor, Maine.

The *White Bird* and its legend lay lost and forgotten
for sixty years until author Gunnar Hanson researched
the aircraft's disappearance in 1986. Until then, it was
generally thought that Nungesser and Coli had gone
down in the middle of the Atlantic, but Hanson
discovered that they had made it across the coast of
Newfoundland, and then some.

Though the sky was heavily overcast with clouds as
low as eight hundred feet, there were seventeen reports
from people who heard it go over. Two claimed to have
actually seen a white plane heading southwest at the
approximate time that it was due to reach the North

American continent. What gave the sightings, or rather hearings, credibility was the fact that they were all in a straight line, so there is little doubt *White Bird* made it across the North Atlantic and beyond Newfoundland. Four more sightings came in from Nova Scotia. At this point, Nungesser and Coli must have cut west for the Maine coastline. The final accounts, again in a straight line, came from people living in Maine.

The last person to hear the plane go over was Anson Berry, a reclusive fisherman who lived in the wilds alone. While fishing in a body of water known as Round Lake, about twenty-five miles north of the village of Machias, Berry heard a plane fly overhead late in the afternoon. He could not see it because it was in the overcast. The white color of the plane would have also made it difficult to spot against the clouds.

His earwitness account became colored through the years. Some claimed that he heard the engine sputtering and then die before a loud crashing sound. Others swore he never said any such thing. The next day, he walked to a small general store and asked if anyone else had heard an airplane fly over. No one had heard anything. But one old fellow, who was a boy when he knew Berry, stated emphatically that Anson never said anything about a plane crashing.

Because Berry was known as an honest man, no one ever doubted his story. His account also holds water because five other citizens of Maine who reported the *White Bird* passing over their head were in a direct line northeast of him.

Anson Berry will forever be a footnote in history as the last man to hear the engine of *White Bird* pass in the clouds above. The next thirty miles along the projected course of the aircraft would have taken it over totally uninhabited, thickly forested country, speckled with lakes and spreading into a vast impenetrable bog. Several miles past the great bog, the landscape becomes populated with towns and people, none of whom reported seeing or hearing the *White Bird* in 1927.

Theories abound. One has the intrepid French pilots, realizing that they can't make New York, turning for Montreal. But that distance was too great for them to make with the fuel aboard. Or, knowing they were lost over land, they might have turned east for the coast and crashed in the sea. Another theory, backed by psychics, has them flying low and crashing into a mountain. Take your pick.

I CONTACTED Gunnar Hanson in the summer of 1984. At that time, he was working with Rick Gillespie of TIGRE, another group interested in solving the mystery. Having other projects on the table, I dropped the matter until a few months later, when Gunnar called me to say he'd had a falling-out with Gillespie. I asked if he would like to pool search efforts with NUMA and me. He did.

We arranged to meet in Maine near the Round Lake area where Berry had lived. Ray Beck of Chatham, New York, also joined us, since he'd reported seeing an old engine half-buried in the ground above the Round Lake hills less than a mile from where Berry heard the plane pass. This was during a hunting trip in 1954. He generously offered the use of his vacation cabin, which was not far from the search area.

We gathered together and began walking the hills south of the lake. As coincidence would have it,

Gillespie and his TIGRE group were also searching the area at the same time. It was raining, and Gillespie stayed in the town of Machias and held press conferences, claiming the discovery was only hours away.

My feeling has always been not to make a big deal out of an expedition until you have something to show for the effort. What was amusing was that we came, we searched, and we went home without Gillespie or his TIGRE group knowing we were present.

We forged through the wilderness of the beautiful country while the precipitation fell in a constant drizzle. For two days, we tramped the hills, Ray Beck trying to retrace his footsteps during the sighting of the engine so many years before. Nothing was found. Discouraged and soaked through clothes and skin, we returned to the cabin and made plans to try again the following year.

If I have learned anything looking for lost history, it is to keep an open mind and not become hung up on one theory and one theory only. Having always had faith in psychics, because they are such amiable and interesting people, and believing they see things that most of us can't, I contacted Ingo Swann. Ingo is perhaps the world's most respected *remote viewer*, a term now in use for people who imagine beyond.

He thought the *White Bird* project would be an excellent opportunity to conduct a controlled experiment. His associate, Blue Harary, well known for his work in remote viewing at Stanford University, came on board, as well as a lady named Fanny from Miami, Florida, who'd worked for many years with police departments in solving crimes. She holds classes for men and women with psychic talents and thought it would be a great chance for them to hone their skills.

And, since they were working in different parts of the country, Ingo felt that there wouldn't be any danger of them referencing or tuning in to one another.

First, Ingo sent them photos of Nungesser and Coli and their aircraft, along with a chart of the North Atlantic. His question was: "Did they go down in the ocean?"

They all came back with a no.

Then maps of Newfoundland, Nova Scotia, and the Bay of Fundy were sent.

Again the answer was no.

Next they received a map of Maine.

This time they replied with a yes.

He kept reducing the maps until he sent them a topographical map of the Round Lake area. Without hesitation, Ingo, Blue, Fanny, and her six students all put the plane wreck within a quarter-mile grid on the southern slope of Round Lake Hills. This struck me as amazing. Never in my dreams had I expected them all to agree on a crash site. If it were this easy for them to find lost historical ships and aircraft, future operations would all include psychic readings.

Now it was time to check out their predictions.

We gathered at Ray Beck's cabin. Ingo and I met at the airport in Bangor and drove into the woods. How I managed to find the cabin during a thunder and lightning storm in the wilds of Maine, I'll never guess. But miraculously I took all the correct turns until the lights of the cabin appeared. Ray was there, along with an old backwoodsman named Andy and two young fellows from New York City. Thunder rattled the log walls of the cabin as lightning flashed all around. It was indeed a haunted night. We sat amid the tempest, the big-time author, the renowned psychic, Ray Beck, who'd achieved fame and wealth inventing methods of plastic manufacturing, and Gunnar Hanson, a huge bear of a man at least six feet six and weighing 250 pounds. Only then did I learn that Gunnar was also an actor and had played the role of Leatherface, the butcher who dismembered bodies in the cult movie *The Texas Chainsaw Massacre*.

It goes without saying that I didn't get much sleep that night.

For the next two days, we combed the site as directed by the psychics. Their visions indicated that the plane had become buried, so I brought along a small magnetometer, but it proved useless. There is so much ferrous geology under Round Lake Hills that the needle on the mag's dial pegged and stayed there.

Then a plague struck. Just as we were wrapping up the search, the infamous Maine black flies appeared. I thought mosquitoes were bad. They're trifling compared to black flies. Two things mystify me. One, how such a teeny-weenie insect can cause such an irritating bite. And two, why anyone would go to live in the wilds of Maine where they proliferate and attack. Ray Beck saved everyone a fate worse than death by passing out hats with nets that covered the head and neck.

The resulting search came as a crushing defeat. *White Bird* was not there. The entire ground was covered twice, inch by inch. Not a shred of an aircraft was found. Swann and the others were stunned with disbelief. How could eight remote viewers, working in separate areas of the country, come up with the same location yet nothing be found? Could they have tapped into one another's minds? Is the plane indeed buried beneath the rocks of Round Lake Hills? Or was it carried off and sold for salvage many years ago without the finders reporting it? There were no solid answers.

I came up with theory number two hundred and thirty-seven. Since the *White Bird* had dropped its landing gear on takeoff from Paris and planned to land in the East River of New York, I figured that if they knew they were about to run out of fuel, Nungesser would have attempted a water landing. It wasn't outlandish, considering the plane was constructed for just such an event. If this were a possibility, then they may have crashed and sunk to the bottom in any one of a dozen lakes along their projected flight course in a line beyond Anson Berry.

IN APRIL of 1997, I called on Ralph Wilbanks, and he and Wes Hall towed *Diversity* up to Machias, where we all stayed at the Machias Inn. Dirk Cussler came along with Craig Dirgo and Dave Keyes, assistant to NUMA trustee Doug Wheeler. Bill Shea also graced us with his presence. There are few people I enjoy as much as Bill. We've been through some harrowing times together.

Connie Young, the noted psychic from Enid, Oklahoma, also joined the search. Connie had worked with the FBI on the Tylenol murders, with incredible results. Connie envisioned the *White Bird* coming down in water and drew a diagram that nearly matched Round Lake.

We hauled *Diversity* over narrow, muddy dirt roads and found a little ramp on Round Lake. Local residents were dumbfounded. They'd never seen a boat that large on any of the lakes in the area and couldn't believe we had pulled it over back-country roads. The effort didn't come easy. Ralph had to stop often so the guys could chop off branches that hung over the road.

Every inch of Round Lake was surveyed with both sidescan sonar and magnetometer. Wes dove on two or three interesting targets, but they all turned out to be old logs. The water, strangely enough, was not blue or green, but a dark, rather attractive brown from the tannic acid in the logs that littered the bottom.

We found no trace of *White Bird*.

The other lakes we planned to search were in primitive areas that Ralph's boat could not penetrate. He made a magnificent effort to take it all the way to the next body of water, Long Lake, actually arriving at a crude ramp, but the water was shallow and too littered with rocks for *Diversity* to be launched without knocking holes in her hull. This called for plan B.

We were lucky in meeting Carl Kurz, a local school-teacher who was also an avid hunter-fisherman and restored rifles and shotguns. He generously offered his Zodiac boat with an outboard motor for our back-country searches.

The rain came down as we tackled Long Lake, which stretched on the other side of the Round Lake Hills. Ralph stayed reasonably dry in his slickers and big red fireman's hat but grumbled most of the time, while Wes seldom muttered a word. The rest of us wandered around the woods between showers, but mostly sat in the cars.

During dinner that evening, Wes rolled out the sidescan recordings of Long Lake and examined them inch by inch. Plenty of rocks, but no sign of an aircraft or a lost fisherman's boat either.

Over the next few days, we searched two more lakes without success. Still no *White Bird,* but we had fun despite the continuous rain. Everyone had their fill of Maine lobsters. I saw one store that had lobster on sale for $2.99 a pound. Our morning breakfasts were enjoyable, as we gathered around the table at Helen's restaurant and planned the day's search. And then there were Helen's scrumptious pies. If he could have, Ralph would have loaded up *Diversity*'s cabin with them for the trip back to Charleston.

Dave Keyes took off early, because he was getting married and wanted a tattoo of his wife's name.

Craig, Dirk, Connie, and I drove back to Bangor to catch the flight to Boston and then on home. I stopped at Stephen King's house and walked up to the front porch. There were three or four cars in the driveway, including a Mercedes-Benz sports car. I rang the bell, knocked on the door, and mugged for the TV surveillance cameras. Nobody answered.

I yelled. "King, get out here, it's Cussler."

Dead silence.

I never knew if he was home or if I was *persona non grata.*

Fool that I am, I'd have probably volunteered for the rack during the Spanish Inquisition. I brought the gang back for another try in 1998. Except for Connie and Bill, the same motley crew returned. This time we were joined by my son-in-law, Bob Toft, and by William Nungesser, distant relative of Charles, who enthralled the team with stories about his famous kinsman.

Ralph and Wes searched the lakes while the rest of us

tramped through the jungles of Maine in a futile search for *White Bird*. And guess what? It rained the whole time. We all came back to the hotel drenched. I'll bet the manager would have turned the air blue with four-letter words if he'd known that I dried my sneakers in his microwave.

No matter how far we hiked, no matter how deeply we penetrated the wilderness, we always found old stumps of trees that had been cut down. It seemed that everywhere we searched, the lumberjacks had gotten there first.

A fascinating piece of history tells us that when the early colonies were formed in the seventeenth century, Maine was like a prairie. Trees grew only in occasional groves. For almost two hundred years, the land was farmed. But over the decades, farmers began to give up the land for other pursuits, or they moved west. Eventually, the open lands became covered with a giant forest of trees. Today it is so thick that it is difficult to walk through.

I mentioned to Carl that it seemed the entire state of Maine had been lumbered.

He nodded, smiled, and said, "Yes, twice."

If that is the case, why hasn't a hunter, a troop of Boy Scouts, or an army of lumberjacks ever stumbled on the remains of an old aircraft and the bones of her pilots? Scores of rumors and accounts of people finding an old engine have floated around for years. All have proven to be dead ends. Personally, I want to hear much more than simple engine sightings. Why haven't they also found the three huge aluminum fuel tanks that were as tall as a man, the instrument panel, the propeller that measured eighteen feet in diameter, or the dozens of other pieces that made up the aircraft?

If she hadn't been found after three-quarters of a century, the odds were only worsening with each passing season. Groups of local people spend their Sundays searching the woods. Perhaps one day some-one will get lucky and walk into the wreck before they recognize it. In the meantime, the stories still thrive of old-timers sighting odd things in the forest, of mysterious engines dragged out of the wilderness and sold for scrap, of aircraft remains on the side of mountains spotted from the air during World War II. None pans out.

Either *White Bird* sank out of sight in a lake, which NUMA has pretty well covered, or she crashed in the vast bog that has never been entered by man or beast.

My bet is on the bog.

Will I ever go back again?

I hate to give up. My NUMA team would have never found the *Hunley* if we had quit after the first few tries. The next step is aerial remote sensing. Even that is a long shot, but every avenue must be traveled. Someday, I'll come back with the gang and give it another shot.

Charles Nungesser, François Coli, and their magnificent *White Bird* lie waiting for discovery. They merit the fame for being the first to fly the Atlantic from east to west. It would not be right to leave them in an unmarked grave in a strange land. They must be found and returned to France as heroes.

They deserve no less.

PART TWELVE

U.S.S. *Akron*

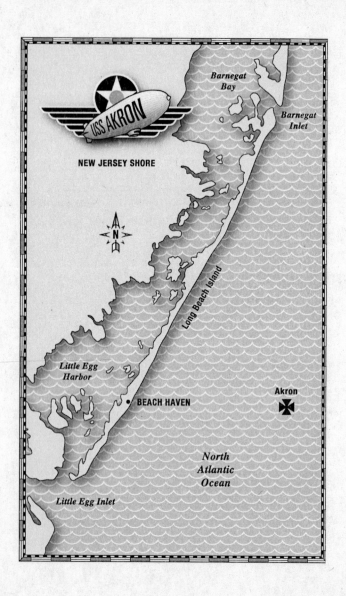

I

Lighter Than Air

1931–1933

"DROP BALLAST," COMMANDER FRANK McCord ordered.

A seaman sprinted across the short space of the control room and twisted the emergency ballast lever. Within seconds, four thousand pounds of water poured into the stormy air surrounding *Akron*.

The blimp rose a few hundred feet. She was now at thirteen hundred feet and holding.

The eight engines were pointed down and running full out—the ballast had been jettisoned. For a time, it seemed they had succeeded. Then the lightning, thunder, and gusts of winds enveloped them again. Within seconds, the rudder control wires were ripped loose, and the helm stopped responding.

Those on board had no way of knowing, but *Akron* had only minutes to live.

Two Years Before

"Damn," Lieutenant (jg) "Red" Dugan said, "you could put an entire circus in this building, with room left over for a couple of Egyptian pyramids."

Dugan was taking his first glance inside the Goodyear Zeppelin air dock in Akron, Ohio. The interior was cavernous, making the workers at the far end appear to be the size of insects. The air dock building was rounded at the top, with skylights in the sides partway up the walls to help with lighting. Huge banks of spotlights also added illumination, and at this moment they were being directed from the floor of the hangar up to the middle.

A single round duraluminum ring was suspended from the ceiling of the building. It was the first of a total of thirty-six rings that would be assembled together to form a lighter-than-air ship that would measure 785 feet in length and stand fifteen stories tall when completed. The ring consisted of inner and outer circles attached to one another by an intricate spiderweb of diamond-shaped aluminum struts. Nearest the floor and inside the inner circle were a pair of humps, where the walkways through the ship would eventually be located. The entire contraption was glowing with the dull silver color of fresh aluminum.

The Goodyear representative, Bruce Harding, was used to such reactions.

"We needed a big building to build the navy a big airship," he said, smiling.

"What does it cost . . . ," Dugan began to say.

"To heat it in winter?" Harding said, answering the unasked question.

"How did you know that would be my question?" Dugan asked.

"Because, Lieutenant Dugan," Harding said, "it's the first one everyone asks."

"So?" Dugan said.

"A lot," Harding said, as he directed Dugan farther inside.

WHEN FINISHED, U.S.S. *Akron* would be a behemoth. The flexible skin would contain 6 million cubic feet of gas. Power would come from eight Maybach Model VL-11 engines that each produced 560 horsepower. The power plants were a twelve-cylinder V-design with a dry weight of 1,200 pounds each.

Housed in eight engine rooms, the Maybachs transferred power via sixteen-foot-long shafts to the propeller shaft. The two-bladed, sixteen-foot-diameter propellers rotated so that they were able to provide thrust in four directions.

To fuel the eight engines, *Akron* would carry 126,000 gallons of fuel stored in a total of 110 tanks. Extensive pipes throughout the ship would allow the aircraft commander to redistribute the fuel as it burned. This, in addition to the unique water-recovery system—a collector was mounted close to the hull above each of the eight engines—allowed the commander to keep the ship on an even keel. But that only touched on what needed to be finished.

"Everything is on schedule, Lieutenant Dugan," Harding said. "It's just a lot to do."

The electrical power needed for radios, telephones,

lights, winches, pumps, and fans would come from a pair of eight-kilowatt internal combustion generators. The radios were state-of-the-art, with both intermediate-frequency and high-frequency transmitters. The high-frequency transmitter gave *Akron* a radio range of 5,000 nautical miles. Future plans called for the addition of facsimile equipment for receiving weather maps and other data. The antenna streamed 100 feet along the hull and sometimes 800 feet deployed alongside.

Because of the 785-foot length and the many systems requiring monitoring, communication aboard the airship would be critical. A total of eighteen telephones would be installed aboard *Akron,* with each able to sound an alarm. Voice tubes, a holdover from days past, would also be used. Mechanical engine telegraphs, similar to those on other navy ships, would be used to communicate with the engine rooms.

"What about the control car?" Dugan asked.

"It will be a streamlined affair," Harding said. "The forward third will house rudder, ballast, engine controls, and the like. The middle third is the navigation station. The last third provides access into the hull via a ladder."

"What about a redundant control station?" Dugan asked.

"It'll be located in the stern at the bottom of the lower control fin," Harding said.

Dugan had studied the plans. Most of what Harding was saying was old hat.

There was to be an airplane compartment of seventy by thirty-two feet, where the five Curtiss F9C2 airplanes would be hangared. Then there were the living accommodations that would be built on each side of the aircraft compartment—a total of eight eight- by ten-foot spaces housing the crew's toilet and washroom, bunk rooms with canvas bunks, galleys and messes for the officers, CPOs, and regular crews.

Akron was to be a minicity, complete with airport, when finished.

"It gets cold up there in the wild blue yonder," Dugan said.

"Aluminum piping from the forward engine rooms provides heat to the control rooms, common areas, and hangars," Harding said, "and I'm sure the navy has some nice warm clothing for those that venture in the walkways while aloft."

"Do you know they just changed the crew roster again?" Dugan asked.

"No," Harding said, "what's the latest?"

"Thirty-eight men, ten officers, and the pilots," Dugan said.

"Over fifty men, then," Harding said easily.

"That's the current plan," Dugan said.

Harding stared at the intricately woven struts that formed the single massive ring suspended from the ceiling of the hangar. "When she's done, she'll carry them," Harding said, "and a whole lot more, if need be."

ALONGSIDE THE FRAMEWORK of *Akron,* the Goodyear workers looked like ants on a watermelon. The workers swarmed from place to place as orders were shouted over radios and through bullhorns. The radio calls went to the operator of the overhead cranes, who carefully maneuvered the completed sections into place to be bolted to the frame. The bullhorns were used by the workers on the hull who were attaching the pieces together.

Today, the nose cone was being mounted.

The bow section was a thing of beauty: gently arcing longitudinal struts that met near the point at a small circular opening crisscrossed with aluminum support beams. It was delicate in design, sturdy in appearance, and detailed in the extreme. The crane operator dropped a hook into the center and waited while a harness was attached.

Then the crane operator raised the piece a few feet into the air to check the balance. Satisfied, the operator radioed down for the workers to attach another pair of lines starboard and port. These were attached to a second set of cranes. Once the cone was rigged, it was slowly hoisted upright, rotated sideways, and then brought alongside the main section of the hull.

Once positioned, the bow section was moved inch by inch into perfect alignment, then temporarily pinned and later bolted into place. By January of 1931, the main sections of the hull were in place and fastened down. The next few months saw the addition of the fins, elevators, and rudders. Once that was done, work began on the outer covering. The covering was sixty-five-pound-strength cotton seventy-four feet long and a foot or two wide with eyelets that were laced to the framework. This was covered with four coats of dope, two regular acetate, the last two containing aluminum powder. More than thirty thousand square yards of fabric would eventually cover the framework.

By July, the engines, propellers, water-recovery system, and other mechanical parts were being installed. On August 8, 1931, U.S.S. *Akron* was christened at a ceremony in Akron, Ohio. September 23 would be her maiden flight.

U.S.S. *AKRON*, the latest U.S. military airship, came from a long line that stretched back to the country's formation. President George Washington witnessed the first U.S. balloon flight in January 1793, when Frenchman Jean-Pierre Blanchard touched down from Philadelphia. Years later, the Civil War brought balloon development on both the Union and Confederate sides. Even so, it was not until the turn of the twentieth century that development truly accelerated.

In France in 1903, Albert Santos-Dumont built a successful powered dirigible, which he flew over the Parisian rooftops. A half-dozen years later, fellow Frenchman Louis Bleriot made a successful crossing of the English Channel in a powered airship capable of forty-five miles an hour. The following year, the U.S. Navy formed her first aviation group at Greenbury Point, Maryland, near Annapolis.

That first group was primarily concerned with airplanes, but there were students of lighter-than-air flight as well. By the year 1911, the British military had proved the worth of airships by successfully using them for North Sea patrol duty. That same year in Germany, Count Ferdinand von Zeppelin began the first commercial airline, with a total of five dirigibles in service.

World War I saw the first airship attack, as German lighter-than-air craft bombed London. Aviation was moving from science to practicality, and the uses continued to grow. By 1921, the U.S. Navy was compelled to form a new bureau to handle aeronautics.

The bureau would be led by Admiral William A. Moffett. Almost immediately, the program suffered losses. On August 24, 1921, while undergoing trials near Hull, England, the airship that the navy had planned to purchase from England, to be designated U.S. Navy *ZR-2*, broke apart. Forty-three men were lost, including most of the infant U.S. Navy aeronautics program.

But the program forged on.

Using *L-49*, a captured German zeppelin, construction was under way on a similar 680-foot airship, to be designated *ZR-1*. She was scheduled to fly in 1923. In the meantime, only two weeks before the crash of *ZR-2*, the navy had taken delivery of an Italian-made semirigid airship they would name *Roma*. Quite honestly, *Roma* was a pile of trash. Her half-dozen Asaldo engines were found to be unreliable and were later replaced with U.S.-made Liberty engines. Her outer covering contained a total of 184 holes needing patching. Once those hurdles were overcome, she took to the air. At this time, hydrogen gas was used instead of the safer helium because of cost. *Roma* made a few flights powered by the unstable gas.

On February 22, 1922, however, all went wrong.

While on a flight from Langley Field to Hampton Roads, Virginia, the pilot was unable to control the unwieldy airship. Striking a telephone pole that sparked, the Italian craft burst into flames. Of the forty-five aboard, thirty-four were killed and eight injured. Remarkably, three on board exited the wreckage virtually unscathed. The incident forced the U.S. Navy to take a hard look at using hydrogen as a lifting agent and at the aeronautics program as a whole.

By 1927, when Charles Lindbergh made his historic solo flight across the Atlantic Ocean, the U.S. Navy had only a single airship in service, *Los Angeles*, which had been constructed in Germany. Around this time, the navy put out contract specifications for the construction of two large airships to supplement the fleet. The bid was won by the Goodyear-Zeppelin Corporation, based in Akron, Ohio. Two years later, in 1929, interest in lighter-than-air craft increased. The German airship *Graf Zeppelin* attempted a round-the-world flight, which was featured daily in the Hearst newspapers.

That same year, the U.S. Navy took delivery of *ZMC-2*, a pudgy, metal-clad zeppelin that featured eight tail fins arranged at equal intervals around the stern. From the rear, *ZMC-2* had the appearance of an airplane nose cone, complete with stubby propellers. *ZMC-2*'s length was just under 150 feet, and she was powered by a pair of 200-horsepower Wright Whirlwind engines.

The next year, initial construction began on U.S.S. *Akron*.

TUESDAY, OCTOBER 24, 1931, was a big day. Today *Akron* was due to be commissioned. In the huge hangar at the Rigid Airship and Experimental Squadron at Lakehurst, New Jersey, the crowd was filled with dignitaries. President Litchfield of the Goodyear-Zeppelin Corporation led the speeches.

The entire affair was broadcast on NBC affiliate WEAF for nationwide consumption. From New York City, John Phillip Sousa and his band performed a lively rendition of "Anchors Aweigh." From Baltimore, Secretary of the Navy Charles Francis

Adams made remarks, followed by Assistant Secretary of the Navy David Ingalls. From Washington, Rear Admiral William Moffett added his comments.

Back in New Jersey, the future commander of *Akron*, Captain Charles Rosendahl, listened to the ceremony in amusement. Rosendahl was no rookie to zeppelins. As senior surviving officer aboard the ill-fated U.S.S. *Shenandoah*, Rosendahl was known as a courageous airman. After that, Rosendahl had spent some years as skipper of *Los Angeles*, and had been a participant on *Graf Zeppelin*'s round-the-world cruise.

Rosendahl was seasoned and ready.

FIVE DAYS after the ceremony, *Akron* made her first official flight. The passenger list included 10 officers and 49 men. This load was complemented by 31 members of the press and 19 other guests. Total passenger load was 109. Once everyone was aboard, Rosendahl began the orders to lift off.

"Engines three, four, seven, and eight," Rosendahl said, "tilt toward ground."

An airman repeated the instructions.

"Course two, seven, zero," Rosendahl said.

"Roger," the helmsman said.

The time was 7:15 A.M. *Akron* was flying south toward Annapolis.

"There's the academy," Milton Perkins, the rumpled Associated Press reporter, remarked.

His compatriot from the *New York Times*, Harold Temper, stared down at his wristwatch. "I make it twenty minutes past nine."

Less than an hour later, *Akron* was above Washington, D.C.'s naval yard.

Lunchtime came with *Akron* high above the Pennsylvania countryside.

Temper stared at his plate of food. "Think the crew usually eats like this?"

Perkins cut a piece of steak and left it on his fork while he wolfed down a shrimp. "Nope," he said, "this spread is just for the special guests and reporters."

"They must want a nice story to come out," Temper said.

"They must want Congress to give them more money," Perkins said, "so they can build some more of these."

"Why not?" Temper said. "Why not?"

Later that afternoon, *Akron* passed over Philadelphia and steered down toward Trenton. Near sunset, she landed back at her base at Lakehurst.

All in all, it was a successful debut.

FOR THE ORDINARY sailor, choosing an airship instead of a water ship was usually rewarded with better working conditions. The fact was, airship duty was dangerous. Crashes at the start of the program were frequent, but they were becoming less so. Still, if an airship went down, the chance of dying was great.

However, if one put that aside, the actual work aboard was a great deal better than that at sea. For one thing, there was almost no rust to contend with—the great bane of sailors at sea. The duraluminum did not rust, and because of weight limitations, iron was almost nonexistent. As far as food and shelter went, airship travel had a lot going for it—for one thing, the crews were smaller.

Instead of the cook needing to feed thousands of

sailors at a single sitting, the pace of work aboard a dirigible lent itself to small groups of men in the mess at one time. Everyone got a hot meal. As far as bunk arrangements went, because of the crew rotation the berths were never crowded. In addition, the motion of *Akron* gently rocked the canvas hammocks while under way.

Even so, the work was not simple and required a recruit with a higher-than-average intelligence and physical stamina. The numerous systems that made up *Akron* were complex and constantly in need of monitoring and adjustment, and it was important that accurate records were kept. As for stamina, movement inside the hull was along a series of ladders and walkways. The distances were great, and there was sometimes a need for speed.

And then there was the view—an endless carpet of America beneath you.

The view made up for any trying times.

COMMANDER ALGER DRESEL thought he was running late.

Steering his 1926 Pierce-Arrow Roadster past the guard gate at the entrance to Lakehurst, Dresel quickly accelerated down the access roads leading to the blimp hangar. The Pierce was a beautiful two-tone blue, with a tan top, and featured a golf bag compartment that was accessible from outside. He patted the thick buckskin leather on the seat in the forward compartment, then stared at the dash, where an ornate windup clock was set in the stainless steel engine-turned dashboard. Like everything aboard the aged automobile, the clock worked perfectly. Dresel was a lover of all things mechanical, and he personally maintained the Pierce-Arrow to perfection. Nine-fifteen A.M. He would arrive right on time.

Quickly parking, Dresel turned off the engine and removed his luggage.

"ASCENDING," the rudder man said loudly.

It was Sunday May 8, 1932, just before 6 A.M. *Akron* rose above Lakehurst on the first leg of a cross-country cruise. So far, only one of the new Curtiss planes, XF9C, had been delivered. The new plane and the older-model N2Y would fly up and attach to the amidships hook hanging under *Akron*'s belly once the airship was over Barnegat Bay, some sixty miles south.

This was Captain Rosendahl's last cruise as commander of *Akron*. His future replacement, Dresel, stood alongside him in the control car. At 7:20 A.M., just past Toms River, the telephone rang. Rosendahl lifted the receiver.

"Captain," a crewman in the aircraft dock said, "both planes are safely aboard."

"Very good," Rosendahl said. He turned to Dresel. "Both planes are secured. How would you like to take over command for a time?"

"That would be fine, Captain," Dresel said.

"Command to Commander Dresel," Rosendahl said.

Rosendahl turned to leave the control car. For the last couple of weeks, he had observed Dresel while on the ground. Rosendahl's observations had led him to believe that Commander Dresel was a calm and sober officer who cared about his men and his command. Rosendahl was not worried about turning *Akron* over to him, he just wanted to give the junior officer the benefit of as much flight experience as possible.

Rosendahl had learned that ground training went only so far.

LIEUTENANT HOWARD YOUNG started back down the ladder into his Curtiss. It always felt odd to enter the plane when she was hanging below *Akron*. Climbing up out of the plane was not so strange—the huge fuselage of the airship was overhead, and the mass signaled safety—but descending was another matter. First, the plane was attached by a hook that did not appear to be all that stable. Second, when climbing down, a person had a bird's-eye view of the ground passing thousands of feet below.

Young made it inside. He retrieved his logbook and a pack of Beeman's gum he had left inside. Slipping the book inside his leather flight suit, he pulled up the zipper so the book rode close to his stomach, then started back up the ladder. Young was no stranger to blimp operations—he had nearly five dozen takeoffs and landings under his belt—so climbing the ladder was nothing new. He quickly bounded up the rungs. Halfway between the plane and the opening into *Akron*, Young missed a rung. Luckily, his hands were firmly attached to the steps above. As Young's feet broke loose, he hung in the air by his hands as the wind outside buffeted him. A crewman above started down the ladder, but Young quickly recovered and continued up the ladder.

"You okay, sir?" the crewman asked, when Young entered the cockpit.

"Fine, fine," Young said, smiling.

"I'm glad," the crewman said, "because that's one long step down."

Young stared out the opening at the ground passing below.

"One real long step," he said.

THE EASTERN SEABOARD passed underneath *Akron* as she cruised south.

With the officers, men, and pair of pilots, the total personnel aboard numbered eighty exactly. Staying over the ocean, *Akron* passed Cape Hatteras, then turned to land. By lunchtime, she was passing over the navy yards at Norfolk, Virginia; just after eight that night she was over Augusta, Georgia.

While the airship was under way, there was a litany of jobs to be performed. Along with the cooking and serving the food, the cooks and mess men were responsible for cleaning the galleys and planning the menu. Electricians prowled the walkways inside the hull, checking connections and tending to any minor or major troubles that might arise. Radio operators handled the communications chores, while engine men tended to each of the eight engines. Riggers climbed inside the hull, making sure that the cloth covering was taut and not leaking, while mechanics tended to the frames and supports. *Akron* was a miniature city while in flight.

MONDAY THE NINTH, *Akron* passed over Houston just before 4 P.M.

An hour later, the first problem arose.

"Sir," the crewman shouted over the telephone, "we have a leak in a port fuel tank. Gasoline is entering the hull."

Rosendahl was in command of the blimp.

"Shut down all the engines save number seven," he said over the telephone to all hands. "We have liquid fuel inside the hull."

Next he adjusted the telephone to recall the crewman reporting the spill.

"How much have we lost?" he asked.

"Fifteen hundred gallons, sir," the man answered.

"Is the fuel still flowing?" Rosendahl asked.

"No, sir," the crewman said. "It was a crack alongside a weld. The level in the tank is now level with or slightly below the crack. If the ship remains stable, we should not have any further flow."

"I'll send a mechanic," Rosendahl said, "to see if we can temporarily patch the tank."

"Yes, sir," the seaman said.

Rosendahl turned to Dresel.

"We need to vent the fumes," he said. "Will you take charge of that?"

"Yes, sir," Dresel said.

Akron limped along on engine seven as the fuel was vented.

An hour later, things were looking up. The thick fumes in the control car were receding, and Dresel was reporting that most of the liquid gasoline had flowed out of the hull between spaces in the covering. It seemed the worst had passed.

"Sir," the radio operator reported by telephone, "San Antonio is reporting thunderstorms."

Rosendahl stared ahead. The ominous black clouds were still miles ahead, and right now the only ones near *Akron* were a few white puffy clouds that looked like cotton balls. Just then the hair on Rosendahl's arms stood out.

"Wow," he said seconds later, as a huge bolt streaked from one of the innocent-looking clouds and struck the ground below, "all this air is charged."

Dresel returned to the control car. "The fuel is vented as best we can," he said. "The rest of the fumes will just need to work themselves out."

"We've got a line of heavy weather ahead," Rosendahl said. "I'm ordering a course change to the north."

That night and all of the following day, *Akron* fought the storm.

Wednesday, May 11, *Akron* reached San Diego.

MOORING A BLIMP is not unlike mooring an aircraft carrier—there is a lot that can go wrong. *Akron*'s planes flew down through the cloud cover and landed safely; now it was the huge blimp's turn to try. Camp Kearney outside San Diego sat on a plateau of scrub brush and dust. Prone to gusts of wind and changing temperatures, she was far from the ideal spot for a blimp base. Still, Rosendahl had little choice— *Akron* was low on fuel.

Fog and clouds made visibility difficult as Rosendahl ordered *Akron* to descend. They were less than 1,000 feet above the ground before the view cleared. Rosendahl caught sight of the primary winch. The time was 11:42 A.M.

"Get a line down to that winch," he shouted over the telephone.

And then it all went wrong.

A freak of nature caused the temperature suddenly to

drop ten degrees, causing a temporary loss of buoyancy. Rosendahl ordered the engines turned downward, but that stirred up the dust, making visibility difficult. *Akron* barely moved.

"Full open on the helium valves," Rosendahl ordered.

But *Akron*'s angle kept growing.

Then several of the water ballast bags tipped over, pouring some three thousand gallons of water on those below. Nothing was going right.

"That's it," Rosendahl ordered. "I want free flight."

Orders were given to cut the cable holding *Akron* to the winch.

Two men were assigned to the forward cable, but one had abandoned ship by sliding down the cable to ground when the ship had taken her last lurch upward. The single man left was unable to cut the ⅞-inch steel cable. He dropped the bolt cutters to a group on the ground, asking them to cut the cable from below.

At numerous points along *Akron*'s hull, sailors from Camp Kearney were holding lines that would later be attached to anchors. Only their weight held them to the ground. Once the cable was cut, *Akron* began rising.

APPRENTICE SEAMAN "Bud" Cowart suddenly found himself dangling from a line some twenty feet in the air. Three other seamen had dropped safely to the ground, while Cowart and two more hung on for dear life. As Cowart watched, one of the men on the rope let go. The man plummeted downward. *Akron* was at a height of one hundred feet and continuing the ascent.

Cowart stared toward the ground in horror.

While the body plummeted down, the other

remaining sailor was hanging on by one hand. Just before the first man struck the ground, the second man dropped. *Akron* was at a height of two hundred feet. A sailor dropped through the air with his arms windmilling. Cowart watched as the man slammed into the earth, bounced a few feet in the air, then came to rest facedown.

Neither man would survive the fall.

Cowart was now alone, and the giant airship continued to climb. Finding toggles on the manila rope, Cowart managed to fashion a crude boatswain's seat as *Akron* hovered at fifteen hundred feet of elevation. On board the airship, the situation was coming back under control.

"Men," Captain Rosendahl said over the telephone, "the landing was aborted and now we have a situation on our hands. One of the landing crew is dangling from our mooring line, and we need to get him aboard. Proceed to that objective at a safe pace."

Hanging the receiver back in the cradle, Rosendahl turned to Dresel.

"You just witnessed the worst that can happen," he said. "Remember it, and don't let it happen to you."

"Yes, sir," Dresel said.

"Now take over the helm. I'm going back to see how Lieutenant Mayer is doing on bringing aboard that sailor."

Cowart shouted up at the *Akron*. "When are you going to haul me aboard?"

"It may take an hour or better," Mayer shouted back, "so secure yourself to ride it out."

"What's the deal?" Rosendahl asked.

"We need to get a line to him," Mayer said, "then try to winch him aboard."

It would be two long hours before Cowart was finally yanked aboard.

Seven hours after the first attempt, *Akron* finally moored at Camp Kearney.

AKRON TRAVELED NORTH from San Diego to San Pedro. For the next few weeks, the airship would take part in training exercises off the West Coast of the United States. On June 6, the weather was right for the trip east to Lakehurst. From San Pedro to Banning, California, over the Salton Sea. Then south to Yuma, Phoenix, Tucson, and Douglas, Arizona. Next came El Paso, Odessa, Midland, Big Spring, and Abilene, Texas. Across the state line and past Shreveport, Louisiana. Mississippi and Alabama, a stop at Parris Island, South Carolina, and then the return to Lakehurst.

Akron had been away thirty-eight days and had traveled more than seventeen thousand miles.

As THE new year dawned, *Akron* received her third captain in nineteen months as Commander Frank McCord assumed leadership of the blimp. McCord wasted no time on the ground—two hours after assuming control, *Akron* set off for a cruise to Miami.

Throughout January and February, McCord kept up a full flight schedule.

On March 4, *Akron* flew over the inauguration of President Franklin Roosevelt. That same night, she returned to Lakehurst and cold temperatures. The cold held for nearly a week, curtailing flight operations. As soon as it warmed enough, McCord set off for the warmer climes of Florida and the Bahamas. The grueling schedule continued throughout the rest of the month.

Then came the fickle winds of April.

AKRON LIFTED OFF from Lakehurst on April 3, 1933, at 7:28 P.M.

Commander Frank McCord was in charge, and he was assisted by Lieutenant Commander Herbert Wiley as his executive officer, as well as Lieutenant Dugan as his engineering officer. The crew would consist of seventy-six officers and men, including Rear Admiral Moffett, who wanted to see *Akron* in operation firsthand.

The temperature at liftoff was 41 degrees Fahrenheit, and the barometer read 29.72. Akron was carrying 73,600 gallons of fuel, enough for six days aloft, though this cruise was scheduled for forty-eight hours. Because of the fog, plane operations had just been canceled. As *Akron* lifted from the pad then turned her bow east, one of the pilots who was securing his Curtiss on the runway turned and stared up at the giant blimp. She was a beauty, no doubt about that—her silver fuselage at bow and stern was lit by the red and blue of the ground lights, while the red and green of her running lights added a festive touch as well. The pilot watched as the airship ascended. In seconds, the upper part of the hull was barely visible in the fog; by the time a full minute had passed, only a hazy outline of the lower hull and control car remained in sight. Then that was gone.

"Set a course east to Philadelphia," McCord instructed the navigator. "The weather report indicates they have only scattered clouds."

"Aye, Captain," the navigator said.

Less than an hour later, *Akron* passed over Philadelphia, finding the visibility fair to good. In the control car, McCord stared at the latest weather report. A thunderstorm was being reported in Washington, D.C., and was said to be moving north and east toward them. McCord decided on a course east by southeast to skirt the storm. If all worked according to plan, he would miss the storm's fury and arrive off Newport, Rhode Island, for a test scheduled for seven the next morning.

The test would never happen.

SAINT ELMO'S FIRE. The brush discharge of electricity was dancing from the flagstaff of *Phoebus*. A flaming phenomenon that never signaled calm or comfort, a sign of disturbances in the heavens, a beacon of foul weather as sure as a snowball in the face.

Captain Carl Dalldorf burped as his ship rocked, tasting the sour tang of a dill pickle. *Phoebus*, a motor tanker registered in Danzig, Germany, was crewed by Germans. Dalldorf and his crew had spent a fine weekend in upper Manhattan, mingling with the German population and frequenting the Bierstubes. Casting off from Pier 6 at 2 P.M., *Phoebus* was bound for Tampico, Mexico. The ship had spent most of the afternoon and evening in a pea-soup fog. Now, just before 11 P.M., lightning began to strike the water around the vessel, while thunder reverberated loudly from the heavens.

Dalldorf stared at his barometer. There had been a sharp drop.

He knew the signs—this was a storm that bore watching.

*

UP THE DELAWARE RIVER, starboard back across New Jersey, hit the water near Asbury Park—that was the course. But the storm kept advancing.

"Get me the latest weather map," McCord said, just after 11 P.M.

Wiley headed for the aerological office above the control car and consulted with Lieutenant Herb Wescoat. Wiley liked Wescoat, who, unlike some of the meteorological officers Wiley had served with, had at least an inkling of a sense of humor.

"What have you got?" Wiley asked.

"We received about two-thirds of the map—it came in code," Wescoat replied, handing Wiley the copy.

"This doesn't look too promising," Wiley noted.

"No," Wescoat said, "it doesn't."

"Do you have any recommendations for the captain?" Wiley asked.

"I'd ask him to land as soon as possible," Wescoat said logically.

"I doubt he'll do that with Admiral Moffett aboard," Wiley said.

"Hmm," Wescoat said slowly. "Then I'd recommend we all pray."

CAPTAIN DALLDORF was due to remain on watch until midnight. By the look of the storm, he might stay on duty a while longer. A rogue wave had just rolled over *Phoebus*'s bow, a most rare occurrence. In addition, not five minutes before, his second in command had come across a sailor lying in the rain on the walkway outside the pilothouse. After he was revived, the man explained that when he'd gone to grip a handrail, an electrical charge had shocked him and thrown him back six feet, where he'd struck his head. That was just bizarre. Lightning usually passes through ships, leaving no damage. Dalldorf guessed that because *Phoebus* was carrying a load of truck batteries to Mexico, maybe the pooled energy had somehow created the shock.

Whatever the case, the storm and the general feeling in the air were disturbing.

"Bring me some more coffee," Dalldorf ordered a crewman. Then he lit an American-made cigarette and took a puff.

THEY WERE minutes from death and miles from safety, as April 3 became April 4.

A lightning bolt streaked through the sky, and *Akron* was lit as though it were in the beam of a spotlight. At just that instant, the control car lurched from side to side.

"Drop ballast," Commander McCord ordered.

A second later, the helmsman lost control of the rudder as the wires parted. The wheel began to spin wildly. Five squawks rang out over the telephone system, signaling landing positions. *Akron* continued to lose altitude.

"Drop more ballast," McCord ordered.

Just then, a horrible shrieking was heard from the hull of *Akron*. The ship's structure was breaking apart. The upper fin had been lost to the violence of the storm, and the strain from the loss of the fin broke frame girders. Some of the broken girders punctured the helium bags. *Akron* began to leak like a water-filled balloon poked by a pin. The airship continued to descend.

Wiley stared from a small window in the control car, as the blimp lowered through the thick fog. At about two hundred feet, he first caught sight of the waves below.

"I see the water approaching," he said ominously.

No one in the control car replied.

Throughout *Akron*, the seventy-plus men made preparations for a water landing. Those with time fastened their coats firmly; a few managed to grab some light personal items. One scribbled a note to loved ones and stuffed it into the pipe forming one end of his hammock, never to be recovered. Many simply awaited the inevitable.

Akron sagged lower, her bones broken and her lungs punctured.

Then, at a distance of less than fifty feet above the waves, she stopped and hung in the air for a moment. There was no doubt she was a beautiful ship. A second later, a final lightning bolt lit her gleaming silver hull and surrounded the ship with a glow of electrical energy.

Then, like a rock dropped from a bridge, *Akron* plunged down into the ocean.

"THE LIGHTS HAVE DISAPPEARED," the lookout declared.

"Are you certain?" Dalldorf asked.

"Yes, sir," the lookout noted, "they dropped below the horizon a minute ago."

"It's probably an aircraft," Dalldorf said. "Fix our position."

The navigator took a minute to make notes on a sheet of paper. "Latitude 39 degrees, 40 minutes north; longitude 73 degrees, 40 minutes west," he said.

Just then his second in command burst through the door of the pilothouse.

"The smell of gasoline is very heavy," he said. "It's all around us in the water."

"Prepare to lower lifeboat number one," Dalldorf said, "and stand by to rescue survivors."

Phoebus remained until first light, when the Coast Guard arrived. Three men were taken aboard the German vessel. They were the only survivors of the crash of *Akron*.

II

No Surfing in New Jersey

1986

ONCE I BEGAN RESEARCHING EARLY AIRSHIPS and their often tragic endings, I became hooked on their fascinating stories. The stories of *Akron* and her sister rigid airships *Macon* and *Shenandoah* tell of a bright future turned dark when all three fell out of the sky and crashed. I wondered if any of their wreckage had gone undiscovered.

Shenandoah's crash site in Noble County, Ohio, is well known and marked in a farmer's field by a memorial. *Macon* went down in deep water off Point Sur, California, in 1937. A search was launched for her resting site because of a desire to find the Curtiss aircraft that she'd taken into the sea with her. An expensive deepwater project was successful in finding her remains and a few of her aircraft, but none was salvaged. Video pictures of the wreckage revealed that the planes were too damaged and corroded by the sea to be restored, so they were left to rest on the bottom of the Pacific.

That left *Akron*.

I wish I could write an electrifying tale of adventure about finding *Akron* that would fire the imagination and leave a lasting impression. But the search was nothing but a struggle against a violent and unrelenting world. A search of the archives at the Washington Library put me on the track of the salvage vessels that recovered pieces of *Akron*'s wreckage and brought it to shore on a barge. An examination of the log of the *Falcon*, the famous navy salvage boat that had raised the submarine *S-51* under the leadership of Commander Edward Ellsburg in 1925, and worked as a dive and survey boat for thirty years, put me on the track leading to the *Akron*'s grave. The logbook gave the coordinates where *Falcon* moored. Her position was reasonably close to the main debris field that was twenty-seven miles offshore from Beach Haven, New Jersey.

The volunteer NUMA team assembled in Beach Haven in July of 1986. Most came from Long Island, New York. Al and Laura Ecke came with their thirty-four-foot boat. Dr. Ken Kamler acted as team physician and diver, along with Mike Duffy, a seasoned oceanographer. Zeff and Peggy Loria also came along to lend a hand, set up logistics, and run things when I had to go home a day early to begin a book tour. My good old pal, dependable Bill Shea, who suffered the seasickness of the damned on our voyages around the North Sea, also came along.

We gathered at a motel on the beach, a short drive from the marina where the Eckes' boat was docked. The lady at the desk stood nearly six feet tall, her blond hair pulled back into a tight bun. She stared at me through steely piercing eyes that I swore were focusing on a calendar hanging on the wall directly behind my head.

"*Ja,* vas du you vant?"

I should have known I was in for it. She had the face of the town rat catcher.

"I have a reservation. My name is Cussler."

She snapped open a ledgerlike book with razor precision and perused the names. "*Ja,* Cussler, a good German name. You *will* fill out the register."

I signed.

"Your credit card." It was a demand, not a request.

She made an imprint and handed back the card, but not before biting one corner as if it were a counterfeit coin. "Now the orders."

I looked at her. "Orders?"

"You *will* not drink alcohol in your room. You *will* have no parties in your room. You *will* not bring animals into your room. You *will* not smoke in your room. You *will* not make loud sounds or play loud music in your room. You *will* not eat in your room."

"Can I watch TV in my room?"

"Twenty-five cents for ten minutes. There is a slot next to the power button."

"Can I use the bathroom?" I said, in a pathetic attempt to beleaguer her.

"If you are hygienically neat."

"But can I sleep in the bed?"

A dark scowl crossed her face as she caught on. "If you do not adhere to the orders, you will have to stay somewhere else."

"My friends are here."

"That's your problem."

I couldn't resist one more. "What time do we fall out in formation for roll call?"

"Here is your key. Room 27."

"That's upstairs," I complained. "I'd prefer a room on ground level."

"We do not play musical chairs," she said, her hostility rising.

I could see it was a lost cause, so I picked up my luggage and hiked up the stairs. The room was dark when I entered. Hanging over the bed was a print of a man standing behind a desk. I walked closer, thinking he might have a spit curl over one eye and a clipped broom mustache.

But, no, it was Elvis Presley. I'd never seen a picture of him standing behind a desk before.

I unpacked and met the rest of the gang at dinner. We met several local divers, but none were familiar with *Akron*. The first three days we encountered miserable weather and stayed ashore. I might have risked the rough seas. I had certainly run search lanes dragging detection gear through much worse in the North Sea, but except for Bill, who would go despite his suffering, this was not a crew who relished eight- to ten-foot waves.

An unforeseen problem was Ecke's boat. Though a nice and comfortable craft for short day trips, it had only one engine. If it faltered in a gale, forget it.

Stormy weather or not, since I was a California beach bum and enjoyed body surfing, I put on my swim trunks and headed to the beach, thinking the storm might kick up some good waves. Never having surfed the East Coast, I was stunned to find that the waves didn't come up much above my knees, a condition that ranges from the Florida Keys until Long Island, New York. I went back to the motel, sat under an umbrella by the postage stamp–sized pool, and read the *New York Times*.

At last, after we enjoyed the preeminent lifestyle of Beach Haven in the rain for three days, the sun appeared, and our jolly band of sea hunters set sail from the dock at Little Egg Harbor and cruised out to sea. With only one engine, the boat drove through the waves with the sensation of a hacksaw cutting marble. It took us four hours to run the twenty-seven miles to our search grid.

The instant we arrived, Captain Ecke peered at some dark clouds on the eastern horizon and proclaimed, "We have to return to port. There's a storm coming."

"Storm, hell!" I protested. "We just got here."

I argued, pleaded, and begged, finally cajoling him into remaining on station. The storm, as I predicted, continued north and we had calm seas for the search. The sidescan sonar went out and we began running lines. After four hours, not so much as a beer bottle could be seen protruding from the surface. Then the sonar recorded a strange anomaly, and I sent Mike Duffy and Dr. Kamler over the side to investigate. Ten minutes later, they surfaced and said the anomaly was nothing but a grotesque rock. Could the sands have buried *Akron*? I didn't think so. The divers said the bottom had the consistency of gravel and seemed quite firm.

With a four-hour trip back to port staring us in the face, I called it quits for the day. We pulled up anchor and chugged home. Later, before we all headed out to a seafood restaurant for dinner, Ecke and I sat at a patio table and studied the charts to see if there was a discrepancy in the positions given by the navy salvage ships. No gleam of joy could have pierced the dismal gloom when I realized Harold had mistakenly converted the *Falcon*'s logbook coordinates to the wrong LORAN coordinates. We had searched over a mile away from where we were supposed to be.

When I called Harold on the error, he became indignant and shrugged his shoulders, as if the entire wasted day were a voyage down the lazy river in the noonday sun. Since he was supplying the boat, I bit my tongue and slinked off to the restaurant, wondering about the meaning of life.

The weather looked good the next morning, so we tried again. Déjà vu. We had no sooner arrived at the search grid than Harold swept his hand toward another front of storm clouds and turned the boat back to shore. These flights of fancy were beginning to get to me, but this time Harold had a point. The Coast Guard hailed us over the radio and urged us to find a safe harbor.

We sailed into the Beach Haven Channel just as the squall struck with fifty-mile-an-hour winds. Harold was in Nirvana. I've never seen a man in the throes of ecstasy before. He seemed to experience an unrestrained joy from motoring four hours out and four hours back without accomplishing anything. Still, I had to hand it to him. Being a fireman, he was as hardy as they come.

The third day was the charm. Clear sky and calm seas. We arrived at the proper coordinates and began searching. We quickly began to record debris scattered around the seafloor eighty feet under our keel. The divers went down and found a galley stove from the dirigible, as well as twisted duraluminum beams. No more were we broken and saddened souls.

I had to fly out the next morning to begin a tour for my latest book. The crew, bless them, then went out again with Zeff Loria running the sidescan, and found the aircraft's lower fin lying on the bottom. Divers searched a small part of the seven-hundred-foot debris field and found piles of twisted beams and support frames half-buried in the seafloor. No aircraft were visible, since none were aboard when *Akron* crashed into the sea. There were few intact artifacts left from the great zeppelin, whose hull was only a hundred feet shorter than *Titanic*. Her career was short, but she and her sisters had made a lasting impression on the history of lighter-than-air craft. It was sad and unfortunate that the great airships could not have been a major stepping-stone into air transportation, but most all met with tragic fates. Now the graves of *Akron*, *Macon*, and *Shenandoah* are all accounted for. I wish that someday professional archaeologists would return to *Akron*, retrieve her artifacts, and put them on display in the museum at Lakehurst, New Jersey.

One final note on a very strange story related to *Akron*. Not long after she was launched, the dirigible was scheduled to fly over a football game in Huntington, West Virginia. The date was October 10, 1931. As thousands watched, a huge zeppelin cruised over the Ohio River and approached the stadium at only three hundred feet. Then, to the spectators' horror, it suddenly crumpled and crashed to the ground. Several men were seen to escape in parachutes. After a thorough search, however, rescuers were stunned to find no sign of the *Akron*. No victims or wreckage could be found. Later investigation revealed that the flight by the navy dirigible over the stadium had been canceled. Not only had *Akron* *not* crashed in full view of a horde of sworn witnesses, but she had been over a hundred miles away at the time, and no other lighter-than-air craft were reported missing.

The eerie apparition has never been explained.

PART THIRTEEN
PT-109

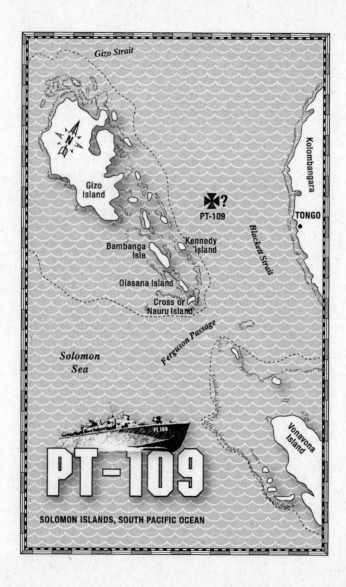

Gizo Strait

Kolombangara

Gizo
Island

PT-109

TONGO

Bambanga
Isle

Kennedy
Island

Blackett Strait

Olasana Island

Cross or
Nauru Island

Ferguson Passage

Solomon
Sea

Vonavona
Island

PT-109

SOLOMON ISLANDS, SOUTH PACIFIC OCEAN

I

PT-109

1943

IT WAS ANOTHER DAY OF TROPICAL HEAT AND humidity, the type of smothering air that brings upon a festering malaise of listlessness and diminished expectations. Even the fact that the crew of *PT-109* was due a night in port was doing little to add enthusiasm to what had become an endless war against sweat and insects. The crew was battle-weary and dulled by exhaustion.

They dreamed of home fires and cool breezes.

"Maybe we can scrounge up some bread," said Raymond Albert.

Albert was from Akron, Ohio, twenty years old and always hungry.

"To make some Spam sandwiches?" radioman John Maguire said dubiously.

"No more Spam," Albert said. "Perhaps we can shoot a few fish and have fish sandwiches."

Just then the sounds of an approaching shore launch

filtered into the cove where *PT-109* was moored.
Seated behind the bosun's mate was a slim, sandy-
haired man who usually sported a broad smile. This
afternoon, however, no smile was visible.

"Maybe Kennedy's brought some fresh rations,"
Maguire said hopefully.

"If he had fresh food," Albert said, "he'd look
happy. He doesn't look happy."

PT-109 LOOKED USED and abused, but it was not
the result of a long life. The trim eighty-foot vessel had
first met water in July 1942, just over a year before, in
the polluted waters near her factory in Bayonne, New
Jersey. Constructed of plywood by ELCO, the Electric
Boat Company, she had first been assigned to the PT
Boat Training Center in Melville, Rhode Island, before
traveling through the Panama Canal on a transport
ship. Eventually reaching Noumea in the South Pacific,
she had been towed to the Solomon Islands and joined
the fighting near Guadalcanal. Powered by three
twelve-cylinder Packard engines and sporting a total of
four torpedo tubes, she was finished in a dark-green
paint scheme that allowed her to hide under a canopy of
foliage when not on patrol.

After training at Melville, John F. Kennedy assumed
command in April of 1943.

THE BASE for *PT-109* was named Todd City in
honor of Leon E. Todd, the first PT-boat crewman
based at Lumberi to die. The island where Lumberi was
located was named Rendova. To the east of Rendova
was the Solomon Sea; to the west, New Georgia Island.
To the north lay Gizo Island and the Japanese base

at Gizo Town, which fronted Blackett Strait. West of Gizo was the tall, tree-covered mountain named Kolombangara that formed the opposite edge of the strait. Rendova was almost uninhabited until the navy base was established, and the jungles nearby were still wild. Brightly colored parrots flitted from one coconut palm to another, while lizards climbed atop the rotting coconuts at their bases. Flies and winged beetles took to the air. When the sun was setting, bats and night birds could be seen taking flight. The waters near Rendova were warm and teeming with life. Coral reefs poked up through the crystal-clear water, and tropical fish abounded.

It could be considered paradise, save for the war raging nearby.

LIEUTENANT (JG) JOHN FITZGERALD KENNEDY climbed from the shore launch, clutching a folder holding orders and operational information. A handsome man at twenty-six years old, he had been raised with privilege. After a childhood in Massachusetts, he had attended boarding school at Choate, followed by graduation from Harvard University. Son of the former ambassador to the Court of St. James, Joseph Kennedy, he had little in common with the men who served under him.

Still, his crew had found their well-heeled skipper both friendly and approachable.

A stern taskmaster when that was warranted, he also showed leniency with regulations he found arbitrary or unsound. And while he was tasked with maintaining at least a reasonable sense of navy decorum, he was more concerned with matters that pertained to crew readiness and operations. There was one other thing that endeared him to his men—there was no job he would not do himself. When cargo needed to be loaded, he helped. When the boat needed scraping or painting, he reached for a tool.

Those who had served under other PT-boat skippers rated Kennedy a favorite.

"GATHER 'ROUND," Kennedy said as he climbed the gangplank. "I have our orders."

Ensign Leonard Thom from Sandusky, Ohio, the second in command, shouted down to the sailors in their bunks. Thom was a large man with light hair and a blond beard. Built like a football player, he had an eternally positive attitude that flowed forth like waves of warmth. Once the crew filtered abovedecks and stood milling on the stern, he turned to Kennedy.

"Men are assembled, sir."

Kennedy glanced around and nodded.

"We've been ordered to go out tonight," Kennedy said, staring at his men.

"Damn," someone said under his breath.

Grumbling could be heard as the men scattered, but all in all they took the news surprisingly well. There was a war in progress, and war demanded unusual measures. Personal desires gave way to sacrifice, weariness to preparation, fear to duty. They had a job to do—and they'd do it.

Still, not a single man could envision the horror they were about to face.

"WIND IT UP," Lieutenant Kennedy said, a few minutes before half past four the afternoon of August 1.

A rumble filled the air as the first of the trio of Packard engines was started. Down in the engine room, Motor Machinist First Class Gerald Zinser waited for the word to engage the drive.

Behind the helm, Lieutenant Kennedy revved the Packard, then adjusted it back to an idle. Satisfied with the sound, he called down for the drive to be engaged. Then he carefully steered *PT-109* away from shore. Slowly the boat made way up the channel. The sun was low in the sky, and the light through the haze cast a pale orange glow over the heights of Rendova Peak.

Seaman Second Class Raymond Albert was on the stern deck. He could see sand crabs scurry from the water's edge as the noisy PT boat idled past. Overhead a small flock of green parrots flitted past, changing directions in midair before heading across Lumberi to find refuge in the tall palms. The wake angled toward shore and washed against the mangrove roots lining the rim of the water.

Ensign George Ross was a friend of Kennedy's who had hitched a ride on *PT-109* for the night. Formerly the executive officer of *PT-166*, a vessel sunk by friendly fire on July 20, Ross was without a boat and wanted to take part in the action. Kennedy offered to let him operate the aged thirty-seven-millimeter army antitank gun that *PT-109* had been tasked with testing. The gun was crudely lashed with planks onto the foredeck, and Ross was staring at the placement and wondering if it would remain on board after it was fired. There was little Ross could do about it now, so he raised his eyes and stared off the bow.

Fifty yards ahead, several bottlenose dolphins leapt in the air, looking for all the world like a flowing arc of wet gray paint. Staring to port, Ross watched the water a hundred yards ahead boil as a school of baitfish danced across the top of the water. To starboard, Ross thought he caught the glimpse of a shark's fin piercing the surface, but when he looked more carefully, he could see nothing.

"ENSIGN THOM," Kennedy shouted above the noise of the engines.

"Sir," Thom said, approaching from the stairs leading belowdecks.

"Go below and tell Zinser that engine three feels sluggish."

"Yes, sir," Thom said as he went belowdecks.

"SKIPPER REPORTS number three feels sluggish," Thom shouted over the din.

Zinser was wiping his hands with a rag. He pointed at a round glass bowl attached to an engine.

"Seems to be okay now," Zinser said. "There was some gunk in the fuel."

"I'll let him know," Thom said, as he started to leave.

"Mr. Thom?" Zinser said.

Thom turned around and smiled at Zinser. "Yes, Zinser?"

"We're going to see action tonight, aren't we?"

The enlisted men respected Thom. One reason was because he was as open and honest with the crew as the rules allowed. "Word is the Express is running. We are going to try to sink a few."

Zinser nodded. "What's the chance we get tomorrow night off?"

"Hard to say," Thom said. "I guess that depends on tonight."

Thom had never spoken truer works, but neither he nor Zinser knew that yet.

THOM WENT to the helm station and touched Kennedy's shoulder. "Zinny had some bad fuel."

"Yeah," Kennedy said, "she's smoothed out now."

Thom stared at the sky. The last flicker of light was washing down the side of the distant peak. In the Solomon Islands, it grows dark quickly. One moment there is waning sunlight, and within half an hour the first stars can be seen. It was as if a switch had been flipped off.

"It'll be clear tonight, sir," Thom noted.

"All the better for hunting," Kennedy said easily.

ON THE JAPANESE destroyer *Amagiri*, there was a level of tension that came from knowing they were being stalked. Somewhere in the night were the pesky American mosquito boats. The fast plywood attack crafts came quickly and disappeared just as fast. This was a strange and new type of marine warfare. The Japanese sailors were not trained for this. Historical rules dictated that ships fired on other ships when they were in sight. Sneaking and hiding in the dark was a little unnerving.

Truth be told, the PT boats had not caused much damage—their torpedoes were notoriously inaccurate, and to use their deck guns, they needed to be close enough to the ships of the Express to be in harm's way themselves. Still, they were out there in the blackness, came quickly without warning, and sped away as if on the wings of eagles.

Gunner Hikeo Nisimura adjusted the chin strap on his helmet and stared to port. From his vantage point in the bow gun, he had an unusually broad view of the areas *Amagiri* steamed past. This evening, the top of the peak on Kolombangara Island was shrouded in clouds. As he watched, the last remnants of the setting sun dropped below the horizon, and the peak began to grow purple from top to bottom, as if a giant had poured on a ladle of plum sauce.

And then, although the temperature was nearly seventy degrees, Nisimura felt a chill.

IN *AMAGIRI*'S PILOTHOUSE, Commander Kohei Hanami stared at the chart, then ordered the speed increased to thirty-five knots. Hanami was both a stern taskmaster and one who believed in rigid schedules. In the holds of his command were 912 soldiers and nearly a hundred tons of supplies that were bound for Munda Airfield, where the Japanese army was fighting a losing battle against the American marines. *Amagiri*'s part in this plan was to arrive at the base at Vila on Kolombangara Island, off-load the soldiers and supplies, then steam back to her base before daylight.

ENSIGN ROSS walked back from the bow to the helm. The flotilla was cruising north through Ferguson Passage. To starboard, barely visible in the black of night, was the outline of Vonavona Island. Ross stood for a moment, hands on his hips, and smelled the air. Salt and seawater, mildew and fungus. From over the water on land came the scent of night-blooming jasmine and limes mixing with the musty smell of mangrove roots at low tide. He sniffed again.

A smell of home.

The scent of baked beans wafted through a hatch. Then the smell of meat being fried in lard. Beans and Spam was the order of the night. Ross just hoped the cook had some powdered lemonade to add to their chlorinated water for flavor.

Reaching Kennedy behind the helm, he smiled. "Smells like dinner's almost ready, Jack."

Kennedy adjusted his orange kapok life vest. "I can hardly wait, Henry," he said, smiling.

"I checked out the thirty-seven-millimeter," Ross said. "She's ready for firing."

"Marney's in the forward turret?" Kennedy asked.

"Yes," Ross said.

"He's a good Massachusetts man," Kennedy said, "from Chicopee."

"I talked to him," Ross said. "He mentioned he's new to your crew."

"Yes," Kennedy said. "Starkey, Marney, and Zinser down in the engine room—all new to *109.*"

"How do you feel about them?" Ross asked.

"All good men," Kennedy noted. "Ready to fight."

"That's good," Ross said, "because I have a feeling they'll soon have a chance."

Kennedy nodded and stared into the black night. "I do too, Henry," he said easily. "I do, too."

The time was half past 9 P.M.

THERE WERE a total of fifteen PT boats on patrol, as the Japanese flotilla consisting of the destroyers *Amagiri, Arashi, Hagikaze,* and *Shigure* steamed south. The boats worked in small groups, with *PT-109* patrolling with *PT-157, PT-159,* and *PT-162* of Division B.

Radar was a recent addition to the PT boats, and only a few of the vessels had been equipped. The radar sets were finicky, unreliable, and subject to interpretation by the operator. Still, they were better than nothing—and when they did work, they added a margin of safety and success to what were for the most part random search-and-destroy missions.

On *PT-159*, the operator stared at the glowing green screen intently. A second later, he shouted to the captain. "Radar contact, four possible barges, three miles distant, along Kolombangara."

The skipper climbed down to look at the radar screen, then back up to stare into the blackness. After repeating the maneuver a few more times, he ordered the deck guns set to fire low. With the crude radar, he was still certain the blips were barges.

In fact, they were the four Japanese destroyers.

PT-159 raced close to fire and was met with fire from the heavy guns of the destroyers. Now knowing his target, the skipper pushed the buttons on the dashboard to launch a pair of torpedoes. Unfortunately, the skipper of *PT-159* chose not to break radio silence to inform the other boats of the flotilla passing. The torpedoes missed and the flotilla steamed south without harm.

WHILE THE WATERS around Kolombangara Island were filled with Japanese destroyers and barges, along with American PT boats and heavy cruisers to the north, there was a different type of war being fought.

It was a solitary and introspective affair of waiting, watching, and reporting.

High atop Kolombangara Island, in a crude camp

consisting of a bamboo hut, was a brave Australian armed with a telescope, binoculars, radio, and little else. Lieutenant Arthur Reginald "Reg" Evans was a member of the Australian Coastwatcher Service. The service had been formed in World War I to help in patrolling Australia's vast coastline. The Australian Navy hit upon the idea of enlisting the help of local fishermen, harbormasters, and postmen to watch the coast and report any suspicious activity by telegraph. The idea proved successful and was reintroduced and expanded as World War II came along. Submarines, aircraft, and small boats transferred the coastwatchers to small islands in the South Pacific to provide eyes on the ground. They reported ship and plane movements, recruited local natives to help the effort against the Japanese, and provided weather reports for the Allied forces. The job was lonely, dirty, and dangerous.

The Japanese knew of the coastwatchers, and they hunted them down with dogs.

Reg Evans sipped a cup of tea and stared down at the black water. He had no way of knowing he would be instrumental in rescuing the man who would one day be elected President of the United States.

AMAGIRI ARRIVED off Vila just as August 1 turned into August 2. Commander Hanami ordered his ship anchored, then waited as a fleet of barges and landing craft approached and swarmed around his hull. Soldiers assembled on deck, then began climbing down landing nets into the rectangular crafts in an orderly line. To the other side, sailors began to unload cases and crates from the hull, then filled stern nets that were hoisted up off *Amagiri*'s deck and down to the barges. Hanami paced the decks, willing the off-loading to go faster. The quicker he and the other ships of the flotilla finished, the less chance they had of being dead in the water when the sun came up.

Twenty minutes passed.

"The soldiers are all off," a junior officer said finally, "and the last of the supplies are being handed down now."

"Secure the landing nets and order the anchor hoisted," Hanami ordered. "I want to be back in our slip at Rabaul before first light."

The officer saluted and made his way forward, as Hanami walked toward the pilothouse.

AUGUST 2 was less than an hour old as Lieutenant Kennedy adjusted the wheel of *PT-109* to port. The boat was off Kolombangara, following *PT-162* and *PT-169*. Heading west at a slow speed, the trio were seeking a target. Slowly, the three boats crossed Blackett Strait and headed in the direction of Gizo Island. Since the actions of a few hours earlier, when *PT-159* and *PT-157* had fired torpedoes at the Japanese flotilla, the night had been quiet. Kennedy accelerated *PT-109* close to the other two boats, then broke radio silence to request the trio head south to attempt to intercept the rest of the Rendova fleet. The other two skippers agreed. *PT-109* made a wide, sweeping turn in Blackett Strait and steamed slowly toward Ferguson Passage.

ABOARD *AMAGIRI*, Commander Hanami stared into the blackness. He was always uncomfortable when his ship was in Blackett Strait. The close quarters spelled danger if the American PT boats ever launched a coordinated attack. He turned toward the helm.

"What's our current speed?" he asked Coxswain Kazuto Doi.

Doi stared at the gauge. "Thirty knots, sir," he answered.

"The other ships are pulling away," Hanami said. "Increase speed to thirty-five knots."

Doi gave the order and *Amagiri* slowly began to gain speed.

Captain Yamashira, *Amagiri*'s second in command, made a notation on the chart. "We will be in Vella Gulf in approximately ten minutes."

Like Hanami, Yamashira preferred the safety of open water.

In the black night, tall wakes lit by the phosphorescence in the water streamed from *Amagiri*'s bow.

DIRECTLY AHEAD, *PT-109* was idling on a single engine. Lieutenant Kennedy strained to listen for the sound of the other PT boats. He thought he heard a throbbing sound from the south, but he was unable to pin down the exact location. The noise was reverberating between the mountain on Kolombangara and the islands to the west. Kennedy stared around his boat as he listened.

Ensign Ross was on the bow near the thirty-seven-millimeter gun. Ahead of Ross in the forward gun turret was nineteen-year-old Harold Marney. By training, Marney was a motor machinist, but tonight he had been assigned deck duty. The rear gun turret was manned by a twenty-nine-year-old Californian, Raymond Starkey.

Maguire was to Kennedy's right; to his left was

Thom, who was lying on the deck. Directly behind the cockpit, Edgar Mauer peered into the night. Mauer, who also functioned as the cook, had been a seaman aboard the tender *Niagara* when she had been torpedoed and sunk. He had no desire to repeat the experience, so he watched the water carefully.

Two of the crew, Andrew Jackson Kirksey and Charles Harris, were off-duty and slept a fitful sleep on deck. Raymond Albert, a seaman second class, was on watch amidships, while Scottish-born motor machinist William Johnston slept near the stern engine hatch. Gerald Zinser kept watch nearby.

Belowdecks was the oldest man on the crew, thirty-seven-year-old Patrick "Pappy" McMahon, tending the engines. At this instant, Pappy was adjusting the flow of raw seawater into the engines to regulate the temperatures. Touching a manifold, he liked what he felt. Wiping his hand on a rag, he listened carefully to the engine-room noises. Something was amiss, but he could not pin down what it was. He climbed over an auxiliary generator to stare at a gauge.

The stray sound would save his life.

LIKE THE EDGE of a knife, glistening wakes flowed from the bow of *Amagiri* as the ship hurtled north through the blackness. Commander Hanami paced the deck in the pilothouse. He knew the enemy was nearby—he could sense it—but so far at least, nothing had attacked.

"Ship to starboard," the lookout suddenly shouted.

"Deck guns fire," Hanami ordered.

As soon as he looked out the window, he could see the PT boat coming into view. *Amagiri* was right on top

of the vessel, and Hanami knew the guns were too close
to find their mark.

"Hard to port," he ordered.

Hanami knew that if it got away, the PT boat stood
a chance of lining up for a shot. He needed to sink the
vessel or his crew would suffer the consequences.

THE MOMENT BEFORE, the horizon had been clear;
now, as if by magic, a massive vessel had appeared in the
blackness. It was all too much to comprehend. For a
second, like a man staring at an avalanche unable to
move, the crew stood mute as the mysterious leviathan
approached.

There was only one chance to save the crew of *PT-
109*. They needed to get out of the way—and fast.
Kennedy rammed the throttle forward.

Belowdecks in the overheated engine room, Pappy
McMahon heard one of the engines race. Unfortunately, the drive was not engaged, and now that the
engine rpm had increased, there was no way for
McMahon to slam her into forward without stripping
the gears off the shaft.

For the next few seconds, *PT-109* was a sitting duck.

ON THE BOW of *Amagiri*, the gunners could not
depress the guns low enough to take a shot.

"Steer straight at the ship," Hanami ordered the
helmsman.

Hanami stared out the starboard window at the
men on the deck of the PT boat. Two blond-haired men
were behind the helm; on the foredeck a man struggled
with an artillery piece.

*

Ross TRIED to fire the thirty-seven-millimeter gun, but he simply did not have enough time. Kennedy, who by now realized he had throttled up the wrong engine, pulled back on the throttle, but it was too late. The Japanese destroyer was now only feet away.

And then it happened.

Metal met wood like a machete hacking off a tree branch.

In the forward gun turret, Marney saw *Amagiri* approach only seconds before he was crushed by the bow. The teenager, who had been with the crew only a few weeks, died in the warm water of Blackett Strait thousands of miles from his home in Chicopee.

Andrew Jackson Kirksey, sleeping on the aft starboard deck, managed to rise to his elbows before *Amagiri* slammed into *PT-109*. He left behind a wife and young son. Neither his nor Marney's body was ever found.

One second Pappy McMahon was staring at a racing engine; the next found him on the deck of the engine room of *PT-109*. As if in a dream, a line of fire came into his view. This was followed by a black shape scraping through the engine room. A few seconds later, McMahon felt water, and when he struggled to regain his footing, he was, strangely enough, looking out the stern of the ship at the sea. He could smell the fire before he felt the pain.

On *AMAGIRI*, Commander Hanami felt his ship pass through the PT boat with barely a shudder.

"Damage report!" he shouted to his second in command, who raced from the pilothouse.

"How's she feel?" he asked Coxswain Doi.

"There is a slight vibration, sir," Doi answered.

"Reduce speed to thirty knots," Hanami ordered, "and see if it smoothes out."

Then he began to write notes in the ship's log about the encounter.

THE STERN of *PT-109*, burdened with an engine, plunged down into the black water.

Pappy McMahon, burned by a sudden fire, was plunging down through the water, spinning like a top from the turbulence caused by *Amagiri*'s propeller wake. Heavily weighted and with a rotting life vest, he struggled to swim toward the light on the surface. He popped to the surface, surrounded by a sea of burning gasoline.

Ensign Thom had been hurtled into the water at the moment of impact, as were Albert, Zinser, Harris, Starkey, and Johnston. Miraculously, the bow of *PT-109* remained afloat and Kennedy, Maguire, and Mauer remained aboard. Henry Ross had first ridden out the collision on deck but then decided it was safer in the water. As soon as he slipped into the wetness, he realized his mistake. The heavy layer of gasoline on the water caused fumes that quickly sickened him. Struggling to breathe, he fainted and floated on the water in his orange kapok life vest.

"Into the water," Kennedy ordered Maguire and Mauer. "The boat might explode."

The three men entered the water, then swam a short distance away. They waited until *Amagiri*'s wake and the strong currents in Blackett Strait carried away the burning slick of gasoline.

"Back to the boat," Kennedy said a few minutes later.

The men swam back to *PT-109* and climbed onto what was left of the wreckage. The boat was riding in the water, bow in the air, with the shattered stern lapping at the edge of the water. She was afloat, but there was no way to know for how long.

"Mauer," Kennedy ordered, "see if you can find the blinker."

Maurer scrambled into the battered hull and searched until he found the metal tube that encased a battery-operated light used for signaling. "Found it, sir," he said.

"Climb as high up onto the bow as you feel safe and start signaling for the others," Kennedy said. "There must be others from the crew in the water."

"What do you want me to do?" Maguire asked.

"Help Mauer, and keep watch for anyone who is out there," Kennedy said, as he began to remove his shoes and shirt. "I'm going into the water to see who I can find."

HIGH ON a peak on Kolombangara Island, Reg Evans scanned the night water with his binoculars.

Just north of Plum Pudding Island, past the halfway point west in Blackett Strait, was a section of water aflame. Evans recorded the position. Then he lay on his cot for a few hours of rest.

AS SOON as Kennedy swam into the blackness, Mauer and Maguire began to hear the faint sound of voices from across the water.

"Help, help," Zinser screamed. "It's Ensign Thom—I think he's drowning."

Maguire had no desire to climb back into the gasoline-saturated water, but he knew he needed to. Grabbing a rope from the locker, he secured it to the hulk of *PT-109* and slid into Blackett Strait.

Ensign Ross awoke from his faint, floating in the black water. For a few moments, he had no idea what had happened and how he had ended up in his situation. A few minutes passed before his head began to clear enough to assess the situation. He could just see the outline of a pair of men floating in the water nearby, and he swam over to them.

"Thom's delirious," Zinser said, as Ross came into sight.

Thom was fighting an invisible opponent. Ross reached behind him and took him in his arms.

"Lenny," he said, "it's Barney."

A short distance away, Maguire swam toward the three men, the lifeline from *PT-109* giving him his only sense of security. Fumes rose from the water, and Maguire's head was spinning.

"I have a line to the boat," he said.

With the blinker as their guide, the men slowly began to make their way back to the floating hulk.

A short distance away, Charles Harris bobbed on the water with an injured leg. Seeing another body floating on the water, he swam closer. The body was the badly burned Pappy McMahon, who was drifting in and out of consciousness. He held on to McMahon.

Yards away, Kennedy swam through the water. Harris heard him shouting for the crewmen.

"Lieutenant Kennedy," Harris screamed, "over here."

Kennedy followed the voice, and soon the pair of men materialized out of the gloom.

"McMahon is hurt," Harris said, as Kennedy came alongside.

"How are you?"

"My leg is injured but I think I can swim," Harris said.

"I'll tow Pappy," Kennedy said. "You just follow behind."

Kennedy grabbed McMahon's life vest and began to pull him back toward the floating wreck of *PT-109*. Harris was having trouble keeping up—his leg was numb, and he was in shock. After Kennedy and McMahon disappeared from view, Harris began to wonder if he was going to die in the water. His will was fading, and the water was warm and comforting. Just when he had resigned himself to death or capture, Kennedy reappeared out of the blackness and grabbed hold. Harris tried kicking, but only one leg was working.

Thom had made it back to the boat and regained some strength. As soon as he felt strong enough, he took the line and slipped back into the water to search for other survivors. He was not a strong swimmer, but any fears or exhaustion gave way to duty.

Alone in the water, William Johnston had swallowed a lot of gasoline. He had vomited until his stomach quivered, and he was shivering like a dog climbing from freezing water. He heard Thom yelling at him to swim for the boat, but he had little energy. A few kicks and he would rest. And then the idea of death began to comfort him. He passed out.

"Come on, Bill," Thom said, upon reaching him, "we're going back to the boat."

"Boat?" Johnston said weakly.

Thom grabbed his life vest and started to drag him back to safety.

Raymond Starkey was alone.

His hands and arms were burned, and he could feel the heat through the water. Minutes later, the current carried him close to a dark outline in the water. He listened and could hear voices.

"Ahoy," he yelled.

"Over here," voices answered.

Paddling closer, he could see Kennedy in the water near the wreckage.

"Climb onto the wreck," Kennedy said.

Starkey managed to slip up onto what remained of the stern, then collapsed.

Just then, Kennedy began to call out the names of the crew. Kirksey and Marney did not answer.

Hours passed while the sky began to lighten. As the sun rose, the situation was grim.

THAT MORNING, Reg Evans built a small fire, warmed some water for tea, and then began to scan the water of Blackett Strait with his binoculars. Noticing wreckage on the water, he concentrated his telescope on the area. It looked like a Japanese barge, and he reported it to his base in New Georgia as such. Three hours would pass before Evans was notified that *PT-109* had been lost the night before.

FOR THE MEN on *PT-109*, at first the rising sun brought a sense of relief. The warm glow on the main mountain of Kolombangara Island allowed the men to see one another and their surroundings, and that brought a sense of reality back to an otherwise unreal situation. They were alive, at least most of them, and they were glad.

But these feelings were quickly replaced by a different reality.

The men of *PT-109* were floating smack dab in the middle of enemy territory.

"If the Japs come," Kennedy asked, "what weapons do we have to fight with?"

After a count, the crew found they had six .45-caliber side arms as well as Kennedy's .38. This was augmented with two knives and a pocketknife—hardly an arsenal.

JUST BEFORE LUNCH, Reg Evans radioed that the hulk was still on the water and floating off Gizo in Blackett Strait. He was now aware that an American PT boat had been lost the night before, and he carefully watched the wreckage to see if he could make out what it was. It might be a PT boat, he thought to himself. But his telescope and binoculars were not strong enough to allow him a defined image. He continued to scan the water and report the movement of the wreckage.

JUST PAST LUNCHTIME, the wreckage of *PT-109*, which had been riding bow-down, turned turtle. The hull was filling with water, and it seemed that the boat might sink at any moment. Kennedy had been studying the nearby islands all morning. The wreckage had drifted closer to Gizo Island, making Kolombangara Island a distant swim. There were more Japanese on Gizo, but there were also a few small islands and coral atolls that might be uninhabited. Kennedy made his choice.

"Men," he said, "we're going to swim for that small island over there."

He pointed to a small sand-ringed island sprouting coconut palms a few miles distant.

"Thom," he ordered, "you and Ross remove the plank we lashed to the thirty-seven-millimeter gun."

Now that the bow was upside down, the gun had broke the lashings and dropped to the ocean floor two thousand feet below—but the plank used to wedge her in place still remained. Thom cut it loose, and he and Ross floated it over to Kennedy.

Pappy McMahon stared at the blistered skin on his floating arms. He was in shock from the burns and weak from exposure.

"Lieutenant," McMahon said to Kennedy, "you'd better leave me here—I think I'm done for."

"No, Pappy," Kennedy said forcefully, "you're going to make it."

The crew assembled on each side of the plank and awaited the order to begin kicking.

"Thom," Kennedy said, "you and Ross keep the men together. I'm going to tow Pappy."

And with that, the crew of *PT-109* began to paddle slowly toward the distant island.

Hours passed as they painstakingly made their way. Kennedy had cut one of the straps of McMahon's life vest and clutched the canvas strap in his mouth. Slowly, using a breaststroke, he towed the delirious man to safety.

Four men were on each side of the plank, with Ensign Thom rotating back and forth to even the paddling. Kennedy was towing McMahon. Eleven men in total—deep in enemy territory.

LIEUTENANT JOHN F. KENNEDY was feeling an exhaustion that ran through his entire body.

To the west the sun was just dipping below the top of Gizo Island, as he slowly paddled the last few feet into shallow water alongside Plum Pudding Island. He was barely able to rise to his feet. Once standing, he teetered unsteadily for a few seconds until he got his land legs, then whispered down to McMahon, who was floating lightly on his back.

"Pappy, I'm going to check for the enemy," he said quietly. "I'll be right back."

"Be careful, Skipper," McMahon said weakly.

Kennedy walked through the coral rocks and sand onto shore, then entered the foliage and disappeared. With his .38 revolver in his hand, he crept through the bush and trees. The island was about the length of a football field and half again as wide. Palm trees were scattered about, but the primary fauna seemed to be some form of long-needled, pinelike tree, along with bushes dotted with bird droppings. There was no sign of habitation save for the thousands of land crabs that scurried about, and a single bat that Kennedy flushed from a sleep.

He walked back through the island, rubbing his aching jaw. The canvas strap he'd used to tow McMahon was a little moldy, and Kennedy had swallowed a great deal of seawater. Suddenly, he felt his stomach roil, and he vomited the salty waste into the bushes at the edge of the beach. When he was finished, he raised his head and stared into Blackett Strait.

The rest of his crew was entering the shallows near the island, and the taller men were finding footing beneath the water. The water was studded with coral outcroppings, and it tore into their feet. Stumbling through the uneven subsurface, the nine men made their way ashore.

Kennedy helped Pappy to his feet, and the eleven survivors stumbled into the brush.

UPON LEARNING of the fate of *PT-109*, Reg Evans had alerted his native scouts to search for survivors. He could still see the wreckage, but now that the currents had changed, it was drifting north toward Nusatupi Island. Earlier he had requested an aerial search, and his last transmission of the night was to seek the results. So far he had received no word. Evans settled in for the night.

AS NIGHT CAME on August 2, the crew of *PT-109* began to understand their precarious situation. Only moments after taking cover in the bushes, a Japanese barge had slowly passed from south to north less than seventy-five yards out into Blackett Strait. The men kept quiet and the barge passed, but it confirmed just how close to the enemy they were.

Once the barge was safely out of sight, Kennedy motioned to Ross and Thom. Walking a short distance away, the three officers held a conference.

"Okay," Kennedy asked plainly, "how are we going to get out of here?"

The men discussed their choices, but in reality there were few. All agreed that as soon as night fell, the other PT boats in their squadron would return to search for them, but how would they be able to intercept the rescuers in the black of night?

"Our only hope is for one of us to try to swim out in the channel with the blinker," Kennedy said finally, "and since I'm the strongest swimmer, I'll go out tonight."

The three officers nodded slowly. They knew the waters around the Solomon Islands contained sharks. That, combined with the Japanese nearby, the strong currents in the water, and the fact that Kennedy was exhausted, made the idea about as risky as borrowing money from an angry loan shark.

"Jack," Ross said, "I don't think this is wise."

"What other choice do we have?" Kennedy said quietly.

It was a question without answer.

AFTER A FEW HOURS of fitful sleep, Kennedy awoke and stared out at the water. It was a black, limpid pool of the unknown. In the last twenty-four hours, his boat had been run down by a Japanese destroyer and lit aflame. To add insult to injury, he and his crew had been forced to swim to a deserted island deep in enemy territory. They had no food, no water, and very little with which to defend themselves. Kennedy was as scared as the others, but he was also their leader. If there was *any* chance for rescue, he would take it, even if it meant a nighttime foray into shark-infested waters.

With his .38 on a lanyard around his neck, he waded into the water and began to follow an underwater reef to the south toward Ferguson Passage. On the northern edge of the passage lay Nauru Island, bordered with a thick coral plate that caused the waves to crash at heights of up to ten feet. The sound of the breakers made it hard to hear the sound of boat engines, and Kennedy struggled to listen. Hard knobs of coral cut his feet and ankles. In places he could walk on the reef at chest depth; other times the coral receded and he would plunge into the black water and swim for a distance. Slowly making his way south, Kennedy awaited the rescue ships he knew were coming.

Hours passed as he stood in the water, waiting.

Once he thought he heard a boat, and he signaled with the blinker. But it was nothing. For hours he stood, with only the blackness of the water and the feeling of marine life brushing his legs. Once the sun rose, he struggled onto a small island south of Plum Pudding and collapsed.

He was out in the open on the sandy beach, but he was too exhausted to move.

A FEW MILES AWAY, a pair of Reg Evans's Gizo Scouts, Biuku Gasa and Eroni Kumana, were awakening on Sepu Island. During the night, the Japanese had landed several hundred more troops on Gizo Island, and the two scouts wanted to report this development. Sliding their dugout canoe into the water, they began to paddle toward Kolombangara Island.

While the men were not large by Western standards, just a shade over five feet tall, they were lean and strong. As their canoe paddles bit into the water, they began to chant. It was a song of the sea in their native language, and the cadence carried them forward. Finding some floating debris, they stopped and placed it in the dugout. Implements for shaving, a few olive-drab pieces of cloth, and a letter they could not read. They continued on.

THE SUN was roasting Kennedy as he awoke on the sandy shore. He tried the blinker and found that he had left it on and the battery was dead. Tossing it aside, he stared to the north. He was about a mile south of Plum Pudding Island, and he began to walk and swim toward the other men.

Ensign Thom had posted night guards, but they reported no sign of Kennedy. Thom feared his friend had been swept away or eaten by sharks, but there was little he could do. He could only tend to the crew as best he could. McMahon's burns were festering. Thom ordered some coconuts felled and then hacked them open with a knife. He tried to rub the oil on the wounds, but it did little to alleviate the suffering. Harris tried to use the coconut oil to lubricate their handguns, but the experiment proved a failure. The oil gummed up the slides, and Harris was forced to strip all the weapons and clean them. Just then, Maguire saw someone in the water.

"Someone's approaching," he said, pointing.

Ross waded into the water and helped Kennedy to his feet. Taking a few steps, Kennedy stopped and vomited up seawater. He was barely coherent as he struggled ashore. Collapsing in a clearing just off the beach, he managed to croak, "Barney, you take it tonight."

"Okay, John," Ross replied.

The day passed, waiting for a rescue that did not come.

Johnston and Starkey passed the time trying to catch

fish. Zinser tried bathing his burned arms in salt water, but it did not help. Whenever he felt sorry for himself, he had only to look at McMahon. The older man was obviously in pain, but he suffered his discomfort without complaint.

That night Ross waded out into the passage, but again no boats were seen.

REG EVANS HAD EXPLAINED to Biuku and Eroni about the wreck of *PT-109* and asked them to keep an eye out for any survivors. They stayed at Kolombangara to rest before beginning the long trip back across Blackett Strait the next morning.

KENNEDY HAD REGAINED his strength by the time Ross returned early the next morning.

"Nothing, Jack," he said disgustedly. "I don't think they're looking for us at all."

"I've been thinking," Kennedy said to Ross and Thom, "that we should move to that island."

He pointed south to an island named Olasana located about two miles away.

"It's closer to Ferguson Passage, as well as larger," he said. "Maybe we can find something to eat there. If not, at least we wouldn't have to swim as far on our nighttime journeys."

Thom was not a strong swimmer, but he was game.

"It looks like the reef runs there," he said. "We should be able to walk a lot of the distance."

"Then it's agreed," Kennedy said. "I'll tell the crew."

Tonight would mark the fourth night of the ordeal, but the men took the news well. The tension was taking its toll, and the crew was glad to be doing *something*. Just waiting for rescue or capture was stressful; doing anything about their situation was preferable. They set off for Olasana Island. Hours later, the crew struggled ashore and made their way into the trees. The currents had proved stronger than expected, and everyone was tired.

That night no one swam into Ferguson Passage. Help would have to find them.

BIUKU AND ERONI were flying across the water. The sea was slick, and the day's rest had given them strength. Mr. Evans had shown them the wreckage of a vessel through the spyglass. It had washed ashore on the south side of Nauru Island, where the breakers crashed on the coral reef. They decided to check it out on the way home—maybe there was food or fuel aboard.

"SITTING HERE doing nothing is killing me," Kennedy told Ross. "Let's swim over to Nauru."

"Our planes should be flying over," Ross agreed. "Maybe there's a clear spot of sand where we can write a rescue message."

Leaving Ensign Thom in charge, the two men made the short swim to the southernmost island bordering Ferguson Passage. Because of the islands' strategic location directly on the passage, Kennedy and Ross figured that the Japanese might have a post there, but they found no sign of habitation. Walking through the trees to the southern side, they stared out on the passage and noticed the wreck of what appeared to be a Japanese barge. A few boxes had washed ashore, and Ross pried one open and found it filled with hard candy. After eating their fill, they decided to return to the others and share the windfall. Walking along the shore, they came upon a pair of dugout canoes and tins of fresh water. The canoes had been stashed by the scouts, but Kennedy and Ross had no way to know that.

BIUKU AND ERONI anchored their canoe near the Japanese barge and set out searching the interior. They found a Japanese rifle, took it, and climbed back aboard their canoe. They were just starting to paddle when they looked toward Nauru.

"LOOK," Ross said, pointing.

Kennedy stared across the water and saw the two men in the canoe.

Were they Japanese?

Kennedy and Ross had no way to know, so they filtered back into the bushes and hid.

"JAPANESE?" Biuku asked Eroni.

"Don't know," Eroni answered.

The men were paddling furiously away from the encounter north on Blackett Strait. If not for Biuku becoming thirsty at just this instant, history might be very different.

"Let's stop on Olasana and drink some coconut milk," he said.

Luckily, Eroni, now clear of the possible Japanese, agreed.

ON OLASANA, Thom watched the men approaching. He stared at them carefully. Even at this distance they appeared to be natives, but were they islanders consorting with the Japanese? At that instant, he made a decision that would seal their fate. He waded into the water and began to call out to the men. The natives stopped and began to turn away. Then Thom got a brainstorm.

"White star," he shouted, "white star."

The natives had seen the emblem on the lower wings of the American planes. In addition, most knew that if they helped an American pilot, there was usually a reward.

"American," Biuku said at last.

So they paddled over. With help from Thom, they stashed their canoe in the brush.

After a hurried conference, Thom convinced them to take Starkey in their boat back to the base at Rendova. It was almost forty miles distant and the sea in Blackett Strait was choppy now, but the three men set out.

KENNEDY HAD LOADED the water tins and hard candy into the dugout. After leaving Ross to guard Nauru, he was paddling back toward Olasana Island. His plan was to share the spoils with the crew, then have them all move south to Nauru.

Biuku and Eroni made it partway into Blackett Strait before they had to turn back because of the worsening weather. At the same time, Kennedy was returning to Olasana with the water and candy. The two canoes met near the island and glided onto shore.

THAT NIGHT, Kennedy and Ross tried to paddle out into Ferguson Passage, but their boat overturned and they nearly drowned. They managed to swim to Nauru and fell into an exhausted sleep.

The night passed slowly on Olasana. A few of the crew were distrustful of Biuku and Eroni and spent the night watching them carefully. Not knowing whether the native men were loyal, they feared the two would slip off into the night and report them to the Japanese for a reward. On the other side, the massive men armed with black handguns intimidated Biuku and Eroni. They wanted to explain that they only wanted to help, but what little English they spoke would not allow them to get their point across. The Gizo Scouts slept, but with one eye open.

The following morning, when Kennedy returned to Olasana, he knew it was time to do something. Kennedy needed to trust the natives—it was their only hope. Taking a knife to a coconut, he scratched out:

NAURO ISL.

NATIVE KNOWS POSIT.
HE CAN PILOT 11 ALIVE NEED
SMALL BOAT

KENNEDY

He asked the two natives to deliver the message, and they set out for Rendova at once. Stopping in Raramana, they showed the coconut to Benjamin Kevu, the English-speaking leader of the scouts. Kevu knew that Evans was moving his base, and he sent a native to deliver a verbal recap of the message on the coconut. Biuku and Eroni continued on toward the American base at Rendova.

*

REG EVANS HAD MOVED from the top of
Kolombangara Island down to water level on Gomu
Island. As soon as the native arrived with the
message from Kevu, Evans began planning a rescue.
Drafting a reply, he ordered seven of his scouts to
leave in the morning for Olasana. The text of the
message was:

ON HIS MAJESTY'S SERVICE
TO SENIOR OFFICER NARU IS.

FRIDAY 11 AM HAVE JUST LEARNED OF
YOUR PRESENCE ON NARU IS & ALSO THAT
TWO NATIVES HAVE TAKEN NEWS TO
RENDOVA. I STRONGLY ADVISE YOU
RETURN IMMEDIATELY TO HERE IN THIS
CANOE & BY THE TIME YOU ARRIVE HERE I
WILL BE IN RADIO COMMUNICATIONS WITH
AUTHORITIES AT RENDOVA & WE CAN
FINALIZE PLANS TO COLLECT BALANCE OF
YOUR PARTY

AR EVANS LT.
RANVR

Before dispatching the trio of canoes, Evans loaded
them with supplies. Rice, C rations, cigarettes, cans of
hash along with native pawpaws, boiled fish and stoves
to cook, tins of water, matches, and fuel. As soon as the
natives reached the shipwrecked crew, they set to work
fashioning shelters out of palm fronds, cooking food,
and lopping off coconuts so the men could drink the
sweet milk. Then they showed Kennedy to a canoe and

hid him under palm fronds, so planes flying over could not see him. They began to paddle back to Evans with Kennedy.

Meanwhile, Biuku and Eroni had reached the base at Rendova.

It was almost six that evening when Kennedy slid from under the palm fronds and shook Evans's hand. Evans motioned to his crude hut. The men immediately began to discuss the rescue plans.

"Have the boats stop here and pick me up," Kennedy noted. "I'll lead them through the reefs."

"You've been through a lot," Evans said, staring at the skinny, sandy-haired man. A beard covered the man's face, and his lips and cheeks were chapped and red. Only the man's eyes were clear—they burned with a conviction that brooked no argument. "Why don't you let us handle it?"

"I'm going back for my men," Kennedy said, "period."

"Okay," Evans agreed. "I'll radio Rendova."

The signal to the boats was to be four shots in the air. After checking his .38, Kennedy realized he had only three shells left and borrowed a rifle from Evans. Then he set off with the natives in a canoe for a nearby island where they would meet the rescue boats.

At 8 P.M. that night, he heard the engines of the boats and fired into the air.

PT-157 pulled close, and Lieutenant Cluster shouted across the water.

"That you, Jack?"

"Where the hell have you been?" Kennedy said.

Hauled aboard, Kennedy took a place on deck with Biuku and Eroni, who were there to help guide the boat.

The PT boats roared up the channel. In half an hour, they were off Olasana.

"Slow down," Kennedy said, "and lower a raft. We will lead you through the reef."

Climbing into a rubber raft with Biuku and Eroni, Kennedy led *PT-157* safely through the coral. Once inside the reef, he began to call to shore.

"Lenny, Barney, come on out," he yelled.

The crew of *PT-109* walked into the open. They could scarcely believe the ordeal was at an end.

The survivors were ferried out to the PT boat in the raft. Once they were all aboard, Kennedy showed the helmsman the way back through the reef. It was almost 10 P.M. when *PT-157* reached open water and the skipper set a course for Rendova. As soon as the boat was gliding over the water at close to forty knots, a bottle of brandy appeared and the crew took a drink.

"Thank you," Kennedy said to Biuku and Eroni.

Biuku smiled, but he could not resist the urge to kid with Kennedy. "You loosim boat, no find ever again, but you still a-number one," he noted.

II

I Have a Special Room in My Mind for You

2001

Craig Dirgo:

"You and Dirk go over there and see what you can find," Clive said.

I was staring at a chart; the water showed two-thousand-foot maximum depth in the Strait.

"What do we use for a boat?" I asked wisely.

"Not to worry," Clive said. "My son Dirk has been talking to the local dive shop owner. He has a few boats for charter."

"What else?" I asked.

"I'd get a malaria shot if I were you," he said, "and typhoid—just get whatever immunizations they have."

It was late July 2001, and I was sitting on the back porch of Clive's house in Colorado. It was all of about sixty degrees outside, we were discussing malaria and tropical breezes, and I was looking at a map of a series of islands halfway around the world.

"What exactly do you want us to accomplish?" I asked.

"Find out where it's not," he said, "and have some fun. That's what it's all about, isn't it?"

Clive has a strange idea of fun.

A few days before, I'd flown from Fort Lauderdale to Phoenix, stayed the night with Dirk, Clive's son and the president of NUMA, then rented a car and driven north. After editing what we had finished on this book, I was due to leave Clive in the morning to drive back to Phoenix.

"Anything else?"

"Stay out of the casinos in Australia," he said, "and don't believe Dirk's system for blackjack. The house always wins."

I left at first light for Phoenix. Somewhere in Arizona, I picked up a Navajo who was hitchhiking and dropped him at the hospital in Phoenix. Strangely enough, this was the same day that President Bush was awarding the Medal of Honor to some of the remaining code-talkers. It seemed fitting, so I asked him about Native American philosophy.

"There is a pace to everything," he said.

"So what's the key?"

"Must be pacing," he said, just before he fell asleep.

THE PACE on July 28 was fast. We raced from store to store, trying to buy anything we felt we would not be able to find on Gizo, the island that would be our base in the Solomon Islands. Batteries, duct tape, tools, and trinkets. T-shirts for gifts, a portable depth sounder from Wal-Mart.

"What about rope?" asked Dirk.

"Buy it," I said.

"Water purifier?" I asked, as we steered a cart through the discount store.

"But of course."

"Check out these *Planet of the Apes* action figures," I said, as we passed an end display.

Dirk's girlfriend wanted us to take her to the opening tonight as a last celebration in civilization.

"We need those," Dirk said.

Into the cart they went.

We bought a large wheeled plastic tub for storage.

THE FOLLOWING MORNING, Kerrie, Dirk's better half, arrived to drive us to the airport in her new Honda. She stared at the piles of equipment.

"No way," she said.

We had managed to cram it all inside, but just barely.

Arriving in Los Angeles that afternoon, we retrieved our luggage, propped the bags on a pair of carts, then rolled them over to the international terminal and checked in with Air New Zealand. Later that evening, we were on our way. Our route was Los Angeles to Auckland, New Zealand, a short stop, then onto a different plane for the flight to Brisbane, Australia. We arrived at the airport in Brisbane, where we had a night's layover before we caught one of the twice-weekly flights to the Solomon Islands, so we rented a car and set out.

Dirk drove us to the hotel, and we checked into our room.

Then we walked across the street to the casino.

The next day, a few hundred dollars lighter, we flew on a 737 to Honiara, the capital of the Solomon Islands. Honiara has all the charm of Manila after the fall of Marcos. Sporadic power outages and deserted buildings seemed the norm. The Solomon Islands had experienced a recent coup d'état, and the U.S. State Department had a travel warning in place. We met with Ms. Keithie Sauders, the American consular officer, who filled us in on the situation. After assuring us we'd have no trouble, she wished us well and asked that we keep her up-to-date on our progress.

By now, the long flight was catching up with us, and we tumbled into bed for a few hours' sleep. The next morning, we gathered our gear, took a cab to the airport, and caught a DeHavilland Otter turboprop to Gizo Island. The flight was uneventful.

From the air, the Solomon Islands look like the tropical paradise that people always imagine. Blue and green waters lap at small tree-clustered islands. The sand ringing the islands forms a white outline, while small boats and canoes form gentle wakes when viewed from the air.

The pilot brought the DeHavilland down on the grass runway, and we rolled to a stop.

The airport for Gizo is located on Nusatupi Island just across the water from Gizo. It consists of little more than a cement block shack, a tank for refueling, and a path that leads to a dock where small boats transfer arrivals across the water to Gizo. We climbed out of the plane and looked around. A man who looked like the cartoon character Yosemite Sam walked over.

"Dirk, Craig?" he asked.

"You must be Danny Kennedy," Dirk said.

Danny has a great story. He worked as an electrician involved in the construction of Disneyland, then took his money and set out to travel the world. After a short stint as a dive instructor in Hawaii, he started to wander throughout the South Pacific, landing in the Solomon Islands in the early 1980s. Finding the people and diving to his liking, he decided to stay. Now he's an institution. I think it's safe to say that most people visiting Gizo will at one time or another bump into Danny. An eternally optimistic and friendly man given to repeating bad jokes and local legends, he proved to be a valuable ally. He lives above town in a beautiful house, with his Australian wife Kerry and their teenage daughter, who was born in the Solomon Islands. Danny knows the history of *PT-109*. In addition, he knows the waters around Gizo like the nose on his face.

"How was the flight?" he asked.

"Not too bad," I answered.

"You're lucky," Danny said. "A couple of weeks ago, the pilot came in too low and hit a dugout canoe on approach—luckily, the islander saw him coming and jumped over the side. He was aggro, though, I can tell you that."

"Aggro?" asked Dirk.

Danny speaks a strange combination of English, Australian slang, and pidgin, the local language.

"Aggro," Danny said, smiling, "aggravated."

Grabbing some bags, he started for the dock.

After loading the luggage aboard a small boat, we crossed the short span of water and docked in front of the Gizo Hotel. We checked in and stowed our luggage, then walked through the town to Adventure

Sports, Danny's dive operation. Gizo is not a large town, and the main business district is clustered along the waterfront. Directly in front and to the left of the hotel is an open-air market. To the right is a concrete pier, where the local island tramp steamer docks. There is a strip of pocked, potholed pavement left over from the time the Solomon Islands was a British protectorate, but for the most part the roads are packed dirt.

This is not a tourist-tainted town.

The few stores in Gizo are owned by Chinese traders, and entering them gave me the feeling that I had arrived through a time warp into a northern California gold-rush hamlet after the vein had run out. The selections ran from tin tubs for washing to bolts of cloth. Food choices for lunch included coconut flour crackers, canned tuna flavored with curry, and cookies.

The town has three restaurants. The one at the Gizo Hotel we quickly grew tired of; the Nest, midway through the town, had an actual television hooked to a satellite receiver so the customers could watch CNN; and the *PT-109* restaurant, which featured the best food.

The *PT-109* is an open-air affair attached to a two-story home that operates as a lodge for divers. Danny's dive boats moor just outside, and his shop is just across the street. If you want to eat there, you need to call ahead—it is open only when there are customers, and since the coup, that's rare.

In general, Gizo is unspoiled by the trappings of capitalism. As a tourist spot, it would have probably dropped off the map save for a few important items. The first is the water—it is a wonderland of undersea beauty. Corals of all types, fish of so many colors that you'd need a prism to duplicate the beauty, temperatures that are perfect.

The second is the people—the Solomon Islanders are some of the friendliest you could ever encounter. Eternally patient, always smiling, they make you feel welcome. With the economy on the skids, the locals make their way as best they can, but times are tough right now. I can only hope it improves soon. The island has a lot going for it.

Gizo Island and these people would be our home for the next two weeks.

DIRK AND I had decided that our best course of action was to see if we could first locate the wreckage that had been reported by Reg Evans on the reef off Nauru Island. Our vessel for the search would be one of Danny's dive boats. The boats are narrow-beam affairs with a PVC tube canopy over the top and twin benches along each side, with holes to place tanks. Approximately twenty feet in length and powered by single or twin outboard motors, they are perfect for small diving groups but a little too exposed to the weather for search operations. Danny supplied a folding wooden chair that fit amidships, and we sat the large plastic tub in front. On the tub we placed the gradiometer, which we took turns operating. For navigation we had a handheld GPS.

The setup was as far removed from the extravagant search boats you see on the Discovery Channel as we were from a Hard Rock Café. This search was on the low end of the high-tech scale. The first few days, the winds and currents were favorable, and we were able to work along the surf line just off the ledge of coral off Nauru Island. Other than a single target of promise, the area under the water was bare of magnetics. The operation went like this: In the morning we would eat breakfast at the Gizo Hotel. This consisted of toast, a few slices of mango or pineapple, and maybe some cold cereal. Then we would carry our tub of equipment the half-mile to Danny's shop. Sometimes the restaurant would make us lunch—egg-salad sandwiches—but usually we would stop at the Wing-Sun store for cans of tuna, crackers, and bottles of fresh water. Lunch in hand, we'd continue on to the shop. Then we'd load the equipment in the boat. Once we were situated, one of Danny's boat drivers would join us and we would set out to search.

Once clear of the dock, we would lower the gradiometer probe into the water and allow it to calibrate itself, a process that usually took a half hour or so. For weight on the probe itself, we used a rock attached to a thin line designed to break away if we struck the bottom—something that happened at least a dozen times—and to keep the cable clear of the propellers, we propped it off the side, using an old oar that stuck from the starboard side.

It was all jury-rigged, but it seemed to do the job.

Once the gradiometer calibrated, we would pull it back in, then set out for the search area. That usually required a half hour or so in transit. Once on-site we would begin to drag, using the GPS to make straight lines. Then we would drive back and forth, seeking a target. Around noon we would pull over to the closest island and climb off the boat. After a quick bite to eat and a few moments spent watering the palm trees, we'd climb back in the boat and start another line.

Afternoons usually brought rain—since we were basically out in the open, we'd try to shelter the gradiometer as best we could. If the rain was prolonged or heavy, we'd head back to Gizo and wait it out.

By the end of every day, we were exhausted. The constant noise from the outboard motor a few feet from our heads, the rocking of the small boat, and the relentless humidity took their toll. After returning to Gizo, usually around 5 P.M., we'd walk the half-mile back to the hotel, take a quick shower, and change clothes. Then, if it was Monday, Wednesday, or Friday, we could read the Solomon Islands paper, which was six to eight pages in length and chock-full of interesting misspellings. A typical headline read "Pregnant Snake Found Under House," with a picture of the finders holding it in their hands. The paper was a constant source of amusement.

Dinner was served starting at 6:30. Waiting to eat was usually passed by playing endless hands of gin rummy or blackjack. The menu for dinner rarely changed. Kingfish with rice and a tiny salad, or chili crab with rice and a tiny salad. There were also a few mock Chinese dishes.

A few divers showed up the two weeks we were in town. Five or six Australians arrived on the plane with us and stayed a few days. They had come to dive the wreck of the Japanese transport *Toa Maru*, a pristine wreck still full of cargo that draws people to Gizo.

Then, a few days after we arrived, more tourists showed up. We'd asked Danny not to mention to anyone what we were doing, as over the years we had found that this just complicates things, but the town was so small and the tourists so few that within hours of arriving, I think everyone knew the score.

A few days a week, Danny has a picnic over on Plum Pudding Island (now called Kennedy Island by everyone) where his workers cook fresh fish and rice over a campfire. The fish is usually eaten as a sandwich with fresh bread, and it is served on a leaf hacked from a nearby tree. Primitive but fun. A week after we arrived, we headed over to the island at lunchtime to hook up with the divers. Along with a group of fifteen to twenty teenagers on a discovery trip of the South Pacific were three new divers. Danny mentioned they were from Arizona, so I walked over to say hello to some fellow Americans. After introducing myself, I said:

"Danny says you live in Arizona."

"Yes," said the man.

Dirk was approaching.

"What city?"

"Phoenix area," said one of the two women.

"Small world," I said. "Dirk's from there."

"Actually, Paradise Valley," the other woman said, with a trace of haughtiness.

Dirk nodded. Paradise Valley is a tiny area where Clive, the late Erma Bombeck, and rocker Alice Cooper reside, along with a host of other celebrities. So do some smart people who bought their homes years ago.

"Where in Paradise?" Dirk asked.

"Do you know the area?"

"Yeah," Dirk said, with perfect timing, "I live there."

It turns out they were neighbors and lived only a few

miles away. Halfway around the world in the middle of nowhere, and we meet someone from Dirk's hometown. The trio turned out to be a gas. Ted and Sally Guenther were husband and wife. Ted's sister, Chris, was along for the ride. The three were taking a month off from the Arizona summer heat and were traveling through the South Pacific, diving up a storm. For most of the rest of our time in Gizo, they would be our dinner companions and would prove to be good friends.

Near the end of the trip, we also met an Australian couple, Catherine and George Ziedan, whom we would see again in Australia on our way home. Nicer people are hard to find. Upon hearing we were stopping in Surfer's Paradise, they located us at our hotel, then came and picked us up and drove us to their home in the hills above town for an old-fashioned Australian barbecue. The steaks were a size that would shame a Texan, and the shrimp were the size of sausages. I would return to Australia just to visit George, Catherine, and their two teenage children, Georgie and Toby. George is a character straight from a gonzo novel. He attacks life with a zest I've rarely seen. He designed and built the beautiful house where his family resides—clearing the brush with a tractor, digging the ponds with a backhoe, and rigging a cable affair from the house down the steep hill to the pond where you can drop into the water.

But back to the search.

The days began to run together as we scanned the shallows off Nauru, Olasana, and Kennedy Islands. Other than the single target off Nauru, which the weather was preventing us from diving, we were finding nothing. Not only that, Dirk and I had yet to dive.

It might be time to address a statement I always hear: "I'd love to go with you."

No, you wouldn't—at least ninety-nine percent of you. The idea most people have of a search is a series of fine days of sport diving interspersed with finding a wreck and reaping untold glory. The reality is hour after hour of being tossed about in small boats, listening to the increasing squawk of a balky electronic instrument, combined with lack of sleep and having to wash your underwear in a motel-room sink. Then you rise in the morning and do it all again. I would guess diving is less than five percent of the equation.

This reminds me of a story a friend named Jedd Ladd told me in Colorado. Jedd had been at Woodstock, and I asked him about the experience. "Don't believe all the hype about fun and free love," he said. "It was a muddy mess, with no food and lots of rain. I lived in a tent that leaked, and the toilets were a hole in the dirt."

"Wow," I said.

"The music was great, though," he said.

The same thing applies here. The work is monotonous, but you have a chance to make history. We always say in NUMA that if it were easy, someone would have already done it. Persistence is the key, repetition the norm. Dirk and I dug in—day after day we scanned the waters in a direction from Ferguson Passage north. We weren't finding anything that resembled a wreck.

About ten days into the search, we were talking to Danny about *PT-109*, and we mentioned Biuku and Eroni, the natives who rescued Kennedy.

"You want to talk to Biuku?" Danny asked.

"What?" said Dirk.

"Biuku is still alive," Danny said. "He's a friend of mine. He lives down near Vonavona."

"Let's go," Dirk said.

"Living history," I said. "Call him up and see if we can visit."

"He doesn't have a telephone," Danny said, "but if we take one of the boats down there tomorrow, we can probably find him. He's getting old, and he doesn't stray far."

The next morning, Dirk, Danny, Smiling John the boat driver, and I climbed into a boat, crossed Blackett Strait, then proceeded on through the channel toward Vonavona. The journey was a trip through paradise. Clear water and tree-lined passages, like passing down a lazy river, would give way to outcroppings of white sands and colorful reefs just below the surface. The trip to Biuku's home took about an hour. We slid up to a pier made from coral rocks and shells and climbed from the boat. Walking through the trees, we came upon a few wooden homes set up from the ground on pilings. A garden was to one side, and chickens roamed freely, squawking at our imposition.

A woman clutching a baby in her arms sat on the porch of a home, puffing on a corncob pipe.

"One of Biuku's daughters," Danny said, as he plopped down the large bag of rice and the betel nut we had brought as gifts.

In pidgin, he inquired as to Biuku's whereabouts and learned he was down at Munda. One of his children was sick, and that was the nearest hospital. We set off for Munda, another forty-five minutes by boat, and splashed ashore. The night before, I had talked with Dirk about what we could give as a gift. This was the man who had rescued one of our presidents, and for the most part the act had gone unnoticed. I had a pair of binoculars—pretty good Tascos—and we figured he'd like those. Danny went inside and found Biuku and brought him outside.

Biuku is small, a shade over five feet tall and slightly stooped from his seventy-eight years. Danny explained in pidgin what we were doing, then helped seat Biuku next to me on a log under the shade of a large tree. Unrolling a chart of the area, we questioned him, using Danny as a translator. The primary question we needed answered was if by chance the wreck he and Eroni had climbed aboard off Nauru might have been *PT-109*. It was six decades ago, but by his descriptions we began to realize that the wreck was probably Japanese. After inquiring about any other wreckage he might have seen around the same time, and learning of none, we thanked him.

I took the binoculars out of the case.

"Danny," I said, "can you tell him this? We wanted to thank you for your brave actions in saving the man who became president of our country and ask that you accept this as a gift from the American people."

Danny translated, and I could see Biuku smile. I handed him the binoculars, and he placed them around his neck and glanced around the hospital grounds.

"Ah," he said, "spyglasses."

Then we got ready to leave and began to say our good-byes. We started to walk away, then Biuku called to Danny.

"I have a special room in my mind for you, Danny," Biuku said in English.

Obviously, the gifts had gone over well.

*

THE EXPEDITION WAS WINDING to a close, and we were both beginning to feel that the wreck was in deeper water. Our searching had failed to locate anything in the shallows. Our hopes for the wreck off Nauru were dashed by Biuku's revelations that it was a Japanese barge, as well as the fact that on the last day the weather cleared and we could dive the target we had located. It was a strange coral-encrusted protrusion about the size of a large engine block. We tried to clear a small spot to see what was inside, but to little avail. The area could use a better analysis in the future to determine what it actually is, but our best guess is an old anchor or something that was encrusted over time. When we return, we'll check it further.

We began to analyze what we had accomplished. We'd done what we'd set out to do—find where the wreck was not—and in the process we had managed to cover all the shallow water in the high-probability areas. All the waters surrounding Nauru, Olasana, and Plum Pudding Islands, as well as a large block to the north, had been scanned to a depth of around two hundred feet. *PT-109* was not there. There were some areas inside the reef that we had missed, but they were low-probability and outside the parameters of reason. *PT-109* was in deeper water, and that was good—it meant it has a better chance of being preserved.

It was time to take our leave and head home. We climbed aboard the turboprop, thoroughly exhausted and welcoming civilization. After a couple of nights in Surfer's Paradise to decompress, we jumped on a flight for the United States via New Zealand.

A few days after I got back to Fort Lauderdale, I spoke to Clive on the telephone.

"Well," he said, "what do you think?"

I'd been saving a line to use for years—it comes from the movie *Jaws*.

"I think we're going to need a bigger boat," I said.

"So, you two know where it's not?" Clive asked.

"Yep," I said, "and we have a pretty good idea where it is."

So stay tuned—NUMA will be back.

PART FOURTEEN

America's Leonardo da Vinci

America's Leonardo da Vinci

1792, 2001

THOUGH WE DON'T OFTEN FIND WHAT WE search for, it is satisfying to bring closure to a piece of history that has been surrounded in mystery. One such project was the hunt for Samuel Morey's boat, *Aunt Sally*.

Legends persisted for almost two centuries of a boat sunk in the waters of Lake Morey in Fairlee, Vermont, about a mile west of the Connecticut River. With the passage of time, colorful variations on the story have obscured the facts.

What we do know is that Samuel Morey was a true genius whose name and accomplishments are known to very few today. Born in 1763, he became a prolific inventor, whose experiments with light, heat, and steam were half a century ahead of his time. Though it is well recorded that James Watt invented the steam engine, Morey is considered the first to put a steam engine in a boat.

His first patent was signed by President George Washington in 1793, for a steam-powered roasting spit. His next patent was for the use of steam to propel a boat and was signed by Thomas Jefferson, who was then the secretary of state. He constructed the hull and the necessary machinery at the sawmill and iron forge he owned. History has at least credited Morey with creating the use of the first paddle wheels. He is also acclaimed—perhaps grudgingly by some historians—as having built the first successful machine-powered vessel.

His first boat was small, with only enough room for one companion, but it worked. To this day, no one knows what he named this little historic vessel. Morey's maiden voyage was from Orford, New Hampshire, up the Connecticut River to Fairlee, Vermont, and back. This was as early as 1792, more than fourteen years before Robert Fulton's first trial trip up the Hudson River.

A short time later, Morey was encouraged to travel to New York and display a model of his boat. He met a wealthy backer of inventions named Chancellor Livingston. The entrepreneur was deeply taken with Morey's creation and introduced him to Robert Fulton, who was also fascinated by the sight of a working model of a steamboat. Morey was treated with great respect by Livingston and Fulton, who suggested minor modifications. The two New Yorkers then offered Morey $10,000 if he would make the alterations and demonstrate a working model.

He returned home and completed the work with great success, mounting the paddle wheel in the stern, an innovation that was not employed until many years later for boats traveling the Missouri and Mississippi Rivers. It was recorded that, during the effort, Livingston made more than one trip to Morey's workshop to study the progress and take notes on Morey's success.

Then, when Morey returned to New York, he was greeted with great coldness and indifference. No mention was made of the $10,000, and Fulton and Livingston simply brushed him off. The two men had seen all they had to see. Morey's secret invention had been fully acquired and was now no longer needed. The result was that Fulton, backed financially by Livingston and with the influence of powerful men in the New York statehouse, succeeded in building a large boat on Morey's principles, mainly the paddle wheels, which went down in history as the first successful steamboat.

Years later, it was clearly proved that Samuel Morey had taken out the necessary patents for the operation of steam-powered boats several years before Fulton, so there was an obvious case of infringement. But Morey, described as a warm and retiring sort of person, did not want the trouble or the expense of a court case, and probably realized he had little chance of winning over the powers that be in New York. To be sure, he made appeals, but he never followed through, lacking time and money.

Truth has always been on Morey's side, but unfortunately his ingenuity has been mostly forgotten, except by local historical organizations.

Morey also devised gaslights and heated his house for years with what he called "water gas." During his life, no other man was granted as many patents as Samuel Morey. He built dams, intricate irrigation canals, and fish-stocking ponds so he could study their behavior. Remains of a flume he erected to shoot logs down to his lumber mill can still be seen. When the Connecticut River was opened for navigation, it was Sam Morey who designed and built the locks at Bellows Falls, Vermont.

After the debacle with Fulton, he returned home to Orford and continued work on his engines, building a rotary steam engine and then a turpentine-vapor engine. In 1826, he patented an internal combustion engine. Far ahead of his time, Morey installed his first small gas engine in a wagon. When he started it up, the wagon lurched forward and smashed through his workshop wall. He beat Charles Duryea's first gasoline automobile by fifty years.

He constructed a larger engine and dropped it in a boat nineteen feet long and five feet wide, painted white with red streaks and black gunwales. Fitted with paddle wheels on the side, the vessel was christened *Aunt Sally*.

After refitting her with a vapor-type engine, Morey operated *Aunt Sally* on Fairlee Lake, later named after him, for a year or more, hauling lumber and other materials back and forth across the lake.

Then, mysteriously, the first internal combustion-powered craft in history disappeared.

Some said that Morey sunk it in a fit of anger, but a friend of Morey's said, "No Vermont Yankee would sink something that was still useful just because he was mad."

Another story is that it was stolen in the dead of the night by Morey's enemies from New York, filled with stones and scuttled. Still another admission, from a group of three boys who claimed they sank the boat, has added to the enigma.

There was an attempt to find the boat in 1874 by dragging a grappling hook. But the pickerel grass was thick and reached as high as six feet, so the grapple had to be cleaned every twelve feet, and nothing was found.

Other attempts were made, with no success. Doc Harold Edgerton, a trustee of NUMA and a grand old inventor himself, gave it a try in 1984. He used sidescan sonar, which he created and developed to search the lake. But Doc did not find *Aunt Sally*. As he so eloquently put it, "I don't like to give up. I've been on many projects where we never found what we were looking for, others where we did find what we were looking for, and others where we found things we weren't looking for at all."

IN JULY of 1999, I received a call from Michael Colin Moore, who I believe was a descendant of Morey. He related the story of the inventor, and suggested that I might be interested in searching for the lost boat.

After researching the matter with the help of Hetser Gardner, curator of the Fairlee Historical Society, I decided to give it a go. I contacted my old survey pal, Ralph Wilbanks, and arranged an expedition. Though Doc Edgerton had swept the lake with his sidescan sonar fifteen years before, Ralph decided to use a sidescan again in hopes that a newer, advanced navigation system might make a difference. I learned that a pole could be easily pushed into the bottom mud up to five feet. This, of course, led me to believe that any chance of finding the long-lost boat would depend heavily on a magnetometer survey to detect any iron that Morey had used to assemble the boat as well as the engine. After 175 years, it seemed likely that the boat had sunk into the soft mud.

In September of 2000, Ralph arrived in Fairlee, Vermont, with *Diversity* in tow, along with his experienced underwater survey associate Shea McLean. He was joined by writer Jayne Hitchcock and her husband Chris.

Lake Morey is in a pretty setting, set in a valley amid wooded hills and surrounded by picturesque homes. Five hundred and eighty acres of water, it is shaped like a sea slug, forty-two feet at its deepest point. Several probes into the bottom revealed it to be very soft up to eighteen feet.

Ralph divided the lake into search lanes on his computer. He began mowing the lawn with a cesium magnetometer towed off the port side, while the sidescan sonar sensor was towed off the starboard stern. Two computers were tied in with the GPS positioning system. The software then tracked the fifty-foot lanes. After two days of recording several small hits, they decided to spend the third day diving on them to investigate. After marking each one with a buoy, Ralph and Shea traded going over the side. They found old barrels at one site and railroad ties at another. The most promising target turned out to be a forty-foot curved section of pipe.

On the final day, while cruising toward the dock, a boat approached and asked if they could search for a wallet belonging to a boater who was lost overboard. Ralph thought that it would be the same as searching for the proverbial needle in a haystack, but the man persisted, saying there was a medal in the wallet that belonged to the boater's son, who had recently died. Ralph and Shea looked at each other, knowing they couldn't refuse.

The general area where the wallet had sunk was pointed out, and Shea volunteered to go in. Everyone thought it was a lost cause, but in less than three minutes Sean broke the surface with his hand raised in the air, clutching the wallet. The boater had tears in his eyes as he showed everyone the medal. Then he gave Shea two soggy fifty-dollar bills. Shea tried to refuse, but the man would not take no for an answer. That night, Shea treated Ralph and the Hitchcocks to dinner.

Ralph covered the entire lake from shore to shore, even dragging the sensor through the growth along the banks. Over two hundred lanes were searched, with no solid results. Ralph and I strongly believe that Morey's boat was never scuttled in the lake. Its most likely demise probably involved being broken up either for firewood or lumber.

The real pity is that Morey's ingenious power plant, possibly the first internal combustion engine in the world, was lost to the engineers of the future, who would have given their eyeteeth to study it.

The residents around the lake believe that Morey's wonderful boat is still out there, waiting to be discovered. But in our minds, the mystery has been solved. *Aunt Sally* is not on Morey Lake. The brilliant inventor most likely scrapped her.

As the man suggested, "No Vermont Yankee would throw away a good boat and engine."

POSTSCRIPT FROM THE AUTHOR

The National Underwater & Marine Agency (NUMA) has a proud record of achievement. Never has so much been accomplished with so few people with so little financial or technical help.

We're not a giant corporation—an oil company or university with large grant funding—nor are we a department of the government with a billion-dollar budget. We have very few donations of consequence. Douglas Wheeler, a Chicago businessman and NUMA trustee, has been a generous contributor, as has ECO-NOVA Productions of Nova Scotia, which has engaged me to narrate a series of *Sea Hunters* documentaries on famous shipwrecks. And, except for Schonstedt Instruments, we have rarely been offered equipment without paying the going rental price.

NUMA is a nonprofit, volunteer foundation dedicated to preserving our maritime heritage through the discovery, archaeological survey, and conservation of historic shipwrecks and their artifacts. Our purpose is also to reinforce public appreciation for our maritime past, present, and future by initiating and supporting projects designed to uncover and explore historically significant underwater sites before they are lost and gone forever.

Our goals include the protection of these historic sites through public information programs and to make available our archaeological reports and data on technical progress while perpetuating the names and legends of the sea-loving men and women who came before us.

I used to beg for funding, but because we search for history with no monetary return, few are willing to step forward and contribute. If I were to say we were searching for treasure, with our track record donors would probably line up for a city block. I wish I had a nickel for every person who has offered to help with funding, a boat, or equipment and then never called again.

Perhaps it's all for the best that NUMA is primarily funded through my book royalties.

Why do I do it? Why do I initiate so many expeditions that are often an exercise in futility? One reason is that if it's lost, I'll look for it.

Why do I pour my money into the sea?

The answer probably lies in how I explain my philosophy to people who think I belong in a rubber room under restraint:

> *When the time comes and I am lying in a hospital bed two gasps away from the great beyond, I'd like the phone to ring. Then as a beautiful, young, buxom blond nurse leans over me and holds the receiver to my ear, the last words I hear before I drift off are those of my banker telling me my account is $10.00 overdrawn.*

That's the way to go.

Or, as I tell the audience when closing the *Sea Hunters* documentaries:

Now it's your turn to get up off of the couch and go into the deserts, go into the mountains, go under the lakes, the rivers and the seas, and search for history. You'll never have a more rewarding adventure.

CURRENT LIST OF NUMA SEARCH
SURVEYS AND DISCOVERIES

1. *ACETON* (H.M.S.)
British fifty-gun frigate that stranded and burned during the Revolutionary War battle off Fort Moultrie, South Carolina, in 1776.

2. *ALEXANDER NEVSKI*
Russian steam frigate that grounded on the east coast of Denmark in 1868 with the Russian crown prince aboard. All aboard were rescued.

3. *AMERICAN DIVER*
Pre-*Hunley* Confederate submarine that foundered under tow off Fort Morgan, Alabama.

4. *ARCTIC*
British steamship that grounded on the east coast of Denmark in 1868.

5. *ARKANSAS* (C.S.S.)
Confederate ironclad that battled the entire Mississippi River fleet and won. Burned by her crew above Baton Rouge, Louisiana, to avoid capture in 1862.

6. *BLUCHER*
German heavy cruiser sunk during the Battle of Dogger Bank in 1916.

7. *CARPATHIA*
Ship that rescued the survivors of *Titanic*. Torpedoed by *U-55* in 1915.

8. *CARONDELET* (U.S.S.)
Venerable Union navy ironclad that fought in more battles in the Civil War than any other warship. Built by genius inventor James Eads. Sank in the Ohio River in 1873.

9. *CHARING CROSS*
British freighter torpedoed by German U-boat off Flamborough Head, England, in 1916.

10. *CHICAGO*
Ten-thousand-ton British freighter torpedoed by German U-boat off Flamborough Head, England, in 1918.

11. *COLONEL LOVELL* (C.S.S.)
Cotton-clad Confederate ram. Rammed and sunk during the battle for Memphis in 1862.

12. *COMMODORE JONES* (U.S.S.)
Former New York ferryboat that became a Union gunboat. Destroyed by sophisticated Confederate electrical mine in the James River in 1864.

13. *COMMONWEALTH*
British freighter sunk by German U-boat off Flamborough Head, England, in 1915.

14. *CUMBERLAND* (U.S.S.)
Union navy frigate. First vessel to be defeated and sunk by armored vessel. Rammed by the Confederate ironclad *Merrimack*

at Newport News, Virginia, in 1862. More than 120 of her crew killed.

15. *DEFENCE* (H.M.S.)
British heavy cruiser sunk during Battle of Jutland in 1916.

16. *DREWRY* (C.S.S.)
Confederate gunboat that fought for three years on the James River before being sunk by Union artillery fire in Trent's Reach in 1865.

17. *FLORIDA* (C.S.S.)
Famous Confederate sea raider that captured and sank nearly fifty U.S. merchant ships during the Civil War. Captured at Bahia, Brazil, and scuttled near Newport News, Virginia, in 1864.

18. *FREDERICKSBURG* (C.S.S.)
Confederate ironclad of the James River fleet. Blown up by her crew at Drewry's Bluff in 1865.

19. *GAINES* (C.S.S.)
Confederate gunboat in the battle of Mobile Bay. Run aground at Fort Morgan and burned in 1865.

20. GALVESTON GRAVEYARD OF SHIPS
Upward of a dozen ships ran aground between 1680 and 1880 off Galveston Island, Texas.

21. *GENERAL BEAUREGARD* (C.S.S.)
Confederate side-wheel ram that fought in the battle of Memphis. Heavily damaged, she sank along the west bank of the Mississippi River in 1862.

22. *GENERAL SLOCUM*
New York excursion steamer that burned and ran aground off Brothers Island, New York, in 1904.

23. *GENERAL THOMPSON* (C.S.S.)
Confederate side-wheel ram damaged during the battle for
Memphis and run aground in 1862.

24. *GLUCKHAUF*
Prototype of modern oil tanker. Stranded on Fire Island, New
York, in 1893.

25. *GOVERNOR MOORE* (C.S.S.)
Confederate gunboat that was converted from passenger steamer.
Fought in battle of New Orleans, then was run aground and
burned by her crew to avoid capture in 1862. Loss of sixty-four
crew.

26. GREAT STONE FLEET
Large numbers of contacts in area where New England whaling
ships were scuttled to block Charleston Harbor during the Civil
War.

27. *HAWKE* (H.M.S.)
British cruiser sunk by *U-9* sixty miles off the coast of Scotland in
1915. Loss of 348.

28. *HOUSATONIC* (U.S.S.)
Union navy sloop of war. First warship in history to be sunk by a
submarine, the Confederate torpedo boat *Hunley* in 1864. Five of
her crew were lost.

29. *HUNLEY* (C.S.S.)
First submarine in history to sink a warship. After torpedoeing the
U.S.S. *Housatonic* off Charleston, South Carolina, in February of
1864, she vanished.

30. *INDEFATIGABLE* (H.M.S.)
British battle cruiser sunk by German navy during the Battle of
Jutland in 1916. Loss of 1,000-plus.

31. *INVINCIBLE* (H.M.S.)
British battle cruiser sunk by German navy during the Battle of Jutland in 1916. Loss of 1,026.

32. *INVINCIBLE* (R.T.N.)
Armed schooner that was the first flagship of the Republic of Texas Navy. Captured arms and supplies from Mexican merchant that were later turned over to General Sam Houston. Sunk in battle off Galveston, Texas, in 1837.

33. *IVANHOE*
Confederate blockade runner captured by Union gunboats off Fort Morgan, Mobile Bay, Alabama, and destroyed in 1863.

34. *JAMESTOWN*
Passenger steamer seized by Confederacy and later fought with *Merrimack*. Later sunk as an obstruction below Drewry's Bluff in 1862.

35. *KEOKUK* (U.S.S.)
Unique Union monitor with twin nonrevolving gun turrets that was referred to as a citadel monitor. Took more than ninety hits by Confederate guns off Charleston, South Carolina, in 1863. Sunk soon after.

36. *KIRKWALL*
British steamer grounded on the east coast of Denmark in 1874.

37. *L'AIMABLE*
Explorer La Salle's flagship. Grounded in Matagorda Bay, Texas, in 1685.

38. *LEOPOLDVILLE*
British troop transport that was torpedoed on Christmas Eve in 1944 off Cherbourg, France. Loss of more than eight hundred American soldiers.

39. LEXINGTON
Extremely fast side-paddle steamboat constructed by Cornelius Vanderbilt. In 1840 she burned and sank in Long Island Sound, New York, with a loss of 151 passengers and crew.

40. LOUISIANA (C.S.S.)
Mammoth Confederate ironclad mounting sixteen guns. Never finished, she was moored along shore and fought in the battle of New Orleans. Sunk by her crew to avoid capture in 1862.

41. MANASSAS (C.S.S.)
The first armored ship built in North America and the first to see battle. Designed as a ram, she burned and sank in the Mississippi River during the battle of New Orleans in 1862.

42. MARY CELESTE
Famous mystery ship recovered with no one aboard. Later intentionally run aground on the Reef of Rochelais, Haiti, in 1885.

43. MERRIMACK
NUMA found scattered contacts at Craney Island, Portsmouth, Virginia, where ship was blown up to avoid capture. Wreckage believed to have been dredged out of existence.

44. MISSISSIPPI (U.S.S.)
U.S. Navy side-paddle frigate damaged in Battle of Port Hudson, Louisiana, in 1863. Later drifted loose and blew herself to smithereens.

45. NEW ORLEANS
First steamboat down the Mississippi River. Snagged on stump and sank across from Baton Rouge, Louisiana, in 1814.

46. NORSEMAN
Confederate blockade runner that was run ashore off Isle of Palms, South Carolina, in 1865.

47. NORTHAMPTON

Confederate supply ship that was sunk as an obstruction below Drewry's Bluff in 1862.

48. ODIN

Early Swedish steamship that ran ashore off the east coast of Denmark in 1836.

49. PATAPSCO (U.S.S.)

Passaic-class Union monitor that fought throughout the siege of Charleston, South Carolina. Sank after striking a Confederate mine in the channel off Fort Moultrie in 1865. Loss of sixty-two.

50. PATHFINDER (H.M.S.)

Second ship sunk by a submarine and first by a German U-boat. Torpedoed by *U-21* in 1914.

51. PHILLIPE (U.S.S.)

Union navy gunboat destroyed by Confederate guns during the battle of Mobile Bay in 1864.

52. PLATT VALLEY

Side-wheel steamer that snagged and sank on the wreck of *General Beauregard* in 1867.

53. PT-109

John F. Kennedy's World War II command. Run through by Japanese destroyer *Amagiri* in Blackett Strait, Solomon Islands, in 1943.

54. RACCOON

Confederate blockade runner captured by Union gunboat when leaving Charleston Harbor with a load of cotton. Burned in 1863.

55. RATTLESNAKE

Confederate blockade runner caught by Union navy while trying to enter Charleston Harbor with a load of arms. Burned in 1863.

56. *RICHMOND* (C.S.S.)
Confederate ironclad that guarded the reaches of the James River.
After the fall of Richmond she was destroyed by her crew near
Chaffin's Bluff in 1865.

57. *RUBY*
Successful Confederate blockade runner that was finally chased
ashore on Folly's Island, South Carolina, and destroyed in 1864.

58. *S-35*
German destroyer sunk during the Battle of Jutland in 1916.

59. *SAINT PATRICK*
Four-hundred-ton steamer that burned and sank above Memphis
in 1868.

60. *SHARK* (H.M.S.)
British destroyer sunk during the Battle of Jutland in 1916.

61. *STONEWALL JACKSON*
Confederate blockade runner that was formerly the British steamer
Leopard. Ran aground on Isle of Palms, South Carolina, in 1864.

62. *SULTANA*
Side-paddle-wheel steamboat that burned in the Mississippi River
with a loss of two thousand Union soldiers, making it the worst
North American ship disaster.

63. TORPEDO RAFT
The remains of the torpedo raft towed by *Weehawken*. Located at
the north end of Marsh on Morris Island, South Carolina.

64. *U-12*
German submarine that sank after being rammed by the British
cruiser *Ariel* off Scotland in 1915.

65. *U-20*
German U-boat that sank the *Lusitania*. Stranded on Jutland shore, Denmark, in 1916.

66. *U-21*
First German U-boat to sink a ship. Foundered while under tow in the North Sea in 1919.

67. *UB-74*
German U-boat that sank after being depth-charged off Weymouth, England, in 1916.

68. *V-48*
German cruiser sunk during the Battle of Jutland in 1916.

69. *VARUNA* (U.S.S.)
Union navy gunboat that was rammed three times during the battle of New Orleans. Credited with sinking six vessels before being forced ashore and burned in 1862.

70. *VICKSBURG*
Britsh freighter stranded on Fire Island, New York, in 1875.

71. *VIRGINIA II* (C.S.S.)
Confederate ironclad that prevented General Grant's army from crossing the James River to take Richmond. Burned by her crew to avoid capture at Drewry's Bluff in 1865.

72. *WARATAH*
Passenger liner that disappeared off the coast of Africa in 1911. Two hundred passengers and crew lost.

73. *WEEHAWKEN* (U.S.S.)
Led the first attack on Fort Sumter. The only Union monitor to capture a Confederate ironclad in battle. Sank as a result of a storm off Charleston, South Carolina, in 1864.

74. *WIESBADEN*

German heavy cruiser sunk during the Battle of Jutland in 1916.

75. *ZAVALA* (R.T.N.)

Passenger steamboat converted to armed warship by the Republic of Texas Navy. Probably the first armed steamship in North America. Grounded in Galveston Bay, Texas, in 1842.

ADDITIONAL HISTORIC SITES AND ARTIFACTS

1. *AKRON* (U.S.S.)

United States Navy blimp that featured docking and hangaring for nine aircraft while in flight. Crashed near Beach Haven, New Jersey, in 1933. Loss of seventy-three crew.

2. *L'OISEAU BLANC (WHITE BIRD)*

French airplane attempting to capture the Orteig Prize later won by Charles Lindbergh. Plane believed to have been heard over Machias, Maine, but no trace has ever turned up.

3. LOST LOCOMOTIVE OF KIOWA CREEK

Area east of Denver, Colorado, where a Union Pacific locomotive and train were washed away in 1876. Later investigation proved that the locomotive was secretly raised and put back into service in what amounted to an insurance scam.

4. SWAMP ANGEL

Remains of the eight-inch Parrot gun that lobbed 150-pound projectiles into Charleston, South Carolina, during the Civil War.

5. TWIN SISTERS

Famous cannon used by Sam Houston at the battle of San Jacinto. Later used in the Civil War, then hidden by Confederate soldiers so they would not be destroyed.

For more detailed information on the above finds, access our website:

www.numa.net.